Europe in Love, Love in Europe

# Europe in Love, Love in Europe

◆ ◆ ◆

## Imagination and Politics between the Wars

Luisa Passerini

NEW YORK UNIVERSITY PRESS

Washington Square, New York

Published in the USA in 1999 by
NEW YORK UNIVERSITY PRESS
Washington Square
New York, N.Y. 10003

First published in 1999 by I.B.Tauris & Co Ltd
Victoria House, Bloomsbury Square
London WC1B 4DZ
175 Fifth Avenue, New York 10010

Extracts from 'Europe 1936' and 'Spain' from W.H. Auden: *The English Auden*, reprinted by permission of Faber and Faber.

CIP data available from the Library of Congress
ISBN 0-8147-6698-6 (clothbound)

Printed in Great Britain

# Contents

# List of Illustrations
## and Credits

# Acknowledgements

This book is the first product of a larger research which was conceived at the Wissenschaftskolleg in Berlin, received nourishment at New York University, and grew up at the European University Institute in Florence. To these three institutions I owe much, both in terms of incentives and of resistances to the experimental character of the research – and resistances are indispensable, even when distressing, to make one's plans more articulate. I am particularly grateful to the EUI, which provided the greatest part of the resources for the research.

I would like to thank the personnel of the EUI Library at the Badia Fiesolana and particularly of the Inter-Library Loan service which has been precious for my work. I am also grateful to the staff of the following libraries: the WissenschaftsKolleg Library in Berlin; the Bodleian Library in Oxford; the British Library, the Libraries of the Institute of Psychoanalysis, the Analytical Psychology Club, the Tate Gallery, the Warburg Institute and the Victoria and Albert Museum in London, the New York Public Library. I am particularly thankful to Michael Bott of the Library of the University of Reading; to Laura Mulvey and Nicole Newman of the British Film Institute; to Violet MacDermot for her help and advice in the consultation of the archives of the New Atlantis Foundation; to Peter Foden of the archive of Oxford University Press; to David Doughan of the Fawcett Library in London; to the curators of the Neuchâtel archive of the Denis de Rougemont Papers. Finally, I am very grateful to Anne Summers for directing me to the relevant collections in the Department of Manuscripts at the British Library as well as for her advice and suggestions.

Many people have provided invaluable information. I am very grateful to Barry L. Phillips, who is writing Mottram's biography, for the material he kindly shared with me; to Christina Scott, who sent me information concerning the work of her father Christopher Dawson; to Drs Violet MacDermot and Ralph Twentyman for their interviews which provided insights into the historical background around Mitrinovic. I am most thankful to Basil Davidson and Professor Michael R.D. Foot for their help and comments on the Epilogue, as well as to Dorothy Thompson and Simon Kusseff for their conversations with me on Frank Thompson. Of course I am solely responsible for the use I have made of the information provided.

Friends and colleagues have read parts of this book, providing criticisms and encouragements: Sally Alexander, Perry Anderson, Andrea Bosco, Jerry Bruner, Jack Goody, Phyllis Lassner, Alison Light, Romano Màdera, Juliet Mitchell, Jan Montefiore, John Reed, Ann Summers and

Stella Tillyard. Others have discussed the progress and regress of the research as it went through its various stages, when it seemed impossible for it to acquire coherence, let alone be concluded: Luisa Accati, Piero Femore, Giovanni Levi, Bruno Mari, Roberta Mazzanti, Hanne Petersen, Andrew Samuels, Marisa Scioratto, Alberto Tovaglieri, Ruth Van Velsen and Marilyn Young. Corrado Agnes shared many of the pleasures and troubles that this research and writing inflicted upon our life, with affection and humour only rarely giving place to sarcasm.

Marina Nordera and Annett Kuester have been the best possible research assistants, respectively in Florence and London. Sergio Amadei has made the book possible with his secretarial support. Because this book is not a translation from the Italian, but was written in the first instance in English, it has been particularly important for it to be revised by Nicki Owtram with her competence as a linguist, while Philippa Brewster has done a literary revision of it. Colleagues and students of my seminars at the EUI and NYU in the years 1993–98 have provided fruitful stimuli with their participation as well as scepticism.

Fiesole, December 1997

To Sally Alexander

*without whom this book would not exist*

# Introduction

## Encounters

The idea of a united Europe has led a respectable life in the field of political theory, from the projects for European peace in the seventeenth and eighteenth centuries, through the proposals of a federation of European nations by politicians and writers in the nineteenth and twentieth centuries, to the ideal of a community which guided the founders of the European union in our own century. The discourse on love which developed in the same period, sometimes interwoven with religion, has evolved mainly in the fields of literature and its history, philosophy, and psycho-analysis. In particular, the theme of courtly love has been connected over the last two centuries with that of romantic love – and considered its continuation – and elaborated by, among others, romance philologists, novelists and poets. These two discursive traditions on Europe and on love came together at various times and in various points of view.

One central encounter between the two is reflected in the stereotype that the Europeans invented courtly/romantic love in twelfth-century Provence. This has a long history, and finds a significant moment of elaboration during the Enlightenment, when European intellectuals defined the shared heritage of the continent as including a specificity of love between the sexes. At that time – and not unusually – the term 'Europe' was subjected to oscillations of geographical boundaries, since Montesquieu in his *Lettres persanes* (1721), did not include Russia in Europe, while Voltaire, in his *Essai sur les moeurs* (1756), excluded from Europe the Balkan peninsula, then under the Turks. However, a central core of the definition of European civilisation – the status of European women and the attitude towards them – persisted, although contrasting values were given to it. For Voltaire, the main difference between the Orientals and the Europeans was evident in the way they treated women, giving them freedom in Europe, consigning them to slavery in the Orient. For Montesquieu, the freedom of European women was the source of their impudence, which he contrasted with the modesty and chastity of Asian women, although at the same time he gallantly acknowledged the spirit and liveliness of the former. This European specificity, defined on the basis of a contrast with Asia, fostered the claim that relations between the sexes had reached in Europe a level of civilisation which was unheard of in the rest of the world. This was attributed to a plurality of cultural influences of various origins which had co-mingled in Southern France at the beginning of the millennium.

Attention and respect towards women was considered to have been born with chivalry, understood as a founding institution of European political and cultural civilisation. Another major contrast was therefore established, that with classical antiquity, which was essential for defining a European specificity and the conception of a 'modern' Europe. The Chevalier de Jaucourt, who wrote both the 'Europe' and 'Poésie provençale' entries in the *Encyclopédie* of Diderot and D'Alembert (1751–1765), considered the European continent as the world's most notable in commerce, navigation, fertility, and for 'les lumières et l'esprit de ses peuples' (which included all the arts and sciences). Jaucourt regarded the culture of Provence in the twelfth and thirteenth centuries as the turning point in the process of change of sensitivity that opposed the moderns to the ancients, and at the same time as the origin of all modern poetry. The main representative of the Enlightenment in this field, Jean-Baptiste La Curne de Sainte-Palaye – who collected the poems of the troubadours after a long period of oblivion – assumed courtly love to be an integral part of chivalry and therefore a cornerstone of modern Europe. For both him and his English equivalent, Thomas Warton, the 'modern' attitude expressed in Provençal love poetry, conferring importance and authority on women and gallantry towards them, derived from contacts with the Celtic nations, Germans, Scandinavian and Scythians (Russians). Warton also attributed the growth of the taste for romantic fiction to contacts with Arabian culture from Moorish Spain.

In the nineteenth century the two discourses on Europe and love underwent important separate as well as connected developments. Intellectuals like the members of the Coppet group around Madame de Stael combined a liberal Europeanism, critical of the Napoleonic conquest of Europe, with a view of love and particularly of the European nature of courtly love. However, with the rise of nationalisms these conceptions were increasingly subjected to competitive and proprietary tensions, as different countries, particularly France and Germany, vied with each other to take credit for their origin. Certainly the French 'invented' the term 'courtly love', although much later, since it was made successful by the French philologist Gaston Paris in 1883, while the troubadours had preferred other expressions such as 'fin'amors', 'amor honestus', 'cortezia'. During the whole nineteenth century the dispute around the possible

Arabic derivation of Provençal poetry and love continued, a derivation opposed by the claim for a purely European origin (see Chapter 5).

From the end of the century on, another, contrasting, definition of Europeanness emerged in the field of concepts of love and became increasingly dominant in the first half of the twentieth century. According to it, the 'Other' in terms of which Europe defined itself was no longer only Asia, but also America, or rather the United States. Texts by travellers, philosophers and writers of many kinds put forward the idea – often in the threatening tones of allusion to the decadence of Western civilisation – that the freedom of American women and the ease of gender relations in the US were setting an example which Europe would sooner or later follow. Romantic love was predicted to disappear in America despite being frequently invoked and translated into daily life. No prediction could have stood the test of time less well than this, since the ideology and mythology of romantic love were developed in the US to an extraordinary extent, due also to the cultural consumption induced through and by the media.[1]

After the First World War, the connection between love and Europe had its last triumphs. During the period between the wars, the idea of Europe played an important role in the efforts to avoid a second world war and to establish values which could bridge the gap between those of the USA and Soviet Russia (in the 1920s) or those of Fascism and Stalinism (in the 1930s). In this context, the theme of the Europeanness of love attitudes took on a new meaning, as a central aspect of the effort to save European civilisation from its own decadence. The 1930s are particularly interesting because in the period this range of ideas and feelings reached a dramatic and urgent pitch as it became clear that a second war was unavoidable. The threat posed by Nazism to the patrimony of a common civilisation also helped to foster a sense of community, together with a sense of what it could mean to lose it; an important resource such as a European space – where cities like Berlin and Vienna as well as London and Paris could represent intellectual fatherlands to many people – was already at risk. It should not be forgotten that the 'good' or 'great' Europeans, as many intellectuals called themselves and one another before the First World War, had moved between countries without passports, equally at ease with several languages and cultures and sharing the predominantly urban environment of the European cities.

In this atmosphere, C.S. Lewis's *The Allegory of Love*[2] and Denis de Rougemont's *L'amour et l'Occident*[3] – both still in print today – conveyed in different ways the same basic idea that romantic love is the supreme expression of the relationship between the sexes, and was invented by Europeans in the first two centuries of our millennium. Both texts became rapidly and enduringly successful, as if a need of the time were the reaffirmation of the centrality of love in European culture as the starting point for a social regeneration. This is confirmed by other trends of thought

3

which were central to that period: in their own way, the Surrealists insisted that the connection between love and freedom promised a global revolution of the Western world. *L'amour fou* (1937) by André Breton[4] contained the exaltation of total love as the possibility of a future 'age d'or', which would rupture the 'age of mud' ('boue') through which Europe was currently going; in opposition to the 'abject trinity' composed of the bourgeois family, the fatherland and religion, Breton's love represented the continuity between the possible (including marriage) and the impossible of total love. In the same years (1937–39), Georges Bataille posited the nucleus of his vision linking the figure of lovers, 'les amants', with community and society in the discussions on the sacred in societies 'without the sacred' held by the group Collège de Sociologie. At its last meeting, in July 1939, Bataille pointed out this link very clearly: 'la communauté formée par les liens du coeur rappelle l'unité passionnelle des amants'[5]; for him, love expressed a need for sacrifice, where each of the two original unities must lose itself in a new unity which would go beyond it, and the unity of the individual would emerge more sharply from its own negation through passion. All this shows the convergence between very different positions on love in the hope of transforming a civilisation in crisis – such as the European one – by an appeal to private emotions expanding towards the public, as if going back to its own ancient roots.

The Europeanness of courtly/romantic love was not the only example of encounter between the idea of Europe and the world of sentiments; a second major example is represented by the myth of Europa. The myth links the continent, considered geographically and politically, with the world of symbolic meanings, where conjunction and marriage do not indicate only the union between a man and a woman, but also that between various levels of spiritual and physical reality. Love and attraction are present, but they are not the only, and sometimes – depending on the interpretation – not even the main, theme of the story. The myth itself has a very long history of literary and visual representation, from Homer to Horace and Ovid to the paintings of Venetians and many others in the sixteenth, seventeenth and eighteenth centuries. The flourishing of mythology in the nineteenth century favoured the increasing presence of the myth through various media, not only in the great figurative arts such as painting and sculpture, as well as in poetry and music, but also in the so-called minor arts, where the myth figured in innumerable representations on plates, vases, boxes, fans, tapestries, clocks and cards.

According to the best-known version, Europa was the daughter of the Phoenician King Agenor and his wife Argiope; it was in Phoenicia that Zeus saw Europa, together with her maids, collecting flowers near the sea, approached her in the shape of a white bull with horns decorated with garlands of flowers, and abducted her to Crete. There, Europa had three sons by Zeus – Minos, Rhadamanthys, Sarpedon – before marrying King

Asterios, whose name means 'king of the stars'. While trying to find Europa, her brother Cadmus travelled further on to the north-west and reached Boeotia, where he founded Thebes. Europa's name was understood as meaning 'with big eyes' or 'with a wide face', an expression referring to the moon and the lunar goddesses venerated through cults and rituals centring on bulls. However, a possible root of her name could also be a Semitic word meaning 'western' adopted by Phoenicians.

The myth has been given manifold meanings by various interpreters. It has been understood as alluding to marriage by capture (as in the cases of Demeter and Persephone or of the Sabines), and as illustrating the transition from a matrilineal society to a patriarchal one. It might have had something to do with migrations from the East to the West of the Mediterranean, with a change of influence in the area from the Egyptians to the Greeks, as well as with a movement of civilisation including the diffusion of writing, supposedly invented in Phoenicia, whence the written alphabet would have expanded to Crete and the Greek mainland. East-West is also the direction followed by the sun, and the bulls were part of a cult of celestial bodies present in the Mediterranean and particularly in Crete: the horns were a symbol of the moon, the divine bull was transformed into the constellation later known as Taurus, and the name of Europa's husband Asterios evokes the stars. Europa herself has been interpreted as one of the lunar deities, typically moving westward. Finally, the bull was a symbol of fertility and strength, a sacred animal linked with the earth mother, while its castration gave rise to work, agriculture and production.

Europa's name was given to the land lying west of Greece but the connection between Europe and Europa has often been blurred, and has been mysterious from its early history. In its geographical meaning the term had been in use at least since the sixth century BC, and Herodotus in the fifth century considered it 'established by custom'; he used it in his *Histories* to indicate one of the three parts of the world, all named after women, the other two being Lybia and Asia. Herodotus reported the myth of Europa, interpreting it as an episode in a sequence of reciprocal robberies and rapes of women between Asians and Greeks, possibly Cretans.[6] However, he also expressed doubts about the denomination:

> But as for Europe, no men have any knowledge whether it be surrounded or not by seas, nor whence it took its name, nor is it clear who gave the name, unless we are to say that the land took its name from the Tyrian Europa, having been (as it would seem) till then nameless like the others. But it is plain that this woman was of Asiatic birth, and never came to this land which the Greeks now call Europe, but only from Phoenice to Crete and from Crete to Lycia. Thus far have I spoken of these matters, and let it suffice; we will use the names by custom established.[7]

Consequently, the myth of Europa and the representation of the continent have led separate lives, converging only at times. Europe was often represented by the allegorical figure of a powerful and beautiful matron, very much like the women portraying the other continents except for the colour of the skin and the allegorical attributes, since not only did Europe have the bull but also the instruments of the arts, while America was represented with bow and arrows and the feathered head-gear (for instance in 1753 Tiepolo's ceiling fresco in Wurzburg). The forerunner of this allegorical image was present in one of the versions of the myth of Europa (by the bucolic poet Moschus, who lived in Syracuse in the second century BC) which opened with a dream of two wonderful women, one familiar to her trying to keep her, the other foreign to her trying to entice her away: the interpretation of the dream was that the two women represented respectively Asia and Europe. On the symbolic level, the representation through the allegorical figure of a woman has often acted as a more direct and simple symbol of Europe than Europa, although this allegory seems to have disappeared in our century. In the nineteenth and twentieth centuries the image of Europa was used as an allusion to the continent in specific genres, such as political caricature; at the same time the distance between Europa and Europe was sometimes very wide, as is shown for instance in the most stereotyped forms of the Europa motif used in interior decoration, where any connection with the continent seems out of place. However, the two images came together at other times, one such being the 1930s and 1940s, when the sense of a Europe squeezed between the United States and Soviet Russia on the one hand and the threat posed to the continent by Nazism on the other favoured a revitalisation and politicisation of the ancient myth through two major transformations. The first took place against the background of the vast debate on marriage, love and sex, which had been going on since the end of the nineteenth century in Europe and in the United States. The debate centred on the so-called crisis of marriage – the increasing rates of divorce after the First World War and the decreasing birth rate – and it was closely connected with the political, social and economic emancipation of women, in the forms of both feminism and the social affirmation of new ways of living and working, especially for young women.

During the inter-war period, the theme of the 'Great Mother' came to be an integral part of this debate, one introduced by anthropologists, archaeologists, psychologists and historians of literature and art, which revived Bachofen's theory of original matriarchy in a revised form. The Great Mother had been venerated in the archaic societies of the Mediterranean, where women had enjoyed a high degree of freedom and respect. For modern women, the Great Mother had an ambivalent meaning: on the one hand it was understood as a warning not to forget their feminine side, on the other it reminded them of women's past power and perhaps of the possibility of regaining it. Europa was considered one of the Mothers: she was listed as such in the Eranos Index of the Jungians (now at the Warburg Institute, London), and mentioned in all the texts on the Great Goddess or Mother.[8] The myth of Europa was revived in close connection with the crisis of European (and Western) civilisation, particularly in relation to gender relations, and therefore had a strong dramatic emphasis (which its use in recent times, when Europa was appropriated as a symbol of the European construction, seems to have lost). In the myth, as in the art depicting it, there is no visible image of men, in spite of its being a story about the virility of Zeus, who in other similar cases appears in the form of a swan or golden rain. It is as if men were in the background, and the potency of love and generation had to be represented by women and animals or supernatural phenomena. By contrast, the myth alludes to a strong feminine sexuality, re-awakened by emancipation but connected with archaic and mysterious roots, to which either positive or a negative value could be given. The threatening aspects of female sexuality are more evident in the myth of Pasiphae (a descendant of Europa), who was in love with the bull and mother of the Minotaur, the monster of the labyrinth, half-human and half-animal, used by painters such as André Masson and Picasso to symbolise violent transformations. The polyvalency of the image of Europa and the bull is such that the myth can be used either to indicate a conciliation or a deep antagonism between the soul and the body, male and female, human and animal.

Another mutation of the myth which is of interest here brought conflict into the foreground and took a strongly political turn. It can be seen particularly in the works of artists active in the Europe of the 1930s and 1940s, but also in the United States (Chapter 6,6). Europa becomes Europe and the bull becomes Nazism, or more generally the forces of violence and oppression. In the political interpretation centring on Nazism a central element of the previous transformation, i.e. gender struggle, was also present. In the versions where the representations of the two struggles overlap, women symbolised the victims, in striking contrast with the triumphant image of Europa in so many representations by artists from the fifteenth to the nineteenth century. Both transformations, while they did not exhaust the myth, which is broader than these two versions, offer space for many possible interpretations of the Europa myth. This could even be understood as an instance of love creating Europe, attraction being at the root of the movement towards the 'discovery' of the continent; a form of love apparently impossible and unacceptable, breaking conventions and insisting on the sacred aspects of sensual love. Another interpretation of the myth could be that a reconciliation was possible, reducing the tight hold of nationalisms, with the instinctive forces of love and death represented by the bull and at odds in European civilisation, although a widespread feeling of the 1930s also seemed to be a growing uncertainty over whether any such reconciliation could ever take place in modern Europe on the political and moral levels. Whatever the interpretation, the transformations of the myth in the 1930s and 1940s showed its vitality in relation to some of the major social and political processes of our century.

## Time and space

Against this *longue-durée* background, I will concentrate on a much shorter time-span because it satisfies some of my methodological concerns. I chose one decade – the 1930s – not only because the idea of Europe had in that decade a particular significance, and so had the connection between it and love, as signaled by the publication of the texts by Lewis and Rougemont, which can be considered the tip of an iceberg of literature on the subject. But the 1930s is of particular historical interest for our theme also because it was the last period when the connection between Europe and love was widely accepted and virtually unchallenged. After the Second World War, in spite of the continual diffusion and elaboration through the mass-media of romantic love on the one hand and the construction of a united Europe on the other, the idea of the inter-relationship between the two was no longer so widespread and no longer occupied a central place. The theme did not disappear: on the contrary it has been revisited recently but with important corrections which indicate the changes in attitude which have taken place in the meantime.

The philosopher Irving Singer has based his criticism of Eurocentric notions of love on the difference between emotions and behaviour on the one hand and ideas about them on the other. In his interpretation, what was new in troubadours' poetry was the self-sufficiency of human love, and the Western concept of love in its heterosexual and humanistic aspects was, if not 'invented' or 'discovered', at least developed in the twelfth century as never before, although under many influences, including those of the Arabs and Sufis.[9] Singer recognises the centrality of courtly/romantic love for Europe, but reminds us that it is inserted in a plurality of notions of love in European cultures. What has vanished in recent times, according to Singer, is the 'extensive ideology of love', whereby the love bond was part of a social order of loving relationships that united all people to one another and mankind to nature as a whole. In the present world, romantic love cannot be wholly ethnocentric, since love is recognised as a universal tendency among human beings.[10] A similar position is taken by the Mexican writer Octavio Paz. Under the influence of de Rougemont's *L'amour et l'Occident*, he had believed that the feeling of courtly/romantic love belonged exclusively to Western civilisation, but later came to realise that similar forms existed in the Arabian, Persian, Indian, Chinese and Japanese cultures. Although Paz still notes that the appearance of that kind of love was contemporary with the birth of Europe and that the first European civilisation was that of Provence, he distinguishes, like Singer, between the feeling of love, which belongs to all times and places, and the idea or ideology of love typical of a certain society and epoch. In the end, for Paz too the image of love is today universal, and love a cosmopolitan passion.[11] Thus two important interpreters from two different fields converge in stressing the universality of courtly and romantic concepts of love, in spite of confirming the centrality of these to 800 years of European tradition.

While the connection between love and Europe has become less obvious in the second half of the twentieth century, thanks to a more widespread awareness of the ills of ethnocentrism and the desire to avoid them, it was still taken for granted in the 1930s. But the 1930s will not be treated here as strictly the years 1930–39. In fact, one of the results of my research is to confirm what others have found, that the 1930s is a plural decade, not a single historical entity with a fixed character, and that there is no way of reducing the period to order except by gross simplification.[12] The collection of judgments on this period by those who lived through it is astonishingly negative, from Auden's definition 'a low dishonest decade' to Orwell's treatment of it as a collective mistake,[13] through the following statements: 'As a period, the Thirties resist analysis';[14] contrasting them with 'the convalescent 1920s', 'it is not hard to paint the 1930s in the darkest colours';[15] the decade favoured 'a disposition [which] made one ostensibly irreverent, pessimistic, disloyal and destructive in attitude of mind'.[16] This ironic or even sarcastic tone is extended by Annan and Graves to the whole inter-war period. At the same time, recent works of history and literature, especially by feminist scholars, have indicated the potential of new interpretations of the 1930s.[17] I do not intend to propose a new interpretation of the 1930s in Britain, partly because my approach undermines the concept of the decade as an historical tool. In fact some of the processes described start in the 1920s and continue into the early 1940s (to take two very different instances, the success of federalism and the transformations of the Europa myth); therefore it is a 'long 1930s' which is taken into consideration here. Generally speaking, it could be said that if there is a turning-point in the history of mental attitudes such as those considered in this book, it is not 1939 but the end of the war or even the late 1940s. Therefore, use of the terms '1930s' and 'the decade' in this book should be seen as referring to a temporal unity which is wider than the numerical decade.

As for space, my research originally covered France and Francophone Switzerland, which are central for both traditions of love and of a united Europe; Italy, which provides an interesting case of the appropriation of both traditions by Fascism, in an effort to impose repressive modernisation; and Britain, generally assumed to host a weak tradition on European ideas, but a strong literary and philosophical one on love. These choices were not so fully rational as they might seem now, since they were made not only on the basis of unconscious or half-conscious desires, preferences, and previous knowledge, but also on the basis of the languages I can read most easily; this again is not by chance, since these languages reflect what has been considered central in education in Europe over the last 50 years.

Subsequently, I chose to concentrate first of all on Britain and to write this first book on the British case, which proved to be particularly interesting in various respects. The geopolitical position of Britain, marginal and central to Europe at the same time, was coupled with the British attitude, which for a long time – certainly in the 1930s and still partially today – considered Europe as an 'elsewhere' and yet at the same time maintained that Britain had a special mission to save Europe from its folly, a belief uniting progressives and conservatives as well as Protestants and Catholics. Daily language reflected the sense of separation, in expressions such as 'going to Europe' with the version 'going into Europe' (an expression with undertones of penetration) used for political and economic processes such as entering the European Community. Curricula in schools and universities helped foster and confirm this general attitude, since European history was taught separately to British history. A *Leit Motiv* of the 1930s among politicians and intellectuals favourable to Europeanism was in fact that Britain should encourage a united Europe, but from the outside, in order to avoid dropping her priority, which continued to be a close liaison with the colonies and dominions of the empire. Given all this, Britain is also interesting because in the 1930s important connections with the issues under debate in continental Europe were made by means of translations, which were numerous in this field, and through echoes in journals such as T.S. Eliot's *Criterion*. Therefore the British case is not only interesting for its own sake, but also as a mirror of European processes which are shown through suggestive reflections and distortions.

The bipolar sense of Britain's distance from and involvement with Europe – which in the second half of the decade moved towards the latter pole – formed the background even for those few who had different ideas or opposed involvement. It was often confirmed by similar stereotypes held by continental Europeans, first of all that of the founder of Pan Europa, Count Coudenhove-Kalergi, at least until 1938. My interpretation is that such bi-polarity fostered a trend of utopianism which, together with Catholic ideas of Europe, I consider the most interesting forms of British Europeanism in the 1930s. Of course, this utopianism was often – not always, as the 'New Europe' groups shows – a small minority affair; but even if it was not politically very relevant, it was interesting from a cultural perspective. Besides, it is important for us today that such dissonant voices existed at all and that history includes them.

'Europe as an elsewhere' – but an elsewhere one cares very much about – is not only an idea connected with utopianism; it has also something to do with the type of implicit European identity which is most widespread today. History and common sense tell us that in most cases consciously European feelings do not arise until after the experience of living elsewhere. It is only when placed in this position that many people suddenly see, as they did not before, the continental affinities which go beyond national and regional differences. Therefore, even for most of those who have lived and live on the main continent and not on one of its islands, Europe has often been an 'elsewhere', in the sense that it was not and is not openly recognised as a fatherland, while being the object of deep and confused feelings of belonging. Only for some was this feeling open and aware, namely for some intellectuals, political refugees and migrants, in spite and perhaps because of their sufferings. They felt European, as Ursula Hirschmann wrote, precisely because they had nothing to lose from the order based on nationality. Today, with the turn of the millennium, the conviction of many people, for instance in Italy, is – perhaps irrationally – that the last hope is to participate in a united Europe; only in this way could the nation states be saved from their inadequacy and corruption. Therefore 'Europe as an elsewhere' is a central theme of European identity in every country. Perhaps the 'elsewhere' is central for all identities, in the sense that any identity should imply a detachment between self and a belonging to place, both physical and political. But this is particularly true of a complex sentiment like Europeanness, which is always mixed with feelings of national belonging, given the history and the state of the continent, where the combination of European and national belonging appears in a different form in each country.

As already mentioned, in the period between the wars the theme of 'Europe' was often forcibly imposed by the fear of an impending second world war and of the 'new Europe' that Goebbels had in mind, which could not exist without war, ethnic purge, and extreme ideological upheaval. Thus one aspect connected with this 'identity from the outside' is that in the 1930s it was a defensive formation, in the sense that those trying to construct Europe started not so much from a positive and creative point of view but from the need to save European civilisation from decline. The theme of decadence, which had found a best-selling formulation in Spengler's *Decline of the West* in the immediate aftermath of the First World War, was all-pervasive in the 1930s; the sense of the imminent death of a whole civilization was linked to and prolonged the sense of mourning for those lost in the war. From the perspective of the present, we can also say that the annihilation of peoples and cultures attempted by Hitler and Stalin was another sign of this impulse towards death, as was the explosion of sadism in all its forms, from the torture of German concentration camps to Soviet trials and camps, together with the brutal bombing campaigns of the Allies. The word 'Europe' had associations of decadence and death to an increasing extent as the decade went on, having in constrast reflected the hopes of a united Europe and a lasting peace at the end of the 1920s. It might be recalled that since 1915 Freud had admitted the existence of a primary aggressive or destructive instinct which, when fused with sexual impulses, becomes sadistic perversion, and is the expression of a death-instinct giving rise to destructive and sadistic impulses. Freud ended the second edition of *Civilisation and Its Discontents* with a much less optimistic view than he had in the first edition, declaring that the final outcome of the struggle between Eros and Death could not be foreseen in a Europe which was home to Nazism.

## Itineraries

When I started researching the connection between the idea of love and Europeanness, I was clear that the two themes were very distinct, but also that many subterranean connections between them existed which only occasionally became explicit. Therefore I felt that I was following two main directions of enquiry: finding the European dimension in the literature on love ('Europe in love'); exploring the idea of Europe in search of its implicit links to sentiments and emotions ('love in Europe'). The results presented in this book separate along this division, which also provides the title of the book: the first direction is clearest in Chapter 5 on C.S. Lewis, while the second is exemplified by the chapters on New Europe (Chapter 3) and on Dawson (Chapter 2,2). However, these two general lines of research have been articulated through specific itineraries suggested by theoretical and historical connections as well as by available sources.

In the course of dealing with the two discursive traditions on Europe and love in Britain, six itineraries have taken shape, open-ended and leading to further exploration. First, the idea of a united Europe as an independent political idea is researched through various moments of its history in Britain: the debate on the United States of Europe, centring on Aristide Briand's proposal to the League of Nations in 1930 (Chapter 2,1); the debate on the future of European civilisation which continued throughout the decade around works such as the translation of Ortega y Gasset's *La rebelion de las masas* and a number of British texts (Chapter 6,1); the proposal of a Fascist Europe by the British Union of Fascists in the second half of the decade (Chapter 6,2); and the debate on federalism at the very end of the 1930s (Chapter 6,7). In all these cases, the political dimension and meaning were predominant, and very rarely does one find in their interstices hints of the emotional dimension (one instance concerns Count Coudenhove-Kalergi (see Chapter 2,1) who enters the scope of this book in its treatment of the first and the last debates). These hints have not been followed up here, but could be in the future. They are based on the connection between emotions, peace and women, who were deemed to have a natural inclination towards peace-making as well as taking care of social issues and the social aspects of political issues. These ideas, not new, were applied to the construction of a united Europe. The enquiry in this direction might be an object of further work concerning the history of women engaged in international peace movements.

A second path follows the idea of love as an independent discourse, considered not from the perspective of intellectual history, but rather from the point of view of a social history of culture, and this is done through an analysis of the correspondence between a couple – a British woman and a German man – in the years 1938–45 (Chapter 7). Their correspondence is an actual embodiment through internal conflicts and difficult choices, of the European dimension of a love relationship at a historical moment when nationality came to be, in spite of intentions, important in intimate relationships. The story of Catherine and Konrad is in many ways exceptional and no direct representativeness is claimed for it in terms of social history. The two protagonists belonged to well-to-do classes, and were both, each in their own way, rather extraordinary; moreover, theirs was a particular kind of European marriage, being Anglo-German, for which a whole tradition exists in Britain. Therefore the nationalities of the two correspondents were at the time more historically significant than others, being those of the major antagonists of the struggle between democracy and totalitarianism. Finally, even if the two correspondents were not political, their relationship showed the effects of the overlapping of the political and cultural spheres under a totalitarian regime and in times of war. In that situation, romantic love found expression in their correspondence as a hope for the future in the form of a stereotype that the two, particularly Catherine, expected and desired to reconstitute in peacetime. The theme of Europeanness was also present in their letters, implicitly in Catherine's case, given her habit of travelling widely throughout Europe, and more explicitly on the part of Konrad, an aristocrat who recognised a common heritage among European nations, even when at war with one another. Further research could be done into letters written between individuals of different countries and continents, between Europeans separated by economic necessities, wars and colonialism. If the view from the outside is often essential for detecting a European sense of belonging, it may be argued that in a way Europe was also created through correspondence between expatriates and migrants and their relatives and friends at home.

In these first two itineraries of research, one of our central notions – love and Europeanness – is uppermost, the other only hinted: in the first, Europe is the theme, love a suggestion, in the second the reverse. Other lines of work have explicitly embodied the encounter between the two discursive traditions. The third itinerary explores the connections between the debate on the crisis of European civilisation and the debate on the crisis of marriage, sex and love. This connection was at the heart of the work by Christopher Dawson, the Catholic historian who proposed a view of the unity of European civilisation from the Middle Ages on, and at the same time pin-pointed the central role of the relationships between the sexes, particularly in marriage but also in art and literature, for the possible salvation of that civilisation. As a consequence he argued forcefully with the advocates of divorce, sexual freedom and emancipation (see Chapter 2,2). Dawson is particularly important because he introduced into the question of love the religious dimension, which has often been connected in European history with the vision of love; this connection had varied consequences, from the affirmation of the inseparability of love from marriage and procreation to an influence on expression: sometimes in the sense that the mystics used love language to speak about their relationships with God, but also, *vice versa*, in the sense that the patrimony of secular love can be understood as the transformation of love for God.

The link between European civilisation and the emotion of love can also be found in the debates which took place among psycho-analysts and psychologists in the 1930s, involving Freud and Freudians and Jung and Jungians (see Chapter 2,3). The starting point was the question of peace and war: a new world war might well represent the end of European civilisation as such, and the challenge was whether psycho-analysis could provide a way to prevent such a catastrophe, as the positive results of psycho-analysts in treating ex-soldiers of First World War traumas suggested. All psycho-analysts and psychologists pointed out the interwoven nature of love and aggression,[18] which Freud had defined as Eros and Thanatos. Some of his British followers – such as Edward Glover – believed that psychological research into the nature of the war impulse might indeed help, since war-like behaviour was a compensation for the repression of infantile drives of love and hatred. For Jung and some of his followers – such as Mary Esther Harding – women were at the core of the social and spiritual crisis in Europe, particularly those emancipated women at the forefront of the process of modernity who were undergoing a mental masculinisation. If these women could act on an awareness that only in the state of love could they attain the best, they would be able to repair the inner wounds left in the European psyche by the war and to foster a new era, when Eros would unite what Logos had divided.

The same debate on the crisis of traditional forms of masculinity and femininity, and on marriage, love and sex, forms the background to another part of this book, the chapter on a novel published in 1930 by Ralph Mottram, *Europa's Beast* (see Chapter 1). The novel depicts the difficulties of male/female relationships after the First World War, a result of the crisis of men and masculinity, which the war had made evident and emphasised, as well as of the transformations in women's ways of life and traditional forms of femininity. Mottram's text – a fairly unimportant novel in the wide-ranging cultural spectrum of the time – is distinctive in bringing together some social aspects of those crises as lived by middle-class provincial people whose hopes were invested in a romantic love which was also sexual, and the myth of Europa, as we shall see.

A fourth itinerary explores the idea that Europeans had invented both the literature and sentiments of courtly love in twelfth-century Provence, ideas which then spread to many other countries in Europe – from Portugal to Italy, Germany and England – and later led to the development of romantic literature and love. In inter-war Britain, among those who approached this theme were Dawson, Robert Briffault in his then well-known anthropological work *The Mothers* (see Chapter 4), and, most important, C.S. Lewis in his *Allegory of Love* (see Chapter 5). The three represent a range of different approaches to the question of the Europeanness of courtly love: Dawson supported the Arabic origins of what he called the 'ideal of romantic love' and insisted that there was nothing particularly Christian or European in it, because he was keen to exalt Catholic marriage and to rule out the relationship between Catholicism and what he considered a type of 'Platonic' relationship. Briffault accepted that at the basis of Provençal poetry and love there was a mixture of influences from Celtic oral literature to heroic romances and Arabic poetry, and vehemently accused Christianity of having not only removed the sensuous pleasure from love as sung of by the early troubadours, but also of having physically destroyed the flourishing civilisation of Southern France with the Albigensian crusade led by Simon de Montfort in 1208–29. For Lewis, the Europeanness of courtly love was unquestionable, in the sense that Provençal love was the starting point of a line of sentiments that, adequately purged, produced the cultural and moral predominance of Christian values in their British version.

A fifth itinerary finds traces of the Europa myth in the British culture of the 1930s. In Britain, elaborations of the myth had been present through the arts and letters of the previous centuries. A musical work for the stage by Richard Leveridge, *Jupiter and Europa*, had first been performed in London in 1723, while in the literary tradition Europa appeared in the verses of Spenser and Tennyson, and in painting she was portrayed by Turner, Crane (in a painting now lost) and Watts. In the second half of the nineteenth century Europa was present in poems by Cory (1858), Landor (1858), Dowden (1873) and De Vere (1884). The Europa myth appears in the present work in various forms: as the mysterious symbol connecting the ages and presiding over the regeneration of masculinity and femininity in Mottram's novel; in an anthropological interpretation of the myth in Briffault's *Mothers* and, in his two best-selling novels, as a symbol of the doom of European civilisation. The myth also surfaces in cultural products which can be considered exemplary of the 1930s: in one of the satirical poems by the Irish Oliver Gogarty (1933), where Europa is compared with contemporary young women who are brought up as boys; in the fashionable photographs by Madame Yevonde (1935), which portray aristocratic and middle-class British women disguised as Olympian goddesses and mythological heroines; and in the tapestry by the artist Frank Dobson (1938), where the repetition of innumerable figures of Europa and the bull in an elegant combination of colours and design accentuates the stereotypical nature of the image. These three examples demonstrate the ambivalence of the new forms of culture, art and the media in transforming an ancient image.

In the last three examples there is no patent connection between Europa and Europe, while in the first two there are some more-or-less latent ones. In Briffault's two novels, the woman who represents Europa and the European tradition of art and civilisation comes from Russia, then the scene of what he considered an effort to produce a totally new civilisation, which like a Phoenix would be resurrected from the ashes of the old one. For Mottram the connections are much more subterranean: his Europa is linked with Europe in a subtler way than Briffault's; his novel hints at the possibility of a relationship with the inner forces of history, nature and sexuality which is not threatening and destructive. Mottram's heroine is a post-suffragette English woman, a figure encompassing the need of many women for emancipation but adding a mixture of archaic and modern, to create an independent woman with deep roots in the past. This woman is somehow the reincarnation of one of the most famous Europas of Venetian art, by Veronese; she acts as the conduit for the transmission of attitudes and values across centuries and millennia. Since Europa is a symbol of matriarchy or at least of a civilisation preceding patriarchal Europe, her reappearance can be taken as an indication of a crisis of patriarchy and of a possible new order in gender relationships.

A sixth itinerary follows the idea of a new Europe as utopia. Although they did not want to be identified with previous utopias, the members of the New Europe group – active in Britain in the 1930s – had the strength of great utopianism when they envisaged a future European federation based on regional autonomy and on the premise of a general psychic change resulting in a new thought and a new feeling; the story of this group also introduces a number of extraordinary characters, from its founder, the Serbian Dimitrije Mitrinovic, to scientists such as Patrick Geddes and Frederick Soddy to less-well-known people who fought for the ideal of a regeneration of Europe (see Chapter 3). The vision of a new and peaceful Europe catalysed proposals for social solidarity, as in those of Margaret Storm Jameson (see Chapter 6,3) but also hopes of new ways for human beings to relate, and specifically new ways of loving. This latter hope was present in some British poets who participated in the Spanish Civil War on the side of the Republic (see Chapter 6,5) and was represented by a figure of exceptional humanity and culture, Frank Thompson, who fought in the Second World War and died in Bulgaria with the partisans.

His enthusiasm for a united Europe which would welcome and respect a plurality of cultures and languages seems the right ending for this book, providing an epilogue which contrasts to some extent the pessimism arising from so many failures and contradictions of Europeanism and Europeanness.

The six itineraries of research are organised chronologically, although they cannot be absolutely sequential. Therefore the same themes, seen from different points of view, appear more than once. The thematic shifts also involve temporal shifts. While Chapter 1, placed in 1930, has its roots in the preceding period and the First World War, Chapters 2 and 3 gradually move from 1930 to the mid-1930s. Briffault's (Chapter 4) and Lewis's (Chapter 5) main works are dated 1935–36, although references to the previous and subsequent periods are also made in these two chapters. Chapter 6 is concerned with developments in the second half of the 1930s, while Chapter 7 and the Epilogue bring us from the last years of the 1930s to the beginning of the 1940s. All this supports a vision of the 1930s not as a monolithic era, but one of great complexity and multiplicity.

To complete the presentation of the itineraries of research, something must be said about the methodological approach, which changes according to the object and problem tackled. Certain lines of research have required a micro-historical procedure. The first example is the chapter on Mottram, which focuses on a single text, its reception and its place in the production and life of the author. The approach is not social, as it has often been the case with micro-history, but cultural – inspired by psycho-analytical literary criticism – and it uses in a larger sense the interpretive tools developed by this method. Similarly treated way are Dawson, Briffault and Lewis; however, in this last case the chapter also contains an excursus on the dispute about the origins of courtly love which is more in the line of a history of ideas, and an analysis of the role of Provence in the European imaginary which belongs more appropriately to cultural history. The combination of procedures in this same chapter is required by the change of object and of viewpoint. A micro-historical approach is also the only kind that could do justice to the types of sources (private letters) and of historical object (intimate relations) in the treatment of a love correspondence (see Chapter 7). The parts of the book dealing with political and psycho-analytical debates adopt the approach of a cultural and intellectual history over the short and medium term (see Chapters 2, 3 and 6). The combination of approaches makes visible both the distances between different ways of treating the same question and the affinities between distant fields and positions.

It should be clear at this point that the present work is not a social history of emotions, but a cultural and intellectual history which takes into account the role of emotions not only as content but to some extent also in relation to method. One assumption of the research is that there are unconscious aspects of history, ideas and themes that do not appear on the surface of literature and that, thanks to the indeterminacy of the past,[19] can be rescued, interpreted, and elaborated. A corollary of the idea of exploring the indeterminate and hidden aspects of the past has to be an interest in the marginal, the unrepresentative, the interstitial. It is not my intention to reduce what is unconscious to the level of the peripheral, in spite of the strong inclination of the unconscious to find a place among the apparently secondary, or even the irrelevant. However, it is true that the two often coincide, as it happens with commonplaces shared by many people and with attitudes held by small and very small minorities, in a combination which it is not always easy to disentangle. In fact, how is it possible to find what is hidden, at least partially, even to those involved? It becomes possible by combining some techniques which are well-known to historians and social scientists with others which originate from literary criticism and psycho-analysis. Thus I have followed procedures which are usual in historiography, such as reading secondary sources and going through journals that cover publications of all sorts such as the *Times Literary Supplement*. The texts that I fished out in this traditional way were novels and essays, both directly and indirectly relevant to the subject. The ones I decided to take into consideration – through choices in which my own *ego-histoire*, understood as the historian's reflections on her work, certainly played a central role – sometimes had to be treated, according to my hypothesis, as symptoms of repressed themes. One example of this is the interpretation of the novels by Mottram and by Briffault, where the connection between Europe and love and sexuality is alluded to through the myth of Europa and the bull. These novels have not been treated as the basis for generalisations, but rather as symptoms of something subterranean such as the presence of Europe in British culture, in both its contradictory and ambivalent aspects. Briffault's novels express the element of anti-Britishness contained in the British love for Europe as well as the lack of hope in the destiny of European civilisation. Mottram's novel owes its privileged position in this book to its undeveloped, mysterious, and somehow obscure character, its use of the myth of Europa in an implicit and allusive way; so that it may be taken to symbolise the atmosphere of Britain towards Europe at the beginning of the 1930s, an atmosphere where the idea of Europe and things European seemed distant and suggestive, buried under many layers and yet deemed essential to the resumption of meaningful life after the horrors of war.

Again, Europe here is something not immediately visible on the surface, but something of the heart, of the inside, an obscure possibility in which a mythological past is confused with a view of a new golden age. The mission of Britain in relationship with Europe could be understood by Mottram, as by many others, in a cultural and spiritual sense, as a mission of leadership allowing itself to be contaminated with the spirit of southern Europe as expressed through art and travel, a structure of feelings similar to that which emerged in travellers' descriptions of the south of Europe, particularly in the literature about Provence. This hints at the fact that the connections between the itineraries of research are more numerous than those described in this introduction, and that readers, if they wish, may trace some others.

## Positionality

By positionality I mean that I now want to call my own place as investigator into question.[20] My original aim was to find bridges between the personal and the political spheres. While I no longer believe in the immediacy of the feminist *mot-d'ordre* of the 1970s – 'the personal is political' – I retain a belief in the need it expressed for thought which goes beyond the dichotomies of the present world. The tension between the two spheres could and perhaps should never be completely eliminated, but the political and public reverberations of what is personal and private can be explored, in order not only to resist the colonisation of the latter sphere but also to evaluate its potentialities. The inter-relationship between the idea of Europe and that of love can be considered as an example of connections (and distances) between the personal and the political. In terms of historical imagination, it could be asked what would happen if one tried to connect the world of feelings and emotions and the world of politics and official culture. Of course the study of the former requires sources such as literary texts or private correspondence, while the latter relies on essays and other documents.

The distance between attitudes to Europe as expressed in novels, which expected deep regeneration to result from reviving some form of Europeanness, and political ideas about Europe in Britain at the time could not be greater, at least at first sight. The public discourse was about war compensation, trade and European federalism as a way out between the pressure of the United States and Soviet Russia, and later Nazism. However, there were also convergences between this public discourse and the one touching on the private and intimate, inasmuch as both seemed to expect the solution to all sorts of crisis, individual as well as collective, from re-drawing the relationships between European states and particularly between Europe and Britain. On the one hand, therefore, the distance between emotions and political Europe was there, and is reflected in this book by the jumps between chapters. One of my hypotheses in this research has been that this distance was one of the roots of the failure of the political idea of Europe, second to nationalist interests and disinterest in a European union on the part of European governments. On the other hand, there are threads connecting the literary and the political perspectives which might have been developed, as the New Europe group, for instance, tried to do.

Maybe now we have hopes that the distance between the two, although even wider today than in the 1930s, can be reduced in the future, and that people's feelings may have some bearing on decisions concerning questions like war and peace. In the last two decades most forms of politics have become more remote from the lives and interests of most people; the connections between democratic politics and socio/cultural movements have, in the Western European countries, become very thin in comparison with the 1960s and 1970s. This process is even more accentuated for Europeanist politics, which have been touched only very partially by the new social movements. In following my lines of research I often sensed missed chances, somehow naive and yet maybe fertile: the sense that potentialities in history had not been developed or not even fully realised, leaving Europeanism to politicism and bureaucratism, while it could have been linked with imagination and feelings.

In fact historical research shows that the idea of Europe has lost, since the Second World War, most of its hopes of regeneration and the aura of utopianism and passion that were still present in the 1930s. By a sort of nemesis, this loss took place at the same time as the actual construction of an institutional European unity began; this nemesis might well have been – at least partially – a reaction to the Eurocentrism present in the idea of a united Europe, which has had a politically ambivalent history. Such syncronicity also has something to do with the fact that the European construction has been largely an affair of political élites, although the influence of the federalist dream retained a meaningful role. Moreover, the loss of the old rhetorics of Europeanism has been welcomed by many as a way of dispensing with redundant ideology. However, if we consider not only the immediate political value of ideas about Europe but also their cultural reverberations, we see that too much has been thrown away. My intention in this book is to explore, and whenever possible criticise, forms of Eurocentrism in some ideas of Europe and in the connection between them and concepts of love. It is also to see whether anything can be saved of the connection between identity and love once the rigid cage of Eurocentricism is broken. Placing love at the core of identity – rather than linking identities with an abstract and intellectual individualism or with an inherited patrimony based on class, race or region – would imply that elective affinities as well as inherited ones are constitutive of individuals and of their relationships with their collectives. A pre-condition is a critical enquiry into the historical discourses on this matter in the Western tradition.

A paradox of discourses on Europe has always been that the universal destiny of civilisation and that of this particular part of the world were made to overlap, generating a confusion that was shared by writers both great and minor. The result of this overlapping was the exclusion from the area of privileged subjectivity of anybody who was not considered to be a full representatives of European culture. Therefore the loving – and speaking – subject was most frequently assumed to be white, male and European, while women, Jews and people of all other cultures were considered either as objects – without a voice of their own – or admitted to the kind of relationship called romantic love only through processes of subordination and assimilation. A striking example of this is that only men were considered to be the authors of that Provençal poetry so often considered the basis of European civilisation: the figure of the trobairitz, women who were poets and singers in the twelfth and thirteen centuries, was most often either ignored or misrepresented in the eighteenth, nineteeenth and twentieth centuries, until the critical corpus established by Angelica Rieger at the beginning of the 1990s began to do them justice and dispel the over-simplifying interpretation that they were mere literary masks of men's voices.

In the course of this book we shall find numerous examples of convinced supporters of European unity or of the importance of European culture, whose positions were flawed by forms of dogmatic ethnocentrism, if not racism. An important example was the attitude of Count Coudenhove-Kalergi who, in his book *Pan Europa* (1923), which launched the organisation of the same name, proposed that the nations involved in the future federation of European states bring their colonies with them and share the spoils of their exploitation, with a form of Eurocentrism which contained elements of racism towards non-European peoples. The most evident form of internal racism, very often coupled with Europeanism, was anti-Semitism, traces of which appear, among the authors and groups treated here, not only in those who made it a point of their programme such as Oswald Mosley and the British Union of Fascists, but also in Briffault, T.S. Eliot, Gogarty, Ormiston Curle, J.B. Priestley, New Europe; unfortunately this list is long. The fact that these traces are often slight does not reduce their weight. Britain was no exception in the European context.[21] While I do not accept the thesis that the idea of Europe cannot be separated from European fascism and the Nazi Holocaust[22] and I consider this book a testimony to the contrary, it is undeniable that the discourse on Europeanness has often included antisemitism. However, it would be completely ahistorical to confuse the diffused type of antisemitism which was rife in public and private discourses in Europe during the first decades of our century and the violent antisemitism of Fascists and Nazis. On the contrary, I believe that Jewish culture and the Jews have been such essential components of European culture that one could paraphrase Cioran's 'a town without Jews is a dead town' into 'a Europe without Jews is a dead Europe', which also means that the attempted annihilation of Jews dealt a mortal blow to the idea of Europeanness and a united Europe. However, this terrain is fraught with difficulties, signaled for instance by the very fact that the quotation from Cioran comes from a literary context where the mixture of judeophilia and antisemitism is extreme. Other tendencies of Eurocentrism were, as directly applied to the discourse of love, the forms of orientalism and anti-Americanism which often accompanied the definition of an assumed notion of European love.

The deconstruction of Eurocentrism in the field of love can be done and has been done, from the outside, by comparing Eurocentric claims with the history of other civilisations. Various authors have insisted on the existence of a refined kind of love, 'impossible' and characterised by absence and lack, in non-European cultures. A similar kind of love was expressed by the nomadic poets of the Arabic desert from the seventh century onwards, as well as in the treatises on love written by Ibn-Sina and Ibn Hazm al-Andalusi between the end of '900 and the beginning of the first century of our millennium,[23] in the work of the Persian poet Nizami, author of the 1188 *Tale of Layla and Maynun*,[24] and in the *Tale of Genji* written by Lady Shikibu Murasaki in Japan at the beginning of this millennium. The universality of romantic love has been asserted by recent studies whereby anthropologists have found forms of it in all sorts of societies, from the Australian Aborigines to the People's Republic of China.[25]

While these approaches from the outside are useful and inspiring, I have chosen to criticise Eurocentrism from the inside, i.e. through the history of some of its manifestations, and to expose their contradictions and hierarchies, trusting that my approach can erode them from within. Therefore I have accepted what the Italian philosopher and ethnographer Ernesto De Martino called 'critical ethnocentrism', with some corrections of his position. I share with him the central conviction that we cannot jump out of our culture and that an absolutely non-ethnocentric perspective is theoretically absurd and practically impossible, because it would imply the capacity to exit history and contemplate all cultures, including one's own. With the diaspora of cultures which is typical of the post-colonial era, we find ourselves trying to avoid dogmatic ethnocentrism on the one hand and cultural relativism on the other. 'Critical ethnocentrism' inherits from the former the need for a centre and roots, and from the latter the radical criticism of any given superiority, and tries to go further, questioning the *ethnos* of the subject in a comparison with other *ethne*. By so doing one recognises the need to relate the present multiplicity of peoples, cultures and histories in the perspective of a unification of humankind now dispersed. This unification is not a pre-ordained plan by any god or by the forces of history, as the 'lazy presupposition' that history has a meaning without us would imply; it lies totally ahead of us as a task. This task is based on the assumption that European or Western culture has been historically at the centre of the impulse to compare, unify and plan. It implies a critical use of Western interpretive categories, the explicit awareness of their historical genesis and of their limitations, and the need to remould and enlarge their meaning through a relationship with other historic-cultural worlds. It also presupposes the idea that a common humankind embraces all cultures and that only in accepting the comparison between them can one discover the sense in which humankind is to be unified. If this task is not performed, the claim to primacy posed by the history of Western civilisation can be definitively rejected.[26]

I would like to add something to De Martino's approach, having undergone the process of controlling my writing through a continual implicit reference to other cultures and sub-cultures, i.e. questioning how my assertions would sound to those belonging to generations, gender and ethnic traditions different from mine. The first addition is that from the first half of the 1960s, when he wrote, the goal of human unity seems to be further away and the claim to primacy of European and Western culture to have already been rejected, from the outside and from the inside, both because the task is not being performed and because Europe is no longer the centre of the world, in either economic or cultural terms. As a result, the two opposites, dogmatic ethnocentrism and cultural relativism, continue to be dominant. The universal values implicit in particular non-European cultures have been only partially recognised, and a concrete universalism, capable of fully taking into account the particularities of human bodies, is still far from being developed. Secondly, it seems to me that anybody placed within ethnocentrism can speak from a position which is not exactly at the centre, but rather somewhat displaced towards the margins, if she is aware of the contradictions which preside at her taking the position of the subject within her own culture. While this 'anybody' can be translated in my case into 'a woman', it might also have different meanings. However, awareness is an indispensable precondition in order to appeal from within, and critically, to the world of culture, the only currently existing one[27] as well as in order to avoid any form of essentialism.

It may seem strange to advocate a gender point of view in a book where women appear rarely. In fact those present here can be counted very rapidly: from those whose action and thought are better documented – such as Margaret Storm Jameson, Margaret Ormiston Curle and Barbara Wootton – to those about whom we know much less in spite of their having been active in the New Europe group – such as Winifred Gordon Fraser, Lilian Slade or Valerie Cooper – or their having supported a man in intellectual and material ways, as Herma Briffault did, to the authors of 'grey' literature such as the travelling books about Provence. No doubt more research would reveal much more. But I would also like to contend that women are present in this book as audiences capable of suggesting certain views with implicit requests (for instance the ambivalent position of Briffault towards feminists or Mottram's intention to create a protagonist expressing women's conditions); if audiences are not passive, we must assume their influence on authors. I am convinced that in this process the high level of women's emancipation in Britain – when compared with

23

other countries such as Italy – played an important role. And last but not least I would like to count among these unseen influences the literary figures of the trobairitz, whose very existence changes the whole traditional outlook on Provençal love and supports the assumption that the loving and creating subject can equally well be a woman, and the silent object of love a man.

What I have done here is a small part of a historical work, although it has drawn inspiration from literary criticism and psycho-analysis, and makes the need for theoretical work in this field acutely felt. Feminists in the 1970s criticised romantic love as 'the pivot of women's oppression', considering 'romanticism as a cultural tool of male power to keep women from knowing their condition' (Firestone), since its false idealisation concealed gender inferiority through the so-called 'pedestal treatment'. In this perspective, gender and class conspired to sustain romantic love and its deceptions. For Germaine Greer romantic love – originating as the idle adulterous fantasies of the nobility – replaced parental coercion when the Protestant middle classes started abandoning arranged marriages in favour of free and equal unions; in that sense romantic love was a prelude to the 'establishment marriages' of modern times. Juliet Mitchell then changed the territory of the polemics observing that at the end of sixteenth and beginning of the seventeenth centuries the woman became the object of the romantic tale, while previously the subject of passion was the man. Therefore the romance shifted from being about a sexual subject – male – to being about a woman, considered the object of love and sex. In the course of this process, romantic love shifted from oppositional, adulterous love in the Middle Ages to being part of a conformist marital love in modern times and to the massification of culture represented by popular fiction and TV culture. However, these feminists scholars did not challenge the Eurocentric paradigm of romantic love: the male subject was implicitly European or Western, but no explicit criticism followed that line of enquiry, which is an important one for the future.

For future research, the most important questions no longer concern the presumed exclusive Europeanness of courtly and romantic love, but the nature of the construction whereby European culture has considered this love a core of its identity. Privileging this form of love – or better a particular interpretation of it as male, Eurocentric and non-physical – resulted in ignoring the plurality of European traditions of love or subjecting them to a rigid hierarchy. Therefore it favoured a conception of life where emotions were extolled but not integrated with intellectual values, where women and men were only formally equal, and the fulfillment of a relationship was confused with the sexual act. The concept of identity related to this notion was monolithic and hierarchical, subordinating the richness of psychic life to a pyramidal system of values. Conceptualising European identity in this way was part of a tradition of dogmatic ethnocentrism which isolated Europe and privileged its dominant role over and against its other contributions. However, the connection between European identity and courtly love also contained some universal points, inasmuch as this kind of love, at least in its original form, stressed the sense that lovers are always two distinct beings and can never reach complete fusion, that desire and fulfillment stay in a complex relationship, that the expression of love has an existence independent from the sentiment. These elements are examples of what could be saved of the connection between identities and love outside the frame of Eurocentrism.

The awareness of these can be part of identities which have no longer claim to be superior to any other, although saving the specificity which derives from place and tradition, and in the end that of the individual. The path to citizenship of the world may for some lead through the stage of European citizenship – and politically this opens heavy questions on 'which Europe' – but it can never avoid the specific itinerary of an individual's life, not only its social, cultural and gender belonging, but also its unique trajectory.

## Notes on Introduction

1   Illouz
2   Oxford, 1936
3   Paris, 1939
4   Breton, pp 88; 136
5   Bataille, pp 807-8
6   Herodotus, *Histories*, Chapter 1, paragraph 2
7   *Ibidem*, Chapter 4, paragraph 45
8   Graves 1948; Jung and Kerenyi
9   Singer 1984
10  Singer 1987
11  Paz 1993
12  Hynes, p 393
13  *Ibidem*, pp 382; 388
14  Symons, p 14
15  Deeds in Holloway, pp 9; 12
16  Muggeridge, p 14
17  Alexander; Light; Montefiore
18  Suttie
19  Hacking
20  Spivak
21  Kushner; Poliakov

22  Delanty,  p 114
23  Cheikh-Moussa
24  Kakar and Ross
25  Jankowiak
26  De Martino, pp 352; 391-8
27  Braidotti 1987

# CHAPTER 1
# EUROPA IN EAST ANGLIA

## *Europa's Beast* by Ralph H. Mottram

… she just dwelt in that state that was beyond or beside argument, her eyes on the faintly illumined ceiling, her hands on her breasts, and her warm comfortable bed, from being that, became a bath of honey, and from that began to move, as the bull in the picture might, and from that became even more intimate and more nearly human, something which upheld her and bore her along and knew that it was doing so. And the silver-starred blue roof became a sky, and the carefully copied four-poster's hangings a canopy, and she was that beloved creature, mateless and needing no mate, for everything loved and enjoyed her beauty.

Slowly the motion stopped, things resumed their normal appearance and meaning, and she came back to her bed and bedroom, and the shaded lamp at her bedside. She glanced at her wrist-watch. Good gracious! And extinguishing the light she turned on her side and slept.[1]

This erotic fantasy of the protagonist of a novel published in London in April 1930 is crucial to its plot and gives it its title, *Europa's Beast*. The fantasy, which the protagonist considers to be an 'incoherent fancy', not to be confided to anybody, stems from her feeling of being a 'reincarnation' – a sort of religious feeling similar to the one she had experienced during her convent schooling – of a 'mythical or symbolic personage' whose name she does not know or remember. The image was based on the recollection of a painting,

... every detail of which was firmly imprinted on her mind – though the name of the painter escaped her – was it Titian – or Paul someone – or Gior-Gione? - showed that dame, with one lovely scarf, a sort of stole or tippet of the Middle Ages, blowing well clear of her, so that she lay expanded like an open flower, reclining, with the admiring assistance of other beauties, upon the back of a great white bull, whose suppressed force was curbed as it knelt, though its eyes looked you through with a meek earnestness not to be found in the world except in the eyes of the man Skene... in a way she could not explain, she, Olive Blythway, was that female form.[2]

This form was, as will become clear in the course of the story, that of Europa riding the bull as Veronese painted her in 1580. Why Olive Blythway should identify herself with Europa and her lover with the bull is the major puzzle of the novel. Olive is the daughter of a wealthy businessman of plebeian origin, Roger Purchas, her grandmother having been a gypsy, capable of forecasting the future. During the war Olive had been a Voluntary Aid Detachment nurse, a member of the staff of the Princess's Hospital, and in that position had discovered an aspect of the male-female relationship that was a mixture of eroticism, aestheticism, narcissism and sublimated maternal feeling. An instance of her narcissism is the fact that during the war Olive wore the colour of her name:

> One of the distinguishing marks of that most distinguished of all British Medical Units was the liberty allowed VADs to choose their own colour and materials. She had come out in olive green, and knew she looked well. Never, in fact, had she hoped for such success. It did not dawn upon her until long after, that men are at their best when flat on their backs and entirely dependent on women, but that the women on whom they are dependent are not so easy to manage. She saw herself clearly enough, the perfectly-turned-out angel, hovering, skilful and noiseless, by the bedside of suffering.[3]

Her marriage with an airplane pilot of aristocratic descent is based on a similar mixture of sublimation and fraternity, and is, of course, doomed to failure. This mixture does not include sexual pleasure, unless in the 'brutal' form of a quick and absent-minded penetration. After a disappointing first night, Olive and her husband make use of separate bedrooms and go on to conduct a routine conjugal existence, respecting external conventions; it is, however, emotionally very unsatisfactory, at least for her. She accepts the situation because she understands that her husband's emotional and physical indifference is the result of the war, of how the war has affected his already egotistical psychic structure.

*Europa's Beast* opens with a religious ceremony in Easthampton, a cover name for Norwich, where Olive is caught sight of by the architect Geoffrey Skene, who, although he doesn't know her yet, falls in love with her beauty. From five years of fighting in the war, Skene has brought back a wide experience of deep relationships with varied people and cultures.

However, he is conscious that 'the War has achieved little or nothing', and finds within himself 'a great emptiness unfilled', reducing him to 'an empty shell with his clothes on, his name known but nothing of him really present'. In this condition – as a psychically displaced person, in spite of his surviving sense of English identity – he finds a job as an architect supervising a post-war reconstruction, the new City Housing Scheme for the Municipality of Easthampton. However, he feels that his loneliness is not assuaged by his job or his social life, his relatives being dead and his friendships 'dissipated by the war'. It is at this point that he meets Olive, and perceives that she is the only person capable of mitigating his loneliness. Olive's husband subsequently dies in an air accident during a reckless performance. Olive and Skene become lovers – the episode describing this shows a complete dedication and satisfaction on the part of them both – and they marry, against the will of Olive's father, Roger Purchas. He, in his capacity as Chairman of the Housing Commission, gets Skene dismissed from his job, but Skene develops a new career selling his drawings.

In the course of the novel the image of the bull reappears many times to Olive, both in her day-dreaming – 'There it was again, as she looked, the sea monster. A grey bull this time, white-maned...'[4] – shortly after which Skene appears, and in a real dream, when, reawakening after the first night with her lover, 'she heard the white bull drinking in the pools of sleep'. But when she wakes up completely, she realises that 'the white bull was Geoffrey Skene drinking out of the ewer on the cottage-lodgings washstand'.[5] 'She was convinced more deeply than by reason that they [Europa and the bull] were as true today as when they were painted by the man whose name she had forgotten.'[6] At the end of *Europa's Beast*, the couple is in Venice, where Olive discovers the painting by Veronese, which they finally see together in the Palazzo Ducale. She is 'transfixed' on discovering the original of her dreams and startled by its difference from and similarity to her own images: 'that's not how I imagined it!' Her attitude involves her husband in the same fantasy:

> ... she was looking covertly at him and then at the picture, comparing it with themselves. Absurd!... there was as little in common between a harassed responsible professional man of the Twentieth Century and that large docile bull that knelt so obligingly, as there was between the daughter of Roger Purchas and the flowery semi-nudity of that Southern beauty, displaying her abduction with such equanimity.
> Then, as he looked, he began to wonder.[7]

Through the painting he recognises her 'superb devotion' and his own resignation to 'a yoke that was self-imposed'; 'he wasn't a bit bull-like, yet his attitude and expression were that handsome animal's'.[8] They are reconciled with their 'destiny', their 'actual fate', which includes their mutual bond and love.

The *Times Literary Supplement* commented ironically about this ending, and particularly the unfortunate phrase 'differences of diet', which Mottram had used in the comparison between Olive and Europa, although the reviewer preferred the ending to the process leading up to it. The relationship between the plot and the title puzzled many, and most did not bother to solve the puzzle. The title was derogatorily defined as 'not very attractive', 'inartistic and misleading', 'strange', 'queer', and even 'quaint'. Some reviewers expressed themselves disconcerted by the allegory of Europa, which was considered 'obscure and rather incredible' (*Evening Standard*); others simply did not mention the title, while those who did showed their uneasiness with the comparison between Skene and the bull, perhaps due to the type of eroticism presented or alluded to in the novel.

*Europa's Beast* was widely reviewed, in national and international women's magazines, such as *Vogue* and *Harper's Bazaar* (which were fairly sympathetic), through conservative dailies and weeklies like The *Evening Standard* or the *Scots Observer*, to more progressive ones such as the *Observer*, the *Manchester Guardian* and Labour's official paper, the *Daily Herald*. Regional broadsheets (*Birmingham Gazette*, *Liverpool Post*, *Norwich Mercury* and many others) gave space to reviews of the book, which for them had the merit of giving an inside view of life in a provincial town. Readers of these reviews would have been unable to detect a difference between attitudes to the book taken by papers of different political orientations. All of them shared respect for the previous writings by Mottram, especially the war trilogy *The Spanish Farm*, based on the author's experience and published in 1924, which had the same protagonist – Geoffrey Skene – as *Europa's Beast*. But the reviewers were divided between those who judged this new book inferior to Mottram's previous literary achievements and those who proclaimed the appearance of 'his very best work' with 'extraordinary effective result' (*Eastern Daily Press*). Among the former, Ralph Straus of the *Sunday Times* considered the book 'dullish' and not 'so virile as the war-trilogy', judging the new Skene – middle-aged and poorly paid – to be 'an unexciting and vaguely disappointed fellow'. The *New Statesman* was ironic about the middle-classness of *Europa's Beast* ('not a flaw in its admirable commonsense'), while Harold Nicolson in the *Daily Express* displayed ambivalent feelings about a novel 'important in its way' but somehow 'wrong', especially for what concerned 'that prim sensualist' Skene (in Mottram's terms a 'sensuist').

In spite of this ambivalent reception, *Europa's Beast* sold well, although it was not a real bestseller (the first book by Mottram, *The Spanish Farm*, sold 257,072 copies, while the trilogy under that title sold 27,456 copies altogether and its German translation 12,049). The public, however, treated it better than the critics: 7,800 copies were ordered and Chatto & Windus delivered 7,870, plus 358 copies of an 'edition de luxe'. According to the publisher's archival documents, the book had sold 7,238 copies by

September 1930, the year of publication; exactly one year before, *The Spanish Farm* trilogy, which also received the Hawthornden Award, was reported to have sold more than double this number. These figures, as well as the price – *Europa's Beast* ranged between 4s 10d per copy unbound and 7s 6d for a bound one – were indicative of a reasonably successful book, presumably with a middle-class audience. This included a consistent number of women, as the author himself was well aware. Mottram's novel can be placed between the literary and mass market, composed of paperback romances or weekly magazines that boomed in Britain at the end of the 1920s and the beginning of the 1930s. Therefore it might be presumed that his audience was to be found in the middle strata of the middle classes, characterised by their moderate political stand and their version of 'conservative modernity' arising out of a mixture of conservatism and novelty.[9] In this perspective, the interpretation of English culture in the early 1930s as polarised between ideas of catastrophe and of rebirth,[10] has to be corrected. We might admit that the cultural area characterised by conservative modernity fostered the idea of a limited rebirth in an intimate sphere without immediate changes in the outer world.

Mottram's own social ideas were a combination of moderate and 'heretical' positions. In his autobiographical three-volume *Vanities and Verities*, he declares that he was fortunate enough to have been responsible, since he was seventeen, for other people's, and the public's, money, safety against invasion, good order and education. On the other hand, he was proud enough to state that his traditional family creed, the Unitarian church, was considered heresy by many good people, and attributed to that 'heretical frame of mind'[11] his religious approach to art. This combination of conformism and independence became clear in his effort to find a middle way between conservation and innovation. Harold Nicolson, in the *Daily Express*, condescendingly noted his irritation at the triumph of 'middleness' in the characters of *Europa's Beast*:

> they are all semi-detached, semi-prosperous, semi-educated, semi-dashing. I dislike their caution and their pretentiousness, their conventionality and their stuffy little parlour manners – an atmosphere in which even sex becomes genteel.

There is a connection between this kind of middle-being as being half-something, the middle-classness of it all ('one of the most middle-class novels ever written', according to the *New Statesman*) and the type of moderate modernity proposed by Mottram.

However, literary success revolutionised the life of Ralph Mottram, a bank clerk in Norwich from the age of seventeen, with only the break of the First World War, which he fought in Flanders. He quickly wrote two sequels, *Sixty-four, Ninety-four!* in 1925, and *The Crime at Vanderlynden's* in

1926; the resulting trilogy became the basis for the film *Roses of Picardy*, directed and produced by Maurice Elvey in 1927. In that same year, aged forty-four, Mottram left the bank and started life as a professional writer, producing novels and poetry as well as biographies and books on banking before his death in 1971. The success of *Europa's Beast* can be understood only in relation to Mottram's previous work: in 1930, Geoffrey Skene was already a well-known figure in the imaginary of the English public, both in literature and in films. He had been the protagonist of Mottram's first book, *The Spanish Farm*, as well as the hero of the film based on it.

## A 'European' love story

In *The Spanish Farm* Skene appeared as a tall and dark Lieutenant of the Easthamptonshire Regiment, fighting in French Flanders and meeting Madeleine Vanderlynden, twenty-year-old daughter of a farmer. Their love story might well be defined as 'European', since it took place on the continent, between two people of different nationalities, in the area where century after century Romans and Franks, French and Normans, English, Burgundians and Spaniards had fought, an area of transit and cross-cultural encounters. In this context, *The Spanish Farm*'s love story is something exceptional and extraordinary: only in a European war could a French woman and an English man from respectable backgrounds have a sexual and sentimental relationship of the kind that Skene and Madeleine had, rich and temporary, with a total closeness and an unbridgeable distance.

Mottram insists on the difference between the two, her coming from pure peasant stock (but having received an education in a convent) and him from the professional and cultured circles of the middle class. The two lovers embody reciprocal views of national stereotypes, and although each of them speaks the other's language well, they never really understand each other. Madeleine was considered by John Galsworthy, in his preface to the first edition of the book, to be 'amazingly lifelike evidence on French character extremely valuable to those among us who really want to understand the French'. She is such, according to Galsworthy, because of 'her tenacity, her clear knowledge of what she wants, her determined way of getting it, her quick blood, her business capacity', and, we might add, because of her determination to wrestle 'for the uttermost sou of compensation due to her'.[12] To Mottram she is symbolic of post-war France and of a French mentality 'with its dominant peasant outlook', by which 'the Germans were beaten. Therefore their money could be got at. This was not piracy. The Germans had invited a contest, and lost',[13] a transparent allusion to the role of France in the imposition of war compensation on Germany?

In actual fact, the Madeleine created by Mottram, notwithstanding his remark that he had tried to write the book 'from the point of view of the woman', is to a large extent a projection of British middle-class men's stereotypes and hopes: in her physical appearance 'she might well have passed for an English girl',[14] a feature she stressed by choosing sombre colours, 'inclining rather to the English model, implacably neat, well-buttoned, without a spot of bright colour or a trace of expression on her face'.[15] She was very independent in an attractive, because 'unconscious', way,[16] since 'her mental attitude contained nothing of an English suffragette's logical, theoretical stand upon "rights"';[17] on the contrary, she had something that the British respected, a 'masterful strain' and 'the habit of command', sustained by a straight glance and erect carriage.[18] On the one hand, the 'European' dimension of the love-story meant for Skene the possibility of escaping some consequences of women's emancipation in Britain. On the other, the charm stereotypically attributed to French women was a good justification for his being attracted. (It is noticeable, as a curiosity, that in the 1950s the Lord Mayor of Norwich could still declare that Norwich girls looked as good as they did and carried themselves very well because of 'a certain infusion of French blood'.[19])

Madeleine represents a femininity which is as ancient and unshakeable as the land she takes care of. In contrast to her wisdom and vitality, the war appeared as 'a crowning imbecility of insupportable grown-up children'.[20] She noticed the 'similarity of men and their talk in England, France, Germany, Italy'. Among them, the Englishmen seemed to be the least stupid and violent. Madeleine is the mirror through which the self-image of the English is portrayed: her eyes saw them as different from other fighting men, ready to pay for reparations, respectful, obsessive about certain habits like breakfasting with an 'incomprehensible meal of hot-soup'[21] and taking a bath every day. However, she had enough good sense to appreciate their value for what it really was, and in particular that of Skene. Madeleine saw very clearly that Skene was 'neither exceptionally handsome, brave or rich', rather 'an average Englishman of the professional classes';[22] she understood that Skene 'was very innocent, well brought up, sharp at money, willing and "rather like a child", "un peu enfant". She rather expected the English to be like that'. Altogether, Skene appeared to her to be more considerate than 'his nearest French equivalent would have been'. In her comparison between him and her former lover Georges d'Archeville, spoiled and perverse, lovable and self-indulgent, childlish and arrogant, it is Skene who comes out better, as she tells him: 'I love you much more. You are more frank, and much more of a man'.[23] Mottram hints at the fact that in the sexual encounter 'she did not miss her spoiled child too much, for she had instead this good child'. But she spends much of the time of their encounters talking to Skene about Georges, whom she still loves more than anything else. He was the son of the baron for whom Madeleine's father acted as chief tenant and head gamekeeper. After leaving for the war, Georges neglected to give Madeleine any news about himself and only reappeared for a brief period of cohabitation with her, for which she left her job, spent all her money and even took from Skene all the money he was left with, 100 francs. After this, Georges disappeared again and died in the war.

The love between Madeleine and Skene seems inspired more by pragmatic considerations than romantic feelings. Pushed into each other's company by the despair and desolation that surrounded them, they lived a relationship which had no future. Their reciprocally strong attraction led to satisfactory sexual encounters, which took place only on two occasions: a few hours in Amiens, and a week in Paris. Skene asked of Madeleine 'simply to be loved – comforted, more exactly, in his starved, war-worn body'. Madeleine, who 'had never read a novel and was innocent of the romantic theories of love', put into the love encounter with Skene 'something almost sacramental'. She merely wanted to have 'for a week at least someone belonging to her; beyond that she did not look'.[24] In the first love-scene, she pointed out to him the cleanliness and tidiness of her room, because she had understood that this would appeal to that 'man of different race, religion, and language'.[25] Her intuition was right, but she had no idea of the 'decent orderliness' of the life he had left, the life of an assistant diocesan architect in a provincial English town, 'with its rooted habit of cleanly comfort and moderate happiness'. In the end, it is he who embodies the hidden romanticism of the situation, due to the unbridgeable distance – a characteristic of romantic love – between the two. Skene has a type of subdued passion that goes remarkably well with his other qualities, calmness and generosity, which single him out as resilient to war-like feelings; in fact, one easily forgets in the novel that he is a soldier; however, in Skene's portrait some elements of autobiography can be seen.

All this proves to be an insufficient basis for a lasting relationship between lovers from two very different cultures. The closest they come to any international understanding is when Madeleine sends Skene a card on which the Union Jack and the Tricolour are entwined, writing on the back: 'I wish to be all yours'[26]. But when after making love he talks for twenty minutes of his home, he sounds incomprehensible to her, and in the end Skene understands that 'she did not want him, had never wanted him, nor any Englishman, nor anything English'.[27] He was too well behaved, Skene reflected bitterly, 'too English; he had in fact, not asked enough of her. Her good child bored her. Her spoiled, imperious one was what she needed.'[28] The end of the story throws some light on the nature of Madeleine's independence and reassures women back in England. *The Spanish Farm*, however autobiographical, could as well be dedicated by Mottram to his wife.

The film based on the novel was directed by Maurice Elvey and made at a high-point in his career, when he was listed as one of the five favourite film directors in the Bernstein survey for 1927 (ranked fourth by male voters and second by female voters). One year earlier Elvey had established a collaboration with Gaumont, one of the two leading companies in Britain in defiance of American domination of distribution. His films were known for their 'Englishness': he believed that 'what the world wanted from Great Britain was real British pictures'.[29] *Roses of Picardy*, 1927, showed the British in a way which was both flattering and thoughtful. The film presents Skene going back to France to visit the places where he had fought and recalling his love story. The techniques of memory and flashback are the same as Mottram used in the second and third volumes of the trilogy, which take up single episodes of the first and enlarge them, while showing the same story from a different point of view. Unfortunately, the film no longer exists, but some stills have been saved, which give us an idea of what the characters looked like. The love triangle is shown much more directly in the images than in the novels, in which Geoffrey and Georges never actually meet, and the contrast between the two men, the Frenchman and the Englishman, is heightened in the film. In some of these stills, Madeleine (Lillian Hall Davis) appears between an earnest, straightforward Skene (John Stuart) and a run-down fascinating baron (Jameson Thomas). She looks much less strong and self-sufficient than the novel makes her, and stares with adoration at the baron, while the good Skene is sympathetic to his rival (Figure 1). In another still, Madeleine's father appears, grotesquely made up as an old wreck. Apart from fresh and lovely Madeleine, the two Frenchmen seem to be the very image of decay (Figure 2).

The film's reception was favourable; reviewers praised its realism and sensitivity (*The Picturegoer*, *Bioscope*), for the 'truest war atmosphere' that the screen had seen, and for 'a *British* view of the British war spirit' (*Kinematograph Weekly*). One reviewer (Orme) insisted on the relevance of the first scene, introduced by the director in order to contextualise the story. The scene contrasted the deep concentration on the past that characterised the protagonist during his visit to Flanders with the 'bored and tired' tourists 'doing the battlefields', whose guide stated that nothing important happened in that village during the war. (The film's end is very different from that of the book, since in the latter Madeleine's fiancé dies, while in the former he ends up blind and dependent, living with Madeleine and her father; the two of them have become her children, she tells her former English lover, shadows of the men that they were before the war.) According to this review, Maurice Elvey had caught the spirit of the story and produced a remarkable, though sometimes uneven, film; some trivial mistakes ('what have the roses of Picardy to do with Flanders?'[30]) did not really harm the production, defined as 'the sensitive response of a true artist'; finally, Elvey had succeeded in probing the deeper emotions of the war as contrasted with the sensational battle pictures

Figures 1 and 2: Two stills from the missing film based on Mottram's novel *The Spanish Farm*, where Geoffrey Skene, the protagonist of *Europa and the Beast*, appears. In both, he is the character on the left.

shown by the American war films. What is important here is that *Europa's Beast* could count on an audience which had seen the film and identified Skene with John Stuart, a decent and pleasant officer, not dramatically charming but deeply attractive and reliable.

The Skene that meets Olive Blythway in *Europa's Beast* has survived all this and gone back to England. He is still afraid of English suffragists, and that is perhaps why he is tempted by a sleeping beauty like Olive. However, he has learned that a real relationship can take place only with somebody of his own culture. He has retained his Englishness, but has not lost his European outlook totally, as becomes apparent when he returns to Europe *en touriste*. While in Paris he had experienced the irreconciliable opposition between his desires to see paintings and Madeleine's to see shops, in Venice he finds with Olive the compromise of keeping himself out of her shopping, and involving her in his visits to galleries. Olive is significant in her continuity and discontinuity with Madeleine: she is a woman who understands without talking very much, and is very independent in her quiet way. But she is very English (the whole book was 'English to the core': *Everyman*), and Mottram meant her to be so, bringing to perfection through her an idea he had already tried out in the character of Marny in *The English Miss*. Mottram had written, between the trilogy and *Europa's Beast*, three Easthampton novels, based on life in Norwich. One of them, *The English Miss*, published in 1928, presented the protagonist as 'a very modern girl' who had survived the death of her beloved in the war and had ended up accepting the courtship of an American doctor. She was very English, her new fiancé recognised, because of 'a strain of that caution, which had kept the island edition of Christianity so conscious of its Sabbath, elements of that love of the essential that had stripped away every saint in the calendar', coupled with a certain idealism and the will to 'do something to tidy up the awful mess the world is in'.[31] Mottram meant to correct this character with the image of 'a young bride looking so dreadfully unhappy at the ceremony of placing the colour of the IX Battalion in the Cathedral', as he wrote in his diary of 15 May 1929. He also wrote that only when he saw this did he realise the possibility of giving literary form to an idea he had had for many years, that 'of the young frightened victim being carried away by a brute force, and finally surviving'. He never felt quite satisfied with the result, but bringing Skene in again had made it possible to present some of the social problems of the initial post-war era in passages that contained 'genuine social documentation'.

With that assertion Mottram was indicating that he still followed the inspiration started by his best-selling novel, based on events of great social significance ('there were hundreds of Skenes and Madeleines', he had written in the introduction to *Sixty-four, Ninety-four!*). The two novels were efforts in similar directions, both trying to reconcile British supremacy and European solidarity. But while *Europa's Beast* has been totally forgotten,

*The Spanish Farm* was reprinted many times during the 1930s and as recently as 1979 was published in a Penguin edition; a television dramatisation was also produced from it in 1968. The writer John Galsworthy, 1932 Nobel prize-winner for literature, who knew Mottram as a clerk and was the moving spirit in encouraging him to write (*Europa's Beast* is dedicated to him and his wife Ada), wrote that the first volume of *The Spanish Farm* represented a new form of autobiography, being 'not precisely a novel, not altogether a chronicle – a new vehicle of expression'. Such new tone, noticeable for its combination of humour, self-irony, nostalgia and lack of sentimentalism cannot be found in his much heavier, sometimes incongruous, sometimes rhetorical, later novel. This difference in tone possibly occurred because the autobiographical vein played a smaller role in *Europa's Beast* or because Mottram had ventured into a difficult undertaking, sensing something obscure and important in his times but not being able fully to express it.

## Modern men

Among the social problems that Mottram illustrated in *Europa's Beast* were the difficulties of reconstruction, depicted through the confusion and corruption of social schemes like the one in which Skene and the profiteering Roger Purchas were involved, and the reinstatement of men who had come back from the war. These problems were made particularly complicated, according to Mottram in his *Autobiography with a Difference*, by the general process of modernity, involving a decline from the previous social and spiritual order which had been based on the values of equality, goodwill and sense of duty, a sort of 'Golden Age' that had started to vanish at the end of the previous century. His contemporaries agreed with him, and insisted that modernity was a key to the novel, quoting domesticity, welfare and emptiness as the main features in it of modern life. The term 'modern' often appeared in the reviews with reference to the characters and the story: a 'modern study', according to the *East Anglian Daily Times*; 'modern love-making' wrote the *Spectator*; 'remarkable insight into the emotional problems of the better kind of modern man and woman,' the *Daily Mirror*. 'A Modern Europa' was the title that *John O'London Weekly* coupled with a contrasting sub-title: 'A girl who thought she was reincarnate', while the reviewer insisted that the novel was 'entirely modern in period and atmosphere', although the 'ultra-modern girl... in spite of her slim, bobbed modernity... remained heir to all the ages'. Modern, too, is Skene, as he accepts, though with some regret, the public demand for 'modern convenience' in preference to artistic design. In the end, perhaps the main reason why the protagonists looked modern to their readers of 1930 is that they are portrayed as 'the inarticulate, seemingly purposeless beings of the twentieth century, a generation just recovering from the staggering influences of the war' (*Eastern Daily Press*). In this sense Skene has something, although in a framework of different literary values and sociopolitical inclinations of the authors, of that feeling of individual isolation that has been seen as a constant theme of the more important novelists of the thirties. Their characters have been considered to be incomplete as individuals, and to attain their full potential only in the consciousness of their intimate relationships, thus reaching a profound communication beneath the level of language and social ritual.[32]

In the triangle centring on Olive, Ray and Skene embody two different ways of experiencing modernity. Ray has emerged not only from the war but also his family life 'frozen, not merely outside, but inside'.[33] He is incapable of loving, either spiritually or physically, and does not recognise the possibility of being saved through Olive's contact with the deep sources of life. He has become like the machine he masters and that will eventually kill him. All the reviewers considered his facile annihilation by an air crash a major weakness of the novel, which it certainly is, but his end is coherent with his persona and with Mottram's underlying polemics against a certain type of modernity.

There is a similar opposition between Olive and those 'plainer-minded girls' of her time, whom she reproaches because they lack any interest in the femininity of the past embodied by Europa as well as by the model who posed for Veronese; those girls are symbolic of a certain kind of feminine modernity, without roots or depth. Although Olive has shown her ability to be active in the war and appears 'extremely independent' in the administration of the money received from her father, she is not modern in the sense that the women studied by historiography on the interwar years are; she does not take up paid employment or want a career, but rather goes on with traditional activities such as organising exhibitions for charity. Neither does she accept, as supposedly did the great majority of British women, a role as embodiment of the ideal of the housewife. In fact she feels relieved when she can yield to 'simple self-indulgence', 'independence and idleness'.[34] Her models are not Hollywood stars, but that of a character from an opera – Carmen – who comes into her mind vividly as she walks quickly down the road humming a little tune to herself from the opera:

> ... she had a momentary vision of a rather splendid dark woman standing on a table, one hand above her head, tra-la-la-ing and not caring a damn for any one. She felt just like that.

Olive recognises the female genealogy of her feelings, 'from her mother and her mother's mother, and from all women before that',[35] in a tradition that she revitalises in her own times.

Through this multiple female image – present and past, real and imaginary – Mottram offers his interpretation of the complexities of the changes in the lives of English women in the inter-war years: emancipation as well as anxiety over the crisis of the traditional and supposedly eternal relationship between males and females. His effort takes on significance when placed against the background of the then dominant debate on love, sex and marriage. If Olive had been 'dormant' before meeting Skene, as one reviewer had pointed out, this was largely due to her husband's lack of ability to love, both spiritually and physically. It is interesting that Marie Stopes had dedicated her most important book, *Married Love* – whose sales between 1918 and 1925 passed the half-million mark – 'to young husbands', who she felt were too often extremely ignorant about the forms of women's desire. Marie Stopes reported that many marriages were unhappy because of husbands' lack of attention to their wives in daily life and especially in the sexual act, and throughout her books gave advice on how to change that while avoiding unwanted pregnancies. While many men's potency had been annihilated by the experience of the war, women had, in contrast, become more outspoken and aware of their bodies through that same experience. In the 1930s, women's magazines increasingly included instruction in matters of sex and dealt with marital problems in special articles.[36] In a 1929 science fiction history of marriage, *Halcyon or the Future of Monogamy* (where the author imagined reading in a dream the history of monogamy in England by Prof. Minerva Huxterwin, a moral historian of the mid-twenty-first century), Vera Brittain noticed that after the 'Great War of European Disintegration' young women no longer shrank from admitting to themselves and their lovers the mutual nature of sexual desire.

Olive is ready to admit this when she meets Skene. Before this encounter, her admission of desire is mediated through the mythical images that emerge from her subconscious. We can say today that Olive is a creation of the male gaze, although at the time some of the reviewers found that Mottram had displayed a 'feminine' sensitivity and touch in creating her. His construction did not satisfy him, as we know from what he wrote, and she is indeed an unfinished character. One significant indication of Mottram's hesitancy about her is a line that he cancelled from the manuscript and therefore is not included in the printed version of the novel. In the very last pages Mottram had written that her dress was 'exposing the slight loosening maternity had lent to her figure', but these lines were amended on the proof copy. Perhaps maternity, after all, could not be reconciled with the economy of the story, whose core had to be left to the couple, but this is also an indication of the special place occupied by *Europa's Beast* in the literature of the 1930s where images of women are concerned. While the book belongs to a genre between best-selling low-brow novels and modernist texts such as Virginia Woolf's,[37] the female image in it follows neither the romance stereotype of the socially ascendant girl nor the image of the independent (and suffering) cultured woman. In her love with Skene, Olive descends from the social elevation she had achieved with her former husband; she is not a mother, and she has a definite sexuality, linked with her own dreams and perception of her body, all features that separate her from other heroines of the 1930s. Mottram's is an engaged type of literature, although not committed on the side of feminism. As distinct from *The Spanish Farm* trilogy, the bias against feminism is not outspoken, and the resulting ambiguity might have appealed to a large female public.

In spite of all this, it is the male figure that Mottram draws more successfully, experimenting with a redefinition of male identity. The war had destroyed an image of authoritarian and triumphant masculinity while killing at the same time the lovers of many women who had been young during the war years. This led to a need for a renegotiation of the significance and content of the male identity. The strategy adopted by the Fascists in Italy, for instance, was to attempt to restore the male image in the realm of the social imaginary, by proposing a spectacular model of it interpreted in nationalistic terms through the public image of Mussolini. Mottram's solution to the problem is much more interesting. His Skene combines Englishness, middle-classness and maleness in an inextricable knot. In the very first scene he is presented as a male stereotype: 'like most Britons' he would not cry in public, not even to mourn over the tragedy of the Great War. However, also in Skene we find a restoration of the ancient values of masculinity – virile potency, quiet strength and patience – from which aggression has been removed. His identification with the bull is a central point of this restoration.

The image of the bull could be connected with the more general theme of the beauty and the beast, which would take up new meanings in subsequent years, from popular images like the film 'King Kong' (1933) to the versions in powerful paintings by André Masson. While the beast could be a monster or a brute overwhelming a fainted creature, it could also be seen with sympathy as the representation of women's desires that men did not fulfill. This could be the interpretation of the theme as given by the English poet Sylvia Lynd (1888–1952) who in 1931 wrote the poem 'Beauty and the Beast', ending with this ironical question:

And that strange Beast you met in fear
And loved in secrecy and shame –
Was it so well when he, so dear,
Became a Prince, and tame?[38]

Mottram has incorporated the good aspects of the monster into his hero. In his version, the bull is a symbol of the forces of nature and life, it represents procreation, and in a civilised version, love. The accent is on his seductiveness, coupled not with brute force but with mildness and gentleness, as well as with firmness and loyalty. To Skene the bull appears the sign of a destiny that he accepts: a survivor of the war, who has seen much and has lost much, he finally understands and accepts that identification, at the end of the novel, when he sees the Veronese painting together with his lover, now his wife. Recognising his dependency on Olive in order to find a reason for life and the strength to continue, Skene represents a masculine identity which is more subdued and thoughtful than the traditional one. He accepts emotions and makes it possible for Olive to do the same; he is the only one to understand that 'she had been denied any deep feeling at all, by her parents, her set, and even her poor young devil of a husband'.[39] Skene's understanding of all this is wide, but it does not find its roots in morality. His way to humanity is instead through an active appreciation of beauty. Skene is an eye, the male gaze that opens the novel. That Mottram's construction of male identity is not entirely free of contradictions can be discerned by the discrepancy between Olive's self-image – which is similar to Veronese's 'Europa' – and what Mottram and Skene imagined Olive to be like: 'The Victim'.[40] Many other images of Europa would have been more appropriate, and she was in fact more usually viewed as the victim of a rape at that time (a comparison might be made with Max Beckmann's drawing of the passive beauty carried by a ferocious bull, 1933). Veronese's 'Europa' was, however, depicted as triumphant (Plate 1 and Figure 3). The twofold contradiction, between victim and mistress and between master and subject, indicated that the transformation leading to a new type of man was still taking its first uncertain steps.

Figure 3: Max Beckman's Europa of 1933: an example of the politicisation of the image of Europa in relation to Nazism.

## Visuality

One of the reviews (*Time and Tide*) had questioned why the publisher had not put a reproduction of the Veronese on the jacket rather than 'a fanciful design, in which bulls are depicted as steeds bestridden by beauteous women'. This design contrasts strikingly with the original that inspired it (Plates 1 and 2). 'Il ratto d'Europa' (where 'ratto' means abduction, not rape), is a large painting by Paolo Caliari, known as Veronese; it is a radiant portrait of Europa, a dazzlingly beautiful woman surrounded by her handmaidens, busily preparing her for a departure that does not seem to be in any way forced. The pretty lips of the princess are slightly parted in what could be a breath of dismay, but also an amorous sigh. She is comfortably placed on the back of the kneeling bull, with elegant sandals embroidered in openwork on her lovely feet. As the American poet William Story had written in a poem composed in the last years of the nineteenth century and dedicated to the painting, 'Europa: A Picture by Paul Veronese':

Luxuriant, joyous, fresh, with roses bound
About her sunny head, and on her cheek
The glow of morn, Europa mounts the steer.

There are no men in the scene, only the deceiving bull, which licks her foot with an erotic movement. He is wearing wreaths of flowers around his ears, and his glance expresses complicity, cunning self-assuredness and devotion. The seduction exercised by the bull is complemented by the affectionate complicity between Europa and one of her maids, who shows her a ring: it is a story of women, and it continues in the two little scenes on the right-hand side of the painting, where the bull is seen from the back, half covered by Europa's golden cloak. Maids and cupids are escorting them to the sea. In the last image, blurred by distance, Europa has turned to wave goodbye, her right arm and hand raised in a final salute under the flying putti. While no man is present, animals are witnessing the temporary triumph of a woman and her friends: a dog sitting composedly on the left side, the snout of an ox on the right.

The new version of the scene, as visible on the cover of *Europa's Beast*, shows some similarities with its famous original: the small figures on the right repeat the development of the story, in which the landscape is the same, and some of the gestures of the maids are almost identical. The bull is, however, quiet and dull, its eye opaque, lacking the powerful appeal of Veronese's beast. By contrast, the women are slim and 'modern' in attire and look, a perfect image of that 'kind of feminine modernity, without roots, without depths' with which the figure of Olive was intended to contrast. The lightness and mindlessness of the girls, as well as the stupidity of the bull in the 1930 design are a striking illustration of how much of the myth had been lost, and how much would have to be recaptured for it to become consistent with the current sensitivity of that period, an operation in which Mottram was not totally successful.

It is quite possible that Mottram had been inspired by Veronese's painting, as the *Times Literary Supplement* insinuated ('rather from the image that gives the book its title than from any imperious demand by his characters to be brought alive'). He was a 'seeing' writer (*Time and Tide*), for whom visual images were extremely important, as he himself recognised in *Autobiography with a Difference*; in this he explained the roots of his fascination with images as linked to the pictures shown to him as a child by their cook, Mrs Bumphreys, who had disclosed the world of vision to him, laying the foundations for his subsequent artistic development. She had given him a book of 'gays' ('pictures' in the local language), showing men and women who had some special function in life, such as the King, the Beggar, and the Cook; it was at that point that the young Mottram had understood that 'the pictures were right' in spite of being different from what he saw in the world. What was 'wrong' – as he had already grasped by the 1880s – was the world, since 'life was just beginning to be too complicated' and the process of modernity to unfold. Artistic and imaginary visions opened up for Mottram an antithesis to 'bad' modernity and a way of opposing the process of decay.

All this explains the importance of visuality in *Europa's Beast*, as well as its connection with love. Skene's love at his first sight of Olive, in the course of a religious ceremony commemorating the war, is a *topos* in the history of love-culture. His glance, partially reciprocated, is crucial to the exordium, as a later small incident will also be, that places the two potential lovers in opposition to the respectable community to which they belong: a photograph taken on a public occasion and published in a local newspaper surprised the two as they stare at each other in total oblivion. Skene and Olive are brought together in the organisation of an exhibition aiming to reconstruct the history of Easthampton through the centuries. Finally, it is a triumph of visuality – represented by Veronese's painting – that welds Olive to Skene, first in the erotic fantasy quoted at the beginning of this chapter and then in front of the actual painting in Venice. They contemplate the painting together in the Doge's Palace, exchanging a tacit vow of mutual acceptance, in a sort of individualised ritual with pagan undertones. Since their wedding had taken place at the registry office, and Olive's first marriage had been celebrated in church, their real ceremony is this entirely private Venetian one, under the auspices of Veronese.

While glances and visuality connect this story with romantic and courtly patterns of falling in love at first sight with an unknown person on the basis of physical beauty and visual communication, another major *topos* of the love tradition is also present, although in a more ambivalent

44

way. Love based on sight has much to do with distance, and cannot exist unless distance is kept. One of the most successful passages of *Europa's Beast* describes Skene looking at Olive as she leaves the memorial service where he has seen her for the first time; he admires her grace, but does not know who she is or whether he will ever see her again. In the novel's subsequent development, the pathos of distance is maintained for a time by the apparent impossibility of the relationship, one of them being respectably married. It is true that divorce is not considered feasible in this novel ('the very little' Skene had heard on divorce 'removed it at once from serious contemplation'[41]) but its very possibility, together with the decline of parental authority, enable the gravity of traditional obstacles to unhappy love to vanish. However, distance is recreated by the very nature of the relationship between Skene and Olive, by their respective spheres of autonomy, and more than anything else by the mystery surrounding Olive, which makes her somehow unattainable. The mythical aura, mediated by art and aesthetics, contributes to this.

The importance given in *Europa's Beast* to visuality is coupled with its insistence on aesthetic values: the two protagonists distinguish themselves from their compatriots thanks to their appreciation of beauty, whether in human form or in art. To them, observed the *Times Literary Supplement* 'nothing really matters but the pretty image'. The pseudonymous Lydia Languish, in the *John O' London Weekly*, recognised that 'from the purely literary point of view Olive is a brilliant success', but expressed feelings very unsympathetic to her, whom she found 'singularly repellent' in her attitude to her husband. Certainly, she could not be said to be a real woman, Languish argued, in Skene's eyes; rather, he simply 'derived artistic comfort from the vision' of her perfection.

Aestheticism is the real value which the two lovers share and which brings them together. It takes the form of narcissism for Olive, wearing the colour of her name. For her, even the photograph that had surprised her and Skene in a moment of intimacy, and that had created a scandal in the community, counted only because 'it gave a very good impression of herself'.[42] Aestheticism takes an object-directed form for Geoffrey Skene, who is first struck by 'the lovely proportion of her back, so simply draped'.[43] While Olive's husband did not provide a sufficiently appreciative mirror for her, Skene is able to appreciate her in such a way as to actually see a beauty that was somehow hidden before. He perceives that under her 'dull expression (whether of suppression, or futility or incapacity)' she was alive and independent, capable of nourishing 'strong feeling and even a sort of passive will power'.[44] The love that unites Olive and Skene, and that could generally be defined as romantic, is in our century reduced to its aesthetic aspect. Its efficacy as a means of existential salvation cannot be based on anything else; it is a religion of art which transmits the vision of love as central to life.

Finally, aestheticism is also the basis of a sort of aristocraticism within bourgeois culture, which separates Olive and Skene from the pleasant and shallow friends that share their visit and shopping in Venice; it acts as the basis of a discrimination that results in the implicit superiority of the couple over the rest of the world. Although faithful to their Englishness, they do not fail to notice that the aesthetic legitimation on which they are founding their alliance comes originally from Southern Europe. While witnessing the decay of Venice, however, they manifest their readiness to give it a new, and more 'modern', northern version.

## Olive/Europa/Europe

All the reviewers of *Europa's Beast* expressed their appreciation of the contrasts portrayed by the novel between the old and the new, but insisted on the prevalence of modernity, as exemplified in the effort to exorcise the role, in the story, of the obscure influence of something non-rational. This effort went against the intention of the text, specifically geared to the re-emergence of a very distant and supra-individual past, an intention supported by the structure and the content, and typified in the use of retrospective narration (which some reviewers deplored (*Evening Standard*), but that increases the suspended atmosphere of the story, set between widely separated epochs). One has the impression that nothing would happen without Olive's visions and premonitions, and it is indeed Olive who is the most puzzling character. Through her female ancestor endowed with second sight, about the future and thereby in direct contact with obscure forces invisible to modern human beings, she introduces a sense of the supernatural. Olive's own relationship with the past and the world of the imaginary, of which she does not seem fully conscious but which permeates her life, makes her a mysterious creature. It may well be that Mottram was in some way uneasy with Olive, whose mystery unbalanced the social concerns of the novel. But this unbalance is at the source of the very originality of the story. In any case, either the stress on social aspects did not allow Mottram to characterise Olive fully enough, or perhaps he voluntarily gave her an air of *non finito*; in the end, the intuition the author felt about her was not totally accepted by himself and had to remain dim and indistinct.

Even if Olive embodies a link with the supra-individual and the transcendent, no completely satisfactory answer can be given to the question of the secret ways in which she received knowledge of Europa. Mottram hints at the fact that in school she was shown art reproductions, which she might then have forgotten; but when she sees the actual painting, she finds it different from how she remembered it. This question is left unanswered, as is that of the meaning of her identification with Europa, which can be considered at various levels. The first and more immediate one is between Olive and the double image in her imagination and in Veronese's painting, while a second level might concern the identification of Olive with the mythical figure of Europa. The first is spelled out, and the second is plausible, while a third level – Europa being symbolic of Europe – is not made explicit.

Can we say that the reappearance of Europa on the British islands at the time at which *Europa's Beast* was set – with the physicality and passion that she has in Mottram's novel – indicates that the myth was to some degree alive also in its political and public meanings? The almost clandestine and disguised nature of its message would not be inconsistent with the conventions of myths, according to Jung and Kerenyi's interpretation, or with the half-conscious nature of European identity in the British islands. Europa could well be assigned the status of a Jungian archetype, reappearing when it has been forgotten, as a compensation for this oblivion, and following the subterranean veins of the collective imaginary and the collective unconscious. The reappearance of the archetype of Europa in this case would indicate the lack of attention of the modern world to the supernatural, to the role of women as powerful creators, to a relationship between man and woman which is at the same time sensual and sacred, and, last but not least, to a forgotten mission towards Europe.

This last aspect is entirely implicit in the novel, but is not incongruous with it. Mottram himself was quite aware of the values of European civilisation (which he wrote with a capital 'C'). Complying with the wishes of his mother, who had been educated in Versailles, he studied for a year in Lausanne. He understood French and German and always approached other countries with an attitude of openness, never of narrow nationalism. His feelings for Europe were possibly similar to those of cultured English people of politically moderate attitudes: when he had fought in the First World War, in Flanders, he had believed that 'we were defending something, not that we were attacking somebody', insisting that he had no wish to fight the Germans; he had experienced the war as 'the great crisis of our lives, of the life of European Civilization perhaps',[45] whose outcome might mean that 'Civilization is defeated, Barbarism has won!' Mottram never expressed political views linked to any party and became Lord Mayor of Norwich as an independent. After the publication of his novels, he accepted invitations to give talks at the Universities of Berlin, Leipzig and Cologne, and at associations in the Netherlands, Sweden and Paris. In 1930, the same year as *Europa's Beast* was published, he went on a walking holiday in the Black Forest, and commented on it in *Another Window Seat*: 'does it seem strange that I, a member of the victorious Britain of 1914–1918, should want to see the Germany I had never invaded?'

Mottram's war stories can be considered as confirmation of a feeling for European affinities, without denying the differences, affinities both between European countries and between Britain and the rest of Europe.

More specifically, the protagonists of *Europa's Beast* find a feeling of identity, which reconciles Englishness with Western and European values, in a type of love that can be defined as romantic, if we accept Bertrand Russell's definition of this in his *Marriage and Morals* (1929): an emotion that has triumphed over all obstacles and established a unique bond between unique beings. In the novel, the expression of this idea is attributed to the male component of the couple; so it is Skene that 'wanted that particular woman, no other one would do'.[46] The aesthetic and emotional values invoked by Mottram to justify his lovers in *Europa's Beast* may well be recognized as part of a common European patrimony, kept alive mainly through art. This patrimony was increasingly transmitted through tourism in a process in the course of which it was tranformed from an élite to a mass phenomenon. The structure of feeling which connected sensual love, the liberation of the body and the inheritance of great European art and culture is exemplified both by Mottram's novel and by travellers' descriptions of southern Europe, particularly the literature about Provence, a sample of which will be given in connection with Lewis's *Allegory of Love* (see Chapter 5).

Mottram introduced onto the stage of English middle-classness the Europa myth and restored at least part of its erotic impact, but stopped short of giving any particular meaning to the reincarnation of Europa in Britain. It is in this lack of political meaning that Mottram's text strikes us; for a historical interpretation, recognizing it means accepting the discontinuity it implies in the chain of conscious understanding, and measuring the distance between the readings made by Mottram's contemporaries and our possible readings today. They and we share an understanding and appreciation of certain aspects of the novel, which I have tried to reconstruct here. However, we lose or add other elements, since we see aspects that contemporaries were not ready to see or to which, on the other hand, they gave more significance than we do. So we share some of the pleasure and irritation that *Europa's Beast* gave to Harold Nicolson, but we also see in it something that goes beyond his 'semi-everything' criticism. If reading a text is not only a question of finding meaning, but also of finding silences, the implication is that we should look for discrepancies between texts and their contexts, since a text may have secrets not evident to a contemporary readership. Meanings, silences and secrets vary with the times of the readers. By accepting the distance of our reading of the text from its original context, we also respect the right of the text not to be treated as an object, to resist the claim that the text can be resolved by interpretation.[47] My present interpretation tries to throw light on one silence, resulting from the involute relationship between a novel and its title, an aspect that in this case its contemporaries found unreadable. That the supremacy of Britain and the tradition of European solidarity could be reconciled on a cultural meeting-ground, where culture means the legacy of art as well as gender relations, is an idea that was never made explicit in Mottram's novel. It has appeared here thanks to the interimplication that I propose to establish between our contemporary context and the text.

My interpretation stretches the text by Mottram by introducing to it an unspoken intention based on the fact that the central ideas of the novel and the character embodying it are not fully developed, as was the case with the very notion of Europe in much of British culture at the time. The hidden metaphor of Britain saving the patrimony of European civilisation, that included romantic love, could be represented by the story of a beautiful dormant woman who ends up triumphantly identified with Europa. This comparison is suggested by the fact that many believed that Britain had a cultural or political mission to fulfill towards Europe and European civilisation. In the next chapter I shall discuss various interpretations of a British mission in inter-war Europe, according to which only Britain could assume the role of Europe's saviour from the threat of a new war; in the political field this idea was formulated at the ideological level, but was not built upon a solid emotional basis, by contrast with the powerful emotions stirred by nationalism. Those who might have contributed to such an emotional foundation of the idea of Europe were either not fully aware of the relevance that it would come to have or did not believe that the gap between politics and private emotions could be filled. One of my aims in this book is to outline the gap between the world of feelings and emotions to which the novel belonged, on the one hand, and the world of politics and socially and politically committed intellectuals, on the other. It is here that the lacuna of political sense that the novel embodies needs to be recognised.

The debates on the idea of Europe and of European civilisation that took place in Britain in the inter-war period have been forgotten in our time, just as European federalism had been forgotten after the First World War, possibly because those ideas had not helped to deter the actual experience of a war; thus the debate started once more from the beginning in the 1920s. Similarly, in the period following the Second World War, the heritage of ideas and debates on Europe and Europeanism in the inter-war period was almost totally forgotten, and very little attention is paid to it today. However, some of that patrimony is very relevant, both in order to understand that period and to contrast it with our own convictions or the lack of them.

## Notes on Chapter 1

1   *Europa's Beast*, p 205
2   *Ibidem*, p 203
3   *Ibidem*, p 41
4   *Ibidem*, p 329
5   *Ibidem*, p 338
6   *Ibidem*, p 202
7   *Ibidem*, p 362
8   *Ibidem*, pp 363–4
9   Light
10  Symons; Bergonzi, p 55
11  *Vanities and Verities*, p 32ff
12  *Sixty four, Ninety four!*, p 292
13  *Spanish Farm*, p 179
14  *Ibidem*, p 22
15  *Ibidem*, p 91
16  *Ibidem*, p 87
17  *Ibidem*, p 75
18  *Ibidem*, p 147
19  *East Anglian Evening News*, 10.3.1954
20  *Ibidem*, p 149
21  *Ibidem*, p 20
22  *Ibidem*, p 115
23  *Sixty four, Ninety four!*, p 183
24  *Spanish Farm*, p 113
25  *Ibidem*, p 99
26  *Ibidem*, p 114
27  *Ibidem*, p 183
28  *Ibidem*, p 126
29  Wood, 1986 and 1987, pp 73–74
30  Orme
31  *The English Miss*, p 293
32  Johnstone, pp 28–29
33  *Europa's Beast*, p 283
34  Beddoe, pp 32–33, 363
35  *Europa's Beast*, p 63
36  White, p 110
37  Fowler, p 37
38  Dowson, p 71
39  *Europa's Beast*, p 344
40  *Ibidem*, p 28
41  *Ibidem*, p 224
42  *Ibidem*, p 277

43   *Ibidem,* p 15
44   *Ibidem,* p 86
45   *Crime,* p 51
46   *Europa's Beast,* p 343
47   Felman 1980 and 1982; Williams

# CHAPTER 2

# IDEAS OF EUROPE

## The dream of the United States of Europe

Federalist ideas, among them the concept of a federated Europe, appear sporadically in the British political tradition. The British did not apply the principle of federalism to their own affairs, but sympathy for the principle emerges both in dealings with Europe and the empire, and from people of different political tendencies. Interesting examples can be found at the end of the nineteenth century, for instance in the lecture given in 1871 to the Peace Society by John Seeley, Professor of Modern History at Cambridge, on 'The United States of Europe'. Seeley, a Liberal Unionist opposed to home rule, was connected with the Imperial Federation League. However, his lecture proposed a European legislature and executive, an armed force, some form of direct link between the individual and the federal institutions, and also a 'completely new citizenship'. 'We must cease to be mere Englishmen, Frenchmen, Germans, and must begin to take as much pride in calling ourselves Europeans', said Seeley. The purpose of such a United States of Europe was to avoid war, at that point an urgent question in the wake of the Franco-Prussian war. In 1899 *The United States of Europe on the Eve of the Parliament of Peace* by W.T. Stead was published. Stead, who died on the Titanic, was a remarkable figure, the inventor of a new journalism which was politically engaged, a convinced supporter of an empire federation and of home rule, editor of the *Pall Mall Gazette* and founder of the *Review of Reviews*, an advocate of equal rights for women, religious freedom and international peace through the limitation of armaments. In *The United States of Europe* he claimed that the establishment of a federated union of European states, in close alliance with the British Empire federation, should be accomplished by means of English statesmanship, which would thereby make its greatest contribution to world peace.[1]

From the start, the supporters of the idea of a federal Europe in Britain were divided between those who understood Europe as including the British islands, and those who considered it to be exclusively the continent. The latter could count on a shared meaning in everyday language and understanding. Even in this more restricted meaning, the concept of a federal Europe was recognised as a powerful antidote to war by those who included it, in more or less explicit versions, within pacifist agendas and discussions. For example, in the decade before the First World War, the Quakers and the British National Peace League supported the idea of the United States of Europe.[2] In 1914, the proposal for a United States of Europe as the only way to guarantee stability and peace in the region, and indirectly in the world, was repeatedly put forward by the *Review of Reviews* and the labour-oriented *Daily Citizen*.[3] The journal *New Europe: A Weekly Review of Foreign Politics* – concerned to promote national self-determination in Central and Eastern Europe – was funded by David Davies and published in London between October 1916 and 1920,[4] on the initiative of the historian R.W. Seton-Watson and other supporters of the small Slavic peoples. As they declared when launching the review, the aim was to provide 'a rallying ground for all those who see in European reconstruction, on the basis of nationality, the rights of minorities, and the hard facts of geography and economics, the sole guarantee against an early repetition of the horrors of the present war'. Following the Czech philosopher Tomas Garrigue Masaryk's line, the journal proposed the 'emancipation of central and south-eastern Europe from German and Magyar control'.[5] Masaryk, who in 1918 became president of the new Czech Republic, wrote a book with the same title, *The New Europe*,[6] (published in London in 1918), by which he meant a Europe consisting of a line of small nation-states between Germany and Russia, contributing to a new European order based on co-operation, open diplomacy and disarmament.[7] Among the contributors to the journal were Anatole France, Emile Boutroux, Leonard Woolf, Wickham Steed, Charles Seignobos, J.A.R. Marriott and J.G. Frazer.

The *New Europe* journal has been seen as the heir of Gladstonian liberalism in foreign affairs, supporting 'the idea of Public Right as the governing idea of Europe'.[8] Harold Nicolson remembered having been deeply influenced by this group at the Paris peace conference at the end of the First World War, in thinking of the new Serbia, the new Greece and the new Bohemia rather than of Germany, Austria, Turkey. A number of adherents followed academic careers (among them were Lewis Namier and Arnold Toynbee) and they devoted effort to campaigns of public enlightenment on Eastern Europe. They helped to create a series of societies concerned with different peoples from Eastern Europe, to establish the School of Slavonic and East European Studies in London, and the (later Royal) Institute of International Affairs (Chatham House). The *New Europe* journal spread the ideas of self-determination and federalism applied to European countries; Seton-Watson, in his last article in the final issue wrote of 'refusing to despair of the Commonwealth of Europe'. *New Europe* had contacts with another group founded around 1910 and which also published a journal, *Round Table*, where various political tendencies were represented, from the Liberal Philip Kerr (Lord Lothian) to the 'leftists' Alfred Zimmern – who provided a link to *New Europe* – and Lionel Curtis, to the Conservative Leo Amery. *Round Table* was empire-centred and advocated the necessity of a better union within the Empire towards a more federal British Commonwealth. During and after the First World War the group developed an interest in the post-war European order and in the various proposals for European settlement.[9]

The economic side of a possible united Europe was of interest to British business. In 1914 the industrialist Sir Max Waechter established the European Unity League, with its headquarters in London, to work for a Federation of the States of Europe on an economic basis, with the intent of fostering economic agreements between some European countries. After the war, one main obstacle to the development of such a concept was the separation between the political and the economic levels of foreign affairs: throughout the 1920s the Foreign Office was kept in the dark on the issue of reparations, which, together with war debts, tariffs, trade finance, capital lending and currency stabilisation, were left to the Treasury, the Board of Trade and the Bank of England to decide.[10] While the Foreign Office records reveal little interest in European unity, the idea became compelling during the 1920s for most observers of economic developments. The impact of the American economic expansion on Europe and particularly on Britain, the main target for US direct investment, suggested the necessity of a European economic bloc. At the end of the decade the idea of the inevitable transformation of the world economy into continent-sized blocs was shared by Tories such as Harold Macmillan, Labour politicians from Ramsay MacDonald to Oswald Mosley (who had been previously a Conservative, then an Independent, and in 1929–30 served in the Labour ministry), and by the 'broad church' group the Round Table. The picture of the British attitudes towards the idea of Europe through the 1920s and into the 1930s was much more varied and contradictory than is usually assumed.[11]

It is, however, true that London was not frequently regarded as in the core circle of continental capitals for European intellectuals, from Vienna to Prague and Berlin, to Paris and Geneva. Those were the cities that Count Coudenhove-Kalergi (1894–1972) considered the 'heart' of his Pan-European activities – Europeanism seems to have been mainly an urban, even metropolitan, affair – although his wider peregrinations included England.[12] In 1923 Coudenhove-Kalergi published in Vienna *Pan Europa*, soon translated into at least 15 languages, proposing a federation of European states, excluding Russia and Britain, based on economic and political co-operation; branches of the Pan Europa organisation were soon created in many European countries. The institutions of Pan Europa were to be a council composed of national delegates, an assembly of representatives of the parliaments of the federated states and a court of justice; a customs union and a common currency would complete the structure. The nations involved in Pan Europa were to bring their colonies with them, and all share the spoils of their exploitation, without any national divisions, in a Eur-Africa that would unite the most civilised white races and the most primitive black ones.[13] This type of Eurocentrism manifested a form of racism towards the non-European, especially African, peoples. A second organisation, called European Co-operation, would have included the British Isles, and was to work closely together with Pan Europa. When the Count visited London in the spring of 1925, no distinguished British person was ready to endorse the participation of Britain in Pan Europa, but he found some intellectuals and public figures in favour of this kind of organisation for the continental European states: among them he mentions in the first place Wickham Steed, who put him in contact with Ramsay MacDonald, Sir Robert Cecil, Philip Kerr, Lionel Curtis, H.G. Wells, G.B. Shaw, Walter Layton, Gilbert Murray and Robert Horne. Steed also formed a committee to study ways of collaborating with the pan-European movement, where the Socialists were represented by Noel Baker, the Liberals by Percy Molteno, and the Conservatives by himself.[14]

It is worth remembering here that in 1927 Coudenhove-Kalergi wrote *Held oder Heiliger*, dedicated to his wife, on the 'European soul' ('europaeischen Seele'), which included a chapter on 'Man and Woman'. According to Coudenhove-Kalergi, the greatest crisis for Europe was the crisis of that love which he considered 'the highest good and value of Europe': erotics, which had played a central role in European culture since the Minnesaenger, was being replaced by sexuality, as part of the general objectification ('Versaechlichung') of life in the modern world. The count believed that European men and women were as different from one another as Europeans and Chinese; this difference should be restored, and the two 'human groups' should become once more, respectively, fighters and mothers. At this point, women could turn out to be essential builders of Europe, engaging themselves in the political mission of peace, following the 'logic of the heart' and taking care of the 'social question', while helping to avoid a violent revolution in the construction of European unity; once this goal was reached, European women would fight for the peace of the world, hand in hand with their American sisters, who already were at the head of movement for peace.[15] The book was not translated into English, and this part of the count's Europeanism was not present in the British debate about his political proposals.

On the political level, the new wave of interest in a united Europe was shown around 1929–30 by publications on the theme in England and in the United States. Some of them originated in Geneva, from the debate in and around the League of Nations. *The United States of Europe* (1929) by Paul Hutchinson, originally a series of articles written from Geneva for the Chicago *Christian Science Monitor*, was a plea in support of 'what so many now call a dream – the formation of a United States of Europe':[16] a pan-European federation constructed along the lines proposed by Aristide Briand and Coudenhove-Kalergi would bring economic advantages to the working classes no less than to industrialists and, above all, peace. *Uniting Europe* (1930) by William Rappard, Swiss delegate to the League of Nations and Professor at the University of Geneva, was 'a clear and balanced survey of economic conditions',[17] encouraging the belief that Europe was definitely recovering but seeing no possible prospect of its union outside the League of Nations. Travel books covering European countries were also relevant, as some of them included material on the question of European unity. For instance, Sisley Huddleston, a political journalist and writer of travel books on France, wrote *Europe in Zigzags* (1929), a survey of 'social, artistic, literary and political affairs on the continent', praised by the *Review of Reviews* for the 'great knowledge of European affairs' and the 'always graceful quality of his writing'.[18] As the title suggests, the book is not systematic: it recounts personal impressions and ideas, such as a defence of tourism as an increasingly important economic factor, or jokes on national stereotypes; but it also supports Coudenhove-Kalergi's Pan Europa, understood as an association collaborating with the League of Nations and aimed to avoid any form of anti-Americanism.

The question of the British role in a federation of European states divided not only Britons but also Europeanists on the continent, between those who believed that Britain should support a possible federation from the outside and the few who thought it should actually participate in it. Some leading Europeanists (like Wilhelm Heile, MP in the Reichstag, vice president of the International Association of Democratic Parties and of the Federal Committee for European Cooperation founded in Geneva in 1926) disagreeed with Coudenhove-Kalergi, insisting that a federated Europe excluding Britain would never be viable.[19] A proposal for an Anglo-American initiative came from Denmark. In 1926 an English translation of *A New Europe* by the medical doctor C.F. Heerfordt was published in London, and at the same time a French and German text were circulated. Heertfordt, who had never belonged to any political party and lived in a small Danish town (Roskilde), had been so deeply disturbed by the prospect of the annihilation of European culture in the First World War that he had lost interest in his profession and started a Scandinavian Initiative for the United States of the European Nations. He obtained the agreement of a number of important Norwegians, Swedes and Danes, and for the whole interwar period propagated his idea, through books, pamphlets, letters and petitions to goverments and to the press in Europe and the USA. *A New Europe*, which went through various editions in England, proposed an Anglo-European United States as part of a reformed League of Nations and as a step towards co-operation and peace between all the states of the world. This union would include North and South America, starting with Canada and the United States. Not only the proposal's content but also its place of origin made it important as a correction to the stereotyped view that limited Europe to some of its parts: in 1933 a book by a progressive like J. Hampden Jackson (*Europe Since the War*) could omit the history of the Scandinavian States and of the Balkans, and still declare that it had considered 'all the universally important developments of postwar Europe'.

Others were also considering the components of a united states of Europe, and particularly Britain's relation to it; it is interesting to report Leon Trotsky's opinion on the question of Britain's relationship to a European federation. In the 1920s Trotsky began developing a 1914 slogan for mobilising militants, 'the republican United States of Europe', which had been for Lenin in September 1914 one of the most important passwords. Between 1900 and 1914 the theme of the United States of Europe had been debated in socialist meetings on the initiative of German, Austrian and French Socialists. But in March 1915 this theme was abandoned and in August 1915 Lenin clarified that the Republican United States of Europe would be desirable only in view of the revolutionary overthrow of the existing order, while under a capitalist regime it would have been either impossible or reactionary, and would have inevitably aimed to destroy socialism in Europe and to protect the colonial empires. In June 1923 Trotsky, writing in *Pravda* in his capacity as the People's Commissar for War, imbued the idea of the United States of Europe with a renewed revolutionary meaning, since the war had changed the economic relationships between Europe and America, the latter being now the leading capitalist nation. He thought that only economic co-operation and the elimination of custom barriers in Europe could save the continent from disintegration and subordination to American capital; only the revolutionary proletariat, not the European bourgeoisie, could oppose American imperialism and its powerful bourgeoisie, the chief enemy of world revolution.[20] The European revolution for him went hand-in-hand with European unity: the Workers' (or Soviet) United States of Europe, based on the connection between Germany and France, were to include the Soviet Union and at a later stage Britain, when Britain had a workers' government. Trotsky emphasised his idea in two speeches of 1924 and 1926, proposing a European economic union controlled by the revolutionary parties as a basis for a Communist Europe, a springboard for the revolution in the United States of America and in Asia.[21] But in 1927 he was expelled from the party and in 1929 from the USSR, and in 1928 the United Socialist States of Europe (USSE) disappeared from the slogans of the Comintern.[22] The Stalinist line discredited Trotskyite ideas, and the Communist parties of Europe followed this, maintaining hostility to any proposal of a United States of Europe, which was considered to have as its chief objective the creation of an anti-Soviet bloc.[23] However, in the inter-war period the British Independent Labour Party, which professed to be a Marxist – though not a Trotskyite – party, proclaimed USSE to be one of its aims.[24]

Faith in a British workers' government could certainly not be sustained by the Labour Governments of 1924 and 1929–30, in spite of the illusion that a Labour Government would look favourably towards a European union.[25] However, it was difficult for the British to take a stand on the issue, because it was for most of them such a new idea; only in the year preceding the Locarno conference and Germany's entrance into the League of Nations in September 1926, was the European idea more widely understood and accepted for the first time. After the first Pan-European Congress organised by Coudenhove-Kalergi in Vienna in October 1926, where Britain was represented by A. Watts of the Royal Institute for International Affairs, the *Manchester Guardian Weekly* wrote: 'the United States of Europe is no longer a dream; it has entered the world of realities'.[26]

However, a dream-like quality, and its connection with laughter, was always present in the public discourse on Europe, as is well illustrated in a cartoon that the monthly *Review of Reviews* (directed between 1923 and 1930 by Henry Wickham Steed) reproduced from a Dutch newspaper in August 1929 (Figure 4). This showed Aristide Briand, who had just presented the proposal of a United States of Europe to the League of Nations, sleeping in a peaceful countryside, dreaming of fantastic images of medieval castles, described in the caption 'castles in the air'. Briand's castle was a continental cartoon, but it reflected the attitude of much official public opinion in Britain, although not of Wickham Steed himself, who had studied at German and French universities, had been the *Times* correspondent in Berlin, Rome and Vienna, and then its editor, and who attended the meetings of the League of Nations in what he called 'my annual pilgrimage to Geneva'. In the years when he was editor of the *Review of Reviews*, the journal gave very good critical coverage of the Fascist press in Italy and Central Europe, was quite concerned with peace, and was generally attentive to the theme of Europeanism. In the same issue that published the cartoon on the 'medieval dream', a debate for and against the United States of Europe was featured between, respectively, the Swede K.A. Bratt, who was afraid of French predominance and in favour of a closer relationship with the USA, and Coudenhove-Kalergi, who made a general appeal 'to all Europeans' without expressly mentioning Britain. Commenting on both, Steed insisted that any movement tending to lower

Figure 4: Aristide Briand's 'dream' of a united Europe as represented in a cartoon from a Dutch newspaper reproduced in the *Review of Reviews*, August 1929.

tariff barriers and to promote freedom of trade would be welcomed by British opinion, but he recognised the danger of creating a competitor to the USA. Steed also wrote that 'war as an institution is a product of the war mind' and that the idea of linking 'European peoples together so that they may the more readily go hand in hand with the peoples of other "political continents"' could well be a wholesome contribution to the advancement of the world.[27] It is remarkable that Steed, with all his experience as a political commentator, attributed such importance to the role of an ideal and to that of the 'mind'. This was in tune with some of the cultural developments of the time, as we shall see later on.

Some of the resistances that the 'war-mind' encountered in converting to peace were due to the nationalist approach, which was unable to envisage the prospect of co-operation or integration. The war-mind could only find laughable and brand as unrealistic any effort to go beyond nationalisms, and could not help considering a united Europe a mere fantasy or a monster. The nature of an imaginary and ridiculous monstrosity is also well illustrated by another cartoon, published by the *Review of Reviews* two months later and taken from an Italian magazine, which made fun of the composite nature of a European union, where different nationalities could not be harmonised, and featured a sign-post indicating that such an absurd animal could travel only in the direction of subordination to the USA (originally the cartoon, Figure 5, drawn in Italy, probably projected Fascist suspicions of any French proposal and particularly of any form of united Europe). These cartoons had a strong political charge, since they were presented in the middle of the debate on Briand's initiative at the League of Nations for a United States of Europe.

The French Premier Aristide Briand, honorary president of Pan Europa, put forward the proposal of a federal bond between the peoples of Europe, with priority given to economic considerations, in his opening speech at the Tenth Ordinary Session of the League of Nations Assembly on 5 September 1929. By that time, according to Brugmans,[28] British public opinion was divided. Numerous observers deemed it more honest to deliver a firm refusal from the very beginning, in order to avoid creating any illusions. A minority preferred to follow the development of the operation

Figure 5: The monstrous nature of a European union from which subordination to the USA must follow, according to an Italian cartoon reproduced by the *Review of Reviews*, October 1929

closely, with the explicit aim of advising caution. Finally, a minuscule fraction believed that it was not a bad idea. In this last group Brugmans places Sir Arthur Salter, head of the Economic and Social Committee of the League, who was at the same time seduced as well as slightly frightened by Briand's idea. Salter was in favour of participation, considering Britain to be 'the indispensable intermediary between the European and the world point of view', believing that 'for economic as well as political reasons, a greater solidarity between the countries of Europe is of the utmost possible importance'.[29] In a note to his government on 20 May 1930 he would warn against the consequences of a refusal without discussion. In reality, Britain's attitude had moved in that direction, given that the Foreign Secretary, Arthur Henderson, at the September 1929 meetings in Paris, where Briand presented the draft of the memorandum, 'stayed silent... remained non-committal', giving no encouragement, in sharp contrast with the enthusiastic support of the German Chancellor Gustav Stresemann, winner, with Briand, of the 1926 Nobel prize for peace. In his autobiography Coudenhove-Kalergi recorded Henderson's attitude – not a gesture, not a word – with particular disappointment.[30] In a subsequent encounter with Briand, Henderson asked for an assurance, which was granted, that the potential European union should be in no way directed against the United States.[31]

Public opinion in Britain viewed the British colonial mission as irreconciliably more important than closer involvement in Europe. After Briand's first proposal, the reactions of the British press were not very favourable. All the major conservative dailies took the same line, expressing the conviction that the British economy was essentially based on the empire. The *Daily Express* of 6 September 1929 considered the British Empire 'as a single economic whole' to have a higher destiny than the building of a part of Europe: the construction of a unity that would be stronger than the USA and Europe, that of the Commonwealth. The *Evening Standard*, *Morning Post* and *Daily Telegraph* felt very much the same way, while the Liberal and Labour papers, slightly more favourable to some kind of European structure, preferred the widening of the League of Nations into a European union.[32] Winston Churchill was among the very few who gave a relatively positive opinion of a united European community, as he wrote in a famous article in the *Saturday Evening Post* of 15 February 1930. The article made a dramatic use of metaphors and was written with more of a historical and cultural tone than a strictly political one. The idea of a United States of Europe was compared to a spark that could ignite the heap of rubbish accumulated by 400 millions of the 'most educated and most civilised parent races of mankind', including 'all the history books of Europe', as well as 'the bones and broken weapons of the uncounted millions who brought one another to violent deaths'. In the end Churchill declared that the conception of a United States of Europe was right and that Britons should rejoice at every lowering of European internal tariffs and martial armaments, but he concluded:

> We see nothing but good and hope in a richer, freer, more contented European commonality. But we have our own dream and our own task. We are with Europe, but not of it. We are linked, but not comprised. We are interested and associated, but not absorbed.[33]

These words expressed attitudes and reservations shared by a large part of British public opinion.

At the second Pan-European Congress, held in May 1930 in Berlin, the British Secretary of State for the Colonies and Dominions Leopold Amery declared that Britain could not be part at the same time of Pan Europa and Pan Britannia, and she could not risk, by involving herself in a European system, creating distance and estrangement between herself and the dominions.[34] However, Coudenhove-Kalergi thought that the tone of sympathy and approval displayed by Amery – who had since their first encounter supported the pan-European idea – was encouraging,[35] and with his typical, often excessive, optimism judged that the evasive answer of the British reflected a position of the government, not of the nation.

In May 1930 the French Foreign Ministry (Briand was no longer Premier, but Foreign Affairs Minister) published the Memorandum on the Organization of a European Federal Union, which showed some differences to the original plan. It emphasised that the European system was not to be created outside the League of Nations, but rather to be understood as a way of strengthening it; that it had to be based upon a general treaty which would affirm 'the moral union' of Europe, whose principal organ was to be a European conference; that, contrary to what had been said earlier on, economic matters should be subordinated to political ones, although the ultimate aim remained a common market. Historians differ on the evaluation of the intentions of Briand's plan and of its destiny. Some stress that, in spite of always having been an enthusiastic Europeanist, Briand's move to present the memorandum was due to his realisation that it was impossible to rely on the United States to maintain peace in Europe.[36] A convincing interpretation of Briand's intentions is that the French had evolved a policy designed to achieve security for France against Germany by europeanising the German question, and by creating an entity that would remove any advantage for Germany in resorting to arms.[37]

As for the British Government's reactions to the final version of Briand's memorandum, the Foreign Office's reply considered the establishment of a European conference unnecessary, since all the objectives put forward by Briand could be fully dealt with within the framework of the League of Nations.[38] A British historian of the League of Nations and fellow of the British Academy was to write a few years later that the memorandum 'was a rather immature document', echoing Ramsay MacDonald's opinion that at least ten years should be left to go by before any such project be presented.[39] The question of the 'strong antipathy of the dominions to further European entanglement of any kind' was also brought forward by some observers.[40] In sum, the Labour Government was committed to the League of Nations, eager to improve Anglo-American relationships, and afraid of French influence in European affairs.[41]

The traditional interpretation has been that the British official attitude in the whole story was a 'particularly skilful demonstration of diplomatic hypocrisy'.[42] However, a different interpretation has been given on the basis of a careful analysis of internal contradictions in the practice of British politics at the time: it has been pointed out that, against a background of indifference and complacency towards a possible European union, the Briand plan was read reductively by Foreign Office officials. Briand was taken to be proposing an essentially economic form of European union, the only form with which official minds could link British interests, and complicated reasons were given for the fact that in the last version Briand's plan subordinated economic to political factors. British officials ended up substituting a League-based Europeanism for Briand's more autonomous version resulting in an 'emasculation' of his idea and an 'anaemic conception of Europe'; what is noticeable is that this operation was carried out by people such as Lord Cecil, Noel-Baker, and Salter – progressives who had always supported the idea of European cooperation – who insisted on the necessity of giving priority to the League and of practising any form of Europeanism within it.[43] The final result was a mere Committee of Enquiry into the European Union, set up within the League frame, which proved to be a sort of bureaucratic burial of Briand's plan.

Many reasons have been given for the failure of the Briand plan, some of them general, such as the economic depression, the rise of National Socialism in Germany, and uncertainties about whether the Briand scheme should have implied a revision of the Versailles Treaty.[44] But certainly the immediate cause of its failure was the lack of support in Germany and Britain. Attitudes in Germany, where Pan Europa had never flourished as it had in France, were fundamentally hostile; Gustav Stresemann, who in September 1929 evinced support for the strengthening of economic more than political links among the states of Europe, was not typical of the mood in his country. He died in October 1929, and his successor from April 1930, Heinrich Bruening, did not support the Briand plan and considered Pan Europa equivalent to Pan Versailles. It should also be remembered that Briand's idea found little support among the 27 European states that were then members of the League –

with the exception of Jugoslavia and Bulgaria, both in favour of the plan – although it should be added that most of them were waiting to see Britain's reaction. In the end British elusiveness was just one of the many reasons, although a decisive one, that led to the failure of Briand's proposal.

According to all the interpreters, this failure was a crucial turning-point for the destiny of the continent. It has been argued by Crozier that the Briand plan might have offered an alternative to the road that led to the outbreak of the Second World War.[45] According to Lipgens, 'Europe missed the last chance to respond to the challenge of history by its own efforts before it was carved up between the new world powers'.[46] On the same day, 14 September 1930, as the European Commission at the League of Nations in Geneva voted an ineffectual resolution, German electors voted 107 Nazis into the Reichstag, where there had previously been 12.[47] Later on, in the years immediately following Hitler's seizure of power, the Nazis tried to appropriate and reformulate the idea of Europe, maintaining that Fascism, in its Italian and German forms, represented a basically new principle of European order.[48]

In 1931, reports from the Committee of Enquiry into the European Union set up as the only result of the Briand plan showed that there was willingness at least on the part of the economic experts to consider a regional customs union. According to Boyce, Britain might have taken the lead[49] in an effort to work together with other European nations on the commercial front towards a European-wide market, but this possibility was not taken up by the British leadership. In the end, the attitude of the British politicians in the years 1929–30 contributed, in Britain, to pushing the idea of a united Europe back into the realm of undreamable dreams, while the majority preferred what Churchill defined as 'our own dream' of the world empire, leaving the dream of Europe to be elaborated by individual scholars and small groups either in the field of culture or in the no-man's-land between culture and politics.

## Dawson's Christian Community

One of the strongest traditions in the history of the idea of Europe is that European unity is based on Christianity. This theme can be played with many variations, from the vision beautifully expressed by Novalis at the very end of the eighteenth century in *Christenheit oder Europa*:

> Those were bright, glorious times, when Europe formed but one Christian land; when one Christianity dwelt throughout the civilized part of the world, and one great mutual interest bound together the most remote provinces of this wide spiritual empire,[50]

to the common inspiration that led Adenauer, Schuman and De Gasperi to European construction after 1945. In England this tradition includes Edmund Burke's description of the Christian commonwealth of Europe in his *Letters on the Regicide Peace* (1796), where he praised the harmony of the European system of life and education based on the values of Christian religion, concluding with the famous passage: 'no citizen of Europe could be altogether an exile in any part of it'.[51] In the Britain of the 1930s an important formulation of the Christian tradition of European unity was proposed by the Catholic historian Christopher Dawson, who acknowledged the value of Burke's concept of a European community (or commonwealth) on his own thought. The idea of a Catholic Europe takes on a particular importance in Britain, in its confrontation with Anglicanism and Protestantism, and in the polemics against the Reformation. As a historian, Dawson never shared the view held by the Oxford Movement and by Anglo-Catholics that the Reformation should not have taken place, but he did think that it had thrown the baby out with the bath water,[52] and that it had destroyed the original unity of European civilisation.

Dawson converted to Roman Catholicism at the end of 1913 (he was born in 1889), after two years of reflection on the difficulties of severing links with the tradition of his family and university. He had entered the University of Oxford at a time when, after a phase of agnosticism, he had returned to his father's Anglo-Catholic faith, the branch of the Anglican Church closest to Rome. It was a visit to the continent that first gave him the spur for his conversion; he also married a Roman Catholic, but the major force behind his conversion was his need for a conception of religion as one organic unity, a spiritual community extending over time and space, an idea he was to apply later to his vision of society and the state. Dawson was part of the British Catholic revival that in the 1930s changed Catholicism in Britain, where, it must be remembered, the Catholic population was at the turn of the century largely working class and of Irish descent, and after the First World War amounted only to around 5% of the population of England and Wales.[53]

Dawson's religious conception, developed in the 1920s, was not affiliated to any particular Catholic group. In fact, for most of his life he was more appreciated outside his church than in it.[54] He belonged to the Catholic intellectual trend, which sought, like similar movements in France and Germany, to encourage interest in the spiritual side of Catholicism and at the same time to avoid subordinating intellectual and creative work to religious considerations. Dawson collaborated with T.S. Eliot on *The Criterion*, a journal characterised by its European inspiration: it published regular contributions from France, Germany, Italy, Spain, the Netherlands and Switzerland, and in 1929 started to collaborate with four European reviews – *La Nouvelle Revue Française, La Revista de Occidente, Nuova Antologia,* and *Die Europaeische Revue* – to award a fiction prize. In a

'Commentary' in *The Criterion* of August 1927 Eliot appealed to a Europe 'of the mind' and commented on what he saw as a new European consciousness emerging among Western European intellectuals as a reaction to the Russian revolution. This 'European idea' originated in a feeling of insecurity and danger, and therefore frequently took the form of a meditation on the decay of European civilisation, as for instance in the work of Paul Valéry and of Oswald Spengler. After 1927, Eliot became attached to the Anglo-Catholic movement within the Church of England and his conception of Europe became explicitly Christian. In spite of these convergences, there was a certain lack of communication between Eliot and Dawson and their relationship never developed into a real friendship.[55]

Dawson also wrote for the *Sociological Review*, edited by Alexander Farquarson, founder with the biologist Sir Patrick Geddes of the group known as Le Play House which attempted a synthesis of the thinking of Comte, Le Play and Bergson. Frédéric Le Play (1806–1882) was a French engineer and professor as well as an economist and sociologist, who organised the Paris Exhibitions of 1855 and 1867. He also wrote *Les ouvriers européens* (1855), a detailed study of workers from Russia to England in which he regarded Europeans not as politically organised groups in perpetual rivalry, but as social groups whose development was determined by their environment. Le Play Society was interested in the borderland between sociology and geography, its membership being composed of university and secondary school teachers, artists, scientists, historians, classical scholars and business men and women. Dawson recognized the social inspiration of the Le Play group as a major intellectual influence, although his approach differed from theirs in the importance he attributed to religion and to the intellectual factor as a dynamic element within culture; this he derived from the German tradition of Herder, Troeltsch and Weber. Although there were several points in common between Dawson and Geddes, the former criticised the latter's inclination towards biological terms and explanations.[56]

It was in this intellectual atmosphere that Dawson, who was lecturer in the History of Culture at University College Exeter from 1930 to 1936, worked on the idea of the Christian origin of Europe. *The Making of Europe: An Introduction to the History of European Unity* was published at the beginning of 1932 by Sheed & Ward, a new publishing house which set out to raise the level of English Catholic culture and make it an intellectual force as well as a spiritual one. It was run very liberally, not caring to have the *imprimatur* of the ecclesiastical censor on its books. In spite of the fact that it did not always have sufficient capital, Sheed & Ward played an important part in the Catholic revival of the 1920s and 1930s. Among other authors, it published Belloc, Chesterton and Maritain. At the end of the 1920s Dawson had decided to leave his previous publisher, attracted both by the Sheed & Ward cultural-religious project and by the prospect of writing for a general educated public rather than simply for academics; this intent was also reflected in the colourful typographic lay-out of their publications, which contrasted with the unappealing format of most religious publishing of those days.

*The Making of Europe* begins its history with the Roman Empire and the barbarian invasions, and ends, after the Carolingian renaissance, with the rise of medieval unity. Dawson sets out to re-evaluate 'the period usually known as the Dark Ages' as 'the most creative age of all', since it was this period which created 'the root and ground of all the subsequent cultural achievements'. For Dawson, European culture resulted from the fusion of four elements: the Roman Empire, the Catholic church, the classical tradition and the barbarian tribes. Precisely because it was deeply creative, this age lacked the superficial attraction of periods of brilliant cultural expansion, like the Renaissance. Dawson thus places himself decidedly in the tradition that finds the cultural roots of Europe in Christianity, as opposed to that which finds them in the Renaissance, understood as a strong anticlerical and antimedieval reaction, as for example Nietzsche did.

For Dawson, the Catholic historian possesses one major advantage: only to him do the Dark Ages appear as 'ages of dawn'; only he can understand fully that 'the foundations of Europe were laid in fear and weakness and suffering – in such suffering as we can hardly conceive today, even after the disasters of the last eighteen years'. Dawson's position spoke to the anguished problems of his own age: the atrocious experiences of the First World War, the prospect of a second one, the evils of nationalism. He could distance himself from the mainstream of modern history, which had 'usually been written from the nationalist point of view', claiming that 'the ultimate foundation of our culture is not the national state, but the European unity'. Dawson recognised that such unity had not achieved political form, and 'perhaps it may never do so', but insisted that 'it is a real society, not an intellectual abstraction', therefore projecting on to European civilization his notion of the spiritual community.

The introduction to *The Making of Europe,* the source of the quotations above, ends with a plea for 'a common European consciousness' as an essential condition for the survival of European civilisation. A historic sense of the European tradition was, according to Dawson, a pre-condition of that consciousness. Re-writing 'our history from the European point of view' would require a long and painstaking effort to understand the unity of a common civilisation, an effort that had hitherto been given to the study of national individualities.

This formulation is new by comparison with Belloc's proclamation in 1920 that 'Europe will return to the Faith, or she will perish. The Faith is Europe. And Europe is the Faith.'[57] Dawson and Belloc share the idea that Catholics see Europe from within, and that their view of Europe is unfamiliar and uncongenial to modern England. But the intolerant and narrow 'Bellocian theorem' – Europe was made by the Romans, who had providentially been sent ahead to prepare for the Catholic Church, while the Gauls were predestined to do the work which the Jewish people had refused to do[58] – was very far from Dawson's attempt at multiculturalism, which he put forward in his balanced conclusion to *The Making of Europe*:

> ... we no longer have the same confidence in the inborn superiority of Western civilisation and its right to dominate the world. We are conscious of the claims of the subject races and cultures, and we feel the need both for protection from the insurgent forces of the oriental world and for a closer contact with its spiritual traditions... it is well to remember that the unity of our civilisation does not rest entirely on the secular culture and the material progress of the last four centuries. There are deeper traditions in Europe than these, and we must go back behind Humanism and behind the superficial triumphs of modern civilisation.

In fact Dawson was critical of the triumphalist Catholicism of Belloc, whose poetry he preferred to his historical writing, for he considered his historical views one-sided and unreliable. Dawson was part of the group that published the journal *Order* and a series of *Order* essays aimed at bringing English Catholicism up to date on themes such as sex, other world religions, and psychology: the writers of *Order* were polemical with the 'Chester-Bellocian' school, and made the point that 'Catholicism was not always a jolly tavern, nor were Catholics necessarily medievalists and Europe was not always the Faith'.[59]

The reception to *The Making of Europe* was one of interest and recognition, but included also some overt criticism. The book was widely reviewed, both in specialised periodicals and in journals for the general public, in Europe as well as in the United States. In France, where its title was translated as *Les origines de l'Europe et la civilisation européenne* by the publishing house Rieder, it received a very positive review by Etienne Gilson in the *Revue critique d'histoire et de littérature*; Gilson had been propounding similar theses to Dawson, concerning the unifying capacity of the medieval church, on a more learned and specifically philosophical level.[60] In the *English Review* of December 1932, Herbert A.L. Fisher, the Liberal MP and Cabinet Minister who was to publish in 1935 a *History of Europe* in three volumes, praised the book as the work of a 'real historian', and claimed that it combined unusual learning, firm grasp, freshness and independence of judgment. Fisher recognised the value of Dawson's criticism of nationalism and of his contribution to an education towards a common European consciousness, which as such 'never existed' in the previous centuries. Dawson's merit was to have shown how composite European civilisation is and how much the different peoples of Europe owed to one another, since no European culture developed in isolation.

This was an idea that Dawson would take up over and over again in subsequent years, in his effort to redefine the role of nationality and to develop the idea of Europe as a spiritual community.

Predictably, Aldous Huxley, whose novel *Brave New World* was also published in 1932, reacted quite critically to *The Making of Europe*. In the *Spectator* of August 1932 he wrote that, although he found the book 'admirable' because it made 'the Dark Ages lose their darkness, take on form and significance', the very title of the book sounded ironic to his ear. Huxley pointed out that the medieval unity of culture and religion 'never prevented good Catholic Europeans from cutting each other's throats'. To that 'Platonic and Pickwickian unity' he preferred a political and economic unification that could stand what he called the behaviourist test: if men behave as though they are not united, then the society which they constitute can hardly be called a unity. In his review, Huxley came close to a micro-historical and structuralist critique of history, writing that historical generalisations of the kind made by Dawson simply collapse when confronted with anthropological data of the type found by Radin or with such sociological material as had been exposed in *Middletown* by the Lynds. They are based upon 'an originally inadequate documentation reduced by the ravages of time to a random collection of literary and archaeological odds and ends'. This criticism does not merely express, Huxley claimed, 'the diffidence of an unlearned dilettante' towards that type of history, but rather the diffidence towards any organic idea of society and civilisation, whose totalitarian implications Huxley sensed acutely.

G.G. Coulton's criticism, in *The Cambridge Review* of October 1932, was even harsher, although of a very different kind, not attacking the historical method, but rather the theoretical premises and implicit assumptions of *The Making of Europe*. Coulton did not deny that the book was well-informed and well written, but he found Dawson's thought 'confused' and 'parochial', ignoring the real difficulties of the modern man. Dawson's insistence on, and exaggeration of, European unity avoided posing the problem 'whether unity in error is really better than divergence in honest search for truth'. But the strongest political argument advanced by Coulton was that real progress might be the gradually growing understanding between the European and the Asiatic; in that sense the contemporary age was more progressive than a past age when 'no orthodox European could excuse the Asiatic from hell', and dissidents were burned alive in supposed service to God. Coulton was well known for his anti-clericalism and his controversiality;[61] he was to develop his criticism of the Roman Catholic church into an attack on 'the dogma of Papal infallibility, which implies fully fledged Totalitarianism'. He considered this to be more absolute than even the totalitarian regimes of Hitler and Mussolini, which had never quite gone so far.[62]

Perhaps in reply to Coulton's criticism on the question of relationships between Asia and Europe, T.S. Eliot's *The Criterion* of January 1933
pointed out that in Dawson's book the debt which the West owed to the
eastern civilisations – to Byzantium, to Islam and to Persia – was freely
acknowledged and discussed in detail. The writer of the review, Frank
MacEachran, author of various essays on European civilisation, pointed
out something that the lay critics could not appreciate: the transcendental
origin of the controversial idea of unity, outside the limits of the immediate, while the world's present disunity, 'the most ominous sign of the
modern condition', was the result of the corroding influence of theories of
progress and amelioration.

The question of modernity was indeed very present in Dawson's
thinking at the time. In the autumn of 1932 the BBC broadcast a programme on a then hotly debated theme: the question of the forces of
change transforming the modern world. The programme included talks by
Dawson, afterwards published under the title *The Modern Dilemma: The
Problem of European Unity*, touching on the issues of democracy, science,
religion and the European tradition. Dawson attacked Oswald Spengler
for regarding 'our doom as inevitable', and praised Joseph de Maistre,
author of the *Soirées de Saint Petersbourg*, as the last representative of pre-
nationalist Europe. Dawson sympathised with de Maistre's certainty that
Providence had allowed the European order to be broken down by the
French Revolution only in order to make Europe move towards a greater
unity. A similar idea could be found in Maritain, according to whom the
material organisation of the world by European ideas and Western science
was a necessary preparation for the spiritual unification of humanity
through Christianity. The political revival of Europe was impossible without a spiritual revival of European culture, i.e. of Christianity: 'Before the
coming of Christianity there was no Europe'. However, Dawson was perfectly aware that Western civilisation was morally discredited, and a great
effort would be required to restore it. Only the Europeans could succeed in
such a task; the United States, while equal to Western Europe in material
and technical organisation, was unequal to the spiritual task of a new
world leadership. This last observation struck the note of anti-
Americanism, a recurrent theme of debates about the idea of Europe in the
inter-war period.

As already mentioned, Dawson's conception of Europe's civilisation
as an organic whole was critical of Oswald Spengler, whom Dawson
accused of considering cultures as closed systems, and indulging in a fatal-
ism according to which Europe was destined to be destroyed. He criticised Spengler for oversimplifying the complexities of cultural interaction
and not recognising the importance of the co-operation of several peoples
in a civilisation, the same criticism he was to make of Toynbee in the
1950s.[63]

A major issue in the historical debate on Dawson has been his attitude to Fascism. In November 1932, he was one of five participants from Britain at the big international conference on Europe, known as Convegno Volta, organised in Rome by the Italian Royal Academy and the Foundation Alessandro Volta. The other Britons were Lord Rennell of Rodd, British Ambassador to Rome from 1908 to 1919, Lord Lymington, member of parliament since 1929, the historian Sir Charles Petrie; and the economist Paul Einzig. Among those who had been invited from the UK but did not accept were Winston Churchill, Lloyd George, Austen Chamberlain, J.M. Keynes, Rudyard Kipling and Hilaire Belloc. Mussolini inaugurated the conference in Campidoglio, and various Fascist personalities were present. Germany was represented among others by Alfred Rosenberg, the Nazi theoretician of racism, and by Hermann Goering, President of the Reichstag. The conference was asked not to adopt any resolution, in order to avoid political commitment; however, many statements teetered on the edge of this. As for the Britons, Lymington, author of *Ich Dien, The Tory Path* (1931), declared that Mussolini was a great leader; Petrie considered him 'the saviour who will show the way to overcome the barbarians' in Europe and to correct the basic fallacies of the French Revolution. On quite another line, Lord Rennell proposed the organisation within the League of Nations of a Council for Europe, one for the Americas, and at a later stage one for Asia.

In this context, Dawson's address at the Convegno Volta was quite noticeable, since it was critical of racism, which was not at the time a central theme of Italian Fascism. Dawson insisted on the absence of racial uniformity in Europe and on the importance of diversity in European culture; in fact, it was the vital tension between a number of different racial elements, he argued, that allowed Europe to develop as the centre of civilisation. Dawson's view of history was expressed very clearly, if somewhat schematically, in his talk: European history was an alternation of syntheses and revolts. The internationalism of medieval civilisation created the foundation of a unity of Western culture that was not destroyed by the spiritual revolt of Northern Europe, the Reformation. The effect of this revolt was counteracted by the attraction that the new Renaissance culture had for the European mind. Thus a second European synthesis had arisen, based on the internationalism of Renaissance scholarship and art. The new synthesis was destroyed by the Romantic revolt, almost at the same time as the old order of European society was overthrown by the liberal revolutionary movement; liberalism and romanticism were the two forces responsible for the failure of the nineteenth century to realise the ideal of European unity. It was the 'early romantics' who paved the way for the fanaticism of the 'modern pan-racial theorists who subordinate civilisation to skull measurements and who infuse an element of racial hatred into the political and economic rivalries of European peoples'. In opposition to them

Dawson maintained that the European nations were the organs of a single European culture, and advocated the renewal of the old collaboration between North and South as the only way out of a crisis that risked the annihilation of European civilisation as a whole.

The only participant to intervene after Dawson's paper was Francesco Orestano, philosopher and member of the Italian Academy, secretary of the section of the Academy (Moral and Historical Sciences) that had organised the conference and author of a book on an 'aristocracy of peoples' (Un'aristocrazia di popoli). Orestano felt the need to respond to Dawson by stating that there were incompatible and compatible races: hybridisms between the incompatible races could not be successful, like those between English and Indians in India or between whites and blacks in Africa. European races were compatible as a result of what he called a 'vigorous selection by war' ('un'energica selezione guerriera'), which had allowed the survival only of those who were fit to combine with each other.

We know from his daughter that Dawson did not like the atmosphere at the Convegno Volta, turning out to be not at all a historical or academic conference but an act of propaganda and legitimation of the Italian Fascist regime, which by then had set up a full police state and was seeking to improve its international reputation. Delegates were followed and spied on, as well as entertained sumptuously at the Excelsior Hotel. For the conference meetings morning dress and top hats had to be worn; for the evenings uniforms and decorations. The conference took place in the splendid Palazzo Farnese, but meetings were often boring. At the official dinner Dawson's wife Valery was seated next to Goering and two places from Mussolini, an honour that, according to her daughter, made both she and her husband rather uneasy.[64]

Dawson's awkward position at that conference and at the formal events surrounding it could be taken as symbolic of his ambivalence towards Fascism, which was to develop further in later years. In four articles written in April and May 1934 for the Catholic Times Dawson analysed the great European crisis, of which the economic crisis was 'only one episode'. The First World War had dealt a mortal blow to European liberalism, and as a result Communism had acquired a new significance and power. Dawson accepted the Fascist claim that Fascism stood for the creation of a social order which was neither communist nor capitalist, and was a genuine third alternative. Soviet Russia was defined by Dawson as the 'Kingdom of the Antichrist', to which 'even a dictatorship would be preferable'. Catholicism refused the philosophy of liberal individualism on which capitalism was based, favouring an organic conception of society based on mutual dependence between its members and on the principles of hierarchy and authority; therefore it advocated the restoration of a corporate social order where vocational groups bind individuals together not according to the position they occupy in the labour market, but according to the different functions that they exercise. The only criticism of Fascism that Dawson offered was of its belief that the state should absorb the whole of human life and replace all other forms of social organisation.

These articles were rather contradictory. While claiming that democracy was the product of the Christian tradition, Dawson attacked the party system and parliamentary tactics, without which, whatever their weaknesses, there is no democracy. While asserting that if Catholics had to choose between Communism and Fascism, they would always decide against the former, he insisted that a genuine English Fascism would be very different in its external forms from anything that existed on the continent. Of course Dawson was never a follower of Oswald Mosley, and he could not be defined as a Fascist, but the vagueness of his alternative proposal, 'the reunion of Christendom', underlined, even as a temporary solution and with reservations, his sympathy for Fascism. Dawson believed in a European spiritual loyalty higher than that of blood or class, but he also felt at ease when quoting Mussolini's words 'it is always the spirit that is the lever of great things'. As a result, his articles were sometimes read as apologies for Fascism.

According to Bruno Schlesinger's 1949 dissertation, the book in which Dawson collected these ideas in 1935, albeit in a less virulent way, *Religion and the Modern State*, was substantially pro-Fascist, since only the good features of Fascism were enumerated while its fundamental flaws were totally overlooked. Dawson defended his book against the accusation of Fascism, and rightly so, because in it he had toned down some of the statements made in the original articles, concluding that the European tradition was much broader that that of nationalism or liberalism or socialism, and affirming that the choice to be made was 'between the mechanised order of the absolute State, whether it be nominally Fascist or Socialist, and a return to a spiritual order based on a reassertion of the Christian elements in Western culture'.[65] It has been argued that in Dawson's view totalitarianism was virtually inevitable once a civilisation had lost its soul.[66] But there was a point on which Dawson never accepted the inevitability of Fascism, and that was racism: he made it very clear in 1939 that the antisemitic policy of National Socialism was 'a deliberate attempt to focus a sentiment of reaction on a definite social figure: to make the Jew the representative and the scapegoat of the mechanical, cosmopolitan, urban mass civilisation which is the antithesis of an organic national culture'.[67] Schlesinger pointed out that, from 1939 on, Dawson's views developed towards an appreciation of liberalism and democracy and a recognition of violence and terror as essential components of totalitarianism.[68]

Dawson's ambivalence towards Fascism is perhaps linked with the particular situation of Catholics in Britain, where a Christian Democratic party never developed, making it more difficult to articulate left-wing and right-wing positions within the democratic dialectics of a Catholic political view. But even if such a party had existed, it would perhaps not have changed Dawson's position. After all a progressive organization like the Catholic Social Guild did exist, along with papers like the *Christian Democrat* or the *Catholic Worker*, whose sympathies were close to the antifascist Luigi Sturzo, an exiled Italian priest who had founded in 1919 the Catholic Partito Popolare Italiano. However, Dawson chose to write in *The Tablet*, a paper that had always supported Mussolini; and in the late 1930s he openly sided with General Franco against the Republic in the Spanish Civil War. In March 1937, writing on 'Spain and Europe', again in the *Catholic Times*, Dawson dismissed any possibility that a true society of nations could be found in the League of Nations. He understood that 'the issue of the struggle in Spain will decide the fate of Europe', and was sure that the victory of Communism in Spain would have been a victory over Catholicism. On the other hand, he saw in a recovery of Christian Spain a victory for Europe, and a return to an essential element without which European civilisation had become one-sided and incomplete. The article ended with the hope that 'the spirit which saved Europe from Islam and turned the tide of the Reformation is not dead'. Dawson's analysis was in the end proved wrong, because Europe was saved from the disaster precipitated by Nazism precisely by those capitalist democracies that Dawson distrusted so much.

The value of a Catholic ideology for European unity cannot be denied insofar as it is potentially capable of tempering nationalisms and reaching some sort of harmony between them. It is highly regrettable that the Catholic idea of Europe was not used more against Fascism and Nazism, since it actually had such potential; in fact, small pockets of Catholic resistance, like the German *Weisse Rose*, did heroically oppose the dictatorships, while the official hierarchies often did not, both in Italy and Germany. At the same time the Christian idea of European civilisation was an essentialist ideology that implied acculturation and paternalism, considering all other cultures worthy of respect but inferior. Threats to this essentialism were not only the political positions of liberalism, communism and socialism – of 'the dictation of Moscow or Bloomsbury' in Dawson's terms – but also the new cultural and anthropological attitudes that discarded the idea, crucial to his notion of European civilisation, of a spiritual community kept alive through intersubjective and gender relations, particularly in the family.

This aspect was important for Dawson. In 1930 he published in *The Criterion* series of booklets an essay entitled *Christianity and Sex*, in which he took a stand in the debate on marriage, divorce and sexual freedom. The debate had been going on since the end of the nineteenth century, when important books advocating a libertarian view of sexual morals had been published by progressive scientists such as J. Arthur Thomson and Patrick Geddes, authors of *The Evolution of Sex* (1889), by Socialist writers such as Edward Carpenter, eminent in the arts and crafts movement (*Love's Coming of Age*, 1896), and Havelock Ellis, who wrote *Man and Woman* (1894) and *Studies in the Psychology of Sex* (first volume 1896), the last of these influencing Sigmund Freud. Such authors were widely quoted when the debate intensified after the First World War, which had accelerated the processes of economic and moral change. In the 1920s the crisis of marriage had become more acute and rates of divorce had increased not only in the United States but also in European countries such as Holland, Sweden and Denmark. When Dawson was writing, in 1930, the debate had been revived by the publication in the previous years of various relevant texts by Calverton, Russell, Freud, and Briffault. Dawson used Malinowski's *Sex and Repression in Savage Society* (1926) in his criticism of Freud's *Totem and Taboo* (1912–13), in order to prove that the psychological complex derives from a social structure and not *vice versa*, Malinowski having shown that the repression at the root of social life is not the prehistoric Oedipus tragedy, but a deliberate constructive repression of antisocial impulses.

Dawson was convinced that the contemporary crisis was different from anything in the past, since the institution of marriage was being attacked from opposing quarters, in America and in Russia, defined by him as 'the outlying territories of our civilization'.[69] Another thread of anti-Americanism emerges here, with the assumption, very frequent in the inter-war period, that in the United States the family was being destroyed by women's emancipation and divorce, while in Russia it was undermined by the state itself. Dawson took issue with Alexandra Kollontai, the first woman plenipotentiary ever sent out by a modern country as representative to a foreign power – as Soviet Ambassador to Mexico and then to Norway – for her contention that the old form of family was passing away. He had not read Kollontai directly, and quoted her from Calverton's *Bankruptcy of Marriage*. This book, published in New York in 1928, had had a wide impact. It drew a picture of the 'present chaos in modern morals', where the New Woman and the New Morality expressed the spirit of the Jazz Age in the Western World. In the United States the rate of divorce had reached in the mid-1920s the figure of 15.3 for every 10,000 marriages. The disintegration of the family was mainly due to the economic independence of women and to the advance of birth control methods, which allowed girls and young women to rebel against the notions, introduced by Christianity, of repression as virtue and sex as sin. Inadequate, though stimulating, solutions to these problems were proposed, such as that of companionate marriage, characterised by love, companionship, co-operation and the open intention not to have children. The only country that Calverton excluded from this picture of decay was Soviet Russia, where woman was 'the equal of man in every activity and every organisation of life',[70] and her rights as well as those of her children, without distinction between legitimate and illegitimate, were protected by the law.

Dawson objected strongly to these views as well to those expressed by Bertrand Russell, who in *Marriage and Morals* (1929) suggested that the institution of marriage was in crisis because of the lack of sexual education and due to women's emancipation. According to Russell, rational solutions could be found for the former, but no repressive measures could ever stop the latter. Divorce should be made easier, even if that would not resolve the crisis. In addition, Russell suggested as a rational attitude that jealousy be controlled so that marriage could be lifelong and include other sexual relationships. He counterposed the Christian principle that sex is sin with the rational belief that 'instinct should be trained rather than thwarted'.[71] The only place where sexual ethics had been determined by rational considerations rather than by tradition and superstition was Soviet Russia. By contrast, Dawson believed that the USA had not gone as far as Russia – where the legislative reorganisation of marriage and the family had given the state the power to directly control the lives of individuals – but that the two societies were similar in favouring the same cult of the machine and the tendency to subordinate every other aspect of human life to economic activity. The complete emancipation of sexual relations from the old restrictions was in both societies a sign, in spite of appearances, of the destruction of individuals in favour of a standardised type of mass civilisation, characterised by the rule of technology evident in the diffusion of contraception. Defending the positions taken by Pope Leo XIII in his encyclical on marriage,[72] Dawson held the view that 'the supersession of the family means not progress, but the death of society, the end of our age and the passing of European civilisation'.[73] Dawson was worried about the model that the developments in Russia and America, as well as the new ideas, could represent, not only for the intellectuals and the higher classes, but also for the middle and lower classes of society: 'the poor' would not bother to marry if marriage was no longer, as Russell advocated, the only framework for sexual activity.

If he was preoccupied with the influence of these scholars, Dawson was even more so with the effect that 'popular writers like Marie Stopes' could have on the 'ordinary Englishman, instinctively favourable to the traditional morality on which English law and social organisation is based', but 'uneasily conscious of his lack of any clear system of defence of orthodox morality'. Marie Carmichael Stopes had written immensely popular books, especially *Married Love*, which had first been published in 1918 and by 1930 had reached 19 editions and 57 reprints, with more than 600,000 copies sold (by 1940 there would be 930,000 in circulation). Stopes had written a real handbook for married couples who hoped 'to make their marriages beautiful'.[74] On the basis of her studies (she was Doctor of Science and of Philosophy), of her own experience and of the experiences of many people who had gone to her for advice, Stopes explained that 'woman's nature is set to rhythms' like the tides of the sea,[75] so that it was not easy for many men to recognise the 'delicate signs' of their wives' ardour. Stopes explained the periodicity of recurrence of desire in women and provided charts of such rhythms. Whatever the consistency of the charts, Stopes's books did much to establish the existence and the specificity of women's sexual desire, with a clear description of what half a century later would be called the clitoridean orgasm. She also made many other suggestions for a happy marriage, including techniques of birth control. Stopes insisted that she wrote primarily for the British educated classes, but Dawson was evidently worried about the effect of her writing on a larger audience, including the vast majority of the middle classes and perhaps those parts of the working classes that were more similar to the respectable 'ordinary Englishman' he had in mind.

The preoccupation with morality, a traditional task of religious professionals, was now, according to Dawson, left increasingly to Catholics, while 'the advocates of the new morality' were only too ready to acknowledge the Catholic Church as the representative and champion of an irrational system of taboo or even, according to Russell, of 'a morbid aberration... tending towards mental disorders and unwholesome views of life'.[76] Dawson defended the Catholic view of sexual ethics as always based 'not on its ideals of asceticism, nor even on its theological dogmas, but on broad grounds of natural law and social function'.[77] He also defended the Catholic Church from Russell's accusation of having degraded the position of women to below the level of ancient civilisation, and argued that Catholic culture fostered the equal footing of husband and wife as well as, on the basis of the ideal of virginity, the full expression of femininity.

It is significant that for Dawson the romantic exaltation of passion and the glorification of the lover who defies social conventions is 'coloured by Christian ideas', but it is no less contrary to Christian morality than the rationalism of the advocates of a sexual reform based on pure hedonism. In the end that does not produce spirituality as it claims, but unhealthy and perverted sexuality, as exemplified by Byron, Shelley, Poe, and the modern romantics. Dawson believed that the old romantic attitude had been killed by psychology and psycho-analysis, and fully accepted the criticism of the romantic view of love expressed by Russell, who believed that romantic love could be 'the source of the most intense delights', but also the origin of disasters in marriage, since it was 'anarchic' and acted as 'a glamorous mist' rather than allowing for 'something more intimate, affectionate, and realistic'.[78] Therefore the opposing views agreed that romantic love was responsible for many unhappy marriages as well as for many divorces. But Dawson was firmly convinced that Russell, as well as all the advocates of the new morality, whatever they wrote, expressed a rationalism inextricably tangled with romanticism, involving an idealisation of sex and a desire to free emotional life from social constraints. Following these intellectual leaders, ordinary men and women tended to idealise their emotions, while rationalism made them sceptical of all ultimate principles; consequently their sexual life lost all depth, permanence and mystery. Dawson's tirade ended with praise of D.H. Lawrence's criticism of the cerebralisation of sex. However, his own position was to restore the religious view of marriage, thus bringing sexual life into contact with a more universal reality. Western civilisation had developed higher ideals of love and marriage than any other culture. If those 'characteristically European ideals' were not saved, the whole of Western civilisation would be lost. *Christianity and Sex* ends with these words:

> [Western civilisation] can be saved only by a renewal of life. And this is impossible without love, for love is the source of life, both physically and spiritually. Love requires faith, as life requires love.

There were historical dimensions to the connection between Dawson's idea of European unity and the position he took on love. In an article in *The Criterion* of January 1932 on the origins of the romantic tradition Dawson entered the one-and-a-half century long dispute on the origins of Provençal poetry and love. This was evidently a theme that touched him personally; suffice it to say that the first quotation in the article, one crucial to his thesis of the contrast between the Provençal ideal and the Christian moral code, is from *Aucassin et Nicolette*. That love *fabliau* from thirteenth-century Northern France, edited in the eighteenth century by La Curne de Sainte Palaye, had been Christopher Dawson's present on the day of their engagement, to his fiancée Valery, to whom he wrote every day on the rare occasions when the two of them were separated. The theme of love was central to his personal experience and, although less prominently, it is also of crucial importance in his work.

Dawson does not deny the traditional stereotype, that the art of the troubadours is the starting point of modern European literature, but he detaches himself drastically from the most diffuse and traditional view on the origins of Provençal culture itself. He denies any direct relationship between Latin and Provençal poetry as well as any influence from the North and any Germanic origin, while he also refutes the hypothesis of a purely native growth. Dawson instead believes that it was the Arabic influence from Moorish Spain which caused the 'ideal of romantic love' to arise in Provence, and he sees the lack of acceptance of the influence of Islam on the West as a nationalist tendency to insist on the independent and native origin of Western culture. He points to similarities of content and form, of style, of concepts and feelings between Provençal and Arabic love poems, as well as to the status of women in Spain, and to the considerable number of poetesses among queens and princesses of the Spanish dynasties. Clearly he rejects out of hand one of the *topoi* of the discourse on Provençal poetry and love, the destructive effects on Provençal culture of the Albigensian crusade led by the Catholic church. However, he is keen to establish that the culture of the troubadours had no essential relation to Catholicism: 'it is a great mistake to suppose that there is anything peculiarly Christian or European in the ideal or 'Platonic' conception of love', which was really Arabic.

Dawson's insistence on the non-Christian origins of a form of love which was widely considered essentially European can be understood on the basis of two considerations: in terms both of personal experience and of cultural history Dawson could assert that only Christianity made love European, drastically redeeming its original, Asiatic, nature and imbuing it with a spiritual nature that it did not have before. In this way the multiculturalism of European civilisation, as well as its Christian basis, was preserved. Secondly, the romantic element of love was discarded as non-European, as were those elements that Dawson considered degenerations in America and Russia. At that point, while romantic love – understood as freedom of choice, guided by emotion – could be seen spreading everywhere, only Europe appeared capable of defending and saving a conception of love linked with marriage and infused with that sense of spiritual unity that was the basis of the community in which Dawson believed.

It is significant that in 1942, when the Second World War was well advanced and Dawson had lost hope of founding a new review called *Europe* – which was to be an independent Catholic journal proposing a non-sectarian cultural programme – he published *The Judgement of the Nations*, a book in which he reanalysed 'the disintegration of Western civilisation'. This time he felt constrained to apply the term 'dark' to his own times, which were going through 'the Hour of Darkness', and he recognised that 'the incongruous fusion of racial materialism and nationalist mysticism which had produced the portentous social phenomenon of National socialism' stood in direct contradiction to the whole tradition and ethos of Western civilisation. His proposal was a United States of Europe, the only solution capable of reconciling the national freedom and cultural autonomy of the Western European peoples with the tradition of European unity and the needs of world order. The organisation of Europe should be as free and as diversified as possible; the resulting European union would co-operate with other world federations, the British Commonwealth, the USA, the USSR, as well as with Latin America and India and China, as a constituent member of a federal world order. As an ironic nemesis, this hope of Dawson's excluded from a united Europe his own country, a sad renunciation of his great dream of a new spiritual community.[79]

His work has had alternating fortunes. In the 1950s *The Making of Europe* was recommended to students as a cultural prehistory of European unification, as it expressed an assumption shared not only by historians but by part of the cultured general public that the merger of the Six was included in the movement of progress of Western civilisation, of which the Carolingian empire was the starting point.[80] In the 1960s this idea was subjected to criticism as over-optimistic and anachronistic. In his Vogelenzang lectures, delivered in Haarlem in April 1963, Geoffrey Barraclough assessed Dawson's contribution as 'persuasive' in the debate about the medieval bases of European unity, but he also suggested that the Carolingian unity had many limits, was 'less than European', so that Dawson's view that it was the foundation of European development amounted to 'an exaggeration'. Barraclough, like Dawson, was convinced that the 'ultimate foundation of our culture is not the national state but the European unity', and in fact quoted this passage from the introduction of *The Making of European Unity*. What Barraclough totally disagreed with was the confusion between European unity and Church unity, a pivotal point in Dawson's work, and he insisted that the unity achieved under papal leadership was always against an outside enemy, as if Europe seemed incapable of unity for its own sake. This well-grounded judgment prevailed and was repeated by historians of the European idea in the subsequent decades.[81]

In recent times, the very search to find the beginnings of European unity in the Middle Ages has been subjected to criticism. It has been underlined that such a search for something which did not exist silences the plurality of medieval voices.[82] A discourse on European cultural unity in that period has been defined as 'a collective fantasy of great strength' which facilitated exchanges and alliances[83] or as 'a deliberate rhetorical strategy' which justified the right of a part of Europe to dominate.[84] In the light of such contemporary research, the historical value of Dawson's work is less important than his contribution to the political debate of his time.

However, it should be noted that Dawson's *The Making of Europe* was among the first histories of Europe that began to appear in the thirties; others were, in Italy by Benedetto Croce (limited to the nineteenth century) in 1932 and in Britain by H.A.L. Fisher in 1935. It has been observed that before 1945 'Europe seldom occurs in historiography' and that, due to the identification between Europe and the world, only after the mid-thirties did Europe as such become the object of historical investigation and did 'historical works [begin] to appear which carried Europe in their titles'.[85] In this respect Dawson must be recognised as far-sighted, in spite of the weaknesses in his historical approach and its political implications. His sensitivity to the crisis of the European culture took a conservative form, but it was a genuine concern, which, as Vera Brittain wrote in a review of one of his books that anticipated later ones, *Progress and Religion* (1929) was worth studying 'by all who are concerned to save modern Europe from another epoch of self-destruction, more complete than that of 1914 to 1918'.

# Minds between war and peace: psycho-analysts and psychologists on the crisis of European civilisation

The political and cultural debates on the unity of Europe at the end of the 1920s and the beginning of the 1930s need to be placed against a background of common language and understanding which amounted to a common mentality. Wickham Steed's notion of the 'war-mind' as one of the ingredients which made the union of Europe difficult was an opinion widespread in his times, and an underlying assumption of the discourse on Europe and its civilisation. An address given by the British colonial and dominions secretary, Leopold Amery, at the Royal Institute for International Affairs in December 1929 interpreted the question of federal Europe in much the same terms. Amery thought that the proposal of Pan Europa expressed a 'mental readjustment in Europe' which was a reaction to the war as well as an effect of the fear of Bolshevism and of latent resentment throughout Europe towards the 'Anglo-American blockade'. A 'new mentality' was growing that tended to see the old type of nation-state as out of date and to favour the emergence of a common European patriotism. Amery believed that Pan Europa was a wise response to this state of things – and of minds – all the wiser since it excluded both Russia and Britain. He sympathised greatly with the pan-European movement, but he would have rejected any suggestion that Britain should actually proclaim itself a European and not a world power.

In 1932 Arnold Toynbee, a historian and one of the figures connecting The Round Table and the New Europe groups and who also developed a strong interest in psychology, opened his analysis of what he defined as the 'Annus Terribilis 1931' with a sub-chapter on 'The States of Mind'. Toynbee observed that in January 1931 the Commission of Inquiry for European Union – what had survived of Briand's plan – had found it necessary to contradict the current rumours of the imminence of another general war by issuing an explicit *démenti*. However, this very denial underlined the general feeling of insecurity:

> In 1931, men and women all over the world were seriously contemplating and frankly discussing the possibility that the Western system of Society might break down and cease to work.

According to Toynbee, for some centuries before the year 1931 'such moods had been utterly alien from the Western minds'. The belief in progress had been shattered by the First World War, and for the first time Western minds were contemplating 'a spontaneous disintegration of society from within', resulting from the processes of economic and political anarchy.

One way in which to understand this sense of impending cataclysm, that many took for granted at the time, is to concentrate on the efforts made by those who wanted to act on states of minds, believing that they had the means to change them. In the inter-war period many psycho-analysts focused on the question of the relationships between social evils and collective tendencies to destruction, on the one hand, and problems within individual development on the other.

Psycho-analysis had been developing in Britain after the First World War, and it had gained respectability and popularity thanks to a variety of works on 'war neuroses' written by psycho-analysts proposing the treatment of war traumas; such treatment had often proved to be much more effective than those of orthodox psychiatry.[86] This attention to social and political themes remained important on the British psycho-analytical scene for the whole inter-war period.[87] Ernest Jones, who founded the British Psycho-Analytical Society (BPS) in 1919, promoted public lectures on social and political issues and launched its International Library series by editing a book on *War Neuroses* (1919), in which the interpretation of history on the simple basis of economics and politics was considered reductive. In 1923, some of the lectures by British psycho-analysts delivered under the auspices of the Sociological Society were published, all of them concerning the social aspects of psycho-analysis.[88] Among them, the essay on *Psycho-analysis in relation to politics* by M.D. Eder insisted on the possibility of applying psycho-analysis to the political world 'because of its extremely practical nature', but lucidly warned that sociologists could obtain no practical help directly from it. Eder, who was then Secretary of the BPS, could certainly not be viewed as uninterested in the 'outer world', having had a career as a Socialist (he had helped to found the London Labour Party), Zionist, Amazonian explorer and pioneer school doctor.[89] He included the League of Nations in his analysis, since it was for him an interesting attempt to create a co-equal authority against the power of one sovereign; the difficulty of doing this was constituted by the connection between the image of the father and the figure of the king, as well as by the psychological fact that 'the band of brothers does not easily exist without a father'. But – Eder concluded – the question needed to be considered in the light of the renewed political activities of women, which were changing the whole picture by introducing the 'mother' into the public scene.

This suggestion was never really taken up, although the hopes of interpreting politics through psycho-analysis as a way of eventually solving some of the evils of politics continued to inspire publications and debates. The illusion that psycho-analysis could, following the example of the hard sciences, solve the problems of society with clear-cut solutions has to be placed in the context of the confidence of those years – a confidence never shared by Freud – in the possibility of using psycho-analysis to better the general condition of mankind and particularly that of Europe, which was felt by many to be particularly dramatic.

With the effects of the economic crisis, the failure of Briand's plan and the rise of Nazism in Germany, the political situation of Europe at the beginning of the 1930s created widespread anxiety. Sigmund Freud shared it and was one of the intellectuals who adhered to Coudenhove-Kalergi's ideas; he admired the Count, supported his plan for the unification of Europe, and in 1931, with others, proposed his name – unsuccessfully – for the Nobel peace prize. Freud had dedicated attention to the question of war and peace and to its relationship with the general question of civilisation in a variety of writings, from *Zeitgemaesses ueber Krieg und Tod* in 1915 to *Civilisation and Its Discontents*, written in 1929 and published in Vienna and London in 1930. This book was immediately very popular: the German language edition sold 12,000 copies in the first year and needed a second edition in 1931.[90] In Britain the Hogarth Press published a translation by Joan Rivière in an edition of 1,860 copies (a second impression was probably made, since by 1943 sales of 2,694 were recorded). That *Civilisation and Its Discontents* addressed a wide series of worries and needs was recognised by the author himself with his usual rhetoric of modesty and dissatisfaction, when at the beginning of Chapter 6 he acknowledged that in none of his previous writings had he had such a strong feeling of 'describing a common knowledge'. The book has indeed the merit of making explicit some implicit commonplaces and of proposing a new interpretation of the general crisis of civilisation.

A first *locus communis* of cultured opinion in *Civilisation and Its Discontents* is that Western European civilisation has reached the climax of the process that limits and controls human sexuality; Freud adds that civilisation draws from such a repression a degree of psychic energy that it uses for its own purposes. Therefore love is 'one of the foundations of civilisation', but in the course of evolution love comes into opposition with the interests of civilisation, while civilisation threatens love with its restrictions. For civilisation to flourish, it not only has to control the individual libido but also to enforce a larger co-operation between a considerable number of individuals, since it could not survive if it consisted simply of 'double individuals', or couples. Society aims at binding its members together in a libidinal way that establishes strong identifications between them. Women, who represent the interests of the family and of sexual life, and who in the beginning had laid the foundations of civilisation 'by the claims of their love', come eventually to oppose civilisation and its demands as inimical to the free developments of libidinal love. Besides sketching this dialectical process, Freud introduced the death drive as an essential part of aggression and destruction, the struggle between love and death being therefore at the basis of the process of civilisation. While the first edition of *Civilisation and Its Discontents* ended with a declaration of hope that eternal Eros would strive to assert himself in the struggle with Death, a last sentence was added in 1931, after the Nazi party's victory in the German parliamentary elections of September 1930: 'who can foresee with what success and with what result' the struggle between the two 'Heavenly Powers' will end? *Civilisation and Its Discontents* showed that, at the beginning of the 1930s, widespread pessimism regarding the destiny of Europe was still tempered by some hopes, though these were frail and uncertain. Altogether, Freud's version of common knowledge was much more subtle and much less confident in the influence of psycho-analysis than the versions of his followers, who translated his ideas into direct recipes for the cure of society.

In the same 'annus terribilis', 1931, the medical psychologist Edward Glover, of the British Psycho-analytical Society, was invited by the Federation of League of Nations Societies in Geneva to give a lecture on the psycho-pathological investigation of reactions to war. Glover, who had been trained as an analyst by Karl Abraham in Berlin, travelled widely, spoke several languages and was familiar with the literature of many countries. He was himself one of those cultured Europeans who found themselves at home in many capitals of Europe, enjoying a network of friends which extended over large parts of the continent.[91] He gave his lecture in Geneva in front of 'a typical cultivated post-graduate audience',[92] which reacted at first with great enthusiasm, apparently conquered by his arguments. Glover asked how many millions were spent by the League of Nations on psychological research into the nature of the war impulse, and in a footnote replied 'not a penny', while stressing the fact that huge sums were spent on research on cancer and other diseases. In the prevention of future wars, Glover argued, the first effective step was the complete investigation and individual understanding of the nature of sadistic impulses, and he ended his speech by proposing 'a new sixth commandment: Know thine (unconscious) sadism'.[93] The premise of his argument was based on the 'fundamental identity between some of the impulses promoting peace and the impulses giving rise to war'.[94] Analysing the aggressive origin of the impulses to peace, he pointed out that the peace fanatic could also be a danger to peace and wished that a peace conference could be held 'purged of all lean-jowled enthusiasts with dilated pupils'.[95] Glover, picking up the subject some years later, went to the extent of underlining how even the League of Nations could 'behave in an obsessive way and with a blind eye to realities'.[96]

The backbone of his original argument lay in his analysis of war behaviour as compensation for the repression of infantile drives of love and hatred. 'Violating' an 'innocent little country', defending the 'mother' country', Glover argued, are first of all 'echoes of baby phantasies in which the 'good' mother or child is defended against the sinister (mostly sexual) designs of the phantasied 'bad' father'.[97] The frustration to which 'primitive loves and primitive hates' are destined can be compensated only on battlefields, where the primitive impulses can be satisfied in reality.[98]

Unfortunately, a few days later, after having listened to another brilliant lecturer, this time on the economic origins of war, most of the Geneva audience lost some of its enthusiasm for Glover's theses and switched to the opinion that the psychological causes of war had been exaggerated and had to be integrated with 'more important and realistic self-preservative or predatory impulses' which required the concentration of energy on international economic factors.[99] Glover thought that the change was a sign of the volatility of attitudes to psycho-analysis as well as to peace, both being easily swayed by the pressure of prejudices in favour of an economic ideology.

Glover's piece, 'War, Sadism and Pacifism', was published in London in 1933 together with other essays by the same author, in a collection of the same name. It was reviewed by Ernest Jones in the *International Journal of Psycho-analysis*, and republished in 1935 and 1946. Jones judged the book 'an admirable and weighty production', stating that 'any politician, indeed anyone concerned with the public weal, who does not give careful consideration to this book, is definitely evading responsibility'.[100] The book had as exergue a long quotation from the letters that Albert Einstein and Sigmund Freud had exchanged on the subject of war and peace. In 1931 the permanent Committee for Letters and Arts of the League of Nations had asked the International Institute for Intellectual Cooperation to promote a debate between intellectuals. Einstein had been approached; he suggested Freud's name, and an epistolary exchange followed. The two letters they wrote between August and September of 1932 were published the following year in three languages, with the title *Warum Krieg?, Why War?, Pourquoi la guerre?*; the publication was banned in Germany. In his reply to Einstein's question, whether there was a way of liberating men from war, Freud resumed his theory of love and hatred, concluding that the establishment by common consent of a central control was the essential condition for peace, while the necessary preliminary union could be brought about by a sufficient number of emotional ties (identifications). Any effort in the present situation that tried, as the League did, to employ only the latter means was doomed to fail, in spite of being a courageous and innovative enterprise in the history of mankind. Freud also asserted that he and Einstein, while recognising that war was in conformity with nature, biologically justified and hard to avoid, had no option but to be pacifists, since war stridently contradicted the psychic attitude imposed by the civilising process.

Ernest Jones's criticism in the *International Journal of Psycho-analysis* of an implicit Lamarckism of Freud's views, which assumed heredity as well as the innateness of the process leading to opposition to war, was not really justified by the text of the letter. By and large, Freud's exposition was much less deterministic than most formulations given by his contemporaries. However, we know that Freud himself was not very satisfied with the exchange of letters, and did not find it very fruitful that theoreticians should leave their specific fields in order to give advice on urgent questions of a practical order. It has been noted that the correspondence between Einstein and Freud takes for granted anthropological generalisations about violence, crowds and élites, as well as the language of social Darwinism on the superiority or degeneration of certain parts of the human species, while Freud himself adopts somewhat too simply the notions of non-cultivated races and inferior strata of the population.[101] However, there is something important and useful in these letters, and it lies in the efforts they represent to emerge from specialisms and to connect individual and collective developments. This latter was indeed a major achievement, tracing the war phenomenon 'to each subject as such', and interpreting the process by which violence had been monopolised by the state as a collective process.[102] The dissatisfaction that Freud felt was probably a combination of feelings, including fear that these writings were not really scientific and uneasiness about his own ambiguity towards the First World War, which at first he had welcomed with joy, this being connected with his relationship with his Jewish father and a desire to avenge persecution of Jews. His disquiet might also have been rooted in his understanding that tracing the path of aggression back to the subject is not enough, and can result in a reductionism which is absolutely as equal and as opposite to the one that expects a radical change in human relationships and subjectivity to arise simply from a successful socio-political revolution.

This double risk of reductionism was – and still is – the most difficult problem for any application of psycho-analysis to politics. There was a shade of mechanicism in Dr Glover's recommendation, which assumed that a cure for society could be modelled on a cure for the individual, and failed to explain how knowledge and awareness, as well as a re-elaboration of the impulses, were to be acquired by large masses of people. In fact, the developments of a group psychology of war in the following years, by Glover himself as well as by others, were only partially satisfactory. Developments in the direction of recognising the relevance of child analysis had been taking place in the 1920s in Britain under the influence of Melanie Klein. In 1925, invited by Jones through the mediation of Alix and James Strachey, Klein had given some lectures in London that were to become the basis of *The Psycho-analysis of Children* published in 1932.[103] In the preface to this book, Dr Edward Glover was thanked for his 'warm and unfailing interest' and 'his sympathetic criticism'.[104] It is true that later Glover, who was analyst to Klein's daughter, joined the daughter in her attack on her mother, but he might well have been influenced by Klein's inclination to stress the individual more than the social aspect of the development of love and hatred, giving great importance to child analysis. He himself, in his historical outline of psycho-analysis in England, acknowledged the decisive impact that Melanie Klein had had on the British

Society from 1925 to 1933, while after 1933 the dissension over Klein's positions had gradually increased.[105] More generally, it was the influence of British empirical traditions, which emphasised direct observation, as well as the cultural processes that in Britain had stressed the centrality of childhood,[106] that contributed to the concentration of Glover's work on the individual's and the child's development.

Edward Glover was part of an intellectual environment where the problem of reconciling the psycho-analytical and the social aspects of society was felt much more acutely than it is today. He himself had proposed a social system allowing any woman who desired it to take care of her children for the first four-to-five years, and instituting a series of small educational units; he believed that this reform required a revolution in social organisation and that it would be necessary to psycho-analyse all the heads of state as well as all important administrative officers.[107] Others, like Ernest Jones and Roger Money-Kyrle, were interested over a long period of time in the problem which was discussed in one of Jones's interventions, in 1943: 'How can civilisation be saved?'. Money-Kyrle outlined a utopia in his *Aspasia* (1932) – after the Greek hetaera celebrated for her beauty and culture – which envisioned a society based on universal love. This goal required a radical change from the system of Western Europe, where emotional deprivations gave rise to internal inhibitions and a curtailed capacity for love, thereby leading to hatred, depression and discontent. Social stability and happiness would be possible after the number of healthy people increased as the result of the conscious action of human beings:

> ... if we may expect that psychology will advance as rapidly as physics, we may hope soon to control our social future, and to mould it according to our whims.[108]

The problem, however, always came back to this sort of solution, at the same time too easy and too difficult. This is not to diminish the value of such utopias in keeping open a critical perspective on the existing world and the possibility of a different way of life and order, but they paid insufficient attention to either the gap between the individual and the collective or to the accumulated weight of economic and political divisions along national lines.

In 1933 a symposium on the 'Psychology of Peace and War' took place between Glover, the sociologist Morris Ginsberg and another member of the British Psycho-Analytical Society, John Rickman.[109] Ginsberg reversed Glover's point of view – that there could not be any dependable science of group relations until the sociology of the first five years of life had been exhaustively determined – saying that there can be no dependable sociology of the first years of life unless and until there is a dependable sociology of group relations, since 'sociology is not identical with psychology'. This was recognised by Rickman, who opened the debate following the two first speakers, but he deemed it most unlikely that a deliberate change in the policy of nursery discipline could affect the occurrence of war. In the end there were some doubts about the capacity of human beings to complete their psychological emancipation. Reviewing the symposium, Roger Money-Kyrle concluded that 'many citizens, if they were told that there would be no more war, might lose their patriotism, which, however inadequate, might be all they are capable of'.[110] He was to develop his ideas on war in the second half of the 1930s and again after the Second World War. For him the origin of war lay in the psychotic distortion of reality that he equated with Glover's unconscious sadism and masochism; such psychic distortions, he argued, generated aggressive impulses which found their way from the individual to collective forms of aggression and to war.

The British psycho-analysts considered here had, according to Glover, a 'centre' vision, and gathered young Tories, Democrats, Liberals, some Radicals and some vaguely socialist labour organisations; this centre, in its effort to influence public opinion, evolved from a romantic and aristocratic conservatism with some anarchist inclinations to a more liberal view influenced by Fabian ideas. But this vision did not lead to any political alliances, even in a wide sense. Their views were taken into consideration by the intellectual left and found insufficiently convincing. In *The Intelligent Man's Way to Prevent War* edited by Leonard Woolf for Gollancz in 1934 (and republished in a cheap edition in 1936), Norman Angell observed that Glover's analysis was a perfectly valid psycho-analytical explanation, but that it was not historically situated. If the Scots no longer went to war with the English, he wrote, it was not because of much change in the psychological make-up of individuals, 'but by reason of political changes which cause the same individual impulses to manifest themselves in a different political fashion'.[111] The difficulty for Angell was not the absence of a general will to peace, which the great mass of men genuinely wanted, but the contradiction between the war-inducing policy they pursued and the end which they desired. To these observations Angell appended educational solutions, such as the proposal of a new teaching agenda for all the social sciences, mathematics and language which would make intelligible to the ordinary intelligent mind both the anti-social side of human nature and the way to shape impulses to social ends. Norman Angell, in another essay (*The International Anarchy*) in the same book, argued that to avoid war a partnership of nations 'bearing very lightly upon national independence and sovereignty' was sufficient. In the same book Charles Roden Buxton, referring to Coudenhove-Kalergi's Pan Europa and to the Briand plan, expressed his scepticism towards a European 'regional' organisation. He feared that its consequences would be the creation of systems of preferential tariffs and the isolation of continental blocks that would weaken the more general intercontinental organizations like the League of Nations. Thus there was disagreement both on the diagnosis of the illness of European civilisation and on the means to save it; even those who accepted Freud's theory of civilisation were unable to say why the normal degree of frustration, typical of all societies according to Freud, was becoming excessive in the 1930s as it had in the 1910s leading to the First World War.

While the general psycho-analytical tendency in Britain was to underline individual stories and the influences on these of the infantile stages, other interpretative traditions went to the opposite extreme. In 1935 Glover was criticised by Otto Fenichel in the *Internationales Aerztliches Bulletin* of Prague, organ of the German socialist doctors in exile. Fenichel was one of the Political Freudians, the leftist psycho-analysts engaged in organizing a resistance to Fascism in Central Europe. He thought that *War, Sadism and Pacifism* assumed that groups in history presented the same neurotic dynamics as individuals and did not take into account economic and social factors. For Fenichel, the central question was which economic and social conditions, in a situation of antagonism between capital and labour, provoke the explosion of the unconscious aggressive drives; therefore he considered as grotesque the idea that the study of the psychopathology of war in the terms proposed by Glover could avoid war. Glover counter-attacked in the same journal, denouncing Fenichel's effort to reduce psychological processes to the class struggle and to subordinate psycho-analysis to Marxism and socialism.[112] This type of debate showed that the relationship between the social and the psychological continued to be understood by most psycho-analysts, whatever their political stand, as one of subordination and hierarchy. At the same time, the intellectual division of labour between the sciences – politics and economics on the one hand and psycho-analysis on the other – was not questioned deeply enough or far enough.

An interesting effort to apply psycho-analysis to the European situation was made by Fedor Vergin, whose book, *Subconscious Europe*, published in Vienna and Leipzig in 1931, appeared in English translation (by Raglan Somerset) in 1932. Unfortunately, all traces of the author have vanished; but his book is worth considering. Vergin, who quoted Freud and Jones, examined figures such as Franz Joseph I and Hitler, nations such as Austria and Italy, and movements such as socialism. He also took up some questions of European civilization as a whole. First of all, he reconsidered the common heritage that was bringing Europe to the brink of disaster. Every European, Vergin maintained, has inherited from the Stone Age some psychological inhibitions, semi-religious conceptions, primitive magic that cause complexes, mass-illusions, and collective hallucinations;[113] part of this heritage is the excessive importance attached to the mother tongue, which fosters nationalism. European political leaders are impotent against the forces that sway their mentality, being incapable of self-analysis.[114] Emotions and emotional complexes play such a part in the political game that politics persists in magical totemism, in childish beliefs. Bureaucracy is an expression of such archaism: its adoration of routine is a form of primitive ritual, its tendency towards censorship a reaction against a personal sense of guilt.

According to Vergin, a few politicians became conscious of being Europeans and struggled against the savage passions of their own countries: among them were Stresemann and Briand, who succeeded in resisting the rage and hatred of their opponents in settling the frontier zones between the Germans and French. It took each of them a long time to overcome 'the spell of war prejudices' and to find the way 'which led from his own conception of a good European to that of his *vis-à-vis*',[115] but through exchange and reasoning the two men proposed the basis of peace and union in Europe. A similar effort was attempted in Britain by MacDonald, who had succeeded in attaining at least temporarily some measure of agreement between opposite political sides.[116] Britain too had been becoming European since the Great War, but the real hope of the present was given by Pan Europa and its founder: 'from the midst of the degenerate aristocracy of Europe an idealist of a new and original type' emerged. The United States of Europe that Coudenhove-Kalergi proposed was a claim put forward by the sleepless forces of reason and inevitable logic. However, European politics were dominated by psychological conditions 'worthy of the African negro'[117] – we have already noticed that Eurocentrism included elements of racism in some Europeanists – conditions that induced the average European to attack the pan-European ideal with scorn and treat it with suspicion. 'Thus it is that a political idea, like that of the United States of Europe, suffers from the lack of essential psychological conditions and propaganda on its behalf. It is rendered useless by ignorance of psycho-analysis'.[118] The League of Nations was simply the indicator of the differences by which nations were divided, while its governing idea should have been their psychological investigation.

Vergin projected the utopia of 'a scientific age', when Europeans would be able to take the pan-European ideal for granted. His ideas were similar to Glover's in relation to introducing 'a joint rhythm into the primitive chaos of the emotions that bind men together', freeing them through psycho-analysis from revenge, sadism and masochism. However, Vergin's formulation has a strong visionary tone, evocative of millenarianism. He emphasised the catastrophes which would result if the utopia was not brought about: Europe would soon find itself rushing into a 'fresh nationalist war with the same fresh, and to many, quite inexplicable transports of joy, which it displayed in 1914'. Vergin explained this joy by referring to the beast within the European, which found it too restrictive to be subjected to the ideals of civilisation; the beast pushed the average European, who hated his own super-ego, to hate himself in his political opponent. *Subconscious Europe* ends with 'a testamentary greeting to future explorers in the European desert', in 20 or 30 years' time, when the poison gas of the last war will have evaporated. As they 'pick their way through the ruins of Europe', future explorers will have to remember that the Europeans went to 'their foolish graves', because they believed themselves to be half-divine but could not bring themselves to understand their own contradictions.

Vergin's book was not well received in England. The *International Journal of Psycho-analysis* did not review the book, although Ernest Jones owned an original edition that he gave to the library of the Institute of Psycho-analysis in 1941. The *Times Literary Supplement* of 24 November 1932 found *Subconscious Europe* 'dogmatically written', its 'defects amusingly displayed in the section on MacDonald'. The unknown *TLS* reviewer was right in criticising the mechanicism of many parts of the book, since this spoiled some of its interesting intuitions. The result was in fact a mixture of commonplaces and valuable ideas, which combined some of Freud's, Jones's and Glover's theses with a vague version of socialism and a strong contempt for any religion, plus some straightforward racism. Notwithstanding its many shortcomings and shortcuts, *Subconscious Europe* tried to connect what was divided – politics and psycho-analysis – out of an intuition that Pan Europa lacked psychological foundations. Vergin could not bridge the distance between the politicians and bureaucrats who gave a political meaning to the words 'Europe' and 'European', but were uninterested in the emotional foundations of such words, and those who could have filled the idea of the European heritage with emotional strength – as expressed, for instance, in literary works referring to the daily experiences of human solidarity in the war (an example could be Mottram's *Spanish Farm* Trilogy) – but did not even use the words 'Europe' and 'European' in their political sense.

The weakness of pacifism in the European culture of the time, as compared with the strength of Gandhian non-violence in the same years (the 1920s and early 1930s), is a sign of a European cultural tradition of war. We should remember that Diderot, in his entry 'législateur' for the *Encyclopédie*, considered the range of European governments, republics and monarchies as the origin of a wide diversity of feelings and customs ('sentiments et moeurs'); as a consequence, according to Diderot, there will always be wars in Europe. The effort to connect the individual and the collective made by psycho-analysis can be seen as a continuation of some of the hopes of the Enlightenment, to shed light on the obscure sides of European civilisation.

The psycho-analytical debate on war and peace continued in the second half of the 1930s and in the post-war period, reaching several hundred writings (as listed in the *Index of Psycho-analytic Writings* by Alexander

Grinstein).[119] The study of the effects of war in generating anxiety among the civil population was pursued, and the question of democracy posed from the psycho-analytical point of view, while new names appeared in the debate, such as those of John Bowlby and D.W. Winnicott. This discussion of psycho-analysis and politics must be limited to the first half of the 1930s in order to respect the boundaries of the present work. However, we might recall that Freud's work sparked off numerous debates over a vast and varied cultural terrain, from art to sociology to political science. It influenced political scientists, the most famous case being that of Harold D. Lasswell, professor of Political Science at the University of Chicago, who in 1930 published his book *Psychopathology and Politics*. Lasswell used as a point of departure Eder's 1924 essay, and quoted Freud frequently, taking from him the psychodynamic view of the mind and the procedure of free association; he also paid attention to non-Freudian developments, such as those led by Jung and Adler. On the basis of this background as well as of his knowledge of politics, Lasswell was convinced that 'political movements derive their vitality from the displacement of private affects upon public objects'. Therefore, according to him political science could not do without biography and he insisted on the usefulness to political scientists of life stories obtained through prolonged interviews. His work contained a series of case studies of individual agitators, administrators and theorists derived from a questionnaire of 56 questions appended to the book.

This approach – which attempts to connect psycho-analysis and politics – may today appear naive and reductionist. However, it retains important historical value. In the debates that we have considered – with reference to the Freudian scene in England – there was a lively sense of the Europeanness of the cultural inheritance which was at stake, as well as of the connection between this and emotions, understood in a very general way. It was clear to all those engaged in those debates that the threat of a possible Second World War was directly linked with the libidinal foundations of European civilisation and with the connection within it between the impulses towards love and death, without denying the more-than-European nature of aggressive impulses and warlike attitudes. While the link between the discourse on Europe and the discourse on love was mediated for Freudians by the notion of a libidinal economy of drives, the same link was interpreted in a very different way by Jungians; although there is less historical documentation and analysis on these, it is important to consider the question at least briefly.

Jung's reputation in England was subjected to ups and downs. His *Collected Papers on Analytical Psychology* were translated into English by Constance Long as early as 1916, and from that date onwards his disciples promoted his views with success, especially since his conception of the unconscious was less sexually oriented than Freud's and his concept of the libido was broadened to a general mental energy.[120] Jung's writings had a favourable press, and in 1922 the Analytical Psychology Club was formed in London.[121] However, some of the important Jungians changed their position in the 1920s. Maurice Nicoll sacrificed his career as a consultant in order to become an exponent of Ouspensky's thought, although he incorporated many of Jung's ideas into his new teaching;[122] James Young became a follower first of Gurdjieff and then of Alfred Adler; and M.D. Eder, who after having helped Jones found the London Psycho-analytical Society in 1913, had become enthused with Jungianism, was analysed by Ferenczi in Budapest and went definitely back to Freudianism at the beginning of the 1920s[123] – the point at which we first met him. Still, Jung was invited to lecture in England nine times between 1914 and 1939, his writings were regularly translated, and in 1936 the Society of Analytical Psychology was founded. Jung's cultural significance in England is evident in the impact of his ideas on intellectuals and artists of many kinds, such as Arnold Toynbee, Herbert Read, J.B. Priestley, and Kathleen Raine.[124]

In the years immediately before and after 1930, the issue of Europe can be found in some of his writings. One of these pieces is of particular interest for the focus of this work: *Woman in Europe* was originally published in 1927 as an article, then as a pamphlet in 1929 (reprinted several times in subsequent years). Its English version was included in *Contributions to Analytical Psychology*, translated by C.F. and H.G. Baynes in 1928. This is a very important essay, for it became the basis for a whole trend of Jungian analysis and debate about women and femininity, exemplified in England by Esther Harding's *The Way of All Women* (1933), such a successful book that it was reprinted on a regular basis until recently. Jung's essay started with a series of questions, the first being 'Have we anything of fundamental importance to say about Europe?'[125] The answer was that Europe's position was now midway between those of the Asiatic East and the Anglo-Saxon, or American, West. This was a commonplace and a common worry of the times; however, having introduced it, Jung did not develop it and instead chose to contrast the West as a whole – with its development of technological and scientific tendencies – to the East, with its awakening of spiritual forces. From a spiritual point of view, writes Jung, the West is undergoing a process of transition, which for the European man takes place in the realm of the scientifically applied intellect, a realm which includes – for him – both 'the banks and the battlefields', while for the European woman it takes the form of a psychic conflict. Therefore, women are at the very core of the social and spiritual European crisis, although Jung stresses that it is only the modern sections of those belonging to the middle and higher classes and living in the cities who form this group. Here, specifically, Jung is thinking of women active in the professions, in politics and in various jobs, including 'secretaries, typists, shop-girls'.[126] These women are caught in a multifaceted contradiction: politically, economically and spiritually they are not visible, so that they do not receive from their jobs the same gratifications as men do from theirs. At the same time they no longer enjoy the traditional recognition of their role, usually conceived as domestic and motherly. These women, according to Jung, are undergoing a mental masculinisation, and sometimes manifest an aggressive, urgent form of sexuality, or even homosexuality in the masculine role, instead of the traditionally receptive sexuality of woman. In contrast, men are not undergoing a process of feminisation to the same extent; they could not – without psychic injury – be a nursemaid or run a kindergarten, 'unless they were Chinese' (in other words, it was possible for men from non-European cultures to be equated with women because ethnic difference disrupts the European boundaries of gender difference). For Jung, some phenomena of feminisation were taking place, such as those connected with the new psychology inaugurated by Freud. Jung maintains that this involves a concession to femininity, because he considers women to have always been far more 'psychological' than men and because the greatest number of classic psycho-analytic cases were women.

There is a passage of dramatic description in Jung's essay where he portrays the millions of working women who cannot marry both because of their masculinisation and because of the unfavourable male/female ratio created by the First World War. Their 'silent, obstinate desire has magical effects, like the fixed stare of a snake',[127] expressing the accumulation in the unconscious of 'too much that has not been lived',[128] at the same time highlighting the dissatisfaction of married women with their husbands. In addition, the availability of contraception brings a release of psychic energy unable to find an outlet. The result of all this is the crisis of marriage, evidenced by the doubts of those who are within it, hemmed in by the unmarried. This Jungian interpretation can be fully understood with reference to two points in Jung's thought: his theory of the collective unconscious and the notion of the gender inversion of the individual's unconscious. According to the former, the human psyche possesses a common substratum transcending all differences in culture and consciousness, consisting of latent predispositions; this substratum is the collective unconscious, the psychic expression of the identity of brain structure, irrespective of all racial differences. According to the latter, each individual's unconscious is characterised by the opposite sex, so that a woman's unconscious is informed by the archetype of the male *animus*, while a man's unconscious takes the form of an *anima*. These personifications translate the fundamental bisexuality, already indicated by Freud, into archetypes, universal primordial images which are centres of psychic energy and appear in the ancient myths of all peoples as well as in today's individual psyches. The *animus* and the *anima* are essential for maintaining the wholeness and balance of the personality, but they may take control of the individual and act in his or her place. Since the masculinity of the woman and the femininity of the man are inferior to their open sexual characteristics, their excessive influence can be dangerously upsetting for the individual.

Jung considers the 'masculinisation' of many European women as a major factor of imbalance. These women can go back neither to 'an antiquated, purely instinctual femininity'[129] nor to the exclusiveness of medieval marriage,[130] which rendered psychic relationships completely superfluous.[131] At the same time they cannot give up the independence and critical judgement they have acquired, and which are recognised as positive values. The modern European woman is conscious of the fact that 'only in the state of love can she attain the highest and the best of which she is capable', but she fears that love 'could bring her in conflict with history'.[132] The present times urge women to live a more complete life, to achieve meaning and fulfilment by inaugurating something new. In so doing women would be accomplishing two major tasks: in the short run they would repair the inner wounds left in the 'European psyche' by the barbarity of the war, while in the long-term they would initiate a cultural commitment which could be the dawn of a new era, when 'Eros [will] unite what Logos has sundered'.[133] We can see from this analysis that the link between Europe and love in Jung's thought is more specific than in the Freudian analysis, which understands love as a general drive. The Jungian interpretation is concerned with love between the heterosexual couple and the cultural components connected with it, i.e. the images projected by poets through the ages of loved women as *animae*, which are such an important part of the European heritage.

Mary Esther Harding developed these ideas in her *The Way of all Women* (1933), based on her rich psychotherapeutic experience, as Jung noted in his introduction to her book. Harding interpreted the claim for independence from men in the bluestocking attitude and the feminist movement as a 'devious route' to woman's goal: this is described by Harding as the goal of 'relationship', i.e. the capacity to relate, for which a certain separateness is necessary. The feminist movement had to go to extremes in its early days, because the individual side of woman's psyche was at that time completely neglected. Harding stated that it was imperative for a woman to bring up and out the masculine side of her nature, that she had to learn to love a thing, or an idea, in order to reach an awareness of herself, rather than seek identification with men or total separation from them. Harding also made an interesting analysis of the cultural phenomenon that she defined as 'the Ghostly Lover', exemplified by the worship of Rudolph Valentino; she considered cults of this type to be forms of depreciation of real men but also signs of an inner or subjective experience. The 'way' Harding indicated for women was by achieving a gradual growth and deepening of consciousness through the daily reality of their lives. As a result, their personal and egotistical desires should recede and be replaced by a supra-personal influence related to the deeper principles of life. In this way woman would find for herself a spirituality based on the principle of Eros, expressed in real life by a new kind of human relationship. The myth of womanhood would fade and the real woman would emerge, releasing herself from the projection of man which made her seem divinely fair and demonically ugly. For the first time she will be humanly responsible for her own qualities.[134]

In spite of the essentialism of Jung's position – which considers unconsciousness and passivity essential components of woman's nature (as his use of the singular form indicates) – we can see from Harding's work that he encouraged the liberation of women's experiences. Moreover, Jung's interpretation of modern women has some relevance for cultural history, since women are placed by him at the centre of the European crisis, which is due to the loss of the meaning of life. In recent times, a debate between feminists has opposed those who consider Jung an anti-feminist and a racist[135] to those who believe in the possibility of reconciling feminist and Jungian thought provided the latter be divested of sexism; a further difference exists between those for whom a feminist archetypal theory can be proposed[136] and those who maintain that feminism will liberate the archetypes from their static and eternal associations.[137] This debate shows the vitality of Jungian thought in this respect and the fruitfulness of combining it with a feminist approach.

The problem created by the decline of traditional ways of giving life a meaning, such as religion, resulted for Jung in an alarming lack of balance in the European psyche. Therefore he believed that what he called 'the Swiss line' in the European spectrum might have an important function. The Swiss heritage comprised an attachment to the land, to backwardness, and to conservatism, all of which led to an intimate connection with the past[138] and which offered the possibility of acting as counterpoises to the modern tendency to forget it. The contrast between the past and the present was a major theme of Jung's reflections at the end of the 1920s and the beginning of the 1930s. Various essays on this theme were translated into English in 1933 in a collection of his writings under the title *Modern Man in Search of a Soul*. Two of the most important were *Archaic Man* (1928), based on his anthropological experiences in East Africa and with the Pueblo Indians, and *The Spiritual Problem of Modern Man* (1928), based on his observation of his own patients and his times.

In Jung's vision, archaic and modern men coexist in Europe, the former being present not only in the lowest stratum of the population, psychologically speaking, i.e. those who live in a state of unconsciousness which differs very little from that of the primitives, but also in the deeper levels of every individual's psyche. The latter is the man who is aware of the immediate present, and accepts the main tendency of the period, which is to become increasingly interested in psychological matters. This tendency has nothing to do with – indeed it is opposed to – 'the spirit of the time', which shows itself in the ideals of internationalism and supernationalism embodied in the League of Nations, but also in sport, cinema, modern dancing and jazz. The extension of the humanistic ideal produces, on the one hand, efforts to overcome national divisions and, on the other, an intensive evaluation of the body, also linked with an increasing fascination with the psyche, and bringing about a new self-appraisal. Since the French Revolution the psyche has become the focal point of man's interest. Archaic man is unpsychological; psychic happenings take place outside him in an objective way.[139] Modern man can no longer refrain from acknowledging the might of the psyche, despite all his attempts to resist it, one such resistance being the belief of 'the enlightened European' that only economic and political questions matter, while spiritual ones are good only for the masses and for women. However, in the end the 'psychological interest' of modern times does emerge, evident not only in the interest in psychology as a science, but in all sorts of psychic phenomena, including spiritualism, astrology, theosophy and parapsychology, all of which are spiritual currents showing a deep affinity with Gnosticism and employing the energies left by the loss of the metaphysical and religious beliefs of the Middle Ages. 'People no longer feel redeeemed by the death of Christ,' declared Jung dramatically in a lecture with a very significant title: 'Psychotherapists or the Clergy',[140] given in Strasbourg in 1932 and included in the English volume *Modern Man in Search of a Soul*.

Jung was aware that most of the new cults were coming from the East, which had developed a superior psychic proficiency, in spite of having been conquered by the material and technical proficiency of the West. He was happy to collaborate with the sinologist Richard Wilhelm in writing a 'European Commentary' to Wilhelm's translation of an ancient Chinese text, *The Secret of the Golden Flower*. Jung welcomed what he considered to be the beginning of a reaction in the West against the intellect in favour of feeling,[141] and believed that the search for 'tao', translated as 'meaning', goes through a process of enacting a reconciliation between the East and the West. He professed to be a 'thorough Westerner in feeling',[142] for whom the most urgent task was to build up Western civilisation. This had to be done by 'the European just as he is, with all his Western ordinariness, his marriage problems, his neuroses, his social and political delusions, and his whole philosophical disorientation'.[143] The 'psychological tendency' meant that the main task for modern Europeans was in consciously taking on responsibility for their heritage and tradition: 'our prime need is to learn a few European truths about ourselves. Our way begins with European reality and not with yoga exercises which would only delude us about our own reality'.[144] This meant diving deep into the self in a process of 'individuation' – the unification of personality through the integration of its conscious and unconscious aspects, including those most feared and deeply hidden – and understanding the spiritual needs of one's own time. A function of this work was to extricate the European 'from the clouds of his own moral incense',[145] and to clear away the smoke of that incense:

> ... how do we strike men of another colour? What do China and India think of us? And what about all those whom we rob of their lands and exterminate with rum and venereal disease?[146]

The task of the 'good European' is to become aware not only of the evil that his civilisation has inflicted upon other peoples, but also of the spiritual wisdom of other continents, which greatly surpassed that of Europe. In 1935, in his lecture at the Tavistock Institute in London, Jung repeated 'we Europeans are not the only people on the earth. We are just a peninsula of Asia', and, Asia, with its millenary tradition of introspective psychology, has everything to teach to a West which started its psychology 'not even yesterday but only this morning'.[147] However, for Jung only modern psychology was able to provide European consciousness with a key to understanding the present world. His position struck a note of optimism, because he saw the spiritual suffering and the psychological turmoil of Europe as the possible beginning of a new era. Jung promised a reconciliation of human personality that Freud believed to be over-optimistic and idealistic.[148] In a historical perspective, we need both the Freudian and the Jungian contributions: the materialist analysis of the discontents of civilisation and the spiritual diagnosis of the modern lack of meaning. They converge in mitigating the Eurocentrism they share, by strong criticism of Western civilisation and of its privileged forms of knowledge.

The Jungian notion of Europe and the Europeans includes an exchange with other civilisations, particularly those from the East. In this sense it is an open concept, free from some of the rigidities of the archetypes applied to nations. It is interesting from our perspective to consider these in connection with the question of the particular role of England in the European situation of the early 1930s. Jungian notions of archetypes and the collective unconscious provided a basis for the interpretation of national and political issues which is relevant for cultural history. In 1935 Helton Godwin Baynes published an essay on 'Analytical Psychology and the English Mind' (in the *Festschrift Die kulturelle Bedeutung der komplexen Psychologie*). Baynes, a medical doctor who was Jung's assistant from 1919 to 1922, translated Jung's *Psychological Types*,[149] and organised his expedition to East Africa in 1925–26. In the essay on the English mind, Baynes considers the idea of the gentleman as a powerful national myth, acting similarly to the Chinese symbol of 'tao', as a symbolic unifier re-establishing a primal unity of feeling. Baynes distinguishes between two opposite directions of development in the gentleman-idea – and therefore two tendencies in the English character – the esoteric one (where this idea is the symbol of what he calls the 'aristocratic interior') and the exoteric (where it is a social and cultural form with roots in the clan-spirit of the British nation). By 'aristocratic interior' Baynes indicates the mythical tradition represented by King Arthur and the Round Table and by the Quest for the Holy Grail, open to spiritual innovation. The second tradition is that of a conservative, collective attitude, fighting against any innovation; the two are apparently incompatible. However, English history comprises both, as it includes the revolution and the killing of King Charles I, an act implying that the king belongs to the nation, and the first affirmation in European history of the principle that the rights of the people were as sacred as the prerogatives of the crown.

However, the struggle between the two opposite principles does manage to reach a balance, producing the reciprocal allegiance between the passionate individualism of the first tradition and the indomitable conservatism of the second. The psychological correlate of the equilibrium between the king and the commons can be found in the practical poise of the English mind. Finally, a result of this balance is the international role played by Britain in the European situation of the mid-1930s, where it acts as 'one of the most powerful stabilising forces'.

As far as the destiny of analytical psychology in Britain was concerned, Baynes hoped that Jung's ideas, and particularly that of individuation, would find a place in the hearts of Englishmen, that they could accept their emotions and release the excessive constraint on their feelings taught by the exoteric tradition. On Europe, Baynes did not express an opinion in this essay, but he had grounds for hoping that the role of England in the continent would be both innovative and conservative, helping not only to defeat but also to exorcise the destructive forces that were taking hold of Germany, as he later on showed in his *Germany Possessed* (1941). He acknowledged that 'to be magnanimous in victory is one of Mr Churchill's great qualities', but he hoped that 'our victory will be won on the spiritual field' keeping the promise that Hitler had made but could not keep: a new social covenant recognising the humble but essential needs of human nature.[150] Archetypes as applied to ethnic and national communities can easily have racist results, unless they are reformulated in a critical way, reducing their essentialist connotations. In Baynes's case, the national archetype was not used in a totalising way, since he, on the one hand, left it open to individuals to correct and change its influence on their actions and minds and, on the other, underlined the cultural aspects of the archetype.

This seems different to the positions taken by Jung himself towards archetypes concerning the Jews and the Germans. In the 1930s, especially in the second half of the decade, his writings showed deep contradictions, including forms of antisemitism and of attraction to Hitlerism. Although he was not antisemitic in his personal dealings with people, his writings included references to the Jews' presumed physical weakness, inability to create their own cultural form, and nomadic nature; at the same time he was fascinated by Hitlerism which he considered the resurgence of the archetype of Wotan, the German god of storm, battle, prophetic inspiration and science (1936). In the essay *Wotan*, he considered the Germans victims of the god, understood as 'a fundamental attribute of the German psyche, an irrational psychic factor which acts on the high pressure of civilisation like a cyclone and blows it away'.[151] Of course, Jung's essay on Wotan was at the core of Baynes' work on Germany, but perhaps writing in 1941 allowed the latter to see more clearly the negative aspects of Hitlerism. He wrote about 'Hitler's criminality' and 'the abysmal crudity of the Nazi attitude to women... the most convincing evidence of its crippled state'.[152] From the end of the 1930s onward, Jung re-elaborated his attitudes, and his legacy has been subjected to a fruitful and harsh criticism in order to let its positive aspects emerge from these 'lingering shadows';[153] his thought contains also an anti-racist potential – the common substratum of the psyche transcending all differences – which can be used as the basis of a pluralistic vision of society.[154] In Jung's case as in many others, the heritage of Europe between the wars cannot be accepted without a thorough analysis of its implications and complicities. Baynes would say that this is not possible without taking over 'Hitler's debt to mankind and giving it a full and generous realisation', which for him implied 'a fuller flame of individual consciousness'.[155]

## Notes on Chapter 2

1    Pinder 1991
2    Heater, p 123
3    Pegg, pp 7, 9
4    Ceadel, p 183
5    I, 19 October 1916
6    London, 1918
7    Bugge, p 93
8    Goldstein
9    *Ibidem*
10   Boyce 1989, p 67
11   Pinder 1989, pp 205–6
12   *J'ai choisi*, p 160
13   Deschamps
14   *J'ai choisi*, pp 133–4
15   *Held oder Heiliger*, pp 195–213

16   *The United States of Europe*, p 225
17   *Review of Reviews*, 15 July 1930
18   *Ibidem*, 15 March 1930
19   Agnelli
20   Berki
21   Trotsky
22   Chabot
23   Palme Dutt
24   Berki
25   Brugmans, p 69
26   Pegg, p 74
27   *Review of Reviews*, August 15, 1929, no 475
28   Brugmans, p 70
29   Salter, p 121
30   *J'ai choisi*, p 177
31   Heater, p 140
32   Pegg, p 126
33   Churchill, p 37
34   Foerster, p 302
35   *J'ai choisi*, p 182
36   Lipgens 1985; Bosco 1989
37   Crozier
38   Salter, pp 123–4; Pegg, p 150
39   Webster, p 75
40   Dawson W. H.
41   Boyce 1993
42   Carlton, p 86
43   White R., pp 245–6
44   Navari
45   Crozier
46   Lipgens 1985, p 7
47   Brugmans, p 72
48   Salewski
49   Boyce 1993
50   Novalis, p 9
51   Burke, p 249
52   Scott, p 64
53   Keating
54   Oliver
55   Scott, p 93
56   Mulloy
57   Belloc 1962 and 1937
58   Woodruff, p XIII
59   Scott, p 96

60   Cantor, p 330
61   Bennett; *Is the Catholic Church*
62   *Ibidem*, pp 6–7
63   Mulloy, p  414
64   Scott, pp 106–107
65   *Religion and the Modern State*, p 140
66   Hitchcock, p 62
67   *Beyond Politics*, p 82
68   Schlesinger, p 83; Hittinger
69   *Christianity and Sex*, p 5
70   Calverton, p 244
71   Russell, p 310
72   *Arcanum Divinum*, 1880
73   *Christianity and Sex*, p 15
74   Stopes, p XIV
75   *Ibidem*, p 25
76   *Christianity and Sex*, p 11
77   *Ibidem*, p 12
78   *Ibidem*, pp 74–76
79   *The Judgement of the Nations*, pp 208–9; 215–7
80   Brands
81   Roobol
82   Balzaretti
83   Rubin
84   Reuter
85   Roobol
86   Hinshelwood
87   Steiner
88   Jones 1924
89   Hobman
90   Jones
91   Kubie; Walsh
92   Glover 1933, p 33
93   *Ibidem*, p 32
94   *Ibidem*, p 10
95   *Ibidem*, p 28
96   Glover 1936
97   Glover 1933, p 26
98   *Ibidem*, p 22
99   *Ibidem*, p 35
100  *IJP*, 14, 1933, p 421
101  Pick, p 117
102  Fornari, p 124
103  Segal

104  Klein, p XII
105  Glover 1966
106  Mitchell 1991
107  Steiner
108  Money–Kyrle 1932, pp 138–9
109  Glover 1934
110  Money–Kyrle 1935
111  Angell, p 469
112  Cocks
113  Vergin, pp 23–24
114  *Ibidem*, p 25
115  *Ibidem*,  p 175
116  *Ibidem*, p 247
117  *Ibidem*, p 324
118  *Ibidem*, p 325
119  Fornari
120  Rapp
121  Samuels 1994
122  Pogson, p 71
123  Glover 1966
124  Prince, p 55
125  *Woman*, 236
126  *Ibidem*,  251
127  *Ibidem*,  251
128  *Ibidem*,   251
129  *Ibidem*,   259
130  *Ibidem*, 260
131  *Ibidem*, 273
132  *Ibidem*, 266
133  *Ibidem*, 275
134  Harding, pp 80; 334–5
135  Goldenberg
136  Lauter and Schreier Rupprecht
137  Wehr
138  *The Swiss Line*, p 920
139  *Archaic*, 128
140  'Psychotherapists or the Clergy', 516
141  *Secret*, 7
142  *Ibidem*, 1
143  *Ibidem*, 5
144  *In memoriam*, 89
145  *Spiritual*, 186
146  *Ibidem*, 183
147  *Ibidem*, p 139

148  Vegetti Finzi, p 142
149  *Germany Possessed*, p 301
151  *Wotan*, 389
152  *Germany Possessed*, pp 189, 298
153  Maidenbaum and Martin; *Cahiers jungiens*
154  Samuels 1993
155  *Germany*, p 302

# CHAPTER 3

# NEW EUROPE

## Mitrinovic and Orage

At the beginning of the 1930s the New Europe group (NEG) was formed in London; among its aims were that European states should unite into a federation and that the British should be made more actively aware of the continent. According to Lipgens, it was 'perhaps the first real European-federal group', which 'with remarkable consistency' championed an 'integral' conception of federation, urging the pooling of all functions of the nation state except the cultural ones, this to be coupled with decentralisation so as to give more power to the regions and a share of management to workers in industry.[1] The aims expressed by the NEG were formed within a context of ideas quite different from those which had characterised the *New Europe* journal published in London in the years 1916–1920 with the subtitle 'A Weekly Review of Foreign Politics' and the motto 'Pour la victoire intégrale'. As had been declared at its start in October 1916, this review was intended to provide a rallying ground for those who saw in a European reconstruction, on the basis of nationality and of the rights of minorities, a guarantee against a repetition of the horrors of the First World War. The aim was to fight against pan-Germanism by promoting the emancipation of central and south-eastern Europe from German and Magyar control.

Both these New Europe groups derived their inspiration from the desire for the emancipation of Eastern Europe, the earlier group having been drawn together by Masaryk's proposal for a new European order recognising the small Eastern nations, the later being created under the influence of Dimitrije Mitrinovic. Tomas Masaryk (1850–1937) was an inspiring figure for the generation of militant Central and Eastern European intellectuals following his own, such as Mitrinovic and his Dalmatian friend Mestrovic, who sculpted a bust of Masaryk. Mitrinovic had been a leader of the 'Young Bosnia' movement (influenced by Mazzini's thinking on the role of the young in the liberation of a nation), which protested against the Austro-Hungarian annexation of Bosnia and Herzegovina, and worked to develop an awareness of the unity of the Southern Slavs. But he added the ideal of a united Europe to a syncretic construction of ideas derived from philosophies and religious systems belonging to both the Eastern and the Western traditions. In so doing, he promoted an idea of Europe which united cultural and emotional elements with political ones. The importance given to the psychology and existential nature of individuals, rather than what they produced, by those who shared this idea makes their lives particularly relevant. Therefore space will be given in this chapter, more than in others, to their life-trajectories.

Dimitrije Mitrinovic, born in 1887 in Hercegovina into a family of Orthodox faith and Serbian culture, had received an education combining Serbian epic poetry and folk music taught him by his mother, an art teacher, and European classical literature, transmitted by his father, a school teacher and agricultural adviser (who ran an experimental farm) in the service of the Austro-Hungarian Government. The eldest of ten children, Mitrinovic attended the Mostar gymnasium, taught himself Greek and Latin, studied philosophy, psychology and logic at Zagreb University, and followed courses at the Universities of Belgrade and Vienna. He also wrote as a literary critic for a Sarajevo radical literary journal, *Bosanka Vila*, where he expressed belief in a special role of the creative artist in society and pleaded for the democratisation of art and the breaking down of divisions between creators and consumers. He was active in creating secret political and literary societies, to which Ivo Andric, winner 50 years later of the Nobel prize for literature, also belonged, as did Gavrilo Princip, who killed Archduke Ferdinand in Sarajevo. However, Mitrinovic never met Princip and strongly disapproved of his act. In 1913–1914 Mitrinovic attended courses at Munich University and became acquainted with Kandinsky and the Blaue Reiter group. He equated, as they did, modern art and political revolution, cultural modernity and the Slavonic cultural milieu, synthetised by mysticism.[2] Kandinsky drew Mitrinovic's attention to the work of Erich Gutkind, who together with the Dutch author Frederik van Eeden – founder of a co-operative colony called Walden in honour of Thoreau – had put forward the idea of a 'Blutbund', understood as an élite of 'chosen spirits who would lead mankind out of the wilderness of materialism'. Mitrinovic was deeply attracted by this idea and decided to dedicate himself to it. He was also in charge of editing the Blaue Reiter's second yearbook, to be called *Towards the Mankind of the Future through Aryan Europe*, on the theme of transforming and unifying Europe and of creating a pan-European culture. In this context the expression 'Aryan pan-humanity movement' indicated an initiative to unite the Baltic States and Russia within European culture, while the antisemitic connotations of the terminology contrasted with the fact that Mitrinovic approached many Jewish would-be contributors.[3] Due to the outbreak of the First World War, the yearbook was never published, and Mitrinovic fled to London in order to avoid conscription into the Austrian army. He was part of the exodus that brought many intellectuals and religious thinkers from Central and Eastern Europe to London at the outbreak of war.[4]

In London, Mitrinovic was introduced to Alfred R. Orage (1873–1934), editor of *The New Age* between 1908 and 1922, in which Mitrinovic wrote a weekly column on 'World Affairs' in 1920–21 (the column was for a time signed together by the two men as M.M. Cosmoi – meaning Macrocosm Microcosm Cosmos, i.e. God man nature – before being Mitrinovic's alone). *The New Age* gave space to translations from Western as well as Eastern European countries, notably from Russia, and to articles by Russian writers, as well as placing a strong emphasis on spiritualism. It acted as a cultural forum in which many of the ideas and some of the people who some ten years later participated in the NEG first encountered each other.

The attempt to combine the idea of a united Europe with a strong interest in spirituality and esoterism was not entirely new. It was present in the Theosophical Society founded in 1875 by the Russian spiritualist Helena Petrovna Blavatsky, whose aim was to promote universal brotherhood and develop the latent faculties of human beings. Mitrinovic had the greatest respect for her, 'the first Superman in the vehicle of femininity, the first woman genius', he wrote in his column (23 June 1921). Blavatsky's English pupil Annie Besant (1847–1933), a Fabian and feminist as well as a pioneer in the birth control movement who became the International President of the Theosophical Society, gave a lecture on 'the United States of Europe' in the Queen's Hall, London, in 1927.[5] Against the dangers of war and of the dissolution of civilisation she proposed 'the great Ideal of the United States of Europe' as a step in 'the whole tendency of the evolution of mankind'. Her dream was of a great federation of free nations, each self-governing, while the only army would be that of the Federal Government; her examples were the USA and the British Dominions. The first step would be the federation of Teutonic sub-races, composed of the United States, Britain and Germany; meanwhile communication with Russia, 'barred out of Europe', should be restored. The means to achieve these aims were 'to travel more freely amongst each other', to interchange communications and thoughts, to eliminate all passports and custom barriers, to create international schools (as the Theosophical Society was already doing) for international education. This programme could be started immediately by the individual's effort 'to spread peace and not suspicion', but Besant warned that 'before we can look for the United States of Europe we must make friends with our coloured brothers everywhere'.

The Theosophical Society was one of the associations in which Orage was active before founding *The New Age*. He too united a sense of appreciation for Europeanism, especially in the fields of letters and art, with an interest in spiritual matters, and his own life itinerary is strikingly illustrative of the eclecticism of certain avant-garde intellectual circles. Born in Dacre, Yorkshire, Orage had escaped a destiny as a plough-boy thanks to his brilliance at school; he had gone to college, and become an elementary school teacher in Leeds in 1893. In 1894 he had joined the newly-founded Independent Labour Party, and in 1895 started writing for its weekly paper. He was also an active member of the National Union of Teachers. One interesting side to him was his effort to combine politics, literature and economics with an attempt to find ways into deeper levels of consciousness, of which spiritualist experimentation was one. Orage's interest in the occult and transcendental matters had led him to the Society for Psychical Research and then, in 1896 – probably through his wife, who was a theosophist – into the Theosophical Society, at that point inspired by the mysticism of Annie Besant and Edward Carpenter. In 1900 Orage was introduced to the writings of Nietzsche, which had a strong impact on him; his lectures inspired by Nietzsche shocked the audiences of the Theosophical Lodges which he regularly addressed as a speaker travelling in the north of England.

In 1903 Orage participated in the founding of the Leeds Arts Club, which was started with the aim of 'reducing Leeds to Nietzscheism' and was to last for 20 years as a 'provincial avant-garde', one of the most interesting examples in Britain of radical thought and experimental art.[6] The club, based on a social stratum of lower-middle-class artists and teachers, which Orage called 'the professional proletariat', did much to modernise the local culture with Europeanism. This meant becoming acquainted with European (especially German and Scandinavian) literature, drama, music and art, as well as encouraging the practice of speaking European languages and Esperanto. The club included feminists and suffragists, Freemasons, partisans of the Celtic renaissance and of the garden-city ideal, all united by a belief in social organicism, which advocated the harmonious union of the individual and society. It combined three major influences: the strand of cultural criticism expressed by Ruskin, Carlyle and Morris; the spiritualism of Blavatsky and Besant, Blake and Neoplatonism; Nietzsche and German romanticism; and, although with a weaker influence, Fabian social democracy.

When Orage left his job as a teacher and moved to London, he and his friend Holbrook Jackson bought *The New Age* with the financial support of

George Bernard Shaw and a theosophist from the Fabian society – to which Orage then belonged – but the journal soon began criticising the Fabians. Subtitled 'An Independent Socialist Review of Politics, Literature and Art', it became an important forum for many brilliant writers, 'a paper of ideas' which encouraged talented young people to write under Orage's invaluable editing skill. According to Storm Jameson, referring to the generation which had gone through the First World War, 'Orage's *New Age* was the bible of my generation. We would far sooner go hungry than miss buying it. We quoted it, argued with it, formed ourselves on it. I suppose he had a sharper influence on intelligent young Englishmen of that time than anyone else'.[7] *The New Age* mediated between specialized fields of knowledge and public understanding, and encouraged a relationship between literary experimentation and literary tradition. It promoted interest in Nietzsche and Bergson, and formed part of the movement for the introduction of psycho-analysis in England. The psycho-analyst M.D. Eder, already encountered here in the debate on war neuroses, was a close friend of Orage and often wrote in *The New Age*; he was one of the first to introduce Freud to a non-specialist audience. Among other contributors to *The New Age* were G.K. Chesterton, H.G. Wells, Storm Jameson, Ezra Pound, Hilaire Belloc, G.B. Shaw, Arthur Kitson, Herbert Read, Hilda Doolittle and Patrick Geddes.

Orage was a dissident Fabian because he believed that political and economic problems were inseparable from the problems of culture as a whole, and that an investigation of the cultural basis of political reform was more important than the study of the 'scientific application' of socialism. His own intellectual formation was very eclectic. He had studied the Hindu *Upanishad*, written between the ninth and the sixth centuries BC, and the great epic poem *Mahabharata* (between the second and third centuries AD) as well as various Indian philosophies. He himself later described the socialism of his youth as a cult, blending among other ingredients arts and crafts, vegetarianism, theosophy, Shaw, Plato and Marx.[8] Orage had also been influenced by the architect A.J. Penty, who devised a theory regarding the guild organisation of industry (1906): Penty proposed the restoration of a sense of craftsmanship to make labour satisfying through the establishment of guilds that would set their own standards of quality, so that craftsmen would receive a 'just price' for their work. The idea of medieval guilds had been taken from Ruskin and given a socialist slant by Morris; S.G. Hobson made use of it as the basis of a complete industrial and political system, in articles that appeared anonymously in *The New Age*. Guild socialism, the supporters of which included George Lansbury, G.D.H. Cole, and Bertrand Russell, was a synthesis of political socialism and industrial syndicalism.[9] Orage believed that a religious aspect was implicit in the restoration of guilds and from 1918 attempted to combine this with Douglas's ideas about 'social credit'.

According to Douglas, technical changes in the accounting system would induce transformations in the financial system and allow money to be administered according to the community's capacity to produce and its needs.

In Orage's eclectic system the role of Europe was important. Among the elements of European culture introduced to the British by the Leeds Arts Club on Orage's initiation was Nietzsche's influence, which was of a deeply 'European' cast. Orage defined Nietzsche as 'the greatest European event since Goethe', an outstanding 'incarnation of European unrest'.[10] The first complete translation of Nietzsche's works into English was published in 1909, but single works had already been translated, in which Orage could have found Nietzsche's remarks about Europe and the Europeans. An American translation of Nietzsche's *Beyond Good and Evil* existed before 1907, when the British one appeared. Nietzsche, in the section on 'Peoples and fatherlands', very clearly states – although with his usual irony and paradox – the need for 'one Europe' ('das Eine Europa') and for a 'European of the future', the necessity for Europeans to overcome the 'atavistic attacks of patriotism', and 'to be restored to reason, I mean to "good Europeanism"'.[11] Nietzsche's insistence on the narrowness of nationalism, his sarcasm on 'the plebeianism of modern ideas' invented by the English, 'an unphilosophical race' lacking 'real *power* of spirituality, real *depth* of spiritual insight', matched Orage's disgust with socialist materialism as well as his search for spirituality.

*The New Age* paid great attention to spirituality, and to the mysterious and 'dark' sides of human subjectivity. It did this through art and literature, as well as through psycho-analysis. Orage, as mentioned, also had a strong interest in occultism. The role of occultism in his syncretism was not only coherent with his interest in the unconscious – which both preceded and exceeded his interest in psycho-analysis – but was also part of the effort to rediscover aspects of the European tradition which had been forgotten and to give them a new meaning, just as the ideas underlying mediaeval guilds were at the time recast in a new formulation and sense within a general regeneration. In European history, the themes of the occult and the esoteric, from Gnosticism to Rosicrucianism to Freemasonry, represented a sort of subterranean trend the wealth of which might be rescued in a progressive perspective. Often, however, only the daily superstitions to which they gave rise became apparent. For instance, Beatrice Hastings portrayed Orage's mysteric tendencies with some malignancy, after the break up of their relationship of collaboration and love which lasted from 1907 to 1914 (she shared a flat with Orage and Katherine Mansfield). In 1936, she accused him of 'paranoiac mystagoguery'. In more benevolent versions, Orage is said to have given to many who met him the impression that he possessed an aura,[12] or some extraordinary psychic secret;[13] besides the hypnotic effect of his smile, there was some 'wizardry' about him, 'the Orage magic'.[14] 'Orage poured out love, and at the end of his life he was full of light.'[15]

In 1922, at a time when esoteric teachers arrived in London from Eastern Europe, Orage went through a conversion. The doctrine of reincarnation that some of these teachers preached found an eager audience in people who had experienced so many deaths in the First World War, and answered questions about death that the war had heightened. Among them was the thinker and healer Georgei Ivanovitch Gurdjieff, of Greek-Armenian descent, who preached a doctrine of continuing reincarnation by which beings moved higher or lower on the spiral of their evolution, and which involved doing in each life what had been left undone in previous ones. After travelling widely over Asia in search of occult knowledge, he met his main disciple, Petr Demyanovich Ouspensky, in Saint-Petersburg; both of them decided to move to Western Europe during the Revolution, although they would later separate with great acrimony. Through Ouspensky, Orage met Gurdjieff and became his disciple. After this encounter Orage left *The New Age* and went to Fontainebleau, where Gurdjieff had established an institute for the harmonious development of man and the pursuit of cosmic consciousness. Connections existed between the esoteric and the literary worlds: Katherine Mansfield died in Fontainebleau in 1923 and Gurdjieff's ideas influenced both Aldous Huxley and Christopher Isherwood. After Fontainebleau, Orage lived for seven years in the US, teaching the doctrine, raising funds, organising groups and translating Gurdjieff's book *All and Everything*. In 1931, rather disillusioned with Gurdjieff, although he never made this public, Orage went back to London, and the following year founded *The New English Weekly*, which published, as the previous magazine had done, work by some of the best literary critics and writers of the time, such as T.S. Eliot, Dylan Thomas, Lawrence Durrell, Allen Tate, Oscar Williams and George Orwell.

The interest Orage's activities hold for our subject is that he devoted attention to the role of emotions in life and in literature and this resulted in a mixture of oriental and occidental doctrines. He induced a contributor to translate Stendhal's *De l'amour* for serial publication in *The New Age* and was himself the author of the essay *On Love*, announced in the title page as 'translated from the Tibetan'. In this he distinguished three types of love: instinctive, emotional and conscious. The first two are the result of either affinities or of disaffinities, in other words, of a Goethian 'chemistry'. Therefore 'the attractions, repulsions, mechanical and chemical combinations we call love, courtship, marriage, chidren and family, are only the human equivalents of a chemist's laboratory'.[16] Conscious love aims at being both wise and skilful in the service of its object. An example from the past is the love of the European troubadours, while in the present it can be achieved through self-training, following the principle 'take hold tightly; let go lightly'.[17] This principle must be placed within the general understanding that 'our life is but one day of our life', a wisdom inspired by Gurdjieff's teachings. In Orage's *Aphorisms*, most of which were read in the groups he held in New York in 1924–30, he reveals his conviction that the emotional centre – one of the three centres (sensation, emotion and thought) which form the unity of a human being – is the driving force of our whole life.[18]

Mitrinovic disapproved of Orage's choice to follow Gurdjieff. When he heard that Orage had been put to work as a garden labourer in Fontainebleau, as part of a route to develop all the centres within him, he commented: 'If he had said 'no', he would not have needed a master. He could have been one himself'.[19] When in October 1921 Orage invited Ouspensky to participate in the discussion group that had included, besides himself, Mitrinovic, the psycho-analyst Eder and the Jungian psychologist Maurice Nicoll (who would also go to Fontainebleau), Mitrinovic ceased to attend and also stopped writing for *The New Age*. He could not take to esoteric teachings which, on the one hand, resembled his own and, on the other, were much less enlightened, in the sense that they did not try to combine the Eastern and Western traditions of thought in the fields of philosophy, religion, and especially psychology to the same extent as he did. In addition, there is no indication that he ever subjected his followers to the physical fatigues and psychological humiliations that many gurus, including Gurdjieff, inflicted on their followers. However, he was for many just as profoundly and mysteriously fascinating as other spiritual leaders were reported to be. Mitrinovic's outward appearance fulfilled the stereotype of the mystery man from the East with 'his shaven head, his swarthiness, his dark garments and his hypnotic eyes'. This is a description by Paul Selver, then a young collaborator of Orage, meeting Mitrinovic:

> Hardly had I shaken hands with Mitrinovic that I found myself so affected by his mere presence that I nearly lost consciousness [...] there was some something, if not exactly sinister, at least uncanny about Mitrinovic.[20]

According to Selver, Mitrinovic was accomplished and erudite, an idealist and visionary. Another of his followers found that he 'was of the splendid type and proportions one so often sees in the Dalmatian and Bosnian peasantry... [with] the intensity of consciousness, the immediate intuition, of those few individuals whose instinctive, emotional and intellectual centres work in unison'. Others found him 'an entertaining companion because he was such an egregious nonsense-monger' or believed that he was a man with a 'home-made messiah complex'.[21]

During the First World War Mitrinovic had worked at the Serbian Legation in London and had started gathering a small group of followers around him, which originally consisted of Helen Soden, the wife of a doctor, 'a fairly conventional middle class lady in early middle age',[22] and Philip Mairet, a young man who had been a disciple of Patrick Geddes whom we shall later meet as the first president of the NEG. Mitrinovic was by then disillusioned with the idea of forming an elite of leading personalities, that aristocracy of persons that he had hoped to create in the Blutbund devised by Gutkind and van Eeden. He had discovered the inability of distinguished people to temper their individualism and to work together for a common cause, and he now believed in working with ordinary people to form a group of equally responsible individuals. In fact Mairet was not so ordinary. In 1917, when he met Mitrinovic, he was working as a labourer on a farm near Ditchling, Sussex, in order to avoid being called up. His wife had a weaving business there, and they were part of a small community of artists and craftspeople, which included the sculptor Eric Gill, who went on to found a number of other mystical communities. Mairet started a training under Mitrinovic which included meditation, the study of books by Rudolf Steiner (1861–1925, the Austrian philosopher who founded anthroposophy), by Vivekananda (1863–1902, the Hindu monk, philosopher and patriot who was a prophet of neo-Vedantism and Vedantic Socialism), and of a handbook called *Concentration*, by Ernest Wood. This went on for a year and a half, after which time Mairet was discovered, forcibly enrolled in the army and court-martialled for refusing to obey orders; in prison, and in solitary confinement, he valued the spiritual exercises learned under the guidance of Mitrinovic. After the war, he took to learning Sanskrit, became an actor in the Shakespeare Company at the Old Vic theatre for four and a half years, and then moved on to become the literary editor of *The New Age*, to start again his old craft of staining glass, and to keep a handicraft shop in Bloomsbury.

After the First World War Mitrinovic felt that he had to expand his ideas and change his position in the world. He had incorporated the cause of Yugoslavia into a pan-human idealism, the more general expectations of which became the priority for him after the creation of the Yugoslav federation in 1918, where he felt his ideals were distorted and corrupted by politicians and diplomats. Around 1920, Mitrinovic left his job at the Serbian Legation and supported himself mainly thanks to his followers, dedicating himself to the development of a system of thought and education which in the 1930s attracted a wide audience. By the early 1920s Mitrinovic had already developed many aspects of what has latterly been defined as an anthropomorphic political philosophy.[23] This interpreted humanity as a great human being, personified as Anthropos, whereby the various nations and races were parts or functions of his soul. It is difficult to summarise Mitrinovic's work, because it is rich in image, full of references taken from all sorts of cultures, and is not systematic in the usual sense of the word; it is rather repetitive, adding some new detail with each recapitulation. He was probably aware of this, as he once told Dr Twentyman that his first series of writings on 'World Affairs' (1920–21) were written with a scientific approach, the second (1933) in a religious mood, and that he would have liked to write a third series in an artistic tone. It was always the same system of ideas, but seen from different angles.

The articles published in *The New Age* between 1920–21 presented Mitrinovic's vision of universal humanity as one great mind in the process of becoming self-conscious, a process moving towards an organic world order, a community of free members. The various races and nations were like organs of this organism, each with a different psychic function, and they should tend towards a reconciliation between themselves and with the whole. The whole was seen, according to the principles of Vedanta philosophy, as a triunity, which Mitrinovic linked with the interpretation of the Christian Trinity given by the Athanasian Creed at the council of Nicea in 325 AD. The Athanasian Creed, which recognised the individuality of the Trinity while maintaining its unity – presenting the three Persons both simultaneously and in succession – was, according to Mitrinovic, the true foundation of European civilisation. The three Persons were not remote mythological abstractions, but were to be interpreted on the basis of psycho-analysis: the Father, as the world unconscious, the Son, as personality and self-consciousness, and the Holy Spirit, whose human side was Sophia. The incarnation of Sophia in universal humanity was both a spiritual process and a practical one; it included moving away from 'democratic humanity' to 'socialist humanity' and to 'seraphic humanity'. In the course of this progression, competitive individualism would give way to shared experience in the community, and nationalism would be superseded by a world order including all races, nations and religions, which would nonetheless preserve their fundamental characteristics and values.[24]

The concept of organic whole applied to the world was central in Mitrinovic's thought and in the associations he created around him. The idea of organism was mediated from science, particularly biology, but the meaning given to the word by organicists went beyond biological data inasmuch as an organism for them was characterised by autonomy, integration, unity and uniqueness, so that the whole was more than the sum of its parts.[25] The application of this concept to the socio-historical reality was crucial to Auguste Comte's (1798–1875) religion of humanity. In Comte's sociology, the historical evolution of humanity, i.e. the 'Grand Etre' constituted by all human beings from the past to the future – the Great Being which alone can give meaning to individual existence – will culminate in an organic society. In such society, where all political contrasts will be overcome, everybody will have the right to work and to welfare, and an indefinite increase in spiritual perfection will accompany material progress. In his 'positive religion', which treated scientists and geniuses as its saints, Comte included a cult of the supreme pontiff (himself) as well as a cult of femininity incarnated in the woman he had loved, Clotilde de Vaux. Comte was convinced that he had succeeded in applying scientific methods to sociology, a term that he invented for what he first called 'social physics'. His work inspired Mitrinovic, who kept a plaque of Comte's head among the portraits near his desk, and often spoke of him in connection with the Russian philosopher and theologian Solovyov. Vladimir Solovyov (1853–1900), emphasised the concept of God-Manhood, which was to be attained by individual human beings recognising their own divine essence. For Solovyov, the divine triunity implies a feminine principle: '... for there to be the possibility of a world, there must an "other" to God, which is as object to God as subject... This is Sophia', the archetype of the eternal feminine receptive principle of the universe. 'This great royal and feminine Being' is the incarnation of the Holy Spirit in universal humanity recognising its own divine nature. To reach the stage when humanity will be self-conscious is a long process, which starts with a few individuals, Solovyov stated in *The Meaning of Love*. Their community would be as significant to each as each individual is to themself.[26] Both Comte and Solovyov attribute great relevance to love between men and women as a gateway to universal love, since for them it can undermine the pervasive influence of egoism and lead to ultimate perfection.

In Mitrinovic's construction Europe played an important part and its role remained substantially the same in the subsequent developments of his thinking. The role of Europe was indicated in an article of 2 September 1920, when Orage was still co-signing with Mitrinovic:

> Europe anthropologically, historically, culturally, by religion and by geography, appears to have been destined to play the leading role in the functional organization of the world.

According to M.M. Cosmoi, Europe is a tempered epitome of all the races; it is placed in the medium of the two extremes of the Far East and the Far West; it is the site where Christianity arose as a sublimation of a Semitic cult. 'The world needs a spiritual Europe, a Europe consciously and self-consciously one.'

The federation of Europe is the primary condition for the Alliance of Humanity. 'Not Columbia [the inner reality of North America], not Yamato [the spirit of Japan] but Europa is the focus and consciousness of the Human Kingdom.' Europe, now a 'broken and criminal continent', must be enlarged into Europa – the ego of the world – by unification with Russia and England.[27] In this view, the League of Nations is incapable of accomplishing such a spiritual task:

> Bourgeois in conception, pedestrian in method, and merely pacifist in aim, the present League of Nations is doomed to sterility; it can create nothing; ex nihilo nihil fit.[28]

Mitrinovic went back to the founding myth of Europa, interpreting it in the light of his convictions: to him, the myth expressed a new fusion of races, brought about by the migration to the West symbolised by the Bull carrying Europa, i.e. the soul of Europe.[29] Typically European was the generation of opposites in order to reconcile them in a higher synthesis. Even the First World War could be viewed as an attempt to bring about a new and greater European synthesis, more inclusive of cultural and other differences, more tolerant of contradictions, more perfectly Aryan. 'Aryan' and 'Aryandom' to Mitrinovic meant the aspect of will and consciousness in the white race, although not exclusively limited to this: 'Europe herself is the synthesis of the Aryan race and of the extra-Aryan mankind'.[30]

At the time the use of the term 'Aryan' was not yet polluted with the meaning it acquired with Nazism. But it could be used in racist systems of thought, as it had been done by Houston Stewart Chamberlain (1855–1927), a political writer of English origin who lived most of his life in Germany and became Richard Wagner's son-in-law. In his *Foundations of the Nineteenth Century*, two volumes published in England in 1911, the foundation of European culture was attributed to Aryan Greeks and Latins, while the entrance of Jews into European history was considered the intrusion of a foreign element, and Christ was not recognised as a Jew. It was, however, for another of his books that Mitrinovic admired Chamberlain, the one on Kant. Mitrinovic based his concept of 'Aryan' on culture, and not on blood and race: for him 'Aryan' was a spiritual quality, something noble and generous pertaining to an aristocracy of the mind, a concept close to the Nietzschean idea of what is aristocratic. The white race was the first to have achieved individual consciousness, although he did not believe that a European cultural tradition already existed from the past, ready to be inherited; this was important because in this way his thinking was differentiated from most of the Europeanist claims to a European inheritance, as for him European culture and identity had not yet been developed, and would be the result of a conscious collective effort. Until then, 'Europe's relations with the Black and Yellow races have been instinctive and not intelligent', perpetrating 'unimaginable... crimes'.[31] Mitrinovic tried to give new meaning to the phrase 'good European', which had lost meaning during the Great War,[32] and to restore a moral obligation to it: 'good Europeans must be ashamed of the chicanery which Europe practices in her relations with the other races. There is nothing Aryan or noble in it.'[33]

Rather than deconstructing the stereotypes of national and ethnic peculiarities, as we would expect today, Mitrinovic tried to revise them, substituting a positive meaning for a negative one. His effort was not, however, always coherent and successful, since the stereotypes tended to be reconfirmed, sometimes with tones that sound racist to us, with reference to what Mitrinovic called anthropogenesis: 'The Black, the Red and the Yellow races are embryological forms of the fully developed Man, the White race',[34] or with reference to the Jews, to whom Mitrinovic put this choice: 'Zion or Assimilation... by deliberate intermarriage'.[35] Jews should not convert to any particular Church, but 'to a Christianity outside the Churches, in common with the more intelligent Aryans and Aryanisers'.[36] Even if Aryandom means simply self-consciousness, even if the collective designations are not binding for the single individual, these classifications smack of Eurocentric, tendentially racist and at the same time meaningless attitudes. No doubt 'many readers found the articles very hard to understand'[37] and possibly to accept, although forms of anti-semitism and Eurocentrism were widespread in the intellectual environments of the period. When some New Age subscribers accused M.M. Cosmoi of antisemitism, Mitrinovic's reply was that as authors they neither recognised themselves in a national or a tribal chauvinism nor felt pro-Aryan on any racial or tribal ground. It is true that, when Mitrinovic was writing in The New Age, the weekly was at the lowest level of popularity, having fallen from the 22,000 copies distributed in 1909 to 4,500 in 1913 and under 2,000 in 1920, possibly due to its withdrawal from the support of guild socialism in favour of Douglas's social credit.[38] C.H. Douglas's programme implied a marked antisemitism, according to which Jews were part of a power-seeking conspiracy, and The New Age's campaign against high finance and for social credit in the following years (1922–32) was tinged with antisemitism.[39]

The articles in The New Age contain a great number of references from a variety of cultures, besides Western philosophy and the Christian religion. A very interesting position adopted by Mitrinovic, which places him as a forerunner of post-modernism, was his conviction that any claim to originality was in his time ridiculous; 'he despised the mistaken notion of originality' and 'regarded the claim to originality as barbarous'. What was appropriate to the time was to review and reassess all the great works of art and the philosohies and religions of the past 'in their mutual relationships'.[40] Later on, Mitrinovic classified the sources he used for his syncretic construction into six categories. These he called – rather enigmatically – 'ultimate', which included Vedanta philosophy, Buddhism, astrology, Hebrew cabbala, Plato, Aristotle, Hegel, Kant and Leibniz; 'canon' (i.e. fundamental and excellent), which included Blavatsky, Steiner, Swedenborg, Nietzsche, Weininger, Stirner, Comte and Feuerbach; 'proximate', which included Freud, Jung, Adler, Kropotkin; 'immediate', which included Solovyov, Gutkind, van Eeden, Groddeck, Kunkel, Buber; 'journalistic', which included Lewis Mumford, Dandieu, Belloc, Geddes, Orage, S.G. Hobson and B. Kidd. Later additions comprised Lao-Tzu, Schopenhauer, Bergson, Husserl, H. S. Chamberlain's Immanuel Kant and Bhagavan-Das. The extent of Mitrinovic's erudition was immense, and was sustained by a knowledge of many languages of the present and of the past, such as Sanskrit and Chinese. He used images and myths from ancient Greek and Egyptian mythological figures such as Dionysus, Prometheus, Osiris, gnostic concepts such as that of Pleroma, the idea of the Aquarian age as well as the scientific principle of evolution. He included among the builders of the 'continent of liberation', Europe, Charlemagne, Napoleon, and Lenin. Even in the *New Age* period, some major elements of Mitrinovic's ideas, which would go on to be practiced in the later associations, were already quite evident, such as the cult for the men of genius, and the effort to create a lay cult based on the faith in science.

In these ideas and in their syncretic combination – an art at which Mitrinovic excelled – we can see some of the ambivalence inherent to his thinking. The idea of society as a living organism, an organic whole, was central to the Fascist conception of society and its relationship with the state. It is true that the idea of organic relationships at the basis of society had also been put forward by socialists, to indicate a social bond different from the economic nexus dominating industrial society. It is indeed difficult to detach any organic conception, however benevolent, from the implications of totalitarianism that it has when applied to social affairs, since it gives only marginal space to dissent and conflict. In Mitrinovic's sense, the term 'organism' can be appropriately applied to total humanity in time and space, while single nations or peoples are only organs. Therefore in his case it is more a question of cultural assimilation than of political totalitarianism: in the end, the task of Europeans is 'before it is too late, to create an all-inclusive European culture'.[41] All cultures can be included within the synthesis of European consciousness, according to Mitrinovic, who probably felt entitled to say so on the basis of his own background and culture. However, it is precisely this assimilationist approach which is today rightly considered to be inadequate as a foundation for real multi-culturalism.

An example of the connection between organicism and assimilationism can be found in a book published some years later by the NEG (after 30 publishers had refused to publish it). *Europe: A Living Organism*, by the Viennese doctor Victor Bauer, also translated into Italian and French, argued that the body of continental Europe was formed by the living organisms of different nations, growing like plants in organic connection with the geographic space which belonged to them (Great Britain was not an organic part of Europe, although it had a vital interest in the continent). The 'biological centre' of Europe was located in Central Europe, where the three elements West, East and Orient were in the process of combining. The Orient, which was the element of fermentation and amalgamation enhancing the mutual action of West and East, was represented particularly by the Jews, more numerous in Central Europe than in the rest of it. In the area of Central Europe where the process of combination was underway, a new European totality was being formed which 'united

Western experience with Eastern vitality and Oriental versatility'.[42] The man who would emerge from the new totality would not feel himself exclusively as a part of any special nation, he would be a European, fostering a European Supernationalism.[43] The final goal of this biologism was to awaken Europe, 'the Mother-cellule of the world's cultured civilisation, into life, and regain for it the lost supremacy amongst the People of the Earth – not by violence, but with prudence and wisdom'.[44]

Mitrinovic was as ambivalent as Bauer on the matter of relationships between cultures, in the sense that while recognising the need for federation and devolution preserving the identity of each cultural unit, he maintained a hierarchical vision of cultures and of the need of European leadership. A similar criticism can be made for what concerns the role of women in his work. A source of his position on this matter was, besides the writings by Comte and Solovyov, *The Science of Power* by Benjamin Kidd (1858–1916) published posthumously in 1918. According to Kidd, woman is the active agent in creating and spreading power, which consists in enthusiasm for an idea; woman is naturally unselfish and is devoted to the interests of the race, both of which are also in accordance with the principles of Christianity. The singular noun, consistently used before second wave feminism for speaking about women, contributes to making an equation of all women together, and between them and some natural principle, so that they remain undifferentiated and unindividuated. Mitrinovic recognised the justice in woman's desire for 'awakening and taking her place in the world', even 'violently', which he expressed in his personified language: 'The Male has provoked the revolt of the Female in the West. Woman is an insurgent and a Prometheus in this era.'[45] But he did not like 'the dangerous though human fact of feminist emancipation, and the feministic tendency'.[46] Thus the recognition of the value of femininity contains the element of 'otherness' – the subject always being male – and implies a fixed role – the role of establishing cohesion – for women, destined to reflect the vision of perfect femininity for the eyes of men; the exaltation of monogamy presupposes that women are ready to incarnate the compassionate spirit of mankind and to accomplish the redemption of the cosmos.

## The Adler Society

From the 1920s onward Mitrinovic tried to combine his ideas with the findings of Western psychology. He became a good friend of Georg Groddeck (1866–1934), the German founder of psychosomatic medicine and author of *Das Buch vom Es* (1923), from which Freud took the term 'Es', derived from Nietzsche ('Es' is translated into 'id' for Freud and into 'it' for Groddeck). Groddeck's last book, *Der Mensch als Symbol* (1932), an analysis of language based on a psychological interpretation of etymology and the history of words, included some of the ideas which he had exchanged with Mitrinovic.[47] Mitrinovic read Freud and recognized his value, but found Jung and Adler more useful for his purposes. The latter especially was to be crucial for him. Alfred Adler (1870–1937) was born in a Viennese suburb, the second son of a Jewish merchant. However, he did not identify with Judaism and converted to Protestantism in order to 'share a common deity with the universal faith of man'.[48] Adler became a medical doctor, and wrote about social medicine and social diseases; in 1902 he was invited by Freud – who held his work in high esteem – to join the Viennese Psycho-analytic Society, which he left in early 1911, two and a half years earlier than Jung. Adler was deeply interested in socialism, and married a Russian socialist, Raissa Epstein, a friend of Trotsky's wife. He did not want to take an active part in politics, but in the period 1920–34 collaborated with the Social Democrats by founding and developing institutions dedicated to advising teachers and to medico-pedagogical consultation, as well as kindergarten and experimental schools. While three-quarters of Freud's patients belonged to the upper classes, three-quarters of Adler's came from the middle and lower classes. His fees were consistently lower, his treatments shorter, and his face-to-face setting reflected an equality between patient and doctor. Adler established a pragmatic or concrete psychology which taught a practical knowledge of oneself and others, but which included some very relevant theoretical insights, such as that on the existence and importance of primary aggressive drives, which he had developed as early as 1908.[49] Together with some colleagues who had also left the Freudian society, Adler founded what was to become the International Society for Individual Psychology (ISIP), and it was in this context that an association between him and Mitrinovic was formed.

Adler visited England for the second time in 1926 (the first visit, in 1923, had been rather brief), and was heard giving a lecture by an associate of Mitrinovic, Lilian Slade (sister of the painter Frank Slade, who shared a studio with another important follower of Mitrinovic, Valerie Cooper, a musician who taught dance and eurhythmics). Lilian Slade was enthusiastic about Adler and introduced the two men, who found that they shared much common ground. Mitrinovic, after various meetings with Adler, asked him to lecture on Dostoevsky and Nietzsche in Valerie Cooper's studio, and in 1927 went to see him in Vienna with Mairet, Cooper and others. Some of these participated in congresses of the ISIP. Through the efforts of a few enthusiastic people, among them Philip Mairet and Alan Porter (later to become professor of literature at Vassar College in the USA), the English branch of the ISIP was founded in London. In the following years the society prospered and provided its adherents with a full cultural and social programme, which included a philosophical group, an educational group, and a sociological group, plus general discussions and social evenings with dancing. The society's activities also included a medical group (whose members were all medical practitioners), a men's group, a women's group, and other smaller study groups. Each group had a leader and a secretary, and lectures were delivered both in the groups and at general meetings. The groups met regularly on a fixed night of the week, usually at the society's rooms at 55 Gower Street. Plays, arts and crafts, music and eurythmics were also available for the members to do, the last two thanks to Valerie Cooper. If so desired, the members could spend most of their days in the environment provided by the society, and the most dedicated actually did so. On Tuesday nights, at the general meetings, Mitrinovic would himself lecture on 'the fundamentals of individual psychology, with discussion, for newcomers and enquirers'.

From the preparatory summaries of some of the lectures as well as the notes taken from them, it is possible to derive some idea of their themes and approaches. For instance, Lilian Slade gave a lecture in 1928 on 'Woman and Society', where she recognised the great changes in domestic work but criticised the notion of women's equality with men including freedom in sex. In order 'to set the standard of values in life', women ought to know the state of world affairs, to have some knowledge of cultural matters, mathematics, philosophy and foreign languages, so as to become as complete human beings as possible. But the goal, as Helen Soden repeated in two other lectures (both probably in 1930), was to create real women, and not imitation men, as was happening with the 'terrible domination of woman over man'. Women felt superior to men who, affected by 'the disease of our time, weakness of will', were good comrades, but lacking in initiative and intellectuality. What was necessary was to restore the complementary nature of the sexes, with the vital significance of human bi-polarity, while, 'if the present ideals of feminism were to be realised the best intelligence of Britain and America would be extinct in three generations'. On 23 October 1929 Philip Mairet lectured the Sociological Section on 'The Family of the Future', criticising the 'Malthusian nightmare' on the basis of the Adlerian idea of the 'human family' and of the anthropomorphisation – an idea taken from Mitrinovic – of the whole of mankind. Mankind was like a great individual that had entered as a whole a neurotic phase, indicated by 'modern hesitancy and nervous crisis'. For the explanation of certain concepts, such as essential humanity, Mairet referred his listeners to other evenings, 'especially Tuesdays', when Mitrinovic spoke. On another occasion, Alan Porter (no date) spoke on Adler's concept of marriage, explaining that neurosis occurs when marriage is considered a romance and the 'amative aspect is made the sole condition of it', while marriage is a discipline, a training in communal relationships.

In June 1930, Lilian Slade gave a lecture on the 'Dialectics of Emotions', interpreting ideas from Adler and Ferenczi. Her table of emotions,

positive as well as negative, and the various relationships between superiors, equals and inferiors reflected the Adlerian typology of interrelations
between individuals, and between individuals and various types of
groups. The theme of emotions was also treated on other occasions, for
instance with reference to the work of the Indian philosopher Bhagavan-
Das, who had provided a classification of emotions, 'the very root of all the
virtues being the Emotion of Love'. This was understood not as born out
of desire, but as the realisation of all selves into the one self.[50] It can be
mentioned here that ideas of love in the groups around Mitrinovic included
among their sources Erich Gutkind's conception of the physical union of
two lovers – contrasted with merely sexual unions – as a form of longing
for the divine. All these can be considered examples of the NEG's contribution to introduce ideas from other cultures onto the British scene, and
not only on the subject of a 'science of emotions'. Other lectures included
a series on astrology, one on the philosophies of Husserl, Vaihinger, Driesch,
and Nietzsche, and one on the questions of 'modern Europe' and peace.

It is worthwhile briefly to explore the basis of agreement between
Adler and Mitrinovic. Already during his Freudian period Adler had elaborated his theory of organ inferiority, which he developed later on,
considering organ inferiority not only as a basis for a proneness to transient diseases in a given organ, but also as the origin of compensatory
processes, and finally as a substratum for neurosis. Organ inferiority sets
in motion a complex psychological process of self-assertion, which may
become a permanent factor of psychic development. Unlike Freud, Adler
always stressed both the physiological and the social origins of neurosis.
However, physical inferiority never forces an individual to adopt a mistaken style of life (Lebensstil); every individual can decide about his
actions and contribute to the progress of human society. Individuals are
wholes, who can reach their wholeness only through co-operation, on the
basis of a community feeling (Gemeinschaftsgefuehl), understood as a
reflection of the general interdependence of the cosmos; the striving for
superiority is not antagonistic to such community feeling. Adler found
confirmation of his notion of the whole in the holistic philosophy of the
South African Jan Christian Smuts, theoriser of the link between holism
and evolution, which he conceived as a rising series of wholes from electrons
and atoms to colloids, plants and animals, up to minds and personalities.[51]

No doubt Mitrinovic preferred the Adlerian vision of each individual
as unique, indivisible and exceptional, to the Freudian conception of
ambivalence and conflicts in human beings. The former better suited his
own attitude as well as his activity as an organiser. He praised Adler for
treating sexuality as secondary, as simply one of the functions of the libido,
and for his interpretation of the libido 'as from the heart, the centre of the
whole man'.[52] It is easy to understand why Mitrinovic appreciated certain
major aspects of Adlerian psychology: the combination of the uniqueness

and indivisibility of the individual with the importance of community feeling, the possibility of transforming society by concentrating on individuals rather than by political action, the consideration of psychic life as teleological, were all themes that struck a sympathetic chord in Mitrinovic, who, with a different terminology, had already developed similar ideas. The same can be said of Adler's view that love and marriage are to be understood as a form of co-operation towards the welfare of humanity, and that they should be lived *as if* (Adler was a follower of neo-Kantian Vaihinger's philosophy of fictions) they involved everybody's well-being. The two men also felt very similarly on the question of women's emancipation. Adler maintained that absolute equality between women and men was essential, and followed Bachofen and Bebel in believing that a stage of matriarchy had preceded patriarchy in human history; he also counterposed to Freud's penis envy the themes of man's inferiority and of 'fear of woman'. But he was diffident of feminism, and warned against 'the masculine protest' that could emerge both in men and women. Both Adler and Mitrinovic insisted on the importance of love as the most powerful means of education, and shared great admiration for Nietzsche.

Mitrinovic himself gave many lectures on Adlerian psychology (50 in the years 1927–1932), some of which were published in the magazine *Purpose* (which claimed to be interested in 'the human purpose: relativity and psychology', and declared that it 'delight[ed] in new knowledge, reverence[d] the pioneer and like[d] revolutionaries better than reactionaries'). Records of the lectures still exist, and these are useful, but cannot really give an idea of what the lectures might have been like. Mitrinovic was a very 'oral' person. He preferred to speak rather than to write, to write in journals rather than books, and he spoke English with a solemn and musical intonation.[53] 'It was the mouth, of a singularly perfect form, that was his organ of power; the mouth of a poet and a orator.'[54] 'He plunged, with a sort of massive but fluid deliberation, into what seemed to me like a river of speech, which flowed on without ceasing and without hurrying... I struggled with all my being to understand what he said, but could only dimly follow' (Valerie Cooper on her first encounter with Mitrinovic).[55] He was able to speak from his 'feeling centre'[56] rather than from his intellectual one, thus capturing the attention of people even if they did not understand fully what he was saying. 'He was speaking to the unconscious', remembered his friend Harry Rutherford, 'intensely personal in his approach'. He would explain philosophical notions to old ladies who others thought unable to understand them, and he remarked that it was 'all going into their unconscious'.

He was, when he spoke, in control both of his tone of voice and his facial expressions, which he adapted to his audience and the impression he wished to convey. He was able to address large audiences as well as small ones with complete clarity of expression and great imaginativeness, so that he could hold them spell-bound.[57]

Thus, we can imagine that it mattered very much how these lectures were delivered. In them, Mitrinovic spoke about Freud, Jung, Adler and Ferenczi, about Hegel, Marx, Bergson and Nietzsche, and he formulated individual psychology in his own terms. It is quite striking that there was never any clear change in direction in his philosophy; perhaps it is typical of a syncretistic philosophy that it can keep adding new elements, without changing or evolving in any distinguishable way.

The theme of Europe was also present in the lectures, although in a subordinated form. In a lecture given at the Adler Society (no date), the American writer and poet J. Gould Fletcher stated that a new system of education should be conceived in order to train new generations to think as European beings. Mitrinovic deduced the meaning of Europe and of the Western World from 'the revolt on the plane of science' as exemplified by Adler. He seemed to imply that the Western World has produced a science which is mechanistic and pessimistic; Freud is an incarnation of such a science, Adler redresses the balance, teaching optimism and humility. This must become the true spirit of Europe if people in Europe can be awakened from their torpor and encouraged to be themselves,[58] and this could happen 'if there were in Europe, in that shattered civilisation, in that decaying culture that is our present (one), spontaneous people here and there... becoming aware that they themselves are culture units'. Culture – explains Mitrinovic – is when we know that every one of us is responsible for the whole race of mankind.

This concept of Europe tried to incorporate a cultural and emotional content which would be meaningful for individuals, and would give 'Europe' a meaning it did not have in political contexts. It became increasingly important to Mitrinovic at the beginning of the 1930s, and had an influence on reorienting his activity. This meant a change in the form and nature of the associations in which he was involved. The Adlerian Society was centred on a nucleus which constituted 'an esoteric school, or school of initiation' around Mitrinovic's personality, and the members were arranged in concentric circles according to the degree of intimacy with him. This group of people were fundamentally motivated to do 'an objective work under public auspices' by their intention to avoid sinking 'into obscure self-regarding inactivities'.[59] In this communal exercise, activites were kept on two levels, the public and the private, the exoteric and the esoteric.[60] This was consistent with Mitrinovic's disposition. While he was no longer, as he had been in his youth, engaged in creating secret societies, he was still, according to the slavophile Stephen Graham, a born conspirator leading a pacific life. In fact, all the public projects set in motion by him were both vehicles for the personal development of the participants and enterprises with social public goals. However, it would be inadequate to consider the latter as simply subordinate to the former, since the very particularity of Mitrinovic's teaching was to keep together the individual and the social.

Differently from other spiritual gurus, who insisted on an initiation process understood as self-perfection, Mitrinovic interpreted initiation as a social process, and more precisely as preparation for a function that he defined as 'Senate'. Since society was to be organised along the principle of threefoldness – the cultural, the political and the economic – a fourth principle, Senate, was to act as the intermediary. This was a self-appointed body whose function would be to mediate the conflicts that would necessarily arise in the highly dynamic, never static, social system which Mitrinovic envisaged. He introduced a utopian spirit into the everyday activities of his associations, in the spirit of one of his phrases: 'utopia now'. Mitrinovic insisted on the importance of personal relationships between individuals, irrespective of race, class, age or sex, as the basis of a new social order. He never wanted to build a separate society in society; for him all forms of association had to avoid becoming institutionalised, and nothing was ever final. Therefore the 'concentric circles' mentioned above were liable to move every day, according to various initiatives, and his associates preferred to call them 'constellations'. Harry Rutherford has vividly described how these groupings worked: Mitrinovic would start an initiative with a very small group of two or three persons, progressively enlarge it to other people, each person being allotted a function in the new project. The course of this process could go in different directions, according to people's reactions and Mitrinovic's judgement: the whole constellation thus sometimes came to be composed of several functional constellations with perhaps a central secret core, or the whole structure might be blown up[61] and a similar process started all over again. Mitrinovic's main goal was that of spiritual education, while his main conviction was to prepare social change through individual transformation. In this sense, it has been rightly claimed that Mitrinovic was calling in the first instance for 'new Europeans' rather than a new Europe.[62]

Such a goal could be compatible with a professional association, as the ISIP partially was, only up to a point. The Adlerian Society had attracted members of the medical professions, but also 'substantial numbers of young, idealistic folk: teachers, artists, students, journalists'[63] who were the ideal audience for Mitrinovic's purpose of preparing a community of the future. Moreover, the pressures from the political developments in Europe, especially the rise of Fascism and Nazism, tended on the one hand to hasten the need for a process of innovation and on the other to dissuade medical people in Germany from political entanglement. In 1930, the division between the medical group and that part of the society which was closer to Mitrinovic became apparent, and in 1931 the decision was taken to separate meetings and subscriptions, while maintaining friendly relationships. The gap became wider in the following years because of the additional pressure, acutely felt by Adler, to keep the society out of public activities which might endanger its followers in the countries where the Nazi movement was attacking it. On the contrary, Mitrinovic and his associates were moving into a phase of renewed and wider public activity, which led to the foundation of various other groups. The most important of these was the NEG, founded in 1931, and made up of very much the same people who had formed part of the Adlerian Society.

## The New Europe group and the New Britain movement

The NEG had its headquarters at the same address as the Adler Society in Gower Street, and its secretary was Winifred Gordon Fraser, whom Mitrinovic had met when she was working in a South Kensington bookshop and had recruited as secretary and organiser. She was very active in taking initiatives and establishing contacts. The NEG not only promoted lectures and meetings, but also published and distributed leaflets and pamphlets. Starting from the conviction that 'politics have failed', it proposed in one of its leaflets 'the active cooperation of individuals' and the formation of groups designed to examine the situation and to inform on 'the possibilities for a reconstructed, renewed social order'.[64] Central in its programme was a European federation as a major step towards a world one. The method was to be a 'revolution of order', guided by the principles of federation and devolution, respectively indicating harmony between peoples and groups and complete liberty for individuals. Devolution meant the application of diversity, and implied that decisions had to be taken by the smallest possible grouping of those who must implement them or would be affected by them.

The psychological approach was not abandoned by the new group, either as a general inspiration or as a specific theme. For instance, on 16 November 1931, one of Adler's collaborators, M.D. Erwin Wexberg from Vienna, gave a talk to the NEG with the title 'A psychologist's view on European crisis'. Wexberg interpreted Georges Duhamel's thesis that the cause of the crisis was fear, as 'the emotional expression of the inferiority feeling, and its compensation produced by the Great War'. 'Balance of power' meant that the nations were afraid of each other – which was really a fear of something in themselves – and used safeguards, like a neurotic. Similarly, the League of Nations was a neurotic fiction formed in order to avoid responsibility, newspapers acting as instruments of this fiction. The German example was a peculiar one: the only real point of the National Socialist programme, antisemitism, was indicative of a neurotic evasion of responsibility; no one was guilty, except the Jews, while all that was good, great and beautiful was German. It was a compensatory delirium of great-ness, springing from a deep-rooted feeling of inferiority, and it was dangerous, like any other form of insanity. According to Wexberg, the treatment to be prescribed was the overcoming of fear, which was at the basis of the whole neurosis, by an increase of insight and by pacific co-operation according to the rules of human sociality.

Mitrinovic too gave a series of lectures to the NEG, in the period 1931–33, on the links between politics and psychology, and particularly on the theme of a united Europe in a world order. He restated his ideas about Europe, insisting on the absolute necessity of federating as the only way out of the disastrous collapse of the European civilisation:

> Europe should be the unity of Byzantine and Roman spirit, the union of sacred-ness, of outer and inner, [of] useful and useless. Europe is fundamentally more Eastern than Western. The American vision is that everything can be organised, there is no soul, there are only reflexes.[65]

Against federating were 'great and small Tories', as well as Mussolini and Fascism, while Russia was in favour, and Liberalism, Diplomacy, Capitalism and the League of Nations fell in between. Europe, being 'an organism doctored by such physicians', existed only in appearance. In the end, all those for, against and in between actually opposed federation. 'Europe has two enemies: the Russian Communist movement as it stands at present, and the American civilisation of materialism'.[66] The apparent contradiction must be understood on the basis of the sharp distinction drawn by Mitrinovic between the 'soul' of Russia and Russian Communism, which was only a part of Russia as a whole.

While the lectures mixed paradoxical statements of this kind, the publications of the NEG were more coherent and propositive. A short but very eloquent pamphlet was published in 1931, possibly that very mani-festo which Mairet remembered 'with a certain complacency' that he himself had written: *Integration of Europe. The Way to Reconstitute the States of Europe as an Organic Society in a New World Order*. The subtitle referred to two themes which were widespread in Europe at the time: 'organic soci-ety', as we have seen, appealed to the hopes of creating a real community; 'new order' was a term appropriated both by the left and the right, from Communists (*Ordine Nuovo* was the title of Gramsci's paper from 1919 to 1925) to Nazis via the radical-liberals, to indicate the necessity of a reor-ganisation of the political, economic and social life of the world. It was a word of order shared with a French periodical, *Ordre nouveau*, published in Paris between 1930 and 1938 by the group to which Robert Aron, Arnaud Dandieu and Denis de Rougemont belonged; one of the founders and chief-collaborators of *Ordre Nouveau* was Alexandre Marc (the pseu-donym of Alexandre-Marc Lipiansky), a Russian Jew whose family had left the country because of the Revolution, and who in 1933 converted to Catholicism. Marc often wrote articles signed together with his wife Suzanne Jean in publications directed by Mitrinovic. *Ordre Nouveau* rejected both capitalist and Communist materialism, and believed in a spiritual revolution, in personalism and individualism; it played a major role as a mediator between different groups of young intellectuals in the 1930s; consistently with this, it gave great importance to the idea of generation.[67]

The NEG pamphlet combined Eurocentrism ('in Europe the intellect and coordinating mind of the human race is centred... [here] mankind has chosen to come to world consciousness') and Anglocentrism (it is England that will 'lead the States of Europe towards an integrated life'), with a 'European socialism' which had nothing to do with contemporary Marxist views in Britain. Indeed, it should not be forgotten that the editor of the British magazine *Labour Monthly*, Palme Dutt, wrote in March 1931 that pan-Europeanism was an imperialist idea intended to isolate the Soviet Union.[68] The programme of 'European socialism' as it was presented in the NEG pamphlet was based on three levels or estates (socialism for Mitrinovic was a self-ordering of man, based on the nature of the individual and collective soul of mankind). On the political level, a 'much greater regional autonomy within England' would be necessary to enable it 'to lead in the greater regional conception of Europe', while the General Parliament of the Federation would be elected by all the regional parliaments, so that it would show full respect for local autonomies. On the economic level, national corporations or associations of all the workers in any given industry would be constituted by manual workers, managers, staff and accountants, whose delegates would compose a General Economic Council of the Federation. On the cultural level, a Cultural Assembly was to take care of education, health and recreation, as well as of science, philosophy and art. In this framework, federation with Europe was considered the best way for England to preserve her colonial leadership, since if England did not take up her responsibility of leading the way towards a federation of the States of Europe, 'it is most unlikely that Western Europe can live for long as a chief world-power, and doubtful if the British empire can long survive'.

This programme necessitated a preliminary reawakening of 'the most aristocratic spirits that still remain' to allow Europe to overcome her 'darkest years', those following World War I, and to enact the 'dawning *consciousness of a common predicament*' (original italics). One pre-condition for this federation was 'a general psychic change', 'a new thought and a new feeling', capable of drawing inspiration from the 'style of life and sense of values' which were developed in the European cultural heritage, and of providing 'a modern and enlightened version of our historic culture'. The priority was spiritual and the first step was to find 'persons who wholeheartedly desire' European unity and would consciously work for it.

Many terms in the pamphlet allude to subjectivity – although without using this term – by referring to the individual capacity not only for decisions and change but also for sentiments and emotions. However, subjectivity is not conceived of as a merely individual faculty; on the contrary it leads to a common way of life, and to the recognition that nations are 'organs, constituting altogether the body of Europe'. The reference to subjectivity is pragmatic, since the whole process can only be started by 'the radical change of outlook' that would be necessary in order for England to identify her destiny with that of Europe.

These themes – the appeal to a spiritual aristocracy, the reference to a common historical heritage, the conception of Europe as a living organism, the association of the 'darkest' moment with the new 'dawn' – were widespread in the literature of the inter-war period. Indeed, they constituted a shared patrimony for the left and the right, for Communists and Fascists, certainly in France and Italy, although they had different meanings and implications. The very notion of Europe was an area of dispute, where opposing factions fought to appropriate the wealth of the European cultural heritage. In this context, to reduce the groups around Mitrinovic to predecessors of or sympathisers with Fascism[69] would mean not only to presuppose an 'imaginary Fascism'[70] occupying a much larger area than Fascists in reality ever did, but also to ignore the real novelty of groups which sought to give priority to the spiritual formation of human beings. The NEG's platform included aspects which the Fascists would never accept, such as the refusal of a central control by the state and the primacy of the individual, the effort to build a higher level of consciousness and to develop personality, the insistence on the importance of inter-subjective relationships. The NEG's concept of authority was also very different from that of the Fascists, in as much as it was embodied in the concept of Senate. Senators would derive their authority solely from personal influence, and they would help contending parties – which included Communists and Fascists – to see their conflicts within the context of the world as a whole.

In the first half of the 1930s an incessant flow of activites occupied the people around Mitrinovic. In the summer of 1932, the NEG organised a series of lectures entitled 'Popular Myths Exploded', including 'That capitalism has anything further to offer us', 'That the press is instructive to the public', 'That there is nothing to be done about it'. C.E.M Joad exploded the myth 'That civilisation is civilised', by reading extracts from a Martian historian's description of the demise of European civilisation, written in 10,000 PMI (Post Martem Incarnatum). The fact that his lecture was chaired by Harold Nicolson, as was another lecture by Leonard Woolf, is taken as an indication of the connections between Mitrinovic's groups and the Bloomsbury Group, other signs being that Valerie Cooper's studio was a meeting place for people from both groups, and that writings by previous groups around Mitrinovic were published by the Hogarth Press.[71]

In October 1932 a quarterly by the title of *New Britain* was launched, which a year later changed its title to *New Atlantis. For Western Renaissance and World Socialism*, and became *New Albion* in April 1934. Meanwhile, in May 1933, a weekly had appeared under the title of *New Britain*. The contributors to these publications were for the most part the same, i.e. Colonel J.V. Delahaye, Philip Mairet, Frederick Soddy, S.G. Hobson, Frank MacEachran, and J. MacMurray. Mitrinovic wrote articles and editorials for them, and acted as director, but very often his name did not appear. The logic of this was to multiply initiatives, groups, journals, in an endless process which counted more than the results, and, indeed, in which the results were sacrificed. In 1931, some other associations had been created, such as the Eleventh Hour Flying Clubs (for European federation towards world federation), and the Women's Guild for Human Order. In a statement of aims and objectives the latter declared to 'accept and work for the sociology taught by the NEG' and to 'wish to rediscover the meaning and function of womanhood'. They asked women of all nations, creeds, classes and ages to join with them in demanding a new human order in a period of crisis and insecurity. They were very aware of the world situation: they referred to 'millions of unemployed – fellow men and women – in every country', and to a war which had begun in the East (possibly the occupation by Japan of Manchuria and China in 1931 and 1932) and which 'must inevitably arise in the West'. The Guild of Women believed:

> Woman's influence is unifying, co-ordinating, she is essentially the preserver of life. Man on the other hand is inventive, analytical, specialist; he reasons for the joy of reasoning… any woman can begin today in her own sphere by making an inspiring background for the men she meets, enabling them to act positively and optimistically in the world.[72]

This programme does not seem particularly radical today. However, Mitrinovic encouraged the women in the NEG and in the other organisations around him to follow their inclinations in job choices and cultural interests. It was important at that time to have somebody saying that women were individuals with the same value as men, although they should not imitate men.[73]

The most important initiative under the auspices of the NEG was the New Britain movement, launched in December 1932. Its objectives included a reform of the monetary system (credit to the nation rather than to banks); the reorganisation of industry through national guilds under the workers' control; the devolution of parliament into a House of Industry, a House of Culture, and a Political Chamber; European federation as a first step towards world federation. The *New Britain* weekly acted as the organ of New Britain (NB) groups. By August 1933 the circulation of the weekly amounted to 32,000, and by November 1933, NB groups were established in 47 towns plus 30 in the London area. This was the closest the NEG ever came to a nationally-organised political movement, with declared aims, a defined policy and a programme of action, as Andrew Campbell and Charles Purdom, the professional journalist whom Mitrinovic had called to edit the weekly, proposed. Purdom understood that the paper met such a favourable response because of the widespread need for a new type of political organisation, which he then proposed in August 1933 with the support of many members.

But his efforts were frustrated. Mitrinovic was absolutely opposed to transforming the NB movement into anything similar to a party, and, together with his closest associates, was also against accepting decisions taken by voting and democratic procedures. During the end of 1933 and the beginning of 1934, the split within the NB movement continued, and in March 1934 a first national conference was held, where a coup manoeuvered by the central group around Mitrinovic took the leadership. Purdom resigned and left, and so did many who believed in organising a national movement for industrial planning and monetary reform. Shortly afterwards, another wing of the movement, the pacifists (among whom was G.E.C. Catlin, Vera Brittain's husband) and those committed to international socialism were outraged by a call by Mitrinovic for Britain to rearm and impose peace on Europe, and they also left. By December 1934, the NB movements had 'devolved' into four leagues, of which only the House of Industry League resembled a public organisation attempting to influence trade unionists; it brought together, besides trade unionists, engineers and scientists and sponsored educational work among other activities.[74]

NB's contradictions in ideas and membership, which included both business people and trade unionists, were such that, even without the coup, the movement might never have developed into a political organisation. However, during its life it established contacts with many people of various political attitudes, including Harold MacMillan, had among its associates the Communist Jack Murphy, and attracted all sorts of intellectuals, such as Bertrand Russell and T.S. Eliot. This last, for instance, contributed an article on 'New Britain as I See It' to *New Britain Weekly* in 1934 (20 July). Eliot saw a 'New Britain' as an order in which acquisitiveness and love of power did not receive the sanction of society, and where passions towards religious ends were not diverted to Fascism and Communism. The whole story of the NB movement demonstrates how greatly the need of an organisation which might combine the regeneration of the individual with political aims was felt. The leadership's refusal to commit itself to becoming a political party brought the movement to an end in 1935, although the NEG continued until after the war.

The four leagues included a British League for European Federation, but it was the NEG which remained the main promoter of Europeanist activities, consisting in lectures, luncheons and discussions. Magazines often appeared only once or twice and then disappeared, to reappear shortly after with a similar title: *New Europe, New Atlantis, New Albion*. Mitrinovic and Orage were the joint directors of *New Europe*, first published in September 1934, announcing that it had incorporated *New Atlantis*; its motto was 'Respublica Europae', the subtitle 'A monthly journal for Federation and Disarmament', while the map of Europe on the endpaper included Turkey and the USSR. The address of the journal in Cursitor Street was the same as the two journals founded by Orage, *The New Age* and the more recent *New English Weekly*. Orage died shortly afterwards, in November 1934.

The choice of names which characterised NEG and NB is significant: *New Atlantis* is taken from the title of the book written between 1614 and 1617 by Francis Bacon (referring to the lost Atlantis of Plato) and published after his death in 1626. *The New Atlantis* is a short and incomplete fable, narrating the visit of an English ship to the island continent of Bensalem in the Pacific, 'a picture of our world as it might be if we did our duty by it'.[75] For the NEG, Bacon's *New Atlantis* illustrated not only the social nature of scientific research after the Solomon's House model (a foundation in which the progress of science and the laws of its legitimate use were under the control of a body of wise men), but more generally the possibility of applying science to society so as to create a welfare state.[76] Names were used by Mitrinovic and his associates to create a link with the cultures of the past, with 'new' added: Albion (Celtic Albio) was the Old English name for England which can be found in Pliny, Ptolemy and Beda; during the Second World War the NEG used the phrase 'Albion-Gallia' to indicate the union of all the British and French, and potentially of all Europeans. Other names were taken from the pre-Roman past and traditions, which the NEG was keen to restore: a Caractacus Club and a Boadicea Club were created in the second half of the 1930s – respectively for men and women – taking their names from the Celtic chieftain who rebelled against Rome in Wales in 43AD and from the queen who led a revolt against Roman rule in East Anglia in 60AD, both dignified and proud heroes. The choice of Glastonbury as the site for a decisive conference of the NEG reflected a similar intention, Glastonbury being the place of origin of Celtic Christianity. The story was that Joseph of Arimathea had started there what would become the Irish monastic tradition, a mysticism which was far removed from the Roman Catholic insistence on good behaviour and deeds, and which could be inspiring for the birth of a new European spirituality.

While Mitrinovic was the founder and leading inspirer of the NEG, the group brought together a number of extraordinary figures, from many intellectual backgrounds, including eminent scientists, all united by the hope of using the advancement of science for the betterment of human conditions. In fact, Mitrinovic excelled in bringing together disparate

people and in keeping them co-operating harmoniously at various levels
of participation: thus, the presidents were prominent individuals who did
not participate in the day-to-day activities of the group, but were present
on special occasions and were ready to give talks and attract new as well
as existing members. The first president was Sir Patrick Geddes
(1854–1932), biologist, sociologist, educationist and town planner, already
encountered earlier as a friend of Dawson's and founder of the Le Play
Society. Geddes, who in the 1890s had begun the assimilation of social
thought from the continent, rejected an over–simple metaphorical comparison of society with an organism; in order to express the continuity of
human social life with the life of other organisms, he developed the triple
relationship of Environment-Function-Organism, and translated Le Play's
formula 'lieu, travail, famille' into 'place-work-folk'.[77]

Besides being professor of botany at University College Dundee
(1889–1914), and holding teaching posts in London, Aberdeen and
Edinburgh, Geddes devoted himself to the planning of country and town.
His town planning was based on the principle that care should be given
not only to citizens' physical health, but also to their spiritual well-being.
He also participated in the debate on sexuality, writing with J. Arthur
Thomson *The Evolution of Sex* (1889), in which the authors expressed
'wholesome scorn for those who, in practice or in theory, would deny to
women the sovereignty of their own bodies'[78] and evisaged an evolution
from the vague sexual attraction of the lowest organisms to a definite
reproduction impulse and possibly further, towards a 'more than earthly
paradise love' of 'the poet and his heroine, forerunners of the race'.[79]
Geddes's travels took him to France, Mexico, Cyprus and India, where as
professor of civics and sociology at Bombay (1920–23) he organised a post-
graduate school. He also created a collegiate life with a summer meeting
at the Outlook Tower in Castle Hill, Edinburgh, a regional geographic
museum with a social purpose in city improvements. Geddes's
Europeanism had first appeared in the idea (developed in the years
1917–1925) of a third alternative, which went beyond war and peace, to
include regional independence, the reconstruction of war-torn areas, and
a new League of Nations. The new league was to be a federation of cities,
not the war-capitals but the provincial centres, aiming at the liberation of
Europe from bureaucratic and financial oppression, and at a material and
spiritual reconstruction which would transform Europe into a Eutopia.[80]
While both 'eutopia' and 'utopia' had already been used by Thomas More
(1516), Geddes preferred the first expression, meaning 'a good place', to
the second indicating 'nowhere'.

Geddes was active in many fields. He promoted a publishing house
associated with Celtic and general literature, art, geography, education.
Asked to do so by some Zionist friends, the psycho-analyst M. D. Eder and
his wife, he planned the Jewish National University in Jerusalem, which,

however, like many of his projects was never implemented.[81] In the last part of his life he built an unofficial student residence (Scots College) in Montpellier, France, where he helped develop the Cité Universitaire Méditerranéenne and where he lived for the last part of his life. One year before his death, he decided to accept the knighthood that he had already once refused; this time he accepted it because it came from a Labour government. Geddes shared with Mitrinovic the idea that the greatest need of their time was to grasp life as a whole, to see its many sides in their proper relations, and to develop both a practical and a philosophical interest in an integrated view of life. As an evolutionist, he stressed the importance of the development of sex as a more profoundly important step in evolution than had yet been realised. Geddes had many followers throughout Britain, who constituted something like a school of thought and action; one of them was Mairet, a disciple of Mitrinovic as well.[82]

With the death of Geddes in 1932, Arthur Kitson (1859–1937) became president of the NEG. An engineer, inventor and monetary reformer, for 50 years an opponent of the financial system and the gold standard, he was the founder of the Banking and Currency Reform League. Kitson was another encyclopedic scientist: he had worked with Thomas Edison on the electric light, with Graham Bell on the telephone and he held about 500 patents for invention (including the Kitson incandescent light). But Kitson also lectured to the Independent Labour Party branches about his idea for financial reform. The titles of his books express his unorthodox views: *A Fraudulent Standard: An Exposure of the Fraudulent Character of Our Monetary Standards* (1917); *The Bankers' Conspiracy, Which Started the World Crisis* (1933). In *A Letter to the Prince of Wales* (1931) Kitson, then President of the Economic Freedom League and Chairman of the Monetary Reform Association, exposed his plan to emerge from the world crisis by nationalising the Bank of England, making the state the supreme money-lender of the nation and not a borrower, treating money as a 'social instrument'. He believed that under a scientific financial system it would be possible to abolish taxation and that there was no need to force down wages and salaries in a world where there was an abundance of raw material, labour and capital. Kitson 'lived in his dream of a better England and a better world', firmly convinced that 'the survival of civilisation depends on us'.[83] Mitrinovic shared with him the belief that a new social order would be impossible without a radical reform of the monetary system.

Kitson's ideas inspired his successor in the presidency of the NEG, Frederick Soddy (1877–1953), who had dedicated to him his main economic work, *Wealth, Virtual Wealth and Debt* (1926). After studying in Aberystwyth and Oxford, Soddy had worked first with Ernest Rutherford and then with William Ramsay on radioactivity experiments; he discovered isotopes, elements with the same chemical qualities but different atomic weights which are considered essential to allow atomic energy to

1.   *The Rape of Europa* by Veronese, 1580, later inspired Mottram's novel *Europa's Beast.*

2. The 1930 version of the jacket of the novel 'modernised' Vernoese's painting.

3. Europa, incarnated in one of Madame Yevonde's Goddesses.

4. A stylised version of Europa and the Bull on a textile by Frank Dobson.

be used for peaceful purposes.[84] Besides being one of the pioneers of research into atomic disintegration (*The Interpretation of the Atom*, 1932), he had, like Geddes, an encyclopedic mind: at virtually the same moment, he received the Nobel prize for chemistry, in 1921, and published a volume on *Cartesian Economics*, in 1922. As early as 1906 he had questioned the wisdom of using gold as a currency material; he wrote many books on monetary reform (*Money Versus Man*, 1931; *A Physical Theory of Money*, 1934), which were not favoured by economists, but were appreciated by Keynes.[85] He belonged to the Le Play Society founded by Geddes, and participated actively in the NB movement. Soddy shared with the NB the belief in 'a national renaissance without violence', based on the principle derived from Ruskin that true wealth was life not money. He was one of the speakers in the series 'Popular Myths Exploded' organised by the NEG in 1932, on the theme 'Poverty Old and New', with a lecture that the NEG published. He seized on devolution as the key theme of the New Europe platform and spoke of it repeatedly and passionately on many public occasions; he also wrote in various journals published by local branches of the NB movement.

Soddy cultivated his many interests until the end of his life, publishing in various fields, and being intensely interested in social and political affairs such as women's suffrage and home rule, of which he had been an advocate since before the First World War. His interests extended to geology, archaeology, farming, family life and budgets. Soddy was both intransigent and uncompromising, a born fighter against anything that he thought unfair or stupid; he was, above all, an individualist.[86] He believed that 'science makes possible a nobler civilisation without the rotting that reared it'[87] and that 'the way lies open for a real democracy with opportunities for all to live an ample and civilised life'.[88] Soddy continued his activity with the NEG after the Second World War and led its delegation to the Congress of the European Union of Federalists held in Rome in 1948. Lewis Mumford, who had met him at the Sociological Society in 1920, wrote that he 'demonstrated, by his own too lonely example, the necessary transcendence of the limits of specialisation... even by his "failure" he has become one of the heralds of a new age'.[89]

The succession of presidents of the NEG is not totally clear. In 1939 the President was S.G. Hobson, but after the Second World War Soddy became President again. Hobson was not a scientist, but rather a political man. However, he shared with his predecessors the belief in an analogy between biological and economic systems, and the conviction that there should be functional harmony between the parts. Born in a Quaker village in Ulster, Hobson was a Fabian from 1891 to 1910 (from 1900 a member of the executive), and a member of the Independent Labour Party from 1893 to 1905. He was the author of *National Guilds* (1910) translated into many European languages as well as Chinese and Japanese. Hobson proposed as a means of abolishing the wage system the establishment of self-governing brotherhoods of producers with a complete monopoly of the labour-power in their industry. These guilds could be chartered by the state and their power vested in the House of Industry – into which the House of Lords was to be tranformed – endowed with powers of control and co-ordination of economic affairs. The House of Commons would still have such responsibilities as state policies, foreign relations, dominions and colonies, army and navy.[90] A third estate would have been the House of Culture, concerning itself with journalism, art and literature. Hobson deplored the 'false inference' drawn from his ideas in Germany and Italy, as well as the blindness of official socialism towards them. He participated in the NEG's activities, and liked to be associated with its young members. According to Hobson, the NEG showed a 'repugnance to machine politics', and preferred to 'visualize Europe as a great political and cultural family, on whose united shoulders rested the future of the New World'.[91]

A high degree of individuation was certainly a common feature uniting these very different men in the NEG: it was part of their charisma. They were interested in the education of youth and for all; they believed that science was producing fantastic possibilities for the reorganisation of society, in spite of social incapacity to profit by them. It has been suggested that Soddy turned his attention from physics to finance because he was not sure that radioactive power could ever be used for the good of humanity. All these men headed the tradition now known as 'the social responsibility of science'.[92] In spite of being immensely interested in knowledge, or perhaps because of this, they all refused to become specialists in only one field, and shared this with Mitrinovic, who never wanted to become an expert in one of his many fields of interest. Therefore they also experienced the difficulty involved in any attempt to achieve encyclopedic knowledge in an age of specialism.[93] Finally, they shared, with various nuances, an organicist view of the social system and its evils, as well as the hope of finding remedies that would allow a functional harmony of all its parts.

It is doubtful whether such men could have kept the group together had it not been for the activity of some women 'of unusual gifts' who composed, according to S.G. Hobson, 'a unique trinity of talents, invaluable to any movement': Winifred Gordon Fraser, Lilian Slade and Valerie Cooper. Gordon Fraser, as secretary of the NEG, took initiatives such as contacting Sir Charles Trevelyan, Lewis Mumford and Salvador de Madariaga, to invite them to give talks or participate in the organisation. Trevelyan replied (7 November 1931) that the aspirations of the NEG sounded very good, but were too vague. He found 'astonishing... the omission of any mention of the League of Nations which is the one real hope of the world internationally'. Gordon Fraser replied on 16 November that the NEG was 'entirely in favour of the League of Nations being made a vital organisation', but added that this could only happen 'if individuals in each nation determine that it shall be so'.[94] In 1939 she asked both Madariaga and Mumford to be vice-presidents; they refused, but expressed sympathy and agreement with the NEG's positions. Winifred Gordon Fraser was not only an organiser; she also wrote articles and gave lectures. Valerie Cooper contributed to the NB journals with articles on eurythmics, nudism, physical health (the journal carried advertisements not only of her school, but also of new initiatives by others, such as the Integrity Food Centre and the First Vitamin Café). Lilian Slade was a powerful and inspired speaker. These women combined practicality and idealism, psychic understanding and warm hospitality. When Hobson visited the group at Gower Street in 1932 he found 'a pervading friendliness and a complete absence of dogma', as well as 'the constant resort to psychological science and terms'. Hobson also defined Mitrinovic as 'the presiding genius' of that 'astonishing congregation of men and women'. During the Second World War the group was run mainly by women and a few young men, those New Order Boys who with the New Order Girls constituted the youngest associates of Mitrinovic.

## Eutopia or Atlantis?

In the 1930s the NEG was a melting-pot of ideas of many sorts, and particularly of Europe's heritage and future. The debate oscillated between the two poles of the threat of a catastrophe in the near future, which would sweep Europe away like a second Atlantis, and the prospect of a harmonious development towards a European Eutopia. These opposite outcomes were contested not only in the lectures, speeches, and debates, organized by the NEG, but also through the books that it recommended, and sometimes published, or that its own members wrote. Among the recommended books were those by Edward Glover, Jung and Groddeck (not by Freud), William Blake, *Aspasia* by Money-Kyrle, John Strachey's *The Menace of Fascism* and the Coles's *Intelligent Man's Review of Europe Today*, as well as *The Brown Book of the Hitler Terror and the Burning of the Reichstag*.

The situation of Europe after the First World War and the attempt to find a third way between America and Russia was a recurrent subject. The NEG's suggested readings included *L'Union Européenne* by B. Mirkine-Guetzevitch and Georges Scelle, containing the complete documentation of the Briand Memorandum and the debate on it; Sherwood Eddy's *The Challenge of Europe*, which warned against postponing the question of social justice until Communism became inevitable. Also recommended was *Europe's New Map* by F.J. Adkins, a description of changes after 1918 in the political map of Europe enlivened by remarks based on travels through Europe, which by 1922 had swollen to the point where the British Passport Office was nearly overwhelmed by prospective European travellers (the NEG had a travelling club which organised travels, preceded by lectures, predominantly to Eastern European countries). One collaborator of the NEG was, as we have seen, the American poet J. Gould Fletcher, author of *Europe's Two Frontiers* (1930), in which he maintained that the conflict between America and Russia was psychological, and that intelligent Europeans should find salvation within themselves. In a lecture given to the NEG, probably in 1932, Fletcher proposed the economic federation of Europe, the abolition of war debts and the demolition of war armaments. He had heard Christopher Dawson's broadcast on Europe and accepted his view that Europe was politically democratic, socially humanitarian, intellectually scientific and spiritually Christian.

The European cultural heritage as an antidote to nationalism was the central theme of the work of Frank MacEachran, a collaborator both of *The Criterion* and of *New Britain*. The NEG published his *The Unity of Europe* in 1933, and he sent them a copy of his other book, *The Destiny of Europe* (1932). MacEachran was convinced that a European tradition went back to Greece, Rome and Judaea. The Jewish contribution was essential in bringing about a universalism, an ethical earnestness and an asceticism unknown to the Greeks and Romans. The modern European, born between 1300 and 1600, derived from the chivalric ideal of the knight the value of 'a man who is in control of his passion and therefore of himself', free and restrained at the same time. In order for the Germanic sources, medieval Christianity and Arabian influence to mix to produce the idea of the 'gentleman', it was necessary to add the ingredients of the Provençal troubadour culture and Gothic pride. MacEachran quoted Briand and Gaston Riou (*Europe ma patrie*), Ortega y Gasset (*La rebelion de las masas*) and Drieu la Rochelle (*Genève ou Moscou*), Maritain and Julien Benda. But he added an English specificity by suggesting England as the mediator between Europe and the rest of the world, on the basis of England's capacity to preserve the European tradition of unity, diversity, tolerance and moderation. At the same time, he believed that 'everything which is good in England exists by virtue of the European connection'. 'The fever of nationalism' had nearly destroyed the unity of Europe, but if Europeans realised that they are Europeans, 'the springtime of Greece will return'.

In contrast to MacEachran's optimism, another recurrent theme in NEG publications was the decline of the West. Spengler was not included in the list of recommended books, but the idea of an impending cataclysm was crucial to others which figured prominently in that list, such as *The Secret of the West* by the Russian symbolist writer Dmitri Merejkowski. This was a vast collection of aphorisms foreseeing a second world war for Europe, which would become the self-destruction of humanity. At a time when 'to be a "European" no longer means being "universal"', Europe – the second Atlantis – might be destroyed by an inner flame rather than by an outer one. Nicolaj Berdyaev's *The End of our Time*, also recommended reading, besides attacking Marxism-Leninism for its incapacity for doubt and critical reflection, proclaimed that 'night is upon us', but also announced that 'a new and unknown world is coming to birth', the world of the new middle ages. A similar feeling was powerfully expressed in the poem 'Genethliacon for the New World Order' by Hugh McDiarmid (pseudonym of the Scot Christopher Grieve), published in *New Atlantis*, January 1934, which struck a note of hope:

All is deepening darkness. I see no shred
Of light at all. I hear no sound
But cries of horror and distress in the night...
The end of the world is at hand...
For the time is at hand – It is always
Darkest just before the dawn – and as
A woman's labour, life's most terrible pain,
Suddenly into joy must pass...

In Mitrinovic's writings from autumn 1933 onward the sense of an impending catastrophe – the annihilation of Europe – became increasingly urgent. To it he opposed the idea of a New West, an Atlantic Alliance, based on the initiative of Albion, 'the world-giant of intermediation and universal thinking', the mediator between Europe and America. 'Immediately now planning and constructing *the New Order of the post-European World*' meant that Britain should take the final initiative for instituting the United States of Europe as the only way to prevent war.[95] If it did not, 'a European war and a civil war of communists and Fascists would shake and destroy every Christian church in Europe and Europe herself'.[96] Mitrinovic had visions of 'great and terrible bloodshed', of 'the hell of bacterial and gas suicide of Christendom'.[97]

In his editorials in *New Europe* Mitrinovic insisted on repentance, redemption and rebirth: 'Beware and repent, Europa Communis! Repent, re-orientate, orientate thyself, O Western Adam! Find the way!'[98] If Albion and Columbia (Britain and the United States) could show the way, New Scythia (Soviet Russia) too would move from the collectivised and mechanised world into the world of redemption of the Personal principle.[99] However, Mitrinovic kept repeating that Britain was not obliged to join the European Union, and might prefer, after having imposed an alliance upon the continent, to establish one between the European federation and its own commonwealth. As time went on, his tones became more and more apocalyptic and prophetic, as he was conscious that he was addressing himself 'to the Deaf, and to the Criminal Idiots and to those who shall Kill and shall be killed unless they Wake up to Hear', i.e. the world's statesmen and supermen.[100] But he still believed that something could be done:

*Finis Europae*? Shall the West and Humanity fail?... Must Germany and France die, O Destiny, O Providence? O Liberty of love and reason, must France,

Germany, Italy, Russia, Europe – must they be destroyed in the disaster of the history of civilization?

Is it not possible to know and to understand truth? Is Federation impossible? Is Federation of Europe and the New Order impossible in Christendom, in Europe? The death of Europe is not decreed. Certain it is not yet. The catastrophe of Christendom and of the Western civilization is not yet necessary and certain.[101]

With a rhetoric which likened the written form to an oral address – probably a pale image of the powerful oratory that he could display in person – Mitrinovic did his best to save Europe and its civilisation. His distrust for politics was total, and although the NEG took initiatives related directly to political events, it of course did so in its own terms. At the end of the 1930s it organised a series of talks on the state of Europe to which well-known federalists and Europeanists were invited, such as Wickham Steed, Salter, Curtis, and Lord Lothian. In 1938, at the time of the Munich crisis, the NEG posted thousands of posters and 20,000 leaflets throughout Britain and Europe, advocating an alliance between Britain and the US and the creation of a European federation with Prague as the capital.

Mitrinovic played the central role in the NEG, where he figured as international organiser. Very different images of him are given by various testimonies. He has been portrayed as 'the Master' by Edwin Muir in his memoirs, who felt 'disappointed and distressed' by the attitudes of his 'devotees', who participated 'reverently' in a 'bogus cult'.[102] However, according to people who were very close to him, Mitrinovic believed that the age of hierarchical leadership had passed, and strongly criticised those who acted deferentially to him.[103] According to oral testimonies, in his actual teaching there was no fixity, because like a Zen sage he used paradoxes, changed his stand suddenly, and proposed to transcend the antithesis between opposites through a mind of higher order. In spite of his stereotyped descriptions of the various functions of races and sexes, his teaching was that one had to find oneself through a process of individuation which involved disentangling the ego from the determinations imposed by sex, age, class, race and nation. The difficulty of this lay precisely in being able to appreciate in oneself and in the other the value of the traditions connected with those determinants, and at the same time to go beyond them. Mitrinovic asked no less of his collaborators, but took into account greatly people's reactions. He believed that a new co-operative order could not be imposed from above, but should grow organically from relationships between individuals. But he differed from other spiritual leaders in linking the process of reaching a higher individual consciousness and more harmonious intersubjective relationships with social change, which included some radical goals. For him the spiritualisation of the individual and the organisation of the world for security and leisure were two processes which were made possible only by each other.[104]

A religious strand ran through Mitrinovic's work, although it was not a confessional one.[105] He hoped to fill the gap that had divided the Christian dogmatics from heresies and the occult traditions as well as from other religions. He felt that his was not a political programme, but rather an attempt to reconsecrate all that Europe had been, a task of reconciliation and acceptance, not of invention. This explains his effort to embrace as much as possible of human cultures, and his commitment to creating an *ante-litteram* multicultural approach, flawed by assimilationism on the theoretical plane, but very open in its practice. In so doing, Mitrinovic also put into practice an extensive educational programme for all those around him, whom he kept constantly alert to what there was to learn from so many cultures, aspects which very often were not taught in British schools at the time. In this way he acted to his associates as a kind of university or encyclopedia of the world's cultures,[106] and he also embodied the spiritual authority of the master in the Eastern tradition, who leads his disciples on a path of discovery in a way which goes beyond Western concepts of superiority and inferiority.

From what we can judge, Mitrinovic was excessively optimistic about his capacity to influence people and combine opposite political visions. For him, syncretism was a way of life, not limited to his philosophical positions. He asserted that his lifestyle combined physical Epicureanism, psychical Stoicism, mental scepticism and spiritual affirmation.[107] Mitrinovic had a vast collection of all sorts of books (those donated by the New Atlantis Foundation to Bradford University Library amount to 4,500), was endowed with a great musical memory, enjoyed many kinds of music and was fond of the Russian ballet. He was a fine art connoisseur, interested in classical sculpture and architecture, but had also an important collection of works by contemporary artists, among whom were Miro, Dali, Braque, Giacometti, Roy de Maistre. He was known to enjoy the theatre and the music hall, and to have, in Willa Muir's word, 'an eye for a pretty woman' (although we know of no sentimental or sexual relationship of his); he loved jokes, including vulgar ones, and was convinced that the joker or trickster represented one of the major dimensions of life. Mitrinovic pushed his eclecticism into food, since he used to dine in the Hungarian, Greek and Russian restaurants in Soho, where he ordered six different dishes and mixed them all up.[108]

One can infer from Mitrinovic's life and writings that for him there was a higher and more important order of things than the realm of politics. But in periods of increasing political polarisation like the mid-1930s this could lead to political blunders. For instance, in the first issue of *New Atlantis*, in October 1933, Mitrinovic wrote a letter to Adolf Hitler, an 'Urgent Appeal', where he invited Hitler 'to take initiative personally as a statesman, to approach Great Britain, and to ask her to take initiative for the Federation of Europe and the Atlantic Alliance'. He declared: 'I refuse

141

to take you [Hitler and his Cabinet] as impostors or great historic murderers', and ended with these words:

> Oh, German! Man! Adolf Hitler! hero and saintly man! Your Germany is leading on to war, to self-extermination of the Continent, of which Germany is the form and spine.
>
> Propose Disarmament, to Germany and to France! Propose the Atlantic Alliance to England and to USA! Your own violence and bloodshed would be consecrated and forgiven.

Although we know that Mitrinovic was not a sympathiser ('As for Fascism, it is not of us'[109]), this letter indicated either an ambivalence or a sense of omnipotence, or perhaps both. The inconsistency of its approach emerges in unfortunate passages like the following:

> ... exterminating the Jewish non-Aryans without oneself becoming of Senate and of Consciousness... invites the Kremlin Nemesis in New Germany.

It may be recalled that *Ordre Nouveau* in France published a similar letter in November 1933, which was heavily criticised by Emmanuel Mounier and Simone Weil. It is mainly on the basis of this letter that Sternhell has included *Ordre Nouveau* in Fascist ideology, but he does not quote the passages from the letter where *Ordre Nouveau* is most critical of Hitler and where it forecasts his descent from nationalism into war, promising to make him responsible for the massacres that the war would bring.

The NEG was similarly ambivalent. It numbered among its members the Communist trade unionist Jack T. Murphy, who had collaborated with Lenin (and was later expelled by the Communist Party in London), Lt Col. J.V. Delahaye, who was Secretary of the People's Front Propaganda Committee, which called on the Labour Party to take initiative for a British People's Front,[110] as well as Maj. Gen. Fuller, who was to become a collaborator of Mosley's *Fascist Quarterly* in 1935–36. John Frederick Charles Fuller (1878–1966) had served in India and fought in the South African war of 1899–1902 and in the First World War in France. Besides many writings advocating a new model army based on modern equipment and books of military history and of the science of war (title of his 1926 book), he also produced essays on *Yoga, the Mystical Philosophy of the Brahmins and Buddhists*, in 1925, and *The Secret Wisdom of the Qabalah*, in 1937. Mitrinovic considered him to be the best specialist on the cabbala in Britain, and Fuller's collaboration with NEG dated from the late 1920s. One of his articles was published and republished in *New Europe* (the most complete version, of September 1934, was called 'Armageddon and the Labyrinth: a vision of war, federation and disarmament'), and made use of an obscure and visionary language charged with symbolic images, such as the Vampire, the Phoenix and the Sphynx. The general meaning was that transformation, assimilation and unification must take place at all levels, in a progression from 'one man, one nation' to 'Europe, Europe-America, the world'. A year later, in 1935, Fuller published a virulently antisemitic article in *The Fascist Quarterly*, in which he presented the usual stereotypes about Jews controlling newspapers and cinema, being the apostles of the new magic cult of psycho-analysis, and Jewry being at the same time a 'worm feeding on the usury system of finance' and dangerously subversive. The usual note – for many antisemites – was added: 'I have met not a few Jews whom I can full-heartedly respect'. Although less virulently, Fuller's attitude had been consistently anti-semitic in the past as well. In *Atlantis, America and the Future* (1926) he had taken an anti-American stance and expressed his antisemitism in a truculent way, describing New York as 'Jew York, crawling with Israelites' and on the way to becoming a 'New Jerusalem'.[111] In his autobiographical *Memoirs of an Unconventional Soldier* (1936) Fuller stated that after the First World War European unification was imperative in the face of a resurgent Asia, and that unification had to take place in the direction of a new morality, of a spiritualisation leading away from pre-war materialism and saving from total disaster the structure of civilisation. He considered the League of Nations essentially anti-spiritual and closely related to bolshevism.

The association of Fuller with the NEG throws a sinister light on the organisation. It is true that Mitrinovic believed that one had to live in a world of perpetual conflicts, that both the conflicting sides were right and that the 'Third Force' should be developed. It is also true that prominent anti-Fascists were invited to write in the group's journals. For instance, in April 1934 Margaret Storm Jameson contributed to *New Albion* with an article on 'Women and Dictatorships'. The role of women in the future world order was a constant concern for the NEG, which included among its suggested readings *Painless Motherhood* by Rennie Smith – distributed free – and *The Way of All Women* by Esther Harding. Storm Jameson countered the attraction that dictatorships had for many women by pointing out that dictatorships imprisoned women in their physiological function of child-bearers, while at the same time asking them to surrender their children to the state. Storm-Jameson concluded by pleading for liberalism and democracy as the political forms most appropriate to women's emancipation and developments.

Writings appearing in the periodicals published by NEG and NB included all sorts of positions on Fascism. In 'An Open Letter to British Fascists',[112] Oliver Baldwin reacted to a parade of Black Shirts through the streets of London by questioning their aims with a series of pointed questions:

> Do you intend to go round the country showing your intellectual level by attacking Jews who happen to be more intelligent than yourself? Do you intend to beat up Socialists because you cannot counter their arguments with better sense?... And what about the power of international finance?

The author counterposed to 'marching, shouting and drilling' the sanctity of the individual, on which a New Britain had to be built, overcoming the intolerance which was threatening 'to throw back European culture into the Middle Ages'. A book review in *New Britain Quarterly*[113] analysed together three books of different political orientation, all published in 1932: *Greater Britain* by Oswald Mosley, *Crisis: The Only Way Out* by Emile Burns, and *The Coming Struggle for Power* by John Strachey. It was typical of the groups around Mitrinovic to counterpose Fascist and leftist positions, as in this case. But the anonymous reviewer treated Mosley's book as the least interesting, criticising the 'mysterious entity known as the "Corporate State"' and the lack of clarity about the proposed rationalisation of industry. Although not adhering to the positions expressed by the two other books, because they too failed 'to face up to the fact of the human individual', the reviewer recognised that the proletariat was not quite so ghostly as the corporate state and advised the reader to study the two latter books, especially Strachey's, as clear, serious, and stimulating.

All ambiguities considered, NEG and the other groups around Mitrinovic cannot be seen as 'looking in the direction of Fascism' or as contributors to ideas developed by Mosley,[114] who is supposed to have derived from them the term 'new party'. First of all, the New Party was not Fascist,[115] remaining in the ambiguity of advocating a stronger executive and economic planning, and secondly, these ideas and terms, as we have seen, were circulating everywhere in Europe, including areas where the left held sway. The NEG not only shared ideas with the left as well, but also shared with other European intellectuals the idea that it was possible to go beyond both Fascism and anti-Fascism. It should be remembered that some of those who believed so went on to become anti-Fascists during the Second World War. The NEG merged these opposite influences with an interest in the esoteric, in spiritual development, and in a higher order of consciousness. Varied experiments, which some people might label superstitions, usually accompany these beliefs, but in these respects the NEG and Mitrinovic were never extreme, on the contrary they were rather moderate. It would be inaccurate and superficial to ignore their particular features and brand them pro-Fascists or crypto-Fascists. A more balanced judgment, while acknowledging their blunders on the questions of women and Jews, is necessary.

The NEG sought to offer an idea of Europe which could include subjectivity by appealing to the individual, the emotions and inter-subjective relationships. Therefore its Europe was not conceived of as isolated, but rather as a part of a dynamic process attempting to move towards a new social order at a world level; the term 'New Europe' indicated an attitude towards change, both in the individual's world and in the social universe. In this audacious plan, which attempted to answer some of the great needs of the modern world, there was too close an identification between the microcosm and macrocosm, and an insufficient recognition of the gap between the two and of the need therefore to find bridges between the different levels. The insistence on the organic and almost physical aspects of a new Europe, as well as the mechanistic link established between the darkest hour and the coming light, is evidence of a deterministic way of conceiving the whole process, including the psychic sphere and subjectivity; the result is that along with some very interesting intuitions, an incoherence is introduced. A similar contrast can be discerned between the organic conception of the state and the economy on the one hand, and the alleged autonomy of individuals and local realities on the other.

A form of determinism was also implicit in the tendency, discernable in Mitrinovic's writings, to take philosophical concepts literally or to make hypostasis out of abstract thinking. An example of literal reading can be seen in relation to Nietzsche, who in *Beyond Good and Evil* had stated the need, in order to solve 'the European problem', to envisage 'the breeding of a new ruling caste for Europe'.[116] One could say that the initiatives of NEG and NB were ways of translating into practice too literally the Nietzschean idea 'to anticipate experimentally the European of the future', and to prepare the new synthesis whereby 'Europe wants to become one'.[117]

As for the hypostatisation, Mitrinovic's thinkings offer many examples of abstract concepts to which an ontological value is attributed – with no proper theoretical foundation – and which are translated into self-subsistent images with a supposedly concrete and autonomous meaning. This is the case of all his personifications, from the whole of humanity conceived as Anthropos or Sophia, to Albion, Columbia, Scythia, etc., personifying the spirit of nations and continents. Europe/Europa too comes into this process of translating concepts into personifications, but since it is described in more detail than many of the others, it escapes some over-simplifications and rigidities. This is the most perishable part of Mitrinovic's heritage, while a more enduring one could well be his attention to intersubjective relations and to the connections between the personal and the political. His ideas about mediation between opposite sides in society – for instance the Senate function – which appeared un-realistic in the political context of the inter-war period, have become a practice for psychologists and social workers resolving social conflicts in some European countries, and might be further developed.

After the Second World War, a new group was formed by Mitrinovic and his associates, called the Renaissance Club. The NEG existed until 1957, being active in post-war Europeanist initiatives; after Mitrinovic's death, in 1953, the New Atlantis Foundation was created in Ditchling, Sussex, in order to preserve the documents of the group and to make them accessible to the public.

## Notes on Chapter 3

1    Lipgens 1982, p 162
2    Behr
3    Behr
4    Rigby, 7ff
5    Besant
6    Steele
7    Storm Jameson, *Journey from the North*, p 329 (see Sources, 6, 3)
8    Mairet 1981, p 40
9    Glass
10   Orage, *Friedrich Nietzsche*, pp 11, 15
11   *Ibidem*, 171
12   Martin, pp 29–30
13   Nott 1970
14   Selver
15   Nott 1969, p 58
16   Orage, *Selected Essays*, p 193
17   *Ibidem*, pp198, 201
18   Orage, *On Love*, pp 50–51
19   Rigby, p 86
20   Selver, p 57
21   Rigby, pp 60–61
22   *Ibidem*, p 54
23   Selver
24   Rutherford 1987
25   Beck
26   Rutherford 1997, p 21
27   *Certainly, Future*, pp 222
28   *Ibidem*, p 85
29   *Ibidem*, p 84
30   *Ibidem*, p 207
31   *Lectures*, 95
32   *Certainly, Future*, p 76
33   *Lectures*, p 92
34   *Certainly, Future*, p 98
35   *Lectures*, pp 114–5
36   *Ibidem*, p 112
37   Rutherford 1987, p 8
38   Rigby, pp 67; 70
39   Holmes, pp 209–10
40   Rutherford 1997, pp 2–3
41   *Certainly, Future*, p 76
42   Bauer, p 19

43    *Ibidem*,  p 51
44    *Ibidem*, p 59
45    *Lectures*, p 255
46    *Ibidem*, p 236
47    Testimony by Dr Twentyman
48    Bottome, p 65
49    Ellenberger, p 605
50    Bhagavan–Das, *Science of Emotions*, p 95
51    Ellenberger, pp 631–2
52    *Lectures*, p 7
53    Selver
54    Mairet in Rigby, p 60
55    Rigby, p 62
56    Rowland Kenney in Rigby, p 3
57    Rutherford 1987, pp 13; 16
58    *Lectures*, pp 29; 33
59    Mairet 1981, pp 102; 131
60    Rigby, p 91
61    Rutherford 1997, pp 8–9
62    Rigby, p 82
63    *Ibidem*, p 94
64    New Atlantis Foundation archives
65    *Lectures*,  p 298
66    October 6, 1932, *Lectures*, pp 305–6
67    Loubet del Bayle, p 166
68    Berki, p 57
69    Merricks, p 140
70    Julliard
71    Merricks, pp 134–8
72    *Statement of Aims and Objectives*, by the Women's Guild
73    Testimony by Dr MacDermot
74    Tyldesley
75    Spedding in Farrington, p 5
76    Farrington, p 11
77    Mumford, p 678
78    *The Evolution of Sex*, p 57
79    *Ibidem*,  p 58
80    Boardman, p 365
81    Stalley, p 93
82    Deffries; Ziffren
83    Wise, *Great Monetary Reformers*, no 2
84    Howorth
85    Gaitskell
86    Merricks

87 Soddy, *The Impact of Science*, p 21
88 Soddy, *Money versus Man*, p 110
89 Mumford, *In Commemoration*
90 Hobson, *Pilgrim to the Left*
91 *Ibidem*, pp 265–7
92 Merricks, p 7
93 Mumford, p 681
94 Archives NAF
95 *New Atlantis*, 1 October 1933
96 *Ibidem*, 9 May 1934
97 *Ibidem*, 4 July 1934
98 September 1934, *Certainly, Future*, p 398
99 March 1935, *Certainly, Future*, p 408
100 *Ibidem*, 8 May 1935
101 *Eleventh Hour*, 15 May 1935, *ibidem*, p 403
102 Merricks, p 143
103 Interviews with Drs Violet MacDermot and Ralph Twentyman
104 Rutherford 1997, p 2
105 Rutherford 1966
106 Rutherford 1997, p 2
107 Rutherford 1987, p 5
108 Rigby, pp 61; 154
109 *New Atlantis*, 8 August, 1934
110 *Left Review*, October 1936
111 Fuller 1926, p 47
112 NB, 26 July 1933
113 NBQ, I, 3
114 Merricks, pp 140, 148
115 Hamilton
116 Nietzsche, p 183
117 *Ibidem*, p 189

# CHAPTER 4

# EUROPA REAPPEARS FROM A NEW EAST

## Briffault's *The Mothers*

It was Peugh, the sculptor, Aloisius Peugh, a name which had at one time possessed a certain academic distinction… His 'Europa', once a Burlington House exhibit, is commonly to be seen in biscuit reproductions among the clutter of Victorian bric-a-brac on the baize of mantelshelves in decayed homes and seedy boarding houses. The beautiful Princess Daria Nevidof had sat to him, in the nude, for the flower-crowned divinity who elegantly rides the amorous bull.

This passage is taken from the second page of the novel *Europa* by Robert Briffault, published in London in 1936, but already a bestseller in the United States since 1935. The 572-page novel presented a vast fresco of Europe between the 1890s and the 1920s, through a picture of the social life of Russian aristocrats at home and abroad, and was largely based on the autobiographical experience of its author, son of a retired French diplomat. The title played on the multifarious meanings of 'Europa': a mythological creature, an artistic image, a princess, a continent in turmoil. The real subject of the novel was the turmoil and destiny of

149

Europe. Iconographically, the imagined sculpture 'Europa' referred to the figurative climate of the second half of the nineteenth century, when classical mythology permeated Victorian social discourse.[1] Why was Princess Nevidof nicknamed Europa? Certainly because of her beauty and her royal aspect, but perhaps also on the basis of her personality, which combined authority with irreverence, a provocative lack of prejudice with an aristocratic genealogy. She came from the East, like her mythological Phoenician predecessor, but the East was now Russia, the place of revolution and of a new order, with which Briffault identified. As in many other cases, the image of a woman was used in the novel to symbolise an identity, this time a continental one, and its epochal change in culture and politics. Daria Nevidof stands for both Europa and the fate of Europe in the novel, because her character alludes both to a process by which decadence give way to the hope of a new world, and to a power which women once had and might in some ways regain in the course of a vast process of liberation.

When *Europa* was published Briffault was at least sixty, and already well known for other works; he had led a nomadic and cosmopolitan life, travelling widely and speaking many languages – French, German, and Italian, besides of course English – but he also knew Latin, Greek, Dutch and Provençal. There is ambiguity about his age, because Briffault's adventurous life starts with a mystery. He maintained, possibly in order to be able to enter the army,[2] that he had been born in London in 1876, but there are some indications that in fact he was born earlier on. A Certificate of Baptism for Robert Stephen Briffault was issued on 8 November 1874 at St Mary's Church, Parish of Walton-on-the-Hill, in the town of Kirkdale, Lancaster.[3] His father had been People's Representative at the French Legislative Assembly of 1849 and chief of the presidential secretariat of Louis Napoleon, but he had retired after the coup d'état. He became naturalised British and married Margaret Man Stewart, a Scot thirty-five years his junior – daughter of a captain and granddaughter of a banker – and they went to live in Florence. Here, Robert attended a private school; he continued his education in Germany, then in Liverpool, and began medical studies in London, where he graduated as a Bachelor both of Medicine and of Surgery.[4]

Some years after his father died in Florence (in 1887), Robert Briffault and his mother moved to New Zealand, where he practiced as a surgeon, married Anna Clarke and had two daughters and a son. In the First World War he served at Gallipoli, in France and in Flanders, and was decorated twice. After the war, his wife died in the influenza epidemic, and Briffault went to live in London where, while continuing to be a doctor, he started his career as a writer of essays in social psychology. The following years were hard, his work alternating between the hospital and writing his *magnum opus* in social anthropology, *The Mothers*. In 1924 his mother died, as did shortly afterwards – probably in 1926 – one of his daughters, Muriel; as a consequence of these blows and overwork Briffault went through a period of severe mental stress and experienced trances lasting up to 20 minutes. Only the support and care of his other daughter Joan allowed him to emerge from this difficult period, having given up medical work in order to finish *The Mothers*, which appeared in three volumes in 1927 and made him famous (in that year he became a member of the PEN club). As he wrote in the preface to the first volume, 'it has been my lot to write books in situations fantastically unsuitable'; he was 'spared no drudgery' while writing the book, and only his daughter 'unwaveringly shared his sacrifice'.[5]

In his first book, *The Making of Humanity* (1919), a political elaboration of scientific data with virulently polemical tones – on which he had worked first in the trenches and then at the British Museum – Briffault had offered a rapid historical exploration of human evolution, a sort of genealogy of European civilization. His brilliance in giving a literary form, drawing from a commanding vocabulary, to a 'galaxy of information' earned him both the applause of *The English Review*, which considered him 'one of the new men of the coming new order', and the antipathy of *The Tablet*, whose comment on the book was laconic and revealing: '... we decline to discuss with him'. His second book, *Psyche's Lamp: A Revaluation of Psychological Principles as Foundation of All Thought* (1921) – written in a ship's cabin – was an attempt to assert the priority of society over the individual and to reformulate psychological principles along materialist lines. Briffault's approach to psychology had been influenced by Alexander Faulkner Shand (1858–1936), an author who had a strong interest in philosophy and philosophical psychology, was never an academic, and became known mainly for his book *The Foundations of Character, Being a Study of the Emotions and Sentiments*, published in 1914. Shand derived the bases of his thought from Herbert Spencer and John Stuart Mill,[6] whose philosophies impelled him to find the principles of a science of character, for him an essential part of a complete science of the mind. He believed that he had found such a principle in the general law that 'mental activity tends, at first unconsciously, afterwards consciously, to produce and sustain system and organization'.[7] Shand distinguished between emotions and sentiments; love for him was the most conspicuous of the systems of sentiments, i.e. a system of tendencies, each giving rise to its own emotions, such as fear, anger, joy and sorrow.[8] His was an objective psychology, which studied 'human nature from the outside' and used introspection for the purposes of interpretation and hypothesis.[9] Shand was original in making a distinctive use of popular opinion and of literary material, largely derived from English and French literature, on the basis of his belief that poets had much more insight than philosophers into the complex nature of love.[10]

The positivistic and evolutionist psychology elaborated by Shand was therefore far removed from that which Freud had been formulating in the decades since the end of the nineteenth century, by transforming introspection into material for psycho-analysis and using as a basis the dynamics of individual emotions. This was one major reason why Briffault preferred Shand to Freud. In *Psyche's Lamp* he argued in his usual vividly antagonistic and provocative way that the human mind is a social product. In an invective against 'the illusion of individuality', he harangued his readers, claiming that 'the individual life is only one step, one link, one phase' in the chain of life, and stated aggressively: 'the only line of demarcation between you and the continuity of Life is that of your cognitive experience';[11] 'you are, quantitatively regarded, a measured portion of energy'.[12] In this perspective, the subject – both the 'I' and the 'we' – appears a mere illusion, like individuality, and Descartes' formula *cogito ergo sum* is seen as fictional and deceptive: there is nothing in us over and above 'the extra-individual, impersonal forces that move us'.[13] In his subsequent work Briffault would transpose these concepts to the anthropological field, continuing with a philosophical-political outlook rather than adopting an experimental or field-based approach.

In *The Mothers*, about one-and-a-half million words long, with a bibliography of 5,000 titles, Briffault amassed a large body of anthropological knowledge about the origins and development of European civilisation. However, the quantity of illustrative material overwhelms the discursive structure, and this accounts for an impressive array of themes, but also for a certain lack of system. In the subtitle, *A Study of the Origins of Sentiments and Institutions*, Briffault takes up Shand's major theme, and coherently begins his exposition with the human mind: this is viewed as a social not a biological product, and he asserts that its 'social characters are traceable to the operation of instincts that are related to the functions of the female and not to those of the male'.[14] Differently from Shand, he is interested in institutions, so that the gender characteristics of the mind lead him to reconsider the early developments of human society and of its fundamental institutions and traditions 'in the light of the matriarchal theory of social evolution'. But Briffault did not follow Bachofen blindly on the thesis of an original stage of universal 'Mutterrecht' (1861); in opposition to the theory of social origins in the patriarchal age of biblical description, he believed that primitive social organisation had as its fundamental unit not the state or the family, but the mother and child within a group of kinsmen. 'Matriarchy' was to be understood not as gynaecocracy, the domination of women over men, but as a state in which women and their influence are much more relevant than in the current so-called civilised societies, where their status is defined by the inequalities typical of a patriarchal social order. Briffault tried to prove his beliefs by a vast *tour de force* covering the cultures of many places and epochs, including a chapter on the herd and the family in animal behaviour.

The Mothers are for him 'the heads of primordial groups, magic women and priestesses credited with supernatural powers, sacred queens in whom the mystic virtue of royalty was thought to reside, fateful goddesses who were the divine counterparts of earthly womanhood'.[15] He finds them in anthropology, in mythology and in literature; he examines the Chinese and Japanese, the Semites, the ancient Egyptians, the Aegeans and Greeks, the Teutons, the Celts and the Romans, as well as many primitive societies. Concerning these last, he is a convinced supporter of the existence of group or collective marriage and of sexual communism.[16] The second volume of The Mothers includes chapters on primitive jealousy and love, the evolution of monogamous marriage, the tabu, the totem, and primitive cosmic religion. Finally, Briffault inquires into the magical origin of queens, the great goddesses of many religions, and he analyses the concepts of modesty and purity, as well as romance.[17] Among the many themes treated in The Mothers, two are particularly relevant for the connection between Europe and love: the theses on marriage and the interpretation of love and romance.

Briffault treats European monogamy as a late development, characterized by the subordination of women, as contrasted with their ancient status of power and influence. The sexual repression of modern times is also contrasted with the greater freedom both of the primitives and of the pagan past. Among Briffault's targets a primary place is given to the Finnish sociologist Edward Westermarck, author of the History of Human Marriage (1891), whom he accused of scientific dishonesty in his support for a theory of 'eternal monogamy' and in lending credence to the objectives of Christian apologists and traditional moralists. This simplification was strongly rejected by Westermarck, who had worked on a polygynous society in Morocco and claimed never to have held the position alleged. He maintained that his arguments were based on his research, not on principles (he accepted divorce and favoured its extension), and confirmed his theory of the family as the earliest social unit and of monogamy as the predominating form in primitive marriage. Westermarck also retorted that Briffault's references, which he had checked, were often inadequate or incorrect.[18]

A pupil of Westermarck and Malinowski, Ashley Montagu, intervened because he felt that Briffault was doing great injustice to Westermarck at the same time as being himself misunderstood on his interpretation of matriarchy. Montague wrote to Briffault, became a friend of his, and organised a meeting between the three men. As a consequence, Briffault gave a paper in Westermarck's seminar at the London School of Economics, and developed a relationship with Malinowski. According to Ashley Montagu, the personalities of Briffault and Malinowski were not dissimilar: 'both were Europeans rather than nationals in any narrow sense, they were urbane, witty and *bons vivants'*.[19] Malinowski even tried to find a job for Briffault, and his first effort in this direction was to ask Briffault to join him in a series of broadcasts which he had been invited to give on BBC radio in 1931. In this series the two men argued over the history of marriage, disagreeing so deeply that in the end Malinowski completed the programme alone. The ground for agreement between them was really narrow if it amounted, as Malinowski said in his last broadcast, to the recognition that marriage 'can be maintained only at a great personal sacrifice of husband and wife' and that maternity is of decisive value in all questions of marriage and parenthood.[20]

The disagreement between Malinowski and Briffault should be placed in the context of the debate on the crisis of marriage, already encountered in the chapters on Mottram and Dawson, the background to this being the growing divorce rate in Western European countries and the USA, and reforms in the Soviet Union abolishing church weddings and the marriage legal contract. The issue of marriage in present times was mixed with the debate on anthropological theories adopted by the Communists on the basis of Engels's *Origin of the Family* (and therefore indirectly of Lewis H. Morgan's *Ancient Society*), theories which included a criticism of the 'bourgeois' conception of the family, the doctrine of the economic determination of all human institutions, and references to primordial sexual communism. In the BBC broadcasts, Malinowski argued that marriage and the family are rooted in the deepest needs of human nature and society and are associated with spiritual and material progress. He strongly disagreed with the interpretation of the original domestic institution as a communal body, the maternal clan, based on group-marriage and joint parenthood. For him the individual family, based on marriage in single pairs even in the case of polygyny, was primeval, while Christian monogamy was a later development; but even for the most primitive peoples marriage was regarded as a sacrament, always had an individual character, and often included love. Therefore he implicitly dismissed Briffault's suggestion that marriage had its foundation in economic relations and that particularly in the lower stages of society it could be reduced to an economic transaction. He considered it a distortion of truth to attack marriage on the premise that it is an enslavement of woman by man; on the contrary, primitive marriage was a contract safeguarding the interests of the woman as well as granting privileges to the man. To the theses of the 'prophets of family doom'[21] – such as those of the behaviourists, whom he ironically labelled misbehaviourists – Malinowski replied with a single word: 'rubbish'. Not only did he believe that in Fascist Italy and in Soviet Russia there would be a return to the old order of marriage and family in the end; he was also convinced that the crisis in the Western World was much more talk than reality.

Briffault brilliantly defended his positions, giving a political turn to his talks: he started by declaring that the criticism of marriage did not come from the Bolsheviks or the behaviourists, but 'chiefly from the women of England', constrained by legal and economic disabilities and obliged to assume their husbands' names and nationalities; he contrasted their status with that of women in matrilocal societies, where the women never leave their social group and people. Among many peoples, he said, the common and poor bring up large families without marrying, 'and live at their pleasure in concubinage';[22] only where property is at stake does the legitimacy of marriage and children gain in importance. He also asserted the 'absence of romantic love among savages'[23] – as we shall soon see in more detail – because in their close communities they do not feel the desperate need to be loved which is typical of the 'essentially lonely' civilised man. Ashley Montagu later supported Malinowski's views, stating that Briffault was brilliant and erudite, but not a scientist, and often inaccurate. According to a Communist interpretation given by *Marxism Today*,[24] the organisation of the broadcasts reflected the existing 'bourgeois' hierarchies: Briffault was given a shorter time than Malinowski, to whom the concluding session was attributed, and he was not allowed to include *The Mothers* in the bibliography appended to the subsequent publication of the debate in *The Listener*. However, Montagu asserted that Briffault's criticism of the marriage laws had influenced legislative opinion in the direction of liberalising marriage and divorce. In spite of his belief in a crude sexual division of labour and his ambiguities towards feminism, Briffault forcefully denounced the injustices inflicted upon women throughout history.

However, given his paradoxical literary temperament, as Havelock Ellis put it, he 'even contrived to alienate in some measure the very sex which he has come forth to champion'.[25] First, in spite of maintaining that some of the crucial functions in primitive societies, such as education, are fundamentally feminine, Briffault assigned to women only a small role in the establishment of civilisation. Second, his statements about the licentiousness of women in various peoples inevitably 'aroused horror in the breasts of many feminists, who still cherish the ideals of prim feminine responsibility'.[26] While Briffault would probably have agreed with Ellis on the latter point, on the former – which was more serious – he came under heavy criticism from Ernest Jones as well. Jones wrote a generally positive review of the book in the *International Journal of Psycho-analysis*, but found unconvincing Briffault's sexual division of labour according to which women were responsible, as a result of the maternal instinct, for the development of love and affection as well as of societal bonds, but were considered 'constitutionally deficient in the qualities that mark the masculine intellect' – abstract and generalising, as opposed to concrete and particularising – so that the process of civilisation, a fundamentally intellectual one, was for the most part the work of men. Only several years later was Briffault to accept 'the view stressed by feminists' that the mind of woman was the product of a tradition which had deformed it in order to conserve irrational attitudes, making it entirely different from what that mind could have been if allowed to develop under rational conditions. Briffault deemed it extremely difficult to determine the extent to which psychic sexual differences are cultural and the extent to which they are biological. But at that point he believed that the feminist view was 'in a very large measure true beyond doubt'.[27]

On the question of love, Briffault's basic assumption was that 'the emotional complex which we speak of as love bears no resemblance to a primary and universal impulse of life'.[28] Briffault demonstrated at length the origin of love as passion as distinct from the maternal instinct as well as its distance from sexual relationship. On the basis of a great abundance of anthropological material, he maintained that strong societal bonds exist in primitive societies and, because of this, that romantic love or jealousy were unnecessary. Among people such as the Eskimos, the Northern and Southern American Indians, the New Zealand Maori, and the Eastern, Western and Central African tribes, 'love as understood by the people of Europe' was unknown and was only now appearing 'little by little', having been 'created' by missionaries and colonisers.[29] Among those peoples, courtship, the kiss as a preliminary to love-making, and love-songs were all unknown.[30] 'That in uncultured societies above the lowest levels 'falling in love' occasionally exists among the young people appears probable; but the sentiment, owing to the unfavourable conditions, seems to have no depth and no stability'.[31] Even among Orientals, according to Briffault, no synthesis between the sexual instincts and other sentiments was to be found.[32] On the contrary, among non-Europeans the love of mothers for their offspring was highly developed. But only in certain conditions imposed by the process of civilisation did it give rise to that 'transferred affection' that has become associated with sexual relations; on such affection literature and tradition have had a decisive influence. This means that for Briffault the sentiment called 'romantic love' emerged only as a consequence of repression, like that exercised by the patriarchal family and the Church, and therefore he regarded it as a product of the middle ages and Renaissance. This position explains his ambivalent attitude towards love, and can be seen in his novels.

In the third volume of *The Mothers*, Briffault dedicates two long chapters to 'Romance', analysing the pre-history and origins of courtly love, from Celtic oral literature to heroic romances and to Provençal poetry. This love, he insists, was first to be found in literary works 'in theoretical and abstract form' and was only subsequently extended to actual life. Historically, the repression that created love as an idealized feeling was the 'crusade' led by Simon de Montfort against the Cathars, which destroyed the flourishing civilisation of Southern France and removed the sensuous pleasure in love sung of by the early troubadours. 'Romance', 'romantic sentiments', 'romantic love' are 'nowadays generally understood to refer to a form of amatory sentiment which is distinctive of European feeling, and to which nothing, either in the ancient classical world or in any other culture, exactly corresponds'.[33] Over three centuries of incessant pressure, the christianisation of that pagan literature was achieved, associating the sentiment of love and the notion of chivalry; while the taste for the latter passed, 'the manner in which amatory sentiments and relations were viewed in the romantic love-poetry of the Provençal poets was handed down to the literary tradition of every country in nascent Europe, and has grown into the blood and bone, as it were, of every subsequent European literature'.[34]

In a long footnote,[35] Briffault faces the question of the influence of Arabic poetry, through Spain, on the Provençal troubadours; he admits that the romance specialists do not regard the question as settled, and invokes the contribution of an Arabist, but seems quite inclined to accept this influence, since he recognises the similarity of the feelings expressed in Moorish and in Provençal poetries, and even refers to the 'elegant semi-Oriental culture of Provence'.[36] During the Second World War Briffault enlarged and rewrote the two chapters on Romance in French in order to produce his book on *Les Troubadours* (1945) showing a remarkable knowledge both of this language and of Provençal poetry as well as of the literature upon it. In *Les Troubadours* he states quite clearly that 'la scolastique amoureuse courtoise tirait de l'Islam son origine'.[37] The very long and complex dispute in favour of and against the Arabic influence on Provençal poetry and sentiments had lasted throughout the nineteenth century,[38] and can be considered a touchstone of Eurocentrism (see Chapter 5). It is significant that Briffault, whose Eurocentrism was evident in the field of courtly/romantic love, took an anti-eurocentric position on this vexed question. In general, he believed, as he made abundantly clear in many of his writings, and particularly in the attack on nationalism in culture to which he devoted a whole chapter of *Reasons for Anger* (1937), that 'every one of the European cultures which pretends today to preserve itself pure and undefiled from alien contamination owes its own growth and development to international contacts'.[39]

What is interesting in this conception is first of all that Briffault indicates the circularity between literature and public taste (the former having imposed on the latter standards that would later be imposed on the former by the latter) as a factor in the genesis of courtly and romantic love, since 'ultimately it is not possible to separate literature from life'. Secondly, he insists on the role of violence and cruelty in enforcing and diffusing the notion of 'platonic love' and the idealisation of marriage, a violence that cancelled two of the main themes of Provençal poetry, those of physical pleasure and of the difference between love and marriage; it was 'the persistent and strenuous influence of Patristic ideals in their fiercest, crudest, and most uncompromising form' for over ten centuries which transformed the heritage of early European poetry into the 'insane vilification of sex and the visionary exaltation of virginity' and introduced 'the sentimental idealisation of the sex relation' into the tradition of European sentiment.[40] The only merit that Briffault awards to romanticism is that in the period following the French Revolution it acted as a revolt, particularly on the part of women, against marriages arranged for reasons of property.[41]

Not only is romantic emotion the product of very recent cultural processes; its power is also being eroded, due to the much greater freedom of social intercourse between women and men, and the greater physical activity and development of sport. In European civilisation the repression of the sexual instincts has resulted in nervous disturbances, religious phenomena, romantic passion and masturbation, all features – of both the highest and the most deplorable sides of our culture – unknown in primitive societies. Therefore, the personal character of sexual attraction is not the cause of monogamous society, but its product.[42] Gordon Rattray Taylor, who edited the abridged version of The Mothers, commented that the whole picture is rendered incomprehensible by the lack of strong fathers and of the Oedipal complex as an explanation of incestuous fears, since The Mothers only studies societies where women were dominant, and ascribes this to the fact that Briffault derived his psychology from Shand and not from Freud.[43] As Briffault had summarized in the first volume of The Mothers his criticism of Freud, he could not accept the concept of the unconscious, which he reduced to 'no other than the natural biological mind as physiologically inherited';[44] as a consequence the idea of an endopsychic conflict was unknown to Briffault, for whom it was only 'the socially and traditionally acquired mind' that exercised a repressing action on the natural mind.

The reception of The Mothers was mixed, with several criticisms which Briffault resented, but the book was also praised and its author became very well known. The Times Literary Supplement considered it 'a swing back to Bachofen', but acknowledged it as a testament to the value of the historical and relativist standpoint.[45] Ernest Jones reviewed it, as we have seen, in the International Journal of Psycho-analysis, while Freud and Suttie used it for their work. Jones, however, was critical not only of Briffault's positions on the sexual division of labour but also of the lack of psycho-analysis underlining his work; the index included neither Totem and Taboo nor Group Psychology by Freud. While this was consistent with Briffault's ideas, it was much less clear why he did not give adequate recognition to the 'number of distinguished workers in this field who have argued along lines similar to his own – of some of the most notable he speaks disparagingly', as Havelock Ellis also noted in the New York Birth Control Review. Ellis thought that this was because Briffault liked to feel that he was standing alone against the world, engaged in a deliberate and violent challenge to what was regarded as orthodox, and this resulted in a severe limitation to the fine working of an 'intensely active mind'.[46] Briffault's reaction was true to this diagnosis. Ten years later, in his novel *Europa in Limbo*, he presented the negative reviews of a book by its protagonist as those of 'Old Haverstock Wallace, the authority on sexual perversion... in a rag devoted to the advertisement of rubber goods', and by 'Professor Bronislawski, who had obtained much honour in England by proving the accuracy of the story of Noah's Ark' and had gone so far as to approach the Home Secretary and the Archbishop of York with a view to having the book suppressed on the grounds of immorality.[47] The reaction of the novel's protagonist, Briffault's *alter ego*, is to entirely repudiate the comments by the reviewers: for Julian,

> [their] animus was so patently unintelligent and unjust that it was deprived of all sting. He laughed heartily over the concentrated bile of the poor anonymous curate of the *Times Literary Supplement*, a clerical and reactionary sheet in which it were a humiliation and condemnation to be praised.[48]

But he also felt a growing sense of isolation and estrangement from his own country, a physical and not simply intellectual loneliness. 'He was made to feel as though he were almost a pariah'. Julian had at first imagined 'with a simplicity which afterwards made him smile, that his own scientific work might be regarded as qualifying him for some teaching post – if not at one of the universities, at least in some school or other'.[49] If we may transpose a similar hope to Briffault, it is true that *The Mothers* did not bring to him – either in novels or in life – any academic recognition or any post, although it did bring some fame to its author.

While *The Mothers* was fairly widely read for the first three decades after its publication – being reprinted as a single volume, reduced and edited by Gordon Rattray Taylor in 1952 – after that period it went into oblivion. It had played an important role in highlighting the question of the power and value of women in an era of strong contradictions brought about by the processes of liberation and emancipation. In this sense not only does it have a crucial place in Briffault's intellectual biography, offering the intellectual basis for similar ideas which were then expressed in his novels, but it is also representative of the cultural debates typical of the interwar period. It anticipates the research and reflection on the great mother and the great goddess which were developed on anthropological, archaeological, mythological and psychological grounds by Robert Graves, Erich Neumann, E.O. James in later decades. In recent times, the theme has reappeared in connection with women's studies and the history and pre-history of religion in the area defined as 'old Europe' – south-eastern Europe including parts of the Middle East – in the period

6,500–3,500BC,[50] and with the psychological transformations necessary to an age which takes 'the return of the goddess' as a symbol of the general re-evaluation of the feminine in our societies.[51]

Europa, the mythological figure revived in Briffault's most successful novels, is already present in *The Mothers* in connection with the theme of the divine bull in ancient Middle Eastern religion, where it represented the soul of the world residing in the moon and symbolising the source of generative power. Such a cult was to be found in Crete, 'as the myths of the Minotaur and of Europa show'.[52] Briffault insisted on the matriarchal character of society in Crete, a veritable 'Isle of Women', on the self-possessed independence of Cretan women, and their dominant role in religion, which he inferred from the predominance of female over male figures in art.[53] Briffault added that in other cultures too, for example the Celtic and North American, an identification was established between the horns of cattle and the lunar crescent, and a contrast was formed between women and bulls, the latter representing agriculture – as pullers of the plough – and being connected with the transfer of agricultural work from women to men. Therefore the myth of Europa was understood by Briffault as a part of the larger mythology of the 'Great Mother' or the 'primitive goddess' associated with the functions and activities of women in early human societies. This interpretation is a clue to understanding the identification between the protagonist of his first novel and the Phoenician princess.

## *Europa* and *Europa in Limbo*

The Russian princess Daria Nevidof appears for the first time in Briffault's novel *Europa* in the Rome of the late 1890s, at an exhibition attended by many local and foreign aristocrats. On her arrival, late as she always is, there is 'a general commotion' which makes people think that royalty has arrived, and they watch Daria admiringly:

> ... people were standing aside, making way for the tall woman who had just entered accompanied by Commendatore Lecci. With a quick athletic step, she walked across the hall. She wore a dress of soft black velvet and a Van Dyck hat with a large white feather... Her eyes looked straight in front of her from under long, dark brows that almost met in the middle and stood out pencilled against her milk-white skin.

In the following scene she meets the only two people in the room who have a sense of art and beauty, the painter Martin, who will admire Daria's competence in art, and young Julian, protagonist of the novel (and a fictional representation of Briffault himself), who remains dazed at the sight of her, since 'he had never seen, he thought, such beauty'. Daria turns out to be not only sensitive to art, but also careless of conventions, since she does not seem to notice, as her sister-in-law has done with disgust, Martin's 'very crumpled suit of tweeds' and the 'lamentable signs of age' of his shoes. On the contrary, Daria finds him 'a very distinguished man', and accepts an invitation to visit his studio and to pose for him. When, later, Julian meets Daria again in Paris, he will be shown her collection of paintings:

> ... [containing] a number of portraits of herself which presented a curious variety of styles. Julian saw with pleasure her picture by James Martin. It contrasted with those of Lavery, Carrière, Antonio de la Gandara, which were concerned with rendering the sensuous beauty and elegance of their subject. In Martin's picture the background of suggested luxurious beauty was subordinated to a tragic light which shone out from the face. It reminded him of Eleonora Duse.

We are not told in how many of those paintings Daria was portrayed as Europa. But the connection through art between the continent and the woman continues in another feature: the two share the tragedy of decline. Daria is perfectly well aware of the fact that she belongs to a sinking world; given her lucid intelligence she has a very clear picture of the global situation, but she also perceives that her fate is doomed like that of the continent, although at the same time she rejoices at the concurrent end of injustice and corruption. The imagined sculpture of Europa/Daria which opens the novel is associated with decay: not only does it end up in an agglomerate of useless objects described by Briffault in negative terms – 'clutter', 'bric-à-brac', 'decayed', 'seedy' – it is also a biscuit reproduction of a marble original. In the epoch of the mechanical reproducibility of art works analysed by Walter Benjamin, it is all too coherent that Briffault gives a central role in his novel to a 'reproduction', alluding at the same time to decay and to a type of art reproducible for the masses. At the end of *Europa in Limbo* – the follow-up Briffault wrote after the great success of the first volume – the equivalence between the woman and the culture she represents is proclaimed explicitly. Daria is by now in Soviet Russia, directing the hospital for civilian women and children into which she has transformed her ancient palace; of all her works of art she has kept only a reproduction of Peugh's statue of herself as Europa. Almost unrecognisable physically due to fatigue and premature ageing, she is still powerful, indeed more so, thanks to her forceful insight. It is almost as if the spirit of continent, in the form of the usual allegory that artists used for Europe, a beautiful and majestic woman, were speaking through Daria's lips:

> I am glad... that I have lived to see the crumbling down of all that gilded putrescence, carious with unspeakable iniquity... But I can never be a part of the new world that will eventually grow out of present ruin. I belong to that

hollow world that is now irrevocably dead. I cannot help it. They used to call me 'Europa,' she said, with a faint flicker of a smile, glancing at the reproduction of Peugh's statue of the symbolic goddess and the bull which stood on a table near by. 'I shall pass away with the old Europe to which I belong, thankful that I have witnessed its end'.

Such a tone is possible because the author of these lines considered himself a communist – although never joining the Communist Party – and felt himself a part of the new world emerging from the ruins of the old. If the East for Mottram's Europa and her promise of regeneration of the male/female relationship was the fabulous Orient concentrated in Venice, Briffault's Europa cannot but come from Russia, and reflect its contradictions. In his other book, *Breakdown: The Collapse of Traditional Civilisation*,[54] Briffault saw the end not only of the cycle of Western civilisation based on class divisions, but of 'traditional civilisation itself', although he was still very optimistic about the whole process: 'when traditional civilisation shall have crumbled down, an opportunity will for the first time be afforded for the re-education as well as for the organisation of mankind'.[55] To create a new humanity 'will require exactly one generation, though it may take longer for the present race of malicious maniacs to die out'.[56] Not only did Briffault defend the censorship of the classics applied by the new education in Soviet Russia; he believed that the classics of Russian literature, which were – like the whole of Western literature – 'saturated with the insane and immoral premises of traditional civilisation', should be not merely expurgated, but 'withheld entirely from the new humanity', so that the mind of the human race would be allowed time to recover. The *Times Literary Supplement* reacted negatively to these views as 'entirely mechanic', millenaristic and devoid of any understanding of the attendant philosophical problems.[57]

While Briffault saw the signs of the collapse of European civilisation everywhere in the continent, *Europa* translates this view into a narrative form. The narrating first person is that of an English journalist, friend of the protagonist Julian Bern, through whose eyes, as a boy, Daria/Europa is first seen. The journalist is writing in London during the early 1920s, when he meets an artist – the sculptor Peugh, maker of 'Europa' – whose flash-backs introduce us to Julian's family's life in the 1890s. Other flashbacks are provided by the journalist, remembering what his friend Julian has told him about his own childhood and adolescence, so that reminiscences in the first person alternate with a third person or impersonal narration. Peugh reappears at various times in the novel, and is significant in its structure, although the sculptor does not play any specific role in the plot. For instance, he reappears at the centre of the novel, at the exact point where the protagonist meets Daria again, after having drifted away from her and her daughter, and starts the slow process of getting in touch with

Zena again. The novel opens with the casual encounter between Peugh and the journalist in a fashionable café in London, where the after-theatre crowd is a mixture of elegant ladies and art critics. Peugh recalls Bern, Julian's father, modelled on Briffault's father Charles, paralleling Julian's link with Briffault himself. Mr Bern is presented in a flattering light as somebody who never made a real career out of his diplomatic post in spite of being 'a man carved in the grand manner', who would have deserved to be made ambassador. But he was 'a bit queer', almost 'a little mad', and had 'curious notions far too original for the fellows in Downing Street', such as the idea that England ought to compel Europe to disarm and federate. As we saw in the previous chapter, this idea had been revived during the 1920s and 1930s. We do not know whether Charles Briffault actually thought this; however, we know that he was a confidant of very important politicians and a friend of the Prince of Wales (one of Robert's earliest recollections was having breakfast with the future Edward VII). His double in the novel is portrayed as closely associated with the European idea, and the association reappears in *Europa in Limbo*: when in Switzerland Julian meets an English feminist participating in a women's congress for permanent peace, and she tells him that they are going to campaign for a League of Nations, he reacts ironically and exclaims: 'Shade of my father! What is a nation?'[58]

In an amusing scene in the first novel, Mr Bern is shown going to see Lord Salisbury with a plan for a united Europe with its capital in Rome, 'the only thing that could have permanently saved England'. Lord Salisbury considers him a madman, proposing an alliance with France with backing from the United States, and dismisses him with contempt: 'My dear sir, that is not within the realm of practical politics'. After that interview Mr Bern dedicates himself to coins and pottery, and keeps a salon in Rome where writers, artists and aristocrats meet and have conversations on all sorts of topics. A major aim of *Europa* is to show that the destiny of Europe, given that any plan such as Mr Bern's was unfeasible because of the politicians' blindness, could only be towards decadence and disgregation. Europe has grown 'from savage infancy to disillusioned age', and Western civilisation 'is cracking', we learn from Mr Bern's guests. Even Nietzsche is introduced into the scene, as a 'strange German professor' coming from Sorrento to visit Mr Bern. Nietzsche explains that Christianity had 'reduced Europe to a stupefied continent' robbing it of its Roman heritage, and therefore of 'all intelligence and meaning'. These words have a particular significance for young Julian, educated as a Protestant, while his sister was brought up as a Catholic, due to an agreement between his Anglican father and his Irish Catholic mother. But Julian dislikes the attitudes of religious people as a whole, their narrowness and dogmatism or their indifference and hypocrisy, 'the gigantic lie' of religion possessing the world. His mother burns books by Zola, and a friend of hers, a Catholic priest, is infuriated when Julian reads Darwin's *The Origin of Species*, a presage of Julian's vocation for biology.

Conversing on Mr Bern's *loggia*, Nietzsche 'called himself a good European and an immoralist', repudiating nationalism, advocating for the European man the task of becoming really civilised, but admitting that 'Europe, as a political configuration, may have, incidentally, to be suppressed and destroyed in the process'.[59] Mr Bern observes bitterly that perhaps only the Japanese, engaged in annexing China, 'might arouse Europe to a sense of unity', and the narrating voice comments: 'Europe was drifting whither they knew not, in the hands of a Fate which seemed mysterious and imperscrutable', because they were unable to discern the realities of facts around them.[60] As in a counterpoint, a Roman cardinal, friend of his mother, explains to Julian that 'the unescapable tradition of the European world' is 'the tradition of Christendom', and so it must go on, 'unless European civilisation should be utterly wiped out'.[61] For the cardinal, who claims descent from the Roman King Numa, the Catholic Church is the only guardian of the tradition of ancient Rome, out of which the European mind grew. And this church will not perish, while the British Empire is already showing signs of weakness.

The Europe presented by Briffault is a continent of blindness and folly. The novel takes place in an aristocratic cosmopolitan ambiance, seen through the eyes of Julian, who does not belong to it by birth, although his paternal aunt has married into it, becoming the conservative and narrow-minded Lady Penmore. She has paid for Julian to continue his education, after a private school in Rome, in an English public school, the only way – she deems – to become an English gentleman. There Julian discovers 'the atrocity of education' designed to keep the minds of the boys 'entirely undergrown',[62] while women are often more intelligent simply because they are less subjected to education. He then proceeds to Cambridge to study biology and starts a scientific career under the guidance of Sir Anthony Fisher, whose views are similar to those of Michurin and Lysenko on the interaction between the germ plasm and the surrounding environment. Such biological views, materialist and dialectical, were actually formulated in the 1930s: Briffault often attributed to his characters ideas which were not current until later.

Julian not only moves freely in aristocratic circles, but also falls in love with a member of the aristocracy. As a boy in Rome (in the 1890s) he had met Daria, independent and wealthy (being divorced). Enchanted as he was by her, Julian will not fail to fall in love with her younger daughter, Zena, 'the very image of her mother'. Julian's love is reciprocated, but is impossible for social reasons. Zena's uncle and Daria's brother, Prince Nevidof, is a fabulously rich man, divorced from the sister of the queen of Serbia, who has frustrated his love with her frigidity, so that he has given himself over to orgies where the knout plays an important part. Prince

Nevidof arranges Zena's marriage to a Russian aristocrat, a gambler and a homosexual, who spends enormous amounts of her money.

Julian does not share his father's hopes for a united Europe, because for him, just like Briffault, Europe is doomed, and its significance lies mainly in the set of traditions that go back to ancient Rome and medieval Christendom).[63] However, in many ways, Julian is a good European. Since adolescence he has been accustomed to moving freely through Europe, and to speaking and reading many languages: the novel includes expressions in Russian, French, Italian, German, Latin and ancient Greek. Julian feels that

> civilised European countries were one community. You went from one country to another, and you could scarcely tell who was the native and who was the foreigner;... it was no more difficult to take a train across Europe than to take a bus or a tram-car. Ever since he could remember he had travelled up and down Europe, to England, or to the Tyrol, to Switzerland, to Florence, and Venice, and the Lakes.[64]

While Julian's father could still remember when people had to have things called passports, nowadays European life was international. Europeans shared customs and feelings, including attitudes towards love and women. While in Africa 'the savages have no sentiments at all about women', European civilisation has built in men a lewd obsession with the female body, and in women a repression of their sexual drives. As a reaction to his own disillusionment with Zena, Julian himself accepts only physical desire, thinking love a fraud, until he discovers, meeting her again, that real sexual satisfaction cannot be separated from love and reciprocal dedication.

In spite of feeling at his ease everywhere, Julian casts on Europe the eye of a stranger. From Rome to the Cote d'Azur, from London to Berlin, from Paris to Bayreuth, he moves in high society and observes its vacuity, its perversions, its dissolute living. But he is not happier with the lower classes. He sees the misery of the English working class as well as its servility; when he goes to Wigan to follow the coal-strike, he recognises the courage of many workers, but also notices their lack of connection with the other classes, of political education, and of adequate strategy. He also remembers meeting 'a collier's son, an exceptionally brilliant and genial fellow' who had succeeded in getting an education and becoming a teacher and a writer. Briffault thus introduces D.H. Lawrence – without mentioning his name – Julian meeting him in the offices of the *English Review*. Julian asked him about the coal strike, but he was 'not in the least interested. He was interested in sex, in some queer, muddled, mystically materialistic views of his which sought to reconcile sexual sensuality with the sublime';[65] Julian reacted by lecturing the man on his 'two million brothers fighting for their mere bread', but the writer just smiled benevolently.

Julian himself, however, did little for the workers, due to his disillusionment with all forms of political ideas and action: Ruskin and Morris represented to him 'afternoon-tea socialism',[66] and the Fabians were prisoners of their illusions about political education; the German Social Democrats, whom he would have supported after listening to Rosa Luxemburg and Karl Liebknecht in Berlin, voted for the war credits. Thus he agreed to leave Germany with Zena, as Daria had advised and already done herself. He realised that men such as Liebknecht and Jean Jaurès would regard him as a coward, an egoist and escapist, and yet 'gladly, gladly would he give his life, in strength of combat or in death, if only he could believe that he would thereby have effected anything'.[67] These could well be words that Briffault attributed to himself and his own attitude to politics.

*Europa* ends with Julian and Zena leaving Berlin. In *Europa in Limbo*, they escape to England from Belgium just before the Germans invade; Zena leaves for Saint Petersbourg where her sister is sick, but Julian will be able to join her only much later, after he has served in the army and has been wounded. He is totally disillusioned, having witnessed the profiteering in munitions supply and international finance which sacrifice the destinies of whole peoples to the interests of a few national governments, banks and financiers (it is in this context that the very wealthy Jewish banker Baron Rubinstein appears, negotiating the exploitation of Prince Nevidof's oilfields). Convalescent, Julian is sent to Switzerland where he meets the Honourable Eleanor Astley, militant feminist, pacifist, social reformer, so depressed by the failure of her efforts that she has just survived an attempted suicide. After meeting Lenin on his way to Russia, Julian goes there too, and finds Zena and her mother, but both of them will later die in the armed clashes between the Reds and the Whites. He returns to England in complete poverty and is found sleeping on a bench in a park by his friend the narrator of both novels. The only job Julian is offered is an editorial post in the United States, and he leaves in order to take it.

The key to understanding the role of Europe in Briffault's vision is the figure of Princess Daria. She is presented as a wise woman, somehow ageless, with an authoritative knowledge of the world, and yet uncorrupted in spite of living in it. Daria is really one of the mothers studied by Briffault, as her identification with Europa shows. She not only poses as Europa, she is actually referred to by that name. Men, Daria tells Julian while she is posing for his teacher painter, have built the world on thought and words, making it 'only a bare, stark skeleton. It is we women who save it from drying up.'[68] Julian is adopted by her from their first meeting and will feel 'monstrously happy' when a few years later Daria, Zena and himself, 'like a family party' make an excursion in Daria's big car from Viareggio to Pisa.[69] Daria becomes more literally his mother when his romance with Zena starts again, at the beginning of 1914. At this point she can legitimately call her two daughters and Julian 'my children', when explaining the situation at the verge of war and advising them to leave Germany as soon as possible. Daria is capable of foreseeing political events, such as the murder of Alexander of Serbia,[70] and expresses deep worry over the destiny of Europe, as when she fears that the intrigues of the pan-Slavists financed by her sister-in-law will bring war and probably 'the ruin of Europe'.[71] Shortly before her death, in Soviet Russia, she undergoes the gender transformation which symbolically affects old women in primitive societies, when they became recognised as able to perform male roles without losing feminine characteristics: her voice has 'taken on a masculine depth, through the harshness of which could yet be distinguished the old undertone of kindness'.[72]

When she appears in the novel as a girl, Zena is presented as similar to her mother: 'her laughter was like Princess Daria's. She had her eyebrows too, long and darker than the hair'.[73] When Julian meets her again, years later, the similarity has become even more striking: 'her beauty had blossomed out into fuller richness, and her likeness to her mother, although she was much fairer in complexion, had become accentuated. She had the same figure and carriage, but she retained her girlish look.'[74] Zena is an example of a good mind which would like to learn, but which has been denied a proper education. She is 'a real grown modern woman',[75] and yet 'overflowing with merriment', but not frivolous, so that she is also the perfect image of the modern child-woman, with a freshness and enthusiasm for life evident in her sexual straightforwardness with Julian: she is the one who pushes Julian to 'leave no drop of ecstasy untasted', reaching 'with untutored ingenuity towards ever new extravagances'.[76]

Zena is close to 'nature', in Briffault's sense, i.e. close to that pagan sensuality that he associates with Italy – where 'peasants still believe in fauns and satyrs'[77] – and far from the denial of heterosexual sex that Briffault attributes to militant women. This denial can take the form of either an ascetic life based on erotophobia, as is the case with a good friend of Julian, the Honourable Eleanor Astley, or of sexual antagonism and perversion (lesbianism, lesbian prostitution), to be found in some feminists and literary *avant garde* women Julian meets (a scene where an English poetess prostitutes herself to a French woman in a high-class brothel in front of Julian and two English ladies was partially cut in the British version of the novel). Suffragists are presented in *Europa* as courageous and right, but they are also ridiculed for their narrowness, being referred to as 'militant virgins of suffrage',[78] 'amazons':[79] for Briffault they fail to perceive that the right of parliamentary franchise is the first step along a long road which should do away with marriage, Christian morality, modesty, pudence and introduce promiscuity in sexual relations.[80]

The love theme cast against the background of European politics and culture is that of reciprocal but impossible and distant love, a *Leit Motiv* of

European culture. In spite of some periods of happiness together, amidst revolution and war, in the end Julian and Zena will be separated by her death (in *Europa in Limbo*), the result of a stray bullet from the pistol of her husband meant for Julian. *Europa*'s subtitle, *A Novel of the Days of Ignorance*, hinted at the gap between two epochs not only in the different political regimes, but also in their gender relations. In *Sin and Sex* (1931) Briffault had explained that the ideal patriarchal wife belonged to the 'Days of Ignorance', and he feared that those days would be continued in the post-Puritanical value of opposing love and lust.[81] *Sin and Sex* defines love as the 'unnatural association of man and woman', 'a superlatively artificial cultural ideal', with no biological basis, yet leading, for cultured humanity, to the most complete fulfilment of human relations. It is above all in this sense that the love in *Europa* embodies Briffault's general conceptions about love. Zena and Julian are prevented from realising their union first by the violence of property and aristocratic descent, then by the state of disintegration of the old society. Zena belongs to it: 'I am too much of the

Figure 6: American edition of Briffault's second book, with a stylised representation of Europa and the Bull.

old world that is dead. But you know that I never loved it... yet I cannot be of the new world because I looked to the joy of life, and am not strong enough for the joy of strife.'[82] The stylised image of a frail Europa on a powerful bull – which appeared in the American edition of this novel (Figure 6) – might allude to the weakness of present day Europe and its inhabitants as compared with the strength of underlying tendencies towards a new emerging society.

The theme of love in the narration is rather thin, because the main subject of the novel is the description of a way of life. Briffault heaps up, in pages which have the flavour of a direct diary, lists of collections of precious books, of exotic foods, of flowers, of fish and molluscs; lists of aristocrats and their titles, displays of famous names: Julian or his friends see Mata Hari dancing in Berlin; Henry James talking in London surrounded by an attentive audience, 'his hand beating the cadence of his clauses like a metronome';[83] young Mussolini in Rome, a 'bull-headed, bony-faced journalist, short in the legs, holding forth with theatrical gestures'.[84] Vladimir Ilich and Bronstein are mentioned by the Russian subjects of Prince Nevidof, Marx as 'an old German Jew dying in London from the effects of long hardship and privation', sent in vain by the director of the Natural History Museum to the Mediterranean in the hope of prolonging his life.[85]

In this European panorama, the fullest perversity is represented by Russian high society, in which the monk Rasputin has enormous power through his influence on the Tzaritsa, and is himself corrupted and perverse. A taste of Russian sadism is given in the novel when Prince Nevidof – Daria's brother – is concluding a transaction in his fabulous villa near Rome with Baroness Rubinstein on behalf of her husband. The baroness, 'one of the handsomest Jewesses in Europe'[86] and yet 'a prude' who finds Kavarsina's costume too short, faithful to orthodox Judaism, is found cheating at cards, and this gives the prince the chance to indulge his anti-semitism and take revenge for her rejection of his sexual advances. The prince has a collection of ancient instruments of torture in the caves of the villa, and the baroness, stripped of her elegant evening gown, is placed on a platform, her wrists tied by ropes hanging from the ceiling, and is whipped by the Cossack guards in front of the other guests. The scene is one of those that the British censor felt the need to have cut from the American version. The lines taken out included references to Baroness Rubinstein 'showing black armpits' and 'dark-circled breasts', while the Cossacks uncorseted her from 'the billowing satin and silk, the cascading lace and lawn, detaching the creaking brocade, the hems of pearl-colored hose', leaving her diamonds and pearls on 'her full-fleshed oriental nudity', which made one of the prince's guests murmur, 'Moreau's Salomé'. In the English version the central part of the flagellation was also cut:

... again and again the lash fell on the full flesh, the big thighs. Grotesquely, the Jewess sprang from one foot to the other, her belly panting, her breasts dancing... Gheorghii followed round the screaming, writhing, kicking Jewess, whipping her. Beads of blood began to appear on the striped, reddened flesh. The prince, who had been watching with gloating eyes the contorsions of the victim, signed to the man to stop... Two nuns... tended the baroness till she could be assisted to her room.[87]

While this last touch adds a grotesque flavour to Briffault's rendering of the story, some more daring words are in Italian, as in the scene of lesbian prostitutes they are in French. Julian is shown to be 'compelled by a horrible fascination'; he first closes his eyes and then gazes, 'spellbound, as in dream'; Zena herself had confessed to having been excited at watching a rebel peasant and two women relatives of his 'stripped naked' and whipped by Cossacks on the prince's Russian property at Kursk.[88] This peasant has become a revolutionary, has been sent by Lenin to Italy to found Communist cells, and is engaged by the prince's wife – the sister of the murdered queen of Serbia and the same woman who financed a 'Greater Serbia' party devoted to unremitting terrorism – to eliminate the prince so that she can have his huge patrimony. But Daria unmasks her, with Julian's help, and inherits her brother's wealth. Actually, in the second novel the agent reappears – greeted by Julian as '*Hic et ubique*, old mole?' and declares that the prince had already committed suicide when he went to kill him.[89] These events add a touch of criminality to the story, while the allusions to orgies titillate the taste for scandals, as the reviewers noticed. But the scene of the baroness also titillated antisemitism, in a far from edifying way.

These were some of the contradictions in which Briffault became involved in his criticism of the old world, whose attitudes he shared in so many ways. One contradiction is evident in his final view on Europe, which he relegates to limbo. Limbo is, in Briffault's definition, the period between two worlds, the decadent one and the new one emerging from the revolution. In the closing pages of *Europa in Limbo* Julian expresses his political convictions. The Europe he sees has changed: 'not one building stone of it, of the essential core and foundation of it, is left standing!'[90] Europe lingers in limbo, waiting to become the decisive battlefield between the forces of the old and the new because 'it was here, in the heart of old Europe, that the right of sanity and reason was first kindled; and here it will be revived'.[91] In this way he reveals a reversed Eurocentrism mixed with the hope of a European revolution, in the face of which any reformist political action is inadequate. Julian severely scolds his friend Eleanor Astley, struggling for disarmament in a commission of the League of Nations, which he defines as 'grotesque': 'a league of bandits,' he says 'cannot prevent banditry. It is far more likely to promote it. Like all shams, it is not merely grotesque, it is dangerous.'[92]

In the end, the sensational tone of the novel does not totally obscure its political message – if politics is understood as a form of culture – and Briffault's insight into the spirit of the time. His attempt to find a sequel to the decadence of the 'old mothers' like Daria and Zena, and to announce the appearance of a new woman is hinted at in the final pages of *Europa in Limbo*. This book concludes with an exchange between Julian and the Honourable Eleanor Astley, the feminist interested in social reform. *The Mothers* ended with a hymn to the eternal feminine quoted from Goethe, and the words 'honour to those who can be mothers, not in the flesh alone, but in the spirit'.[93] At the end of *Europa in Limbo* Eleanor tells Julian that she wants a child, indirectly replying to the questions that Malinowski had posed in his broadcast debate with Briffault:

> Will women cease to be interested in becoming and being mothers?... will the mothers of the future prefer to carry out individual maternity or will they give over their infants into the hands of the State?... to have the father of their child as their mate and husband?[94]

Eleanor gives a reply which anticipates the behaviour of some women half a century later, choosing a maternity without the commitment of being a wife. To her – a mother in flesh and spirit – the last word is given. When Julian leaves for New York to take up a job as a journalist there, because in England he is suspected of being a Communist and is no longer allowed to write, he receives a telegram from Eleanor saying, 'He lives who will see it'. Julian has no hopes or illusions left; Eleanor – a political militant and a feminist – represents with her child the only hope for a possible future.[95]

For Briffault, the imposing task of summarising the European situation in a book that could be read by vast numbers of people was based on his political and existential convictions as well as on the need to make money to support himself and his second wife. In a letter to his daughter he stated that he had constructed *Europa* very carefully in order to make it a widely-read book: 'I tried to get in every aspect', producing 'a remarkably good salad in which everybody can find something'[96] and added: 'I never had any doubt – not through conceit, on thinking that the book was good, but just from a business point of view'.[97] Briffault did not consider the novel as scientifically important as his other books, among which he valued especially *The Mothers*.

The novel is written with a pedagogical intention: as a popular 'Bildungsroman', it tries to sum up the major intellectual and spiritual trends in European thought during the period considered. But at the same time it aims to become a bestseller, so that the general tone is sensationalist and betrays a taste for scandals that recall pulp fiction and popular magazines. *Europa* is certainly more refined than these, and yet manifests the same curiosity and complacency about the aristocracy's habits and vices, coupled with an implicit revolutionary morality through portrayal of

Prince Nevidof's sadistic pleasures in orgies, Rasputin's rapes of girls, the huge waste of money on extravagant luxuries, and intrigues to bring about war. All these stories are narrated by a participant, and although there is some artificiality in the dialogues, for instance on philosophy and art, a sense of discovery is also perceptible: here is somebody who was lucky enough to be born in that setting, but – like, and more than, his heroine – was able to reveal and expose the intricacies of the old world as well as some of its magnificence.

*Europa* was first of all a success in the United States, where its fabulous sense of atmosphere appeared even more evident than in Europe, and where its criticism of European decadence as well its sensationalism possibly found an audience and a climate nurtured by the media. *The Chicago Journal of Commerce* compared Briffault to Zola and Proust, seeing his 'very great book' as a continuation of Jules Romains's *Men of Good Will* and Thomas Mann's *The Magic Mountain*. However, dissent was also expressed. The *American Review*[98] in a review by Dorothea Brande entitled 'A Bad Novel', attributed the popularity of 'a book so long, so dull, so windy' to its pornography.[99] *Time*, while seeing the similarities, deemed that 'Briffault's old fashioned, awkwardly written first novel cannot be compared with the great post-war novels on the same subject', and judged that the famous historical figures presented in *Europa* were little more than mouthpieces for ideas and opinions. Two years later, when *Europa in Limbo* appeared, *Time* recalled that the first volume had sold as well as it had because 'readers were titillated by its scandalous scenes of pre-War continental society' and judged the second volume 'an earnest, disillusioned, clumsily Voltairian novel'.[100]

The critics' reception of *Europa* in England was not enthusiastic, and its American success invited criticism. For Peter Quennell, writing in the *New Statesman*,[101] it expressed an American, rather a 'Middle-Western view of Europe, excited by a vision of Europe as a hotbed of picturesque debauchery'; the narrative was vivid, but lacking in a genuine sense of style, and the result was an extremely readable melodrama, not a work of any historical or literary importance. 'The result is calculated to keep simple-minded readers in a condition of shocked and envious bewilderment from the first to the last chapters.' In *The Spectator*,[102] Peter Burra found that the main characters of the novel were little more than the links in a cavalcade of glittering scenes, through the sites of the royal, the rich and the famous, and that they did not seem much the weightier for their author's encyclopaedic culture and the parade of knowledge which resulted. Edith Shackleton in *Time and Tide*[103] compared Briffault to the more highly-paid gossip writers in his giving readers an effect of close intimacy with the aristocratic and powerful, making Europa 'a lavish catalogue of luxuries and follies rather than a novel'. *Europa in Limbo* was treated no better. Cyril Connolly in *The New Statesman and Nation*[104] considered it a work of propaganda by a passionate Communist giving free rein to his rabid detestation of English imperialism and English democracy, 'just a bad cartoon' in spite of many interesting glimpses of Europe in wartime.

These harsh criticisms were accurate in their assessment of the book's lack of artistic value, and we have seen that Briffault himself was lucid about them. However, the two novels on Europa remain interesting as examples of a popular genre trying to combine autobiography, history and fiction with a political intent, and it is unfair to judge them as if they were failed works of art. They were written explicitly without any pretentions to literary innovation, often with the immediacy of good reportage,[105] while many passages contain a strong denunciation of political and moral ills. The narrative technique à thèse never allows readers to forget that they are reading about the degeneration of Europe – and, we might add, also about the degeneration of the novel, if we can attribute to Briffault's way of writing some irony about the traditional novel. Briffault mistrusted the 'bourgeois conception' of literature as a series of works of art, reserved for the few and entrenched in old values and privileges, as we have seen with respect to his views on Russian literature and the education of a new humanity. He had a similar outlook towards experimental writing and painting, as we learn from his letters to his daughter, married to a painter, whom he advised to 'cultivate a side-line, such, f.i., as internal decoration. There is no future anywhere for abstract art'.[106] Briffault could have placed himself in the domain of mechanical reproducibility, in Walter Benjamin's sense, where instrumental goals predominate.

This raises a problematic aspect of the writing, the particular inter-connection between it and Briffault's nomadic and cosmopolitan life as well as his political beliefs. His life was relevant to his success as a writer as was implicitly recognised even by his critics. When Europa was published in Britain (1936), the Times Literary Supplement found the book both 'tedious', for the over-display of learning in philosophy and biology, and 'interesting', inasmuch as 'a philosopher and a historian of very considerable erudition', who knew many countries and had met a large number of distinguished people in every rank of life, had 'decided to record something of his experience'.[107] Transforming it into a novel like Europa was the only way of recording that experience for Briffault, who would later turn down all the efforts of his wife and his publisher to induce him to write an autobiography. This refusal was consistent with his suspicion of individualism, which he viewed as part of the heritage of Western civilisation and which he strongly criticised (in spite of being himself individualistic to the extreme), considering the individual a biological and social product.

But the relationship between writing and living is more complicated than can be assumed by interpreting Briffault's life as simply offering material for his novels. Let us consider Julian, his alter ego: he too is a wanderer, and considers himself a Communist, but not one who would ever belong to a party. Like Briffault, Julian displays an intelligent understanding of the European situation, with rage and hatred for the 'monstrous enemy'. He is in dispute with the social system and with education, which 'amputates the mind', is critical of everything, and cannot identify himself with anything, not only in politics, but also in daily life. In *Europa in Limbo* Julian fails to find an adequate job in Britain, turns to writing and takes up an editorial job in New York. Briffault too had no settled place, and could not accept the relationships and the compromises that would have allowed him to have one. (By a bitter irony of destiny, Briffault was denied the possibility that Julian had – a revenge of reality over the novel.)

The tension between living and writing should not, however, be lost by seeing the two as indistinguishable, as some critics and biographers have done. Julian Bern is not a simple imitation of Robert Briffault, however romanticised. His characterisation is a way of vindicating and healing the autobiographical experiences of his writer, sometimes rather crudely, as when Julian defeats his adversaries in the public school or goes to the United States to find a job: the narration seems almost a daily reverie, whereby Briffault corrects his own life story, as we have already seen with the fictional book reviews of Julian's work, which satirised the detractors of Briffault's books. However, this role disadvantages the fictional character, over-subordinating him to his author's need to be a pedagogue: Julian is often petulant, like a boring preacher, purporting to know better and explaining everything to women who love him (more so in *Europa in Limbo*), thus taking on too often the role of the teacher that its author was never allowed to be, although he probably would have made a very good one. Writing his novels gave Briffault the chance to appropriate a world which still attracted him, but also of throwing upon it his contempt, his sarcasm, his malediction and his hopes of regeneration; his readers were offered the same possibility, and they appreciated it. However, the instrument for performing this operation remained too much of a tool for compensation and revenge. If 'loss and rage have a dominant role in the creation of the text's subjective world',[108] the two novels by Briffault do not go far enough in creating that subjective world, and therefore the fantasies embodied in them lead to the world which they seemed to have left behind[109] in only a very partial way, with too limited a strength. The core of the drama remains the experiences of its author in his time.

## Life and death of a nomadic subject

For Briffault, the interconnection between life and work is seen not only in his novels, but also in the attitudes expressed in his essays. Briffault's attitude of praise, but no great intellectual respect, for the cultural role of the mother found its counterpart in his attitude to Britain. He developed an increasing resentment towards Britain, a sort of love/hate relationship based both on political convictions, which made him oppose the imperialistic nature of his country, and on personal grounds, since he felt insufficiently appreciated in his homeland. According to a psychological interpretation, Briffault reproduced in his feelings towards England the love/hate that he had nourished towards his own severe and unaffectionate mother, his father having been warm and understanding.[110] A document has been saved that lends strength to this hypothesis: a letter from Briffault's father to his son as a boy, after he had made his mother cry by telling her a lie, that Easter vacations started on Holy Thursday rather than on Friday. The letter, dated 9 April 1882, adjured nine-year old Robert never to lie again and affectionately bestowed upon him a duty:

> Mon cher petit Robert bien aimé,
> Je voudrais beaucoup que tu saches bien que je compte sur toi pour me remplacer auprès de ta mère quand il aura plu à Dieu de me séparer de vous deux… ta mère ne m'a jamais fait un moment de peine et je lui dois le seul bonheur que j'aie eu dans la vie.[111]

In the second part of his life Robert showed a certain indifference to family ties. He corresponded intensely with his daughter Joan, but saw her very rarely, and never met his grandchildren (by his son), who lived in New Zealand. However, he translated his father's recommendations into a fierce battle for truth and justice in his books and political beliefs.

For an orphan of Britain, the United States might have been a good stepmother. Briffault had been welcomed there and invited to give lectures in colleges and universities, often greeted with 'quite an ovation', as happened in Hanover, New Hampshire in March 1929.[112] He was asked to sign many copies of his book besides autograph albums, and enjoyed the atmosphere of the college:

> … browsing room, log-fires burning in the manorial chimney… the people, the professors, are charming… I don't think I ever so much appreciated the company of men. There are practically no women.[113]

In the US Briffault was given the chance to enjoy something that he had never had in Britain, the intellectual homo-eroticism of an academic environment. This could well be coupled with an appreciation of American women, who 'do take the biscuit for daintiness and elegance – even beat the French women at that game – and at others!'. In 1930 Briffault married an American divorcee, Herma Olive Mullins, then Hoyt, twenty-five years younger than him. After spending some time in New York, the two went to live in Paris, although they continued to travel overseas quite often. Both he and Herma, Briffault wrote to his daughter in 1932, had often thought of 'transplanting' themselves to New York, but he did 'not really believe in silly optimism, in toothpaste advertisement grins, which is the faith of this country'.[114] But he had written *Europa* at the suggestion of some American friends, and found it easier to publish the novel in the US than in Britain. The original American version was dedicated to Kyle S. Crichton (1896–1960), born in Pennsylvania of Scottish parents, his father a miner. After working in coal mines and steel mills, Crichton became an editor and author of biographies and plays (under the pen name of Robert Forsythe). Briffault stayed with him in his house in the Bronx when he went to New York and made him his representative in the US.

In the early months of 1935, Briffault complained from Paris to his daughter Joan that in London 'they are still debating whether a book can be published which speaks disrespectfully of the Habsburgs and hints that they all have the pox'.[115] In the last years he and Herma had money problems, like many others, with the collapse of the pound and dollar, and lived in 'frightful uncertainty'.[116] They succeeded in finding a 'very cheap tiny cottage' at Cagnes-sur-mer and moved there, where he received the first copy of *Europa* in September 1935 and announced triumphantly to his daughter:

> ... over 6,000 copies were sold long before publication. It is an enormous success and they are reprinting editions as fast as they can. All the chief American papers had long front-page reviews... Dollars keep rolling in by every mail (letter of 18 September). [117]

News kept coming that the sales were up to 15,000, and a third edition was being printed in the US. The cover was not to Briffault's liking: 'not the style we are used to in England' (it looks in fact dull in colour and design), and he 'chaffed' Scribner about it; 'but nothing matters as long as it sells,' he added, informing Joan that the book was 'topping the bestseller list, beating well-known authors like Willa Cather, Hugh Walpole, Thomas Wolfe. Scribner's manager writes that they simply can't keep pace with the orders, and the printers are working day and night.' His insistence on money was due not only to the fact that he badly needed it in order to repay a huge bank debt taken on in the previous years, but also to his attitude of detachment from his novel, which he defined as 'Roman ohne Wert', the 'worthless novel', joking with Joan on the pun 'Muster ohne Wert' [sample only] – words that had to be written on parcels containing books – and not 'a real thought book'. This was why he did not care to receive the reviews, but Herma kept the advertisements for the book, which were getting 'bigger and bigger' in the American newspapers.[118]

By 1937 *Europa* had sold 200,000 copies in the USA, showing that the public loved the book. In England too, after an initial coldness, there were several editions of the book. Offers for translations kept coming in from many countries, but the German one was doubtful, as 'there is no Germany now'. Joan and her husband Willi were still living in Berlin, and

Briffault insisted that they leave. When he went to Moscow in October 1935, he stopped for a night in Berlin in order to see Joan, although no more than a night, because he was always rushing from place to place. From Moscow he went to Paris, then on to Brussels and London. Later that year he visited Bolivia, about which he sent information to Joan and Willi as a possible place to migrate. A German translation was fixed up with Piper in Munich in 1936, but they published it in Vienna so as to avoid censorship.[119] At that point Briffault was 'losing count' of the translations, and the 'damned book was going in England almost as well as in America. 10,000 copies sold before the end of the first week.'[120] There were rumours about transforming the book into a play and into a film. In the autumn of 1936 Briffault was convinced that both were well under way,[121] and there was news that the well-known American scenarist Robert Buckner was working on a dramatisation of the book, although nothing came of these possibilities. In August 1937, the *New York Times* reported that Kyle Crichton, as Briffault's representative in the US, had declared that no deal for a motion picture would be contemplated until the second novel was published.[122] No subsequent trace of such plans has been found in the available documentation.

At the beginning of 1937, Briffault was again in Paris, working intensively on the sequel to *Europa*, at the insistence of Scribner. Joan had moved to Chile, and her father, again in New York for *Europa in Limbo*, could write 'from – at least – the same continent'. Of the new book, which the publishers had sent to the printers without reading, so that he could have the proofs ready in a week ('a fair record for a long book'), Briffault wrote: 'I don't think it will be as popular as the last, though I fancy it is really better'.[123] Success had not changed his life-style. He still wandered, forcing Herma to move frequently, which she hated. In the tiny cottage at Cagnes, she had found a friend in the painter Stella Bowen, who lived next door as a guest of Ruth Harris from New York. Bowen described the village as 'that charming old muddle of houses which crowns a steep conical hill between Antibes and Nice', and admired the Briffaults' cottage, which did not look very good from the outside: but 'once inside, you found yourself on the top story of an old house that clung to the side of a cliff'. It had a garden and overlooked the sea. While in Paris the Briffaults had been 'hard-up, hard-working and worried'; now, owing to the success of Robert's book, Herma was having a chance to exercise those domestic gifts 'that were her special glory. There was never such a cook, such a born home-maker, such a trainer-up of docile little maid-servants as Herma Briffault'; her culinary standards were so high that Stella Bowen was very worried when she invited the Briffaults to dinner. Herma told Stella Bowen that they had moved eleven times in twelve years: 'each time she had transformed a mediocre habitation into a home of charm'. The fact that 'Robert was an inveterate rolling stone was a real grief to her', because in the end he 'always pulled up his stakes and the maid-servant wept and the siamese cats got upset and Herma had to start all over again'.[124]

Herma Briffault – as she continued to call herself until her death at some point after 1975 – had many other skills from which she made her living: she was an excellent translator, editor and ghost-writer who could turn incoherent material into lucid and persuasive prose. She ghosted several books doing a significant amount of research for them, such as a biography of César Ritz (1936) signed by his widow; she 'learned a lot about food and wine interviewing the great chefs that had trained under Escoffier in the various hotels where Ritz and Escoffier – an inseparable team – had reigned'. In 1936 she edited *Reasons for Anger* by her husband, 'almost a year's work, running to earth widely-scattered essays and arranging them coherently – without a byline, alas'.[125] During all the years in Paris she typed and proof-read her husband's writings, without any public recognition of her work. Among her few recognised translations are those of essays by Curzio Malaparte, published in the *Yale Review* in 1935–36.

In March 1938, in Paris, Briffault had a clear and desperate sense of his own contradictions in the disastrous situation of Europe, which he blamed on Britain as the real culprit in the 'barbarisation of Europe'. In the same year, 1938, he published his book on *The Decline and Fall of the British Empire*, in which he prophesied the end of British domination in Asia and the collaboration of the English people with the rest of the human race, when 'England will have ceased to exist':

> Heaven knows that no one detests and despises England as I do now. It is the real villain of the barbarisation of Europe which is now in full swing – the real culprit. As I said in one of my pieces lately, if a monster casts men, women and children to the wild beasts, one does not blame the wild beasts.

Worried by the possibility that his daughter and her husband would return from South America to Europe (which in the end they did not), by the prospects of his own survival based totally on freelance writing, by the vicissitudes touching the great figures of Europe ('old Freud has had all his belongings confiscated and is a prisoner'), and by his own contradictions, he burst out in despair:

> I am denouncing the infamy of England all the time, but I write in English, and couldn't switch to another language and another culture.[126]

In the same month of March 1938 the Nazis entered Vienna, seized the whole German edition of *Europa* and burnt it. Briffault commented that it was 'the highest honour' ever paid to him, as he wrote to Joan in a letter from Paris, on 15 September 1938.

In the same letter he described the mounting tension over the Nazi threat in Europe:

> I have a powerful radio and we heard every word of Hitler's Nueremberg speech – could even hear the steps of the troops marching to Goetterdaemmerung [twilight of the Gods] music. It was all so schrecklich [terribly scary] that we fell ill with it.

Still, Herma and Robert decided to stay in Paris for as long as they could. Herma was so tired of moving that she absolutely refused to leave; when the 'sense of isolation' and the 'gnawing depression' became unbearable, it had become impossibile to move. By October 1939, there was no longer any possibility of entertaining, which Herma had enjoyed so much; on 1 December Robert wrote: 'one feels the world crumbling within oneself, till one feels very weary'. In 1940 he was arrested and detained by the Nazis, released after one month, but after that 'he looked and acted like an old man', as Herma wrote in a letter that she wrote from London on 11 April 1945, three months after leaving Paris, in which she summarised the war years:

> There is too much to tell. We lived five years in inferno, Robert spent one month in prison, we were both arrested afterwards, but freed; the Gestapo paid us frequent visits; our telephone and radio removed... we gradually sold everything of value we possessed: my few poor jewels, my good fur coat, an Oriental rug, some linen, some silver, some books.

She recalled the starvation diet, the lack of fuel, the long queues to buy something to eat. During the war – 'several years full of hunger and cold and fear' – she went on typing 'with chilblained fingers in woolen mitts, Robert Briffault's books *The New Life of Mr Martin* and *Les Troubadours*'.[127] After the war she moved to London, while Robert was still in Paris, where he lived alone for six to seven months, during which he 'did it, the washing up, and all, and all, besides working (my real work)'.[128] By June 1945 *Les Troubadours* was having a fair amount of success, and he was hoping for an American edition.

In mid-September 1945, Robert too went to London, but the relationship with Herma had deteriorated. He reproached her for having thrown her parties 'up to the last', and for liking partying 'a little too much'. They were living separately, she in South London and he in London's East End, which he liked much more than 'the gentility of Kensington', and they saw each other two to three times a week. Briffault was living 'from day to day', anguished by the feeling that 'time is so short', blaming his state on the experience of two wars: 'The first war undid me, the second has finished me'.[129] He returned to thinking about his son, confessing that he had often wondered whether any of his grandsons were in the war, in the wilds of New Zealand, and that he had thought much of the tragedy of being so entirely cut off from my son and of his being buried in a Godforsaken New Zealand village. Ah me! thank goodness I have my own world of thought and work in which I can live a sort of dream life of my own.[130]

But he did not try to reach his relatives and remained in his 'dream life', without finding a way out of a style of life that required him to be eternally young and active. He felt worn out, and yet was compelled to go on working, since he was totally dependent on his writing for money to live. Meanwhile, Scribner had decided not to publish *The Troubadours*, judging that its readership in the US would have been too small. But in 1946 Briffault published the novel *The New Life of Mr Martin*, which sold 18,000 copies in the US, and went on writing articles for reviews and journals.

Although Briffault enjoyed working in the Bethnal Green library and was flattered that it had all his books, he felt unhappy to be in England:

... it is inconceivable to what degree of sillyness England has fallen. Even compared to other European countries. Writing people are simply afraid to think, much more to write. The reason is simply that they have for centuries been used to think that England could dictate her sillyness to the whole world – and now they begin to suspect that she can't, and that simply upsets all the foundations of their thoughts and opinions... Both materially and spiritually England has become wholly unhabitable to me.[131]

I am too anti-English, and that is a thing they never forgive here.[132]

How does Briffault's hatred for England, which had been growing in the late 1920s and in the 1930s, compare with a similar antipathy towards their country among the British intellectual travellers described by Fussell? Briffault's attitude had in common with them certain stereotypes about English weather and food, as well as a distaste for its narrow moralism and repressive attitudes, but it distinguished itself in the sense that it had a strong political basis. He was always very political, of a type of politics closely connected with his existential ways and beliefs. As hinted, Briffault's hatred for England possibly had psychological roots, and not only political ones, as Britain was the land of his austere mother, while France belonged to his mindless and charming father, whom he considered very similar to himself. In the end, Briffault shared with non-political, sometimes reactionary people the exaltation of Southern Europe. He dreamt of moving to somewhere in the South, in Italy or France, where the food was abundant and varied, and not rationed.

The last period of Briffault's life was beset with difficulties. Herma had succeeded in leaving for New York, and had started divorce proceedings, although she decided to drop them when it became clear that Robert was offended by her initiative. She and Robert still exchanged affectionate letters in the last two years of his life and she tried to help him, attempting to place his work with publishers in the US. Herma was herself having a very difficult time finding secretarial or editorial work in New York. All her papers had been lost and she was finding it very hard to prove that she had ghosted many books. Robert had no place to live, either in England or elsewhere. For some time friends lent him their country cottage, which was certainly the one that Stella Bowen and her husband had bought and renovated, since it had the same name, Green End, and was close to Purleigh near Chelmsford. It lay 'in an insignificant little lane in an insignificant little hamlet', had a high-pitched mansard roof of ancient tiles with a charming dormer window, walls of apricot-washed brick and a front door framed by a red rose and a white; oak beams, a beautiful fireplace, water from the mains laid on, while fruit trees, currants, gooseberries, scarlet runners and peas were grown in the garden. All this made the cottage seem to Stella Bowen 'shaped to every domestic pleasure one could wish'.[133] But when Briffault stayed there in the summer of 1946, he described it to Joan as 'a real farm labourer's cottage in Essex, completely isolated', and he was unable to enjoy its beauty:

> I have touched the lowest depths, unable to see how I could go on... I am tired, tired, tired, and the end will be a release... I am just a homeless outcast. The first war undid me, the second has finished me. This may well be the last you will hear from me.[134]

With a touch of complacency and self-pity mixed with genuine sorrow and affection, Briffault expressed loneliness and sadness:

> ... bless you, my dear! All luck to you. And never mind your poor old father. I am very calm and quiet, waiting for the end. I shall not be sorry when it comes. All my love, Joanie dear
>    your old dad[135]

> What I miss most is love. Yours, my dear, is the only real love I have in the world now.[136]

> Must look round the cupboard and see what tins there are.[137]

Joan and Willi had invited him repeatedly to join them in Chile, but he felt that his life coincided with his writing and that in Chile he would no longer be able to work. He showed in this way his ambiguity towards Europe, which he believed doomed; and yet he could not detach himself from Europe and European culture even when his situation was really difficult and precarious. Often Joan sent him money, which he at first refused and then accepted. In October 1946 he was back in Paris, enjoying 'orgies in all the great restaurants', paid for by an American fan of his.[138] There

Robert Briffault found his old friend Mala Stalio, ready to help him like a 'perfect angel of tenderness and devotion'.[139] He kept moving from Paris to London, then to Antibes, then back to Paris. In July 1947 he was in Florence, then travelled to Rapallo, Nice, Paris, Lausanne, Milan, Torri di Benaco near Verona and back to Florence again. In Rapallo he had met

> ... Schussnig, the successor of Dollfuss, who was bullied by Hitler into the Anschluss. I recognised him and we had a talk. Told him I was one of those terrible Communists... [he] remarked very seriously: 'You are on the winning side, then'.[140]

With his individualistic and idealistic form of Communism, Briffault was actually on the losers' side, a loser himself after some time of success and fame. On 3 February 1948 he spent his seventy-fifth birthday in Florence, but was left without money and ended up in hospital. Then he travelled to London in May and to Paris in July, where he complained that 'Mala let me down, went off to Nice for her "holidays"'.[141] In November 1948 Briffault was taken to a hospital in Paris for his 'état de dénutrition très sérieux et tracheo-laryngite aigue'.[142] At that point he would have accepted going to Chile, but was no longer in a state to face such a long trip, as Mala wrote to Joan.[143] He was then transferred to a hospital in London, where the diagnosis was 'tubercular pneumonia',[144] and where he died – presumably alone – on 11 December 1948.

In the United States his fame had lasted longer than his fortune as a best-selling author. In the last two years of his life, when he was desperately trying to get a visa to go to the US (which was refused, possibly on the grounds that he declared himself a Communist in a letter to the *New York Times* of 1 April 1946), people still remembered him as a great writer. He was 'one of the great lights in the world today', according to a female doctor who visited Herma in New York, while a psycho-analyst told her that he knew 'many people in the world today who say they were made by Robert Briffault'.[145] And not only middle-class professionals were his fans, Herma insisted; it was 'the opinion of all sorts of people that you are the greatest writer in England alive today' and she listed booksellers and shoesalesmen among those who told her so.[146] Very probably these were remarks made not only in order to lift Robert's depression; Herma was usually ready to be very honest to him, as she was when reminding him: 'you are misinformed regarding your books here. Publishing is in a slump. Your books are all out of print and have been for years'.[147] There is some reason to believe that she was actually echoing other people, when she repeated to Briffault, two weeks before his death, that his 'life has counted for a great deal in the world'.[148] But after the Second World War his books lost their market, because the society that he portrayed had disappeared, and he had come to be seen as belonging to that past. The experience of 'being a success' in the United States has been vividly presented by Vera

Brittain, who had gone through it with *Testament of Youth*, which had sold 35,000 copies in two years (1933–34). While recording that in 1936 *Gone with the Wind* became the first book to sell a million copies, Brittain noticed that such a success was 'a very deceptive experience, for only a miracle can keep a stranger in the benignant limelight for long', since 'these dynamic enthusiasms are always transitory, and in America, perhaps, more than anywhere else'.[149] But in Britain too, after the abridged version of *The Mothers* was published in 1952, Briffault's fame either vanished or faded. Bertrand Russell, who had written the introduction to *Sin and Sex*, defining him in 1931 as 'a distinguished anthropologist', in 1968 remembered Briffault in his *Autobiography* as 'a general practitioner from New Zealand who ventured into sociology'.[150]

Briffault's life story was one of a brilliant and successful nomadism which turned into tragic and desolate self-exile. He had embodied some of the contradictions of his age: he had been violently anti-European and at the same time had entrenched values, such as romantic love, that he believed to be exclusively European. When his nomadism became frenetic, in his last years, his love for his daughter manifested itself as a pale version of courtly love: linked with self-pity and narcissism, a love that was possible only at a distance, while no close relationship was left to him, after the separation from Herma. On 4 April 1947 he was writing to Joan from Paris:

> My only choice and prospect is how to die, and I would rather do so holding your hand, my dear, than seek like a dog my end in a corner.

But he did not go to Chile when it would have been possible, and was not given a visa when he was willing to move to the US, so that his death took place in the 'corner' that for him was London, where he had no friends left. He was not able to leave that Europe, whose situation he judged, when dissuading Joan from coming back, 'worse than the war', as he had written in the letter of 16 April 1946. In the same letter he had defined himself: 'I am truly a homeless vagrant in my sad old age', describing his scattered life, with all his books and possessions stored in warehouses in various towns, with very few memories of his family and its past. It was thanks to his daughter Joan, who kept and made available his letters, that a memory of him was transmitted to the future.

## Notes on Chapter 4

1   Kestner, p 5
2   Searle
3   Add.58442
4   Cairns
5   *Mothers*, vol I, p VI
6   Stout
7   Shand, p 520
8   *Ibidem*, p 35
9   *Ibidem*, p 51
10   *Ibidem*, p 54
11   *Psyche*, p 223
12   *Ibidem*, p 229
13   *Ibidem*, p 227
14   *Mothers*, vol I, p V
15   *Ibidem*, p VI
16   *Mothers*, vol I
17   *Mothers*, vol III
18   Westermarck, pp 222–4, 334–5
19   Montagu, p 5
20   *Ibidem*, pp 71–72
21   *Ibidem*, p 8
22   *Ibidem*, p 59
23   *Ibidem*, p 58
24   Sloan
25   Ellis, p 168
26   *Ibidem*, p 169
27   *Breakdown*, pp 224–5
28   *Mothers*, vol I, p 143
29   *Mothers*, vol I, pp 125–6
30   *Mothers*, vol II, pp 142-3
31   *Mothers*, vol II, p 150
32   *Mothers*, II, pp 151–2
33   *Mothers*, vol III, p 427
34   *Mothers*, vol III, p 469
35   *Mothers*, vol III, pp 469–71 n
36   *Mothers*, vol III, p 487
37   *Les Troubadours*, p 83
38   Menolocal
39   *Reasons for Anger*, p 81
40   *Mothers, vol* III, pp 505–6
41   *Reasons for Anger*, p 183
42   *Mothers*, vol II, pp 138–140

43  Taylor, p 20
44  *Mothers*, vol I, p 75
45  *TLS*, 14 July 1927
46  Ellis, p 161
47  *Europa in Limbo*, p 55
48  *Ibidem*, p 56
49  *Ibidem*, p 452
50  Gimbutas
51  Whitmont
52  *Mothers*, vol III, pp 191–195
53  *Mothers*, vol I, p 392
54  New York 1932, London 1935
55  *Breakdown*, p 231
56  *Ibidem*, p 234
57  *TLS*, 18 January 1936
58  p 265 of the American edition; in the English edition the quotation marks are given only to the second phrase, with the curious effect that the father who is invoked is not Julian, but the author's, p 284
59  *Europa*, p 19
60  *Ibidem*, p 22
61  *Ibidem*, p 66
62  *Ibidem*, p 76
63  Lehman, pp 106–7
64  *Europa*, p 28
65  *Ibidem*, p 451
66  *Ibidem*, p 100
67  *Ibidem*, p 551
68  *Ibidem*, p 68
69  *Ibidem*, p 152
70  *Ibidem*, p 62
71  *Ibidem*, p 403
72  *Europa in Limbo*, p 382
73  *Ibidem*, p 139
74  *Ibidem*, p 410
75  *Ibidem*, p 533
76  *Ibidem*, p 520
77  *Ibidem*, p 31
78  *Ibidem*, p 186
79  *Ibidem*, p 195
80  *Ibidem*, pp 244–6
81  *Sin and Sex*, pp 160–1
82  *Europa in Limbo*, p 355
83  *Europe*, p 431
84  *Ibidem*, p 311

85    *Ibidem*, p 259
86    *Ibidem*, p 196
87    *Ibidem*, pp 302–3 of the American edition, p 345 of the English one
88    *Ibidem*, p 140
89    *Europa in Limbo*, p 270
90    *Ibidem*, p 510
91    *Ibidem*, p 510
92    *Ibidem*, pp 493–4
93    *Ibidem*, pp 520–1
94    Montagu, p 78
95    More than half a century later Nicholas Molsey has written a historical novel with the same ambitions as Briffault, although at a much higher literary level, where he describes the political, cultural, scientific, and psychological developments of Europe in the 1930's as the background for a love between a young man and a young woman who are often separated by distance in their travelling for work, politics, and the family. *Hopeful Monsters* (1990) testifies to the need to produce literary narrations which make sense of the intellectual and existential changes of our age, mixing the real and the imaginary, and projecting an image of the future based on the hopes for freedom and social justice, racial and gender understanding, and communication between different generations.
96    Add.58441, letter of 29 September 1935
97    *Ibidem,*
98    *American Review*, VI, November 1935 – March 1936
99    *Time*, 9 September 1935
100   *Time*, 27 September 1937
101   *New Statesman*, 19 September 1936
102   *The Spectator*, 2 October 1936
103   *Time and Tide*, 3 October 1936
104   *The New Statesman and Nation*, 16 October 1937
105   Goldstein
106   Add. 58441, 8 October 1935
107   *TLS*, 17 October 1936
108   Schapiro
109   Rose
110   Taylor
111   Add. 58442
112   Add. 58441, letter of 24 March 1929
113   Add. 58441, letter of 20 March 1929
114   Add. 58441, letter of 28 August 1932
115   Add. 58441, letter of 10 February 1935
116   Add. 58441, letter of 6 March 1935
117   Add. 58441, letter of 18 September 1935
118   Add 58441, letter of 29 September 1935

119   Add. 58441, letter of 10 June 1936
120   Add. 58441, letter of 2 October 1936
121   Add. 58441, 2 October 1936
122   *New York Times*, 16.8.37
123   Add. 58441, letter from New York of 6 July 1937
124   Bowen, pp 234–5
125   NYPL, HB Papers, Personal file 8
126   Add. 58441, letter of 31 March 1938
127   NYPL, HB Papers, f 8
128   Add. 58441, 15 September 1945
129   Add. 58441, letter of 19 June 1946
130   Add. 58441, 12 January 1946
131   Add. 58441, 12 January 1946
132   Add. 58441, 16 April 1946
133   Bowen, pp 245–8
134   Add. 58441, letter of 19 June 1946
135   Add. 58441, 19 June 1946
136   Add. 58441, 11 July 1946
137   Add. 58441, 5 August 1946
138   Add. 58441, 8 October 1946
139   Add. 58441, 15 December 1946
140   Add. 58441, 29 July 1947
141   Add. 58441, 25 July 1948
142   Add. 58443, medical certificate of 6 November 1948
143   Add. 58443, 26 November 1948
144   Add. 58441, letter from Herma to Robert of 24 November
145   Add. 58441, letter of 10 November 1946
146   Add. 58441, letter of 13 January 1947
147   Add. 58441, letter of 12 August 1948
148   Add. 58441, letter of 24 November 1948
149   Brittain 1993, pp 113–5
150   Russell, p 435

# CHAPTER 5

# PROVENÇAL LOVE

## The Allegory of Love by C.S. Lewis

Every one has heard of courtly love, and every one knows that it appears quite suddenly at the end of the eleventh century in Languedoc... Many of the features of this sentiment, as it was known to the Troubadours, have indeed disappeared; but this must not blind us to the fact that the most momentous and the most revolutionary elements in it have made the background of European literature for eight hundred years. French poets, in the eleventh century, discovered or invented, or were the first to express, that romantic species of passion which English poets were still writing about in the nineteenth. They effected a change which has left no corner of our ethics, our imagination, or our daily life untouched, and they erected impassable barriers between us and the classical past or the Oriental present. Compared with this revolution the Renaissance is a mere ripple on the surface of literature.

This is the assertive thesis that C.S. Lewis put forward in the initial pages of his book *The Allegory of Love*, published in 1936 by the Clarendon Press. The book has since then enjoyed a continuous and even increasing success, never going out of print. Apart from the correction of mispellings and minor mistakes, made by the author in 1937 for the first reprint, nothing has been changed in the *Allegory of Love*, and the most recent edition is identical with the first corrected one. In 1958 the press thought 'it would be worthwhile having a new Preface' for the next reprint and asked Lewis whether he would be ready to write it.[1] Lewis evidently refused, because not a word has ever been added to the original.

Such permanence must be seen against the background of Clive Staples Lewis's life. He was born in Belfast in 1898, of Protestant Anglo-Irish descent, and was raised in the Anglican faith. On his mother's death from cancer when he was ten years old, his father sent him and his elder brother Warren to an English boarding school, run with extreme brutality by a clergyman who resorted to beating and caning for any minor reason; later Lewis was moved to a preparatory school, but the early experience of loss and victimisation, both physical and psychological, left a deep mark on 'Jack', as everybody called him. He rarely went back to Ireland, and found it difficult to communicate with his father, something which left him with a strong sense of guilt. His studies in Oxford were interrupted when he was conscripted into the army, and into the trenches of the First World War in France, where he was wounded in 1918; he did not go back to the front and was thus able to resume his classical studies. Between 1925 and 1954 Lewis was a fellow of Magdalen College, Oxford; in 1954 he was appointed to the newly-created Cambridge Chair of Medieval and Renaissance Literature. Lewis did not travel often and spent most of his life between Oxford and Cambridge, going to Europe rarely: to France for the war, and to Greece on a holiday trip with his wife and another couple in April 1960. This apparently quiet and circumscribed life was, however, animated by deep emotional tremors. A major one was his conversion to Christianity from the atheism he had chosen as a student, a transformation which started in his later twenties, in the second half of the 1920s, and which was made public in the early 1930s. In *Surprised by Joy*, Lewis sets the summer of 1929 as the time of his first admission that 'God was God'. Therefore, the process of collecting material for and writing *The Allegory of Love* partially coincided with that of his conversion, although some critics accept his declaration that he had written most of the book as an agnostic, and regard 1931 as his time of conversion.[2]

The most important emotional relationship which C.S. Lewis had, for the thirty years between 1920 and 1950, was with the mother of a close friend of his, Paddy Moore, who had died in the war. Mrs Moore 'adopted' Jack, who went to live with her and her daughter Maureen. Jack's brother Warren Lewis – who joined them – called theirs an 'incomprehensible ménage', in which Mrs Moore exercised over Jack 'an autocracy that developed into stifling tyranny'.[3] Biographers are divided over whether C.S. Lewis and Mrs Moore (some 25 years his elder) were lovers, a question made more problematic by his admission of being strongly attracted to sadomasochism – not so strange, given his traumas at boarding school. The majority, however, are inclined to believe that the relationship was not physically sexual. Another biographical element emerges here which corresponds, on the private level, to Lewis's scholarly interest in a love like that of the Provençals, at the same time sensual and distant. In January 1951, Mrs Moore died, and at the end of the following year Lewis met Joy

Davidman, an ex-Marxist Jew from New York with two small sons, who greatly admired his work and through it was converted to Christianity. In 1956 Lewis married her in a civil marriage – a formality to secure her the right to stay in Britain – not intending to fulfil the husband's role, then fell deeply in love with her, love which she reciprocated; a religious marriage followed in 1957. Again, an autobiographical motif alluded to literary themes: falling in love with his own wife recalled the stereotype of Provençal true love existing out of marriage, in a new light which was consistent with Lewis's religious view of life. In spite of the diagnosis of a terminal cancer, Joy lived three more years, until 1960, while Jack died in 1963.

Lewis's great fame is based on a variety of reputations and reader-ships. His academic reputation was established in the 1930s, and during the Second World War he became a very well-known Christian polemicist, participating in many live and broadcast debates. His religious writings were also the basis of the cult which developed around him in the US – largely ignoring his literary criticism and his fiction – and which has existed steadily since the 1950s. Another separate reputation was built on his space fictions, such as the trilogy *Out of the Silent Planet*, *Perelandra* and *That Hideous Strength*: he belonged, together with J.R.R. Tolkien, author of *The Hobbit* and *The Lord of the Rings*, to the Inklings club – a circle of literary friends more than a formal club – formed in 1933 and lasting well into the 1940s. This reputation was reinforced in the 1950s, with the publication of *Chronicles of Narnia*, a seven-volume children's fantasy. Finally a dramatic treatment of part of his life, with the title *Shadowlands* – both a play and a film – played to audiences between 1985 and 1993, more than 20 years after his death, giving rise to a different type of fame altogether, and presenting a version of his life sometimes resented by his other publics.

Lewis mentioned in a letter to his father of 10 July 1928 that he had by then collected all the material – 'three quarters of the battle' – for *The Allegory of Love*, and had finally started writing the first chapter. The book, he wrote, was 'about mediaeval love poetry and the mediaeval idea of love, which is a very paradoxical business indeed'.[4] The paradox lies in the combination of attraction and distance, since, on the one hand, this type of love is 'extremely super-sensual and refined, and on the other it is an absolute point of honour that the lady should be someone else's wife'.[5] However, due to the author's own teaching commitments and the many domestic engagements with which Mrs Moore encumbered him, the writing proceeded no faster than one chapter a year. Since the book was seven chapters long, only by September 1935 could Lewis announce that it was finished to R.H. Chapman, who was then director of Oxford University Press (OUP); soon afterwards Kenneth Sisam, acting as his substitute, asked Lewis to 'by all means send the MS straight to this address'.[6] OUP's reader, Dom André Wilmart of St Michael's Abbey, gave a favourable judgment and defined the book 'intéressant, vivant et suggestif', though he commented that the supporting literature 'aurait besoin d'etre rajeunie' and warned against the danger of falling into a journalistic genre.[7] OUP did not mind taking this risk; but they did not accept the original title, *The Allegorical Love Poem*, and counterproposed a new selection of titles, from among which Lewis chose *The Allegory of Love*. The book was published on 21 May 1936, in a print-run of 1,000 copies at a price of 15s. OUP did not expect 'great sales' from the book, as stated in a letter.[8]

The fame of *The Allegory of Love* – 'immediately and permanently a success by every standard'[9] – did not rest on the number of copies sold by comparison with other best sellers of the time, such as *Europa*. Although it received the Hawthornden Prize for 1936 and was widely acknowledged by the press, sales remained within the usual limits of an academic essay. It was only in 1942, with the publication of *The Screwtape Letters*, that Lewis achieved 'wide public success of the kind that brings money rolling in'.[10] In a statement sent to Barclays Bank in July 1943, OUP noted that royalties between 1 October 1937 and 1 October 1942 amounted to £119, 18s and 6p, which at the agreed rate of 10% on the published price meant that about 1,600 copies had been sold. The second printing, in 1937, was again of one thousand copies. OUP continued to reprint *The Allegory of Love* regularly over the following years, going in 1950 from the usual 1,000–1,500 copies to 3,000 and in 1953 to 5,000, so that by 1953 13,250 copies had been printed altogether. But it was only with paperback editions that a wide public would come. In February 1956, Penguin proposed its publication in paperback but OUP refused, on the grounds that the book was 'selling well at 600 a year and this sale would be killed if a Pelican edition appeared. We have still a substantial stock...'[11] In fact they stored 'close to 4,000 copies in bound stock or in quires', which they calculated should last between five and seven years (letter of 1 March). In 1958 OUP accepted the proposal to publish a Galaxy paperback edition limited to the US, refusing an agreement to import Galaxy to the UK. Figures projected by its experts suggested a first printing of 10,000–15,000 copies, with sales of 5,000 expected for the first year. The actual sales in the first year amounted to over 6,600 copies; the letter from Galaxy that announced this good news to OUP also indicated that the book was 'the only one of our Galaxy series which is consistently recommended on Catholic reading lists!'[12] In Britain, a new reprint order of 5,000 was issued in March 1959. No figures are available after this date.

Even if it was not for the public at large, *The Allegory of Love* was immediately adopted as 'holiday reading' by a public of 'busy but not uneducated' readers, to quote Harold Nicolson. One reason for this certainly lay in Lewis writing very readably on an appealing subject, cleverly intertwining two major lines of research. Lewis himself described the book as composed of:

... two themes: 1) the birth of allegory; 2) the birth of the romantic conception of love and the long struggle between its earlier form (the romance of adultery) and its later form (the romance of marriage).[13]

This combination of the two themes was criticised by some; for example, Albert Guerard of the *New York Herald Tribune* thought it gave rise to 'two books, both excellent, but each vitiating the other', and added that he preferred the literary analysis to the history of love.[14] Lewis himself judged the first chapter – the one on 'Courtly Love' – 'the least original chapter' of the book, and yet it was the part which met with the greatest success. It dealt with a well-known *locus communis* of romance studies, which we have already encountered with Briffault, the invention of courtly/romantic love in Europe at the beginning of the second millennium. Lewis was convinced that 'real changes in human sentiment are very rare – there are perhaps three or four on record', but also 'that they occur, and that this is one of them'.[15] For him, that epochal change had taken place in circumscribed time and space, i.e. on only one continent and 'suddenly' – as is said in the opening quotation – distancing 'the erotic tradition of modern Europe' from every other, including the two most outstanding traditions of *ars amatoria*, those of the Ancients and the East. Celtic, Byzantine and Arabic influences were dismissed by Lewis in one sentence: 'it has not been made clear that these, if granted, could account for the results we see'.[16]

This type of Eurocentrism was accompanied by anacronisms that he shared with many others, such as calling the Provençal poets 'French' and interchanging 'courtly' and 'romantic' as adjectives pertaining only to European love. In fact, most reviewers of *The Allegory of Love* had no difficulty in sharing these stereotypes. For example, the *Times Literary Supplement* entitled its review 'A History of Romantic Love', with the subtitle 'Provençal sentiment in English poetry'. A strong component of such Eurocentrism in passions took the form of literary nationalism, which led the *Times Literary Supplement* reviewer to 'feel proud that English poets contributed so much to the final perfection of the sentiment' and to recall that 'we English sanctify romantic love'. Indeed *The Allegory of Love* outlines for this theme – what Lewis called his second – an evolutionary design, starting from a supposedly adulterous courtly love and ending with its reconciliation to marriage, through a pre-ordained series of steps along an inevitable progress which finds its culmination in English literature. The logic of the evolutionary scheme was in fact dictated by the final point, which selected in the initial one only those aspects coherent with later developments, such as the spiritual counterposed to the material. For Lewis the spiritual did not so much indicate – as it did for many others – a sexless relationship, as one counterposed to the atheism of his century. He meant by this a relationship allowing the experience of an intense longing, a desire for the unattainable, also representative of a relationship with the divine. This type of longing was for Lewis characteristic of romanticism as well as of much Provençal poetry, not only considered by itself but especially as the point of origin of the tradition that through Dante and Petrarch moved the centre of European poetry and literature from war epics to love. In such a framework, based 'on a broad view of European literature as a whole', the romantic epic that travelled through the centuries on a 'noble viaduct' from Italy to England was 'one of the great trophies of European genius'.[17] In England, it was Chaucer who

> brought the old romance of adultery to the very frontiers of the modern (or should I say the late?) romance of marriage. He does not himself cross the frontier; but we see that his successor will soon inevitably do so.[18]

A further step was taken by King James, in the *Kingis Quair*, where love-longing becomes 'more cheerful', 'more moral', and 'the poetry of marriage at last emerges from the traditional poetry of adultery'.[19] Some uncertainty was shown by Lydgate in *Black Knight*, while an 'apparent retrogression' appeared in the anonymous poem *Court of Love*.[20] But a decisive reconciliation took place with Stephen Hawes in *Pastime of Pleasure and Example of Virtues*: for Hawes the 'Graunde Amour' looked forward to marriage as the only conceivable form of fulfillment.[21] The story finds its triumphant conclusion in Spenser's *Faerie Queene* – the great Christian poet of the Protestant tradition - which restores love, wrongly separated from marriage by the ideals of courtly gallantry, to chastity, i.e. to the union of romantic passion with Christian monogamy.[22] This conclusion can be understood, as Lewis himself puts it, as 'the final defeat of courtly love by the romantic conception of marriage'.[23]

Only two reviewers out of almost 20 expressed doubts on the Eurocentric twist of Lewis's thesis on courtly love, a twist that was probably crucial to its success with the general public. The first of these was Harold Nicolson; the title of his review in the *Daily Telegraph* was quite sceptical: 'The Greatest Revolution in Literature?'. Nicolson appreciated *The Allegory of Love* as a welcome companion and expressed his gratitude for the book's 'ingenuity and wide erudition', but noticed that Lewis had to ignore Sappho and the bucolic poets in order to support his thesis on love as a novelty of the second European millennium. The second critic was William Empson, who suggested in the *Spectator* that Lewis 'had only to open the *Tale of Genji* to find the practice of courtly love in full blast in tenth century Japan', while the 'main troubadour theory, the comparison of a noble successful love to the vision of God' had appeared in Islamic poetry, earlier than the troubadours. Empson, a poet and critic of the Auden generation, as well as contributor to Eliot's *Criterion*, had written the literary-historical *Some Versions of Pastoral* linking proletarian art to the pastoral tradition; he also led a much more cosmopolitan life than Lewis, teaching in the 1930s and 1940s in Japan and China. Empson exercised some well-founded irony on Lewis's 'vast and vague claims for this theme':

> One does not need to claim Moslem influence (never adequately disproved) to refute this idea that love was discovered, like matches, only once, which Mr Lewis has to support by calling Catullus an exhibitionist and hiding the *Song of Solomon*.

Apart from these critics, nobody really discussed the evolutionary Eurocentric scheme, on the contrary it seemed to be taken for granted. The book's reception by fellow critics might well have been 'guarded'[24] on other grounds, such as the excessive weight given to Andreas Capellanus or some exaggerations and some omissions, but was not on this. As for the non-professional public, it was recognised that the great value of the book was to reveal the beauty of the works by English poets that most readers found too difficult to read by themselves.

The idea of the moralising influence of civilisation perfecting an original core of poetry was not new. One of the secondary sources that Lewis quoted with praise was *Euphorion: Studies of the Antique and the Mediaeval in the Renaissance* (1884) by Violet Paget under the pseudonym Vernon Lee, and dedicated to Walter Pater. Paget was a novelist, essayist and critic who achieved an international reputation with this book. She struggled for recognition of her rights in her family, was a pacifist and anti-fascist, travelled widely and lived for many years in Florence, counting among her friends Aristide Briand and many European intellectuals.[25] Lewis drew from her the hypothesis on the origins of courtly love that can be defined, in the current classification of theories on courtly love, as 'sociological': Paget draws the image of a castle, of comparative leisure and luxury in a barbarous countryside, with numerous men and very few women, the lady and her damsels. The males are largely feudally inferior to the lady and her lord; they all depend for courtesy and charm on these few women, whom they cannot marry.[26] This description is not too far from that given by Norbert Elias – writing in the 1930s – and more recently by the sociological school, as exemplified by Koehler. According to the former, the affective disposition of the troubadours' lyric and the 'Minnesänger' is marked by the inferior social status of the majority of minstrels, while for the latter a homology exists between the unfulfilled aspirations of the lesser noblemen for social ascent and the unreciprocated love of the troubadours, a major example of which is the love at a distance ('amor de lonh') sung of by Jaufre Rudel.

However, having accepted the sociological setting as 'very near to being a "cause"', Lewis considers it insufficient to produce courtly love, which he treats as an essentially literary phenomenon. At least this is the thesis that he himself criticised more than 20 years later in *The Four Loves* (affection, friendship, eros and charity): 'I was blind enough,' he writes, 'to treat the mediaeval religion of love as an almost purely literary pheno-menon. I know better now'.[27] The implication here is that only after his experience of reciprocated love with Joy Davidman did Lewis understand that 'Eros by his nature' invites a sort of religion. Whatever his later thoughts on the matter, in *The Allegory of Love* Lewis writes:

> ... life and letters are inextricably intermixed. If the feeling came first a literary convention would soon arise to express it: if the convention came first it would soon teach those who practised it a new feeling.[28]

By this observation Lewis was trying to give a Solomonic solution to an old question, whether the Provençal poems were mirrors of reality, reflecting actual feeling or independent literary inventions. Related questions were the situation of women at the time – higher in status only on literary grounds? – and the physical aspects of love – including the possible homosexuality of some poets. However, these questions were somehow out of synch with Lewis' approach, which is worth exploring. He maintained that, in spite of the introduction of extra-literary elements in critical judgement, such as ethics and religion, a work of poetry is 'like life itself, not like the products of life', and 'the experience of reading is like living'. We know that this was certainly true for Lewis who, for instance, experienced his 'heart at once broken and exalted' when he read *Hippolytus* by Euripides – the story of the stepson who rejects the all-powerful Phaedra and is then unjustly punished by the gods invoked by his father – a reading that shook his decision 'to live without the emotions' and was a step in the process of conversion.[29] Lewis avoids interpreting Provençal poetry either as a mere convention or as an autobiographical act. As we will see, it is true that he shared with many others the view that what was considered a major feature of Provençal love, its adulterous nature, indicated a primitiveness or backwardness in the history of modern Europe. For Violet Paget too, 'the many unclean necessities of adulterous passion' risked making 'the new poetic element of chivalric love remain useless', until another country, Italy, took up the mission to 'prevent such waste' and 'cleanse' mediaeval love, thanks to Dante, Cavalcanti, and Petrarch.[30] Then the 'great and unexpected action of England' began

> ... uniting in itself all the scattered and long-dormant powers of Northern poetry... And one of the great and fruitful things achieved by English poetry was to give to the world the new, the modern, perhaps the definitive, the final ideal of love... based on the old domestic love, quiet, undemonstrative, essentially unsinging, of the early Northern (as indeed also of the Greek and Hindou) epics.[31]

For Vernon Lee, this Northern tradition of domestic love allowed women to choose their own husbands and gave the world the most noble type of love yet seen on earth.

However, in the case of Lewis, the correspondence between poetry and reality must be understood on the level of literature and its emotional value, therefore within a history of consciousness. It is at this level – fusion between poetry and emotional life as a stage in the historical development of subjectivity – that his position must be understood. The key to this understanding is his interpretation of *The Allegory of Love*'s 'theme no. 1' – allegory – which is really the most interesting and innovative part of his work, where Lewis unbalances the Solomonic equivalence between literature and life in favour of the former. 'Allegory, besides being many other things, is the subjectivism of an objective age.'[32] This brilliant definition stems from the conviction of a 'fundamental equivalence between the immaterial and the material', to the extent that the latter can be understood as a copy of the former.[33] The study of allegory thus becomes one way of understanding the history of what Lewis calls the 'inner life', which many would today call subjectivity. This 'inner life' is perceived as a *bellum intestinum*, a conflict embodied by the abstract personifications known as allegories; and the *champ clos* of that combat is characterized by perennial strangeness, adventurousness and a 'sinuous forward movement'.[34] In this, Lewis conjured up 'a history of the imagination', to be understood as a third world of myth and fancy, to be set alongside the actual world and the world of religion.[35] Accordingly, allegory belongs not to mediaeval man, but to man in general; it acts as the pretext for fantasy, and preserves the pagan gods for imaginative uses. This is why it is not an escape from reality, but the disclosure of a deeper reality, allowing the various selves or facets of personality to be represented.[36] The machinery of allegory may thus be regarded as 'a system of conduit pipes which tap the deep, unfailing sources of poetry in the mind of the folk';[37] these sources, that poetry can tap, are not easily accessible to discursive thought.[38] Lewis's disagreement with Freudian psycho-analysis is implicit here; usually he is reported to have been both critical of what he considered its reductionism of spiritual life to sexuality and afraid of being subjected to that interpretation. While Freud recognized the deep connection between art and psycho-analysis as well as the expertise of poets on love,[39] he was convinced – unlike Lewis – that the true knowledge of love could now be developed only by psycho-analysts.

However, the very recognition by Lewis of the autonomous status and the irreplaceable role of literature allowed him to accept indirectly the reality of psychic life and its dynamics. Indeed, it was not by chance that *The Allegory of Love* was saluted by some reviewers as a form of 'history of human psychology' (*Times Literary Supplement*). In his twofold attempt to explore the inner life and to stay free of Freud, Lewis developed a vision that was in some ways very close to that of Jung, with a radical redefinition of the place of sexuality in the psychic life, the importance given to archetypes of the imagination and to long-lasting symbols – 'the constant reappearance of certain basic ideas, which transform themselves without end and yet ever remain the same (eterne in mutability)'[40] –and the recognition of a reservoir of inspiration called by Lewis 'sources of poetry', and by Jung the 'collective unconscious'. A major difference between them, however, is that the internal personifications are for Lewis objects of aesthetic contemplation,[41] while in Jungian psychology they are elements of a dynamic economy that connects the individual and the collective; in addition, Jung's acceptance of the sacred is not personified. However, they have important similarities, probably due to a convergence between two lines of thought on the history of subjectivity which tried to dam the radical materialism of Freud and to incorporate supra-rational or irrational aspects of the psyche and of culture. As a further instance of such a convergence, it might be interesting to compare the revival of Greek mythology proposed recently by the Jungian James Hillman – for whom the Greek gods and myths represent archetypes of our mind and culture, images acting in our souls – with Lewis's idea of the allegorical use of 'the old gods', who found salvation in allegory as a 'temporary tomb, for the day when they could wake again in the beauty of acknowledged myth and thus provide modern Europe with its 'third world' of romantic imagining'.[42]

Lewis's notion that the value of literature rests on the basis of the fundamental equivalence between the material and the immaterial is confirmed by his interpretation of a work which was in certain aspects similar to *The Allegory, L'amour et l'Occident* by Denis de Rougemont, published in Paris in 1939. This book was to become a sort of manifesto of the connection between Europeanness and love, widely read by intellectuals as well as by the general public in many countries, and translated into English with the title *Passion and Society*. Lewis, who received a copy with a dedication by the author, wrote him a letter (unpublished) on 29 March, 1940, and published a book review in *Theology* in June. In the letter, Lewis stated that he had read the book 'with continuous excitement'; he considered it 'a sermon on a most important theological and moral issue', particularly the last chapter (dedicated to the idea that the decision to be faithful in marriage is a foundation of the person), which he defined as 'a work of real greatness', although he was 'very doubtful' about the historical thesis. He announced that the review would not be 'wholly favourable', adding, 'but, I presume, between two Christians, that will give no offence'. The review reacted to the book's historical thesis as interpreted by Lewis, 'that the earliest medieval literature of courtly love was not really an expression of sexual passion, but the exoteric expression of a wish for death and pain' induced by the Catharist version of a widespread pagan Eros-mysticism – by declaring this thesis 'formally impossible'. Lewis's main objection to de Rougemont's ideas was that the latter lacked any 'general theory of story' to mediate his psychological interpretations, so that for instance Rougemont concluded that an unhappy end was due simply to a death-wish. For Lewis this meant a lack of recognition of the peculiar status of the literary – the 'story' – in relationship to psychic reality, and offered an opening to any 'Freudian' interpretation that cut short the autonomy of the story. On these grounds, the two authors were at opposite poles, Rougemont's novelty being precisely the introduction of a psychological outlook into the myth of courtly love, while Lewis' strong point was his stress on its literary nature within a history of the imagination.

What Lewis liked about de Rougemont's argument was

> the incompatibility between the Christian conception of marriage and the modern notion according to which every marriage must have 'falling in love' as its efficient, and worldly 'happiness' as its final cause.

Lewis especially liked one sentence in the book: 'Eros ceases to be a demon only when he ceases to be a god'; he repeated this quotation many times – in the 'Christianity and Culture' debate, in his introduction to The Four Loves, as well as in letters of 1940 and 1955.[43] In his private letters he was much harsher than in the publications, declaring that de Rougemont 'talks manifest nonsense'.[44] Lewis's review was reductive of de Rougemont's work in two ways. First, as the author of L'amour et l'Occident argued in the introduction to the second version of his book (1956), he had not established such a drastic and direct connection between courtly love and poetry on the one hand and Catharism on the other. Secondly, simply stating the predicament of the relationship between marriage and love without indicating the way out proposed by de Rougemont – which was a decision of fidelity made on the basis of a direct relationship between the person and God, in the Protestant tradition – could result only in defending the existing order and undervaluing the challenge and innovation of de Rougemont's approach. In the chapter on 'Eros' in his later book The Four Loves, Lewis confirmed his attitudes about marriage and love, writing ironically on young couples bedevilled by psychologists on the infinite importance of 'sexual adjustment' so that they needed 'the complete works of Freud, Krafft-Ebing, Havelock Ellis and Dr Stopes spread out on bed-tables all round them'.[45]

Not surprisingly, Lewis was defined as 'a conservative iconoclast',[46] as implied in the very last page of The Allegory of Love, where he disclosed the preoccupations which were the basis of the book:

> Feminism in politics, reviving asceticism in religion, animalism in imaginative literature, and, above all, the discoveries of psycho-analysts, have undermined that monogamic idealism about sex which served us for three centuries.[47]

The Times Literary Supplement echoed his discomfort, observing that one of the landmarks of progress, romantic love as a basis for marriage, was 'being seriously challenged', while ideas about marriage were 'again in the melting pot'.

Therefore, the lasting success of *The Allegory of Love* was due to its capacity to give a scholarly but quite accessible expression to a central core of that 'Old European, or Old Western Culture' that was under siege and of which Lewis saw himself and his friends as spokesmen.[48] The book supported a Eurocentric concept of love and exposed its historical nature by showing the steps through which it had come into being through the centuries; thus it opened a way not only to acknowledging the limitations of this love in time and space but also towards possibly going beyond Eurocentrism. For the time being, it meant simply the recognition that if a certain type of love was part of a civilisation whose beginning and end could be marked, its values could be re-enlivened, as this telling testimony by John Heath-Stubbs, poet, critic and translator, born in 1918, implies:

> I belong to a generation for whom such books as C.S. Lewis's *The Allegory of Love* and Denis de Rougemont's *L'amour et l'Occident* were, when we were undergraduates, a stimulus and a revelation. One may no longer agree with their arguments, but surely they illuminated something that we otherwise might have missed. If they were right much of Western art and poetry, our conventions of courtesy and courtship, even our presuppositions as to the respective roles of the sexes in society, were the products of a specific cultural and historical experience.[49]

The relevance of Lewis's *The Allegory of Love* is that it expressed a deep level of identity, and prejudice, at which British people could define themselves as Europeans, a European identity that implied the leadership of Britain on cultural and moral grounds. The belief that they were the repositories of the highest form of love which ever existed, at the culmination of a continual progress which had lasted some eight centuries and was now under threat of degeneration, brought highly cultured scholars and a larger middle-classes public together. The kind of reassuring ethno-centrism implicit in the notion of the exclusively European nature of courtly-romantic love is made explicit by Lewis when he describes the 'bareness' of the mental world that existed prior to it: 'bare' because empty of the ideal of 'happiness', 'a happiness grounded on successful romantic love – which still supplies the motive of our popular fiction'.[50] This bareness might also allude, in autobiographical terms, to the experience of loss and solitude in his childhood, just as the experience of a long-lasting love with a much older woman might reflect his desire for a kind of love which was both very close and inaccessible. However, these links with his life story, either suggesting predispositions induced by experience or on the contrary as 'literary' attitudes suggesting experiential choices, are only a small part of the story. Lewis expressed forcefully and artfully a belief that connected the worlds of high and mass culture, placing it in a conservative restoration of the values of religion and of the heterosexual couple. In that view, the world was 'bare' without the traditional European forms of relationship.

Lewis was aware of the European basis of the values that Christianity propounded, without believing – like Dawson – that Christian Europe could be restored. In an article on the relationship between 'Christianity and Culture', published in *Theology* in 1940, which initiated a debate, Lewis maintained that some of the principal values implicit in European literature – the first two being honour and sexual love – were 'sub-Christian', meaning 'the highest level of natural value lying immediately below the lowest level of spiritual value'. He therefore saw as a value of European culture its potential as a path to Christianity, while acknowledging that there might be 'other ways' to God.

By means of *The Allegory of Love*, Lewis placed himself in what has been defined as the long-lasting tradition of 'romantic protest in British intellectual and cultural life' against the progress of industrial society, reclaiming or remaking traditional meaning and values.[51] Part of this tradition was medievalism, which understood the middle ages as the symbolic representation of a meaningful and creative universe, a world of essential values lost in the process of industrialisation, and as giving form to the nostalgia for a rapidly disappearing England whose culture stretched back to the Middle Ages. While on the one hand Lewis derived his medievalism from Ruskin and particularly from Morris, who was a strong influence in his pre-Christian youth, on the other hand he was part of the movement to reconcile orthodox Christianity with Romanticism; Lewis and some of his contemporaries found in certain experiences of the romantic imagination a way to resist the atheist thought-forms of the twentieth century.

Given the importance of the middle ages in Western civilisation as a basis for cultural identity, Lewis's position in the medievalist debate was an essential element of his success. According to Cantor, *The Allegory of Love* 'was a watershed in the invention of the Middle Ages because Lewis legitimated the subject of the idea of love and gave academic authority to inquiry into romantic patterns within medieval literature'. Lewis proposed an interpretation of high medieval culture which was at that time an innovative one, that the world view in twelfth and early thirteenth century literature was the product of the coming together of two traditions, those of courtly love and of the learned structure of cosmic order, retaining in a subordinate position the values of a warrior society. This view was compatible with the principles of neo-thomism developed in the 1930s and 1940s by liberal French Catholics such as Jacques Maritain and Etienne Gilson, who projected an image of medieval culture as a synthesis of contrasts, as against the fragmentation of modern life and culture.[52]

Lewis's vision of courtly love was linked with the particular 'story' that he and others were telling about their own time and its relationship with the middle ages. In that vision, the fusion of and confusion between a history of poetry and a history of love was consistent with the general assumption of the formation of European subjectivity as a self-contained linear process whose active subjects were literate men, while the people, and women, were sources of inspiration. The meaning of Provençal poetry today is derived from a different set of values, whereby it is very important not only to differentiate between the history of the ways of loving and the history of literature, at the same time as finding connections between them, but also to recognise the multiplicity of contributions to both from various areas of the world and of European society. In this light we are inclined to see certain aspects of Provençal poetry which were in shadow 50 years ago, such as the presence of the body in the songs and the role of women as singers and creators and not only as an audience or as inspiration. With this shift of focus, the theme of the Europeanness of courtly love has almost been forgotten. It is worthwhile to go through a rapid survey of the theme, in order to situate Lewis (and Briffault) in its context.

## A long dispute: the Europeanness of courtly love

The European character of Provençal love has been a long-lasting stereotype, whose basic elements were formulated and systematised during the Enlightenment. For at least two centuries – from the mid-eighteenth to the mid-twentieth – many scholars, writers and intellectuals of various kinds have assumed that Provençal poetry represented the origin not only of European poetry but also of a specifically European way of loving and of the European way of defining individuality and consciousness. These assumptions have not gone unchallenged, as we shall see in a brief excursus on this story, which will touch on developments pertaining to three moments of a very complex process, namely the 1770s, the period between 1810 and 1830, and the 1880s, all three being major points of change.

The Europeanness of the troubadours' love was attributed by some early authors to the peculiar mixture resulting from the encounter between the Northern sagas and the Southern culture. At the origin of this interpretation we find a French and an English scholar, Jean Baptiste La Curne de Sainte-Palaye (1697–1781), with his *Mémoires sur l'ancienne chevalerie* (1753) and the *Histoire littéraire des troubadours* (1774, three volumes of poems and lives of the troubadours, edited and published by the abbé Millot, who also wrote an *Avertissement* and a *Discours préliminaire*) and Thomas Warton (1728–1790), with his *History of English Poetry* (1774) and particularly the *First Dissertation, Of the Origin of Romantic Fiction in Europe*. These authors were not the first to have given attention to Provençal poetry, since this had been done since the sixteenth century, but they initiated a period of renewed attention to the texts: Sainte-Palaye had travelled twice to Italy to find rare manuscripts of the troubadours, which, however, he edited rather freely.[53] In the *Discours*, Sainte-Palaye/Millot put forward the idea that, in a period when barbarity and ignorance still predominated in Europe, and Europeans themselves were immersed in a state of anarchy, the troubadours coaxed Europe out of its torpor and placed 'les esprits' on the road to reason and perfection, till their influence covered most of the continent. Chivalry contributed to the renaissance of culture and creativity, but in the South of France it did not need to create a new system, simply to make the ancient one more widespread and subtle. This was because the people of the French provinces were the descendants of Germans and Gauls, and this derivation was shown primarily by their attitude towards women, very similar to that of the peoples of the North – namely the Celts: Germans, Scandinavians and Scythians – a veneration, a sort of cult as if women had something divine, and a recognition of women's authority in oracles and religion.

Warton further developed an aspect touched on by the two French authors, by insisting forcefully on the origin of romantic fiction. He linked the development of the new attitude to women and love – which he considered to be a major change from that of the Greeks and Romans – with the sensitivity displayed by 'that peculiar and arbitrary species of fiction which we commonly call romantic', also entirely unknown to the writers of Greece and Rome. Its appearance in the popular beliefs of the Europeans was due to two influences: firstly, that of the Gothic scalds and the Scandinavian bards who diffused their adventurous spirit, their tales and their veneration of women in a Europe where 'revolutions, emigrations, and invasions were almost universal'; and secondly, that of the Arabians, who from their settlement in Spain transmitted their romantic fables to other parts of Europe, especially to the French. 'No sooner was the Roman Empire overthrown,' wrote Warton, 'and the Goths had overpowered Europe, than we find the female character assuming an unusual importance and authority, and distinguished with new privileges, in all the European governments established by the Northern conquerors'.

These French and English authors shared a vision of the origins of European culture as resulting from the same ingredients, new views of life and love in which the attitude to women represented a major divergence from those of antiquity. They also shared a certain contempt towards the troubadours and their poetry and attitudes, due to the barbaric origin of European gallantry: Sainte-Palaye/Millot found 'mille traits de libertinage et débauche' in Provençal poetry, which they sought to purge of all the indecencies and outrages to prudency. Warton considered the troubadours of Provence 'an idle and unsettled race of men' who treated love with profound pedantry and affectation, while at the same time encouraging the greatest liberties and indecencies, verging on extravagance and religious fanaticism. Since both Sainte-Palaye/Millot and Warton believed that poetry was a faithful mirror of society, they ascribed such characteristics to the low level of civilisation at the times of the troubadours. Yet, they thought, the language and poetry of the Provençals could have reached the highest perfection, had they not been crushed by the Albigensian crusade (1209–1229) led by Simon de Montfort in the name of the Roman Church, an unjust and cruel enterprise, which all people of feeling still found shameful and revolting.

Some of the basic themes – or my themes – of the long-lasting stereotypes about Provence and its love were thus put in place. What is relevant in this myth of origin is that the specific difference between European love and the classical past is indicated in the combination of cultural heritages of Northern and Eastern Europe, as well as from the Arabs. The role of the North was that it opened the way to a taste for the wonders of oriental and romantic fiction, as well as introducing the 'unusual importance and authority of the female character', while the South elaborated and gave form to these new attitudes, since at this point they had become as different from those of the Romans and Greeks as from those of contemporary Asia. In this view, Europeanness coincided with the capacity to combine creatively a set of multicultural elements, and to give rise to what may be called modern sensitivity. The transmission of these themes in Provence and its culture was accompanied by the publication of the critical editions of the Provençal poems and with the development of the discipline of romance philology.

The next important edition of the poems, *Choix des poésies originales des troubadours*, was published in 1816–1821 by François Raynouard (1761–1836) and it included a very important novelty, a grammar of Provençal, at that point no longer either spoken or understood. In addition, its author compiled a dictionary on which to base his theory of Romance linguistics. An important element in Raynouard's interpretation was the attention he gave to women not only as objects but as subjects of Provençal poetry; he observed that one of the most significant trobairitz, the Comtessa de Dia, spoke a different language to Sappho, who still lived in a period when 'la sensibilité était toute matérielle'. With the countess, it was the heart and its sentiments which counted: tenderness, coupled with intellect, and the desire of love for love's sake. And he interpreted in this way one of her most famous poems:

III

Estat ai en greu cossirier
per un cavallier qu'ai agut,
e vuoill sia totz temps saubut
cum eu l'ai amat a sobrier;
ara vei qu'ieu sui trahida
car eu non li donei m'amor,
don ai estat en gran error
en lieig e quand sui vestida.

III

I've lately been in great distress
over a knight who once was mine,
and I want it known for all eternity
how I loved him to excess.
Now I see I've been betrayed
because I wouldn't sleep with him;
night and day my mind won't rest
to think of the mistake I made.

| | |
|---|---|
| Ben volria mon cavallier | How I wish just once I could caress |
| tener un ser en mos bratz nut | that chevalier with my bare arms, |
| qu'el s'en tengra per ereubut | for he would be in ecstasy |
| sol q'a lui fezes cosseillier | if I'd just let him lean his head against my breast. |
| car plus m'en sui abellida | I'm sure I'm happier with him |
| no fetz Floris de Blanchaflor | than Blancaflor with Floris. |
| ieu l'autrei mon cor e m'amor | My heart and love I offer him, |
| mon sen, mos huoills e ma vida | my mind, my eyes, my life. |
| | |
| Bels Amies avinens e bos, | Handsome friend, charming and kind, |
| cora·us tenrai en mon poder, | when shall I have you in my power? |
| e que iagues ab vos un ser, | If only I could lie beside you for an hour |
| e qe·us des un bais amoros? | and embrace you lovingly – |
| Sapchatz, gran talan n'auria | know this, that I'd give almost anything |
| qe·us tengues en luoc del marit, | to have you in my husband's place, |
| ab so que m'aguessetz plevit | but only under the condition |
| de far tot so qu'eu volria | that you swear to do my bidding.[54] |

For Raynouard, the poems of all the trobairitz expressed 'un abandon plus vif, plus passionné' than those of the troubadours. Thus another element of the mythology was positioned.

Raynouard was in contact with the Coppet group around Madame de Staël (1766–1817), which greatly contributed to the knowledge and re-evaluation of the troubadours. The intellectuals at Coppet – a little village and castle on the lake near Geneva where the Baroness de Staël withdrew when Napoleon exiled her from Paris for her influence on the liberal opposition – read the collection by Sainte-Palaye, but also corresponded with Raynouard. Among them was Simonde de Sismondi (1773–1842), author of a *Histoire de la littérature du midi de l'Europe* (1813), based on the courses he gave at the University of Geneva. This work took as its base Sainte-Palaye/Millot, and it also maintained that chivalry and Provençal poetry were born together, generating at the same time the cult of women and the cult of honour, while anticipating the taste for romantic poetry: 'les troubadours, les premiers-nés de l'Europe pour la poésie romantique'.[55] Sismondi, a protestant and liberal, accepted the thesis of the Arabic origin of Provençal poetry based on the theory that the Arabs had invented the rhyme. But he added another important feature: these ideas had already existed in the people, 'dans le peuple', where they found their real source, but the people were able to follow them in a consistent way only after poetry had given them full expression.

The Coppet group contributed greatly to re-evaluating the middle ages as the beginning of a process of perfectibility of the human species, and chivalry – understood as the search for freedom – as the predecessor of liberalism.[56] Viewed from this perspective, nationalism was linked with cosmopolitism, although often the latter succumbed to the former, and this turn of thought is visible in the changing conception of Provençal culture. In 1810 Madame de Staël had written *De l'Allemagne* (destroyed as soon as it was published on the orders of Napoleon; when the book reappeared in 1813, it was very successful), where she ascribed much more importance to chivalry than in her previous works; it was through the development of her friendship and collaboration with August Wilhelm Schlegel that she came to praise many positive qualities of chivalry, including love and respect for women.[57] In this book,[58] she claimed that the term 'romantic' had been introduced in Germany to describe the poetry which originated from chivalry and Christianity through the troubadours. At this point a competition between nations for ownership of this heritage was perceptible, since Madame de Staël stated that the German 'Minnesänger' were also poets of love, but that they were in no way comparable 'à nos trouvères et à nos troubadours', who were at the roots of French national literature.

A.W. Schlegel played a very important part in redefining the role of the troubadours in European culture. His interest in it was first expressed in his correspondence with his brother Friedrich on the subject of literature in Southern Europe from 1795 on; he studied the manuscripts, and in 1803–4 gave a course in Berlin including the troubadours. In his *Observations sur la langue et la littérature provençales* (1818), he demolished the old prejudice that the troubadours' songs were naive, spontaneous and primitive, showing that they were instead an elaborate and cultured poetry. He was critical of Sainte-Palaye, whose zeal he admired but whom he judged incapable of producing a correct version of the original texts. However, in particular, Schlegel argued with the doctrine of the Arabic origins of Provençal poetry.[59] He had never seen – he claimed – any real evidence of the Arabic origins of Provençal poetry; neither could he be persuaded that the inspiration of a poetry founded on the adoration of women and their social freedom could be taken from a culture in which women were slaves, or that Christian knights could accept models from those they were fighting to the bitter end. 'Mais les sectateurs de Mahomet n'ont jamais eu la moindre influence sur rien de ce qui constitue le génie original du moyen age.' Thus, even if they were the first to use rhyme – although he claimed that many other peoples began to use it at the same time – they certainly did not invent love. Schlegel went so far as to question another imitation, that of the Provençals by the 'Minnesänger', preferring the interpretation that 'impulsions pareilles ont produit des phénomènes analogues'.

The tone of these quotations indicates the change of attitude that was taking place in the conception of Europeanness under the influence of nationalism. The idea of Europe at the time was torn between two opposing political factions – those of Metternich and the Holy Alliance (1815), on the one side, and of the liberal revolutionaries in Naples (1821) and Spain (1823) on the other. The Coppet group, defined by Stendhal as 'les Etats généraux de l'opinion européenne', aspired to become as European as possible,[60] placing the national spirit at the service of the continental one. They believed that nations must keep their differences and even their national egoisms, while the Napoleonic wars were trying to impose forced union.[61] Their Europeanism included some elements of Eurocentrism, on the basis of an idea of European superiority which had been unquestioned since the end of the eighteenth century and which became increasingly apparent at the time.[62]

However, there were various lines of thought in the Coppet group. A frequent visitor there was the romance philologist Claude Fauriel, whose *Histoire de la poésie provençale* (1846) was published only after his death; it was Fauriel who gave Stendhal material on the Arabic origins of Provençal love for his treatise *De l'amour*, first published in 1822. Stendhal's ideas of Europeanness and of love included a division of labour on national grounds, which had for a long time been a theme with many variations (in the *Encyclopédie* the entry 'Nation' included the attribution of national characteristics: as light as a Frenchman, as jealous as an Italian, as solemn as a Spaniard, and so on). In Stendhal's framework, Italians are the only people to know about love and to spend a lot of time talking about it (*De l'amour* was started in Milan, when its author noted on a concert programme the gossip concerning five or six love stories taking place during Carnival in 1820); the French have sacrificed love to the needs of the 'passion nationale', and young Germans show a mystical enthusiasm for women and love; as for European women, the Viennese are loyal and not at all coquettish, while the Scottish are melancholic and for this reason very seductive. In spite of their differences, Europeans are grouped together as superiors to Americans, who experience promiscuity without understanding passion. However, Stendhal's Europeanism in the field of love was not Eurocentric. For him, the Mediterranean was the *foyer* of European civilisation, a meeting-place of Western and Oriental influences; in the chapters on Provence he stated that the Provençals had learned from the Spanish Moors a pleasant way of living, and had developed their 'génie éminemment gai', giving rise to a culture of happiness: 'l'amour régnait avec l'allegresse, les fêtes et les plaisirs dans les châteaux de l'hereuse Provence'. The Moors' conception of love was based on an equality between the lovers, unknown 'dans notre triste Occident' and originated with the Arabs, who had the greatest respect for women (according to Stendhal, wives were able to divorce simply by turning their tents to face away from those of their husbands). In the chapter on *L'Arabie*, Stendhal claimed that Arab gallantry and its literature were born together, and that it was Mohammed, a puritan who proscribed pleasures which do not harm anybody, who killed love in the countries that became Islamic.

In the course of the nineteenth century, various processes addressed the question of Provençal poetry and love. The study of this poetry became a specialised branch of the scientific discipline called romance philology: by 1830–31 courses on the troubadours were offered at the Sorbonne by Fauriel and in Bonn by Friedrich Diez, author of *Die Poesie der Troubadours* (1826), dedicated to A.W. Schlegel, and of *Leben und Werke der Troubadours* (1829), works which had a major influence in the process of this specialisation. This included an increasingly rigorous philology, but also, given its positivistic nature, a narrowing vision, almost repudiating interpretation.[63] Secondly, 'le genre troubadour' became fashionable in various fields of art, such as painting, and daily life, such as clothing (a typical accessory in the 'toilette troubadour' was the scarf, as Jacoubet pointed out). The theme of distant love was widely diffused during this period, in the story of the Provençal poet Jaufre Rudel, who fell in love with the Countess of Tripoli without ever having seen her, travelling over the sea and dying after meeting her. In England Robert Browning's *Rudel and the Lady of Tripoli* (1841–6) and Swinburne's *The Triumph of Time* (1866) are worth mentioning, along with the Pre-Raphaelites, Dante Gabriel Rossetti in particular. In Italy, Giosuè Carducci's *Jaufré Rudel* (1888) as well as Giuseppe Verdi's opera *Il Trovatore* (1853) should be cited. However, it has been claimed that in all these developments science and imagination, between which the Coppet group had found a balance, lost that equilibrium and unfolded along two divergent lines.[64]

While these processes were going on, the crystallisation of a concept of Europeanness and its ancestry was taking place which stressed the superiority of Europe in relation to the imperial and colonial experience.[65] Thus Romance studies came of age as part and parcel of a general tendency to define modern Europe in a way that excluded influences from the Orient. An exclusive insistence on the 'adulterous' character of courtly love came into being, giving rise to a cliché which is now seen to be illusory: 'interdicted' seems to be a more appropriate term than 'adulterous', because it designates not the technical state of love outside the marriage contract but the lack of permanent and fulfilling union with the desired one; the obstacles in the way of the fulfillment of love and the establishment of a satisfying union are more internal and poetic than they are external and social.[66]

By the end of the nineteenth century these stereotypes were crystallized by both specialist and general texts. In 1883, the term 'courtly love', which was to gain widespread currency in the following century, was introduced, over the troubadours' preferred terms 'fin'amors', 'amor honestus' and 'cortezia'. The French philologist Gaston Paris, analysing the poem by Chrétien de Troyes on Lancelot – and describing his total devotion to Guenevere in accepting from her the extreme test of appearing a coward – proposed a definition of this kind of love as 'amour courtois', an absolute love characterised by fascination, idolatry, extasis and tyranny. For Paris, such love has the following features: it is illegitimate, i.e. opposed to marriage and to possession; the woman is superior to the man because she runs the risk of betraying her husband for her lover; the lover (who can only be male for Paris) finds himself in a position of inferiority, trembling and shy, while the lady is capricious, cruel, disdainful and ready to break the relationship if the lover breaks the code of love. But her whimsical requests are trials allowing the knight to better himself through a process where love becomes an art, a virtue, a science, a 'gay saber'.

Some very influential books of a very different nature published in that decade reflect the spread of some of the stereotypes on Provençal love. For Friedrich Engels, in *Der Ursprung der Familie, des Privateigentums und des Staats* (1884), one cannot talk about individual sexual love ('Gechlechtsliebe') in antiquity, when marriages were organised by parents and love in marriage was not a subjective inclination, but an objective duty. According to Engels, only slaves were capable of passion in ancient society, and questions of love were the products of its fragmentation. Modern love is very different from that of the ancients, in the sense that it presupposes equality between women and men. Modernity is equated by Engels with democracy, as far as it explodes the old form of marriage based on the interests of the household and brings individuals' inclinations to the fore. For Engels too, the Provençal poets were central to such a development and represented a pinnacle of European civilisation: they gave classical form to the love of the mediaeval knights; this form included adultery, and poetry celebrated it.

In 1886, Nietzsche published *Jenseits von Gut und Böse* (*Beyond Good and Evil*), in which he brought together Europeanness, love as passion, and the Provençals:

> This makes it clear without further ado why *love as passion* – this is our European speciality – absolutely must be of aristocratic origin: it was, as is well known, invented by the poet-knights of Provence, those splendid, inventive men of the 'gai saber' to whom Europe owes so much and, indeed, almost itself.[67]

These words were extracted from Stendhal and Madame de Stael, to whom Nietzsche referred respectively with enthusiasm and with contempt. For him, the Provençals had invented that *gay saber* which he chose as the title of one of his most important works, *The Gay Science* (1882). The *Fragments*, written between 1885 and 1888 and published posthumously, include the title of an unwritten chapter: 'Gai saber, Prelude to a philosophy of the future', and prophetic thoughts, such as on the danger of a German Reich, and of an antisemitic party, as well as reference to two contradictory features which characterise modern Europeans, the principle of individualism and the vindication of equal rights. The passage on the troubadours is quoted from that part of *Beyond Good and Evil*, on 'Peoples and Fatherlands', in which Nietzsche is interested in establishing a teaching discipline for a caste of Europeans that might govern Europe; it must be an aristocratic teaching, because the democratisation of Europe will lead to the emergence of tyrants. A central strand in this vision is the idea of the South, the Mediterranean, where 'the Provençal and Ligurian blood from time to time foams over' and people are 'good Europeans' by birth.[68] It is here that the famous formulation: 'Europe wants to become one' can be found; beyond the lunacy of nationalism, it is Europe – 'das Eine Europa' – which has been anticipated by artists and great men and 'whose soul now forces its way longingly up and out'.[69] For Nietzsche, the spiritualisation ('Vergeistigung') of sensual love carried out by the Provençals has taken a step forward from the Greeks, who idealised Eros and spiritualised pederasty, without affecting heterosexual love.[70]

The Eurocentrism of this stereotype is evident, although its ambivalence is also clear: it can be used in the service of very different ideologies, by the left and the right politically speaking, and this is particularly true for the period studied here, the 1930s and early 1940s. In the 1930s the progress of romance philology had taken an important step forwards with *La poésie lyrique des troubadours* (1934) by Alfred Jeanroy of Paris University. His work, cited as authoritative by Lewis, was a complete overview of the troubadours' works and life and historical context, and of the previous positions held over these. Jeanroy was very skeptical about the Arabic origins of courtly love and poetry, and quoted Schlegel on the subject without dissent.[71] He coupled this with prejudices about women, as often happened, in spite of quoting two enthusiastic admirers of the trobairitz's poems, Raynouard and Fauriel. But Jeanroy transformed their surprise at the fact that the trobairitz decided to step down from the role of idols to that of *adoratrices*, by asserting that the trobairitz were slaves of tradition, incapable of finding new themes, and that they simply inverted the gender roles: he accused them of laziness of spirit and lack of taste, shame and decency. However, one of the important contributions he made is his polemicising on what he called a misunderstanding about women's poetry, the belief that it was more 'natural' than that of men. He also demolished the opinion (supported in the sixteenth century by Nostradamus) that love courts headed by women had actually existed, by demonstrating that they were a literary exercise developing from a *jeu de société* consisting in questions and answers on love such as: do the lover and the loved have equal rights over each other? does love produce greater joy or grief? is it better to love somebody who hates you or to hate somebody who loves you?[72]

The theme of the Europeanness of courtly love was by then a commonplace, implicitly accepted by large groups of people from various social and cultural backgrounds, so that it offered a resource which could be appropriated and used as a weapon by different political factions. Nazi racist propaganda was one such. On the occasion of the European Youth

Congress in Vienna (in September 1942), Baldur von Schirach, the Reich Youth Leader of the NSDAP and Gauleiter of Vienna, delivered a speech containing the following passage:

> The song that once filled the valleys of Provence and is to this day a triumphal song of Europe and of its civilisation – the song of the troubadours as an expression of those higher feelings that distinguish us from the Jews and jazz-playing American negroes – is something that people of Jewish mentality never can understand. Its whole ethos is foreign to the Jews.[73]

The mytheme connecting Europeanness and Provençal love was distorted by this interpretation and taken to an extreme.

On the opposite side of the political spectrum can be quoted Simone Weil's writings in the same year for *Cahiers du Sud*, the review created between Carcassonne and Marseille by Mediterranean critics and writers such as Joe Bousquet, Jean Ballard, and René Nelli. Simone Weil (who signed her articles with an anagram of her name, Emile Novis), focused on the idea of happiness that the culture of Provence had achieved, based on order, freedom, intelligence, the harmony of different classes, civic sentiment, a conception of subordination that implied equality between those who serve and those who are served, and an idea of fidelity imported by the Moors; the civilisation of Provence was created thanks to its tolerance towards different traditions, since it combined nordic influences with those from Arabia and Persia. Indeed, it is likely that it would have reached the degree of spiritual freedom and fertility found in Greece, had it not been killed by the Albigensian crusade. But 'les patries mortes' cannot be resuscitated; after that crusade, Europe never again reached the same spiritual freedom. According to Weil, the rejection of violence was taken to its extreme in the Provençal idea of love, which was understood as the founding principle of an order without dogmas ('amour ordonnateur'), a love that was devoid of avidity, a waiting directed towards another being that required the latter's consent. Love in the Pays d'Oc had the same inspiration as love in ancient Greece: the latter chose homosexuality in the same way as the former chose adulterous love in order to express the sentiment of impossible love, which is nothing other than chastity. Christianity and the greater purity of customs imported from the Germanic people substituted the identity of sexes with the sacred link of marriage; the love of the troubadours was in the end love for God by means of a beloved human being. The spirit of that love is best expressed in the song by Bernart de Ventadorn:

| | |
|---|---|
| Can vei la lauzeta mover | When I see the lark a-moving |
| de joi sas alas contral rai, | For joy his wings against the sunlight, |
| que s'oblid'es laissa chazer | Who forgets himself and lets himself fall |

per la doussor c'al cor li vai,    For the sweetness which goes into his heart;
ai! tan grans enveya m'en ve    Ai! what great envy comes unto me for him whom
    I see so rejoicing!

de cui qu'eu veya jauzion,    I marvel that my heart melts not for desiring.
meravilhas ai, car desse    Alas! I thought I knew so much
lo cor de dezirer nom fon.    Of Love, and I know so little of it, for I cannot
Ai, las! tan cuidava saber    Hold myself from loving
d'amor, e tan petit en sai!    Her from whom I shall never have anything toward.
car eu d'amar nom posc tener    She hath all my heart from me, and she hath from
    me all my wit
celeis don ja pro non aurai.    And myself and all that is mine.
Tout m'a mo cor, e tout m'a me,    And when she took it from me she left me naught
e se mezeis'e tot lo mon;    Save desiring and a yearning heart.[74]
e can sem tolc, nom laisset re
mas dezirer e cor volon.

This love is aimed at awakening Europeans to the search for the spiritual dimension of life; the roots of European spirituality are the same as those of ancient Greece, and different from that of the Renaissance, which was 'false'. In Weil's image, the idea of Europe implicit in the happiness – *le bonheur* – of the Provençal 'real' renaissance can act as a normative ideal guiding the contemporary search for spiritual freedom.

Briffault and Lewis can be placed in the tradition which we have briefly explored. They shared the convictions, as Howard Bloch has underlined by always quoting them together, that Western romantic love is not 'natural', but has been specifically constructed by European poets and aristocrats of the eleventh century.[75] For the difference between them, we need simply to remember Briffault's vehement attacks on the Christian Fathers for the moralising effects that they imposed upon Provençal love, as well as his hatred of the presumed supremacy of Britain, while for Lewis Provençal love was the starting point of a line of sentiment that, adequately purged, produced the cultural and moral predominance of Christian values in their British version.

The Eurocentric conception of courtly love continued after the Second World War as an implicit assumption in the works of a wide range of authors.[76] Only in the 1960s, when *The Allegory of Love* was enjoying a revived success with the paperback editions and translations into Spanish and Italian (1968 and 1969), did scholars express their reservations about the Eurocentrism implicit in that conception; some went to the extent of considering the expression 'courtly love' as 'inherently absurd' and 'an impediment to the understanding of medieval texts'.[77] For example, Peter Dronke maintained that the feelings and conceptions of *amour courtois* are universally possible in any time or place and at any level of society, in popular as well as aristocratic love-poetry, and introduced the term 'courtly experience' to designate both a particular type of sensitivity and a whole way of looking at life. E.T. Donaldson stressed the fact – well known but usually left unexpressed – that the Provençal equivalent of the French term *amour courtois* was apparently used only once by the Provençal poets themselves, who preferred other expressions; he underlined not only the anacronism implicit in the current use of the term but the lack of agreement about its meaning. For Donaldson, the insistence on a phantom cult of sexual immorality was a projection, occurring at a time – the late nineteenth and twentieth centuries – when sexual morality was once more threatening to replace all other forms of morality, and the scholars who placed most emphasis on a supposed cult of adultery were 'often the very ones who, like Lewis, *were* most anxious to moralize the Middle Ages'. In spite of these attacks, other authors such as Bloch in 1991 continued to assert that romantic love came into being in the first half of the twelfth century, first in Southern and then in Northern France, and that it was transmitted through a remarkable continuity, while it 'did not exist in Judaic, Germanic, Arabic, or Hispanic tradition, in classical Greece or Rome, or in the early Middle Ages'.[78]

However, Bloch has displaced the concept of 'the invention of Western romantic love' at the same time as accepting it, by interpreting such invention as a shrewder form of medieval misogyny, a 'usurping appropriation of woman at the moment she became capable of appropriating' masculine modes of wealth.[79] Of course, the other societies where similar expressions of love existed outside Europe were no less misogynous than Mediaeval European society; the hypothesis could then be made, following Bloch, that the attitude 'putting women on a pedestal' signals a cultural contradiction aroused by important changes in gender relationships. At the same time, insisting only on the continuity of misogyny in various epochs and societies seems reductive, since it forgets that courtly love means not only 'women on a pedestal', it also indicates – more importantly – an attitude which exalts the object of love, woman or man, and the unfulfilled aspect of desire.

The interpretation of Provençal love as a sentiment expressed only by men, with little or no physical satisfaction, and uniquely characteristic of European civilisation, came to be dominant in the second part of the nineteenth century and the first part of the twentieth, in the course of a process which negated Arabic influences, the importance of women as composers and performers of poetry, as well as forms of sexuality and sensuality for purposes other than procreation, such as the 'asag' (sexual encounter which respects feminine chastity[80]). Changes in mentality concerning all these aspects have accompanied the development of a less Eurocentric view. Our understanding of Provençal poetry has increased with new critical editions and discoveries of manuscripts; one major step forward has been the critical edition of the trobairitz's *corpus* by Angelica Rieger, presenting the songs of poets such as N'Azalais de Porcairagues, Na Castelloza and the Comtessa de Dia. All this, while contributing to challenging a merely spiritual conception of Provençal love, has helped to undermine a conception of love which integrated the superiority of Europe over the other continents and of men as authors with a vision of women merely as objects of poetry.

Eurocentrism in the field of love has not been solely a matter of high culture, it has existed in popular and mass culture, often in a connection of circularity with the former. One telling example can be found in the role of Provence in the European imaginary.

## Travelling to Provence

The consideration of Provence as the heart of a European civilization found a parallel in the construction of Provence as the essence of the South, which has been a *Leit Motiv* in travel literature since the nineteenth century. In his *Mémoires d'un touriste* (1838), Stendhal wrote about the natural joy of the Midi, and the lack of interest in money of the people in Southern France, attitudes he saw as similar to those of Italy and Spain. In this century it was Ezra Pound who travelled to Provence and rendered the troubadours' poetry a source of constant inspiration for his work.

Pound started learning Provençal in 1904–5 at Hamilton College with Dr William Pierce Shepard (a distinguished scholar who had studied in Grenoble, Paris and Heidelberg), and continued at the University of Pennsylvania under Hugo Rennert. In the previous 50 years almost 30 editions of Provençal poets and seven grammars and dictionaries had been published, testifying that Provençal studies were flourishing. In the period 1908–1910 Pound translated nearly 50 poems by troubadours, which he published in *Personae* (1909), *Exultations* (1909), *The Spirit of Romance* (1910), and *Canzoni* (1911), although he eliminated many of them from subsequent editions (such as *Personae* of 1926). In 1911–12 he published in *The New Age* (his relationship with its director Orage was an important one) translations of poems by Arnaut Daniel, on whose manuscript he worked at the Ambrosian Library in Milan and whom he valued, after Dante, as a major source of inspiration; Pound's translations awakened a new interest in Provençal poems. He also wrote essays on the Provençals and their poetry, which were included in *The Spirit of Romance* and in *Pavannes and Divisions* (1918). These translations and essays prefigure many of the themes and techniques of the *Cantos* (1917–1968) which, however, abandon mannerisms of the earlier versions. The early poems and prose writings can therefore be used as glosses on passages in the *Cantos*.[81] Although Pound was often technically incompetent, his translations had vivid intuitions and liberated the poems from 'the overriding and all-exterminating cliché 'courtly love" used and abused by critics such as Jeanroy and Paris.[82]

Such experiments in transforming romance philology into contemporary poetry were part of Pound's sense that 'all ages are contemporaneous', while medieval values had for him a particular 'contemporaneity'. In his search for 'inventors' and 'origins', Pound saw the Middle Ages as a period of awakening and Provence as playing a central role in this process.[83] The troubadours' interest in prosody, their continuation of Greek mysteries, their critical relation to the established Church of Rome, their use of medieval mystics, and their engagements with political issues and events made them important predecessors for him,[84] giving them the role of his *personae* or masks of the self or *alter ego*. Therefore his translations and reflections aimed at making the Provençal poets his contemporaries and at reformulating their heritage in modernist terms. Suffice it to quote here as an example a strophe of his version of the famous poem by Jaufre Rudel:

| | |
|---|---|
| Lanqand li jorn son lonc en mai | When the days are long in May |
| m'es bels douz chans d'auzels de loing, | Fair to me are the songs of birds afar. |
| e qand me sui partitz de lai | And when I am parted from her |
| remembram d'un'amor de loing. | I remember me of a love afar, |
| Vauc, de talan enbroncs e clis, | And I go with a mind gloomy and so bowed down |
| si que chans ni flors d'albespis | That no song or white thorn flower |
| nom platz plus que l'inverns gelatz. | Pleases me more than the winter's cold. |
| Ja mais d'amor nom gauzirai | Never more will I take joy of love |
| si nom gau d'est'amor de loing, | Unless it be of this love afar, |
| que gensor ni meillor non sai | For a nobler and fairer I know not of |
| vas nuilla part, ni pres ni loing. | In any place either near or far. |

Crucial moments of Pound's recognition of the troubadours' heritage were his walking tours through Provence. He made the first in May and June 1912, armed with Michelin maps and guidebooks (Baedeker's 1907 *Southern France*, the 1877 *Guide Joanne* to the Pyrenees, and Justin Smith's 1898 *Troubadours at Home*). The tour started from Poitiers, site of the court of the first troubadour, William IX, who Pound believed had 'brought the song up out of Spain', and proceeded through Toulouse, Carcassonne, and Narbonne. Pound intended a book based on the notes taken during the tour, with the title *Gironde*, to be published, but Ford Madox Ford – to whom he had shown part of the manuscript – discouraged him by ridiculing his prose as archaic. The typescript of *Gironde* was left unpublished and was in the end lost, but the notes have been deciphered and published recently. In them, the description of the terrain 'as a chessboard of strategic possibilities transforms the local geography into a topographical allegory of Bertran de Born's embattled psyche', by which Pound projects his own scenarios onto the landscape.[85] In 1919, Pound returned to Provence with his wife Dorothy and Eliot, whom he transformed into Arnaut (*Canto XXIX*) for the occasion.

In 'The Troubadours: Their Sorts and Conditions' (an essay first published in the *Quarterly Review* in 1913 and then in *Pavannes and Divisions*), Pound used some passages included in the fragments remaining from the lost *Gironde*. In one of these he lists three ways of "going back", of feeling as well as knowing about the troubadours': first, by way of the music; second, by way of the land; third, by way of the books themselves, meaning the illuminated manuscripts; in the essay he adds a fourth way, by reading the 'razos' or lives of the troubadours (which were prose introductions to the poems). The first three ways include an experience going beyond that of the oral or written word, such as the music (Pound worked on musical settings of troubadour poetry with the composer Walter Morse Rumel in Paris in the spring and summer of 1912), the visual images of the illuminated manuscripts, and the physical relationship with the landscape through travelling on foot through the land, exposed to the wind, rain and sun.

Travelling was above all a way of retracing emotions, as Pound wrote in his travel notes: 'I am a lover of strange and exquisite emotions',[86] and he found them on his trip, in spite of his occasional disappointment at seeing people dressed in clothing from Milan and Paris. He was seeking contact with that 'aristocracy of emotion' which for him characterised the troubadours as continuators of the Greek mysteries: 'the "chivalric love" was an art, that is to say, a religion'.[87] This religion endowed Provençal love with an esoteric component, whereby the Lady served as a sort of *mantra* of great spiritual strength.[88] In Pound's interpretation, the troubadours' love ethic expressed in the idea of *fin'amors* included a 'chastity' that regulated sex and kept it 'holy', as part of an illuminating wisdom; if lovemaking was at the centre of his Provence, it was so in this idealised sense.[89]

Going to Provence was for Pound a way of travelling back to its civilisation, just as leaving America for Europe was for him a way to live through and express his veneration for the European culture of the past. His cosmopolitism and multi-culturalism had deep historical roots, since for him a close connection existed between poetry, the past, and his own nomadic life through places consecrated by the European literary memory, in the search to regain the 'inclusive man' of Confucius.[90] The moving line that he wrote much later in the *Pisan Cantos* – 'As a lone ant from a broken ant-hill/from the wreckage of Europe, ego scriptor'[91] – expresses his deep sense of belonging to a European cultural heritage which was in the process of being destroyed by the world wars. Provence stayed in the *Cantos* as a concentration of symbols dear to the poet. Thus one of the very last *Cantos* shows traces of the poem *Can vei la lauzeta mover* that he had translated from Bernart de Ventadorn, and the voices of the two poets are both fused and autonomous:

La faillite de François Bernouard, Paris
or a field of larks at Allègre,
   'es laissa cader'
so high toward the sun and then falling,
   'de joi sas alas'
to set here the roads of France.

In the 1930s, many aspects of the attitude expressed by Pound in relation to Provence were shared by the authors of some of the numerous travel books of the period, contributing to spread the Provençal myth, and to extend it to an area with indistinct boundaries stretching from the South of France to most of Italy. This tendency was part of a more general attraction for the South and the Mediterranean, with which the British had an 'imaginative intercourse' and which became increasingly frenetic in the inter-war period in order to escape the growing sense of decadence in Britain.[92] The adoration of the South of France found its expression in the glowing comments about the weather – contrasted with that of Britain – wines, landscape, and a lifestyle which stayed closer to nature, while the people of the South were considered less hypocritical than northerners, more passionate and more sincere. The identification of the *South* with the Mediterranean, with the corollaries of fine food and love – both symbols of real life, sincerity and authenticity – had by now become a theme of international tourism, and was 'a version of the pastoral' that became increasingly widespread in the 1930s.[93] In the travel literature – where women often figured as authors – these themes were repeatedly played with only slight variations.

In travel books published in the 1930s, Provence was approached through its literary memory: 'places like Orange would be uninteresting if the fragrance of old romance did not hang about the streets' with those of aïoli and marron glacé.[94] Literary reminiscences were essential in this discourse, which borrowed from Anatole France the request for the Provençals to teach the world 'effortless joy, the arts, the tilling of the soil, peace, a brilliant peace'.[95] Thus the area was understood as 'a realm invisible, a state not of the mind so much as of the heart, a kingdom to be conquered only by love of it', which lies 'anywhere around the corner' on the Riviera and in Provence.[96]

The historical heritage, freely interpreted, was a major component of this image. Mediaeval Midi had enjoyed intellectual freedom, wealth and luxury, as it had been the home of a love which defied restraint, addressed exclusively to married women.[97] This 'Utopia'[98] included a high status for women, who were held in great respect, directed the ceremonies of the

Courts of Love, and some of whom could become trobairitz as well, like the Comtessa de Dia. Even if the Midi never recovered from the Albigensian crusade and the Inquisition,[99] Provence remained the only pagan spot, apart from Sicily, which was left in godly Christendom.[100]

Together with the wine, the food and the climate, the main component of this 'happy kingdom', as reads the title of one of these books, was its people. Provençals were presented as being as exuberant as their own soil, warm-hearted, generous, wayward and hospitable, with many racial strains mingling in their veins, Christian by conversion or adoption and pagan by heritage.[101] When used as workmen, they were 'perfectly maddening, entirely without initiative, and quite irresponsible, but most lovable', as true 'children of nature' should be. These were words by a Lady Fortescue who had bought, 'before the pound collapsed', a little house in the region, where she had the pleasure of behaving like a feudal lady to the fifty-six-year-old gardener, Hilaire:

> I held out my hand at him, asking him if he would stay on and take care of the garden, Monsieur, and me... he took my hand in both his hard brown paws and bent his head low over it as he thanked me, rather as though swearing fealty to a queen. Then he straightened himself and gave me a long look of promise and fidelity in his eyes. He did the same to Monsieur, and so the bargain was sealed.

Hilaire turned out to be 'very, very wise' and to have 'an instinct for weather which is almost animal and quite unerring'.[102] Thus Lady Fortescue 'had grown to love these excitable emotional men of the South – she pulls together Southern French and Italian – and to regard them as *her* children – for they were little more'.[103] But they were in fact something more, even to her:

> I wonder what woman could resist the unconscious way an Italian peasant makes love to her with his eyes while he is taking her orders?

Through the eyes of Lady Fortescue Provence is transformed into an exotic 'enchanted land' – where she and people like her live 'a queer, fascinating life' – and its inhabitants into primitives living lives close to nature; thus the myth of Provence, its ladies, and its love, is shaped to suit the colonial mind and customs of a British upper-class woman. The success of that myth was possibly also due to its malleability, its capacity to adapt to various types of dreams and projections, whether of upper- or middle-class provenance.

Ford Madox Ford's *Provence from Minstrels to the Machine* (1935, revised in 1938) epitomised these attitudes. The author was a close friend of Ezra Pound, who had written a piece on him in 1914 – when he was still called Ford Madox Hueffer – pointing him out as not only 'the best critic in England, one might say the only critic of any importance', but also 'significant and revolutionary because of his insistence upon clarity and precision' both in prose and in verse. Ford Madox Ford's father, Dr Francis Hueffer, was an authority on the troubadours, of whom he had written an important history in 1878.

His son's Provence is a place of the spirit more than a geographical area; therefore *Provence from Minstrels to the Machine* is largely set in London, which is made 'infinitely more supportable' to its author by reading Mistral and being sure that he will see Provence once more.[104] This land is the opposite of the 'glorification of Mass',[105] and stands for the hope that the number of machines and of machine hours worked in the modern world can be reduced to a minimum. Ford Madox Ford – who declared that he did not care whether Fascism or Communism of the Russian type would eventually prevail in the Western world – claimed that he would prefer to go back to Dark Ages and agricultural communities rather than to suffer a mass 'civilisation'. For him, Provence was a symbol of that past, and therefore of a Europe liberated from the clutches of Fascism and Communism. Between a long digression on garlic, 'allium officinale', and some descriptions of Vaucluse, Ford Madox Ford gave the literary points of reference for his Provence: Caroline Gordon, Allen Tate, but above all Ezra Pound. Curiously enough, Provence in the above sense extended to Italy but not to Spain.

The myth of Provençal love as the heart of European civilisation was expounded in various forms at very different levels. Amy Oakley's version in *The Heart of Provence* expressed a belief regarding ancient Provence that might well have appeared as a vulgarisation of Lewis's *The Allegory of Love*, had the two books not been published in the same year, 1936:

> ... romantic love was considered to be non-existent between husband and wife, therefore a poet might not continue to sing her praise in the event of marriage with his lady. The love of man for woman was extolled, perhaps for the first time in the history of mankind, with spiritual ecstasy.[106]

Oakley's intention was for this myth to provide the 'romantic approach' – as the title of one of her subchapters claimed – that would guide tourists along the routes from Aix-en-Provence to the Camargue to Avignon and Aigues-Mortes to find 'echoes of the troubadours'. It was a similar, although more refined, idea that should guide Europeans, according to Lewis, to reconcile Christianity and romanticism, to restore the relationship between love, marriage and religion, as well as the respect for spirituality and the values of the individual. It is not surprising that much later on, in the 1960s, on the occasion of a debate on whether Britain should 'go into Europe', he would express the hope of connecting Europeanism with federalism at a regional level, of a 'super-national state built up of units like Wessex and Picardy' which would combine unity with the greatest local diversity.

## Notes on Chapter 5

1   OUP Archive, Letter of 22 August 1958
2   Watson, pp 1–2
3   Lewis, *Letters*, p 21
4   *Ibidem*, p 127
5   *Ibidem*
6   OUP Archive, Letters of 18 and 24 September 1935
7   OUP Archive, Letter of 27 October 1935
8   OUP Archive, Letter of 3 November 1935
9   Warren Lewis, in *Letters*, p 20
10  *Ibidem*
11  OUP Archive, Letter of 23 February 1956
12  OUP Archive, Letter of 15 October 1959
13  OUP Archive, Letter of 18 September 1935
14  *New York Herald Tribune*, 18 October 1936
15  *The Allegory of Love*, p 11
16  *Ibidem*
17  *Ibidem*, pp 298; 305
18  *Ibidem*, p 197
19  *Ibidem*, p 237
20  *Ibidem*, p 257
21  *Ibidem*, p 282
22  *Ibidem*, pp 344–5
23  *Ibidem*, p 298
24  Watson, p 6
25  Gunn
26  Lee, pp 136–8
27  *The Four Loves*, p 102
28  *The Allegory of Love*, p 22
29  Wilson, p 109
30  Lee, pp 174–6
31  *Ibidem*, pp 212–4
32  *The Allegory of Love*, p 30
33  *Ibidem*, p 44
34  *Ibidem*, p 69
35  *Ibidem*, p 82
36  *Ibidem*, p 117
37  *Ibidem*, p 120
38  *Ibidem*, p 358
39  In *Beiträge zur Psychologie des Liebeslebens*, 1924
40  *The Allegory of Love*, p 358
41  *Ibidem*, p 83
42  *Ibidem*, p 82

43    *Letters*, pp 346; 451
44    *Ibidem*, p 449
45    *The Four Loves*, p 91
46    Watson, pp 1–2
47    *The Allegory of Love*, p 360
48    Cantor, p 210
49    Boase, Foreword
50    *The Allegory of Love*, p 4
51    Veldman, pp 3; 12
52    Cantor, pp 214–5; 217
53    Gossman
54    See Sources, Chapter 5, pp 324–5
55    Sismondi, t. 1, 10
56    *Groupe de Coppet* 1974 and 1994
57    King
58    Staël, XI, II, *"De la poésie classique et de la poésie romantique"*
59    Schlegel, 67 ff
60    Pellegrini
61    Marcelli
62    Woolf S.
63    Mancini, p 12
64    Duranton, p 366
65    Menolocal, p 6
66    *Ibidem*, pp 103–7
67    Nietzsche, p 198
68    *Ibidem*, § 254; p 188
69    *Ibidem*, § 256; p 189
70    Mancini, pp 64–5
71    Jeanroy, p 70
72    *Ibidem*, 263 ff
73    Lipgens, p 103
74    For this poem and the one quoted on p 214 see Sources, Chapter 5, pp 324–5
75    Bloch, p 8
76    Denomy; Nelli
77    Newman
78    Bloch, p 9
79    *Ibidem*, p 196
80    Nelli, p 335
81    McDougal, pp 40; 137
82    Wilhelm, p 137
83    McDougal, pp 3–5
84    Dennis in Taylor & Melchior
85    Sieburth, XV
86    Pound in Sieburth, p 7

87  *Psychology and Troubadours*, pp 90; 87
88  *Ibidem*, p 97
89  Makin, pp 183–5; 250
90  Holder, p 216
91  *Canto* LXXVI
92  Green; Fussell, pp 130–1
93  *Ibidem*,
94  Day, p 49
95  Oakley, XVIII–XIX
96  Peattie, p 2
97  Day
98  Oakley
99  Day
100  Peattie, p 5
101  Day, p 1
102  Fortescue, p 54
103  Ford Madox Ford
104  *Ibidem*, p 90
105  *Ibidem*, p 320
106  Oakley, p 258

# CHAPTER 6

# BETWEEN CULTURE AND POLITICS

## The future of the European spirit

I n October 1933, a conference called 'Les entretiens sur l'avenir de l'esprit européen' was held in Paris at the International Institute for Intellectual Cooperation, which formed part of the League of Nations. The conference, opened and chaired by Paul Valéry, gathered together well-known intellectuals from 14 countries, all male. The meeting had been called on the peremptory assumption that it would avoid politics and keep the debate within the boundaries of intellectual and cultural problems. These conditions were due to the difficulty of managing the simultaneous presence of men so politically distant as the Italian Fascist Academic Francesco Coppola and the British writer Aldous Huxley, author of the satire on dictatorships, *Brave New World* (1932). As Salvador de Madariaga put it, at the conference there were Europeans who belonged to the centre and Europeans 'banlieusards' – on the outskirts or peripheries – among whom he included those from Russia, Spain, Portugal, and England; these countries, he believed, represented, respectively, the connection with Asia, South America and North America.

In fact, the main intervention in the debate, by Aldous Huxley – the only delegate from Britain – seemed fairly marginal to the tone of the conference, although he posed problems which were central to its topic. He declared that those who had spoken before him – including Valéry, Count Keyserling, Huizinga, Brunschvigc, Benda and Duhamel – had presented only preliminary observations to what he considered to be the central problem. Huxley claimed that this was the intellectual life-style of the masses, and he spoke of a general denigration of intelligence and logic on the one hand and a vulgarity and lowness of the style of life on the other. He felt that anti-intellectualism was triumphing in its various forms – such as Bergsonism, Freudism and Watson's behaviourism – and saw the philosophy of National Socialism as the most dangerous example of the readiness of anti-intellectualism to justify nationalism and its mixture of hatred and vanity. This philosophy constantly dealt with 'particular truths', attempting to justify the 'nordic instincts and the infallible intuitions of blond men', while it treated 'objective truths' as the vain claims of intellectuals.[1] Huxley's first point was that, while the political union of Europe would not be possible without a renewed faith in reason and logic, the masses would accept logic only if it was embodied in a work of art; he hoped that 'an artist of intellectuality' would appear, but stressed the fact that no organisation could provide that logic. Secondly, the increasing prosperity in Europe meant that millions of Europeans could now afford to pay for their bad taste; language was itself corrupted by commercial publicity, while literature and popular music were dominated by second-order material. According to Huxley, the only possibility of stemming these tendencies lay in the education of taste and critical sense through examples taken from the contemporary world. He spoke with lucid pessimism, moderate hope and some humour. His two main points were really central to the question of culture in Europe in the 1930s, but they were not picked up by other delegates. Valéry kept referring to the humorous side of Huxley's speech, but doubted that they as intellectuals – victims themselves of the existing system of dissipation and vulgarity – would ever have the power to do anything. He also issued a very precise warning: 'we should not penetrate the political realm that you have touched, my dear Huxley – not even for an instant'.[2]

The rest of the debate was largely a series of general and often bombastic declarations about the need for Europe to return to its humanistic inspiration, with a vague insistence on the need for education. The only moments when the discussion came to life were those when the taboo on politics was broken, and this happened only twice. The first time it was broken by the Fascist Coppola, who refused to accept the dualism between themselves and the younger generation, dominated – as Count Keyserling had said – by 'telluric forces, instincts, and vital needs'. Coppola's refusal was a mark of his support for the political forces that exalted the 'telluric forces', i.e. National Socialism and Fascism. Indeed, he went even further, declaring that 'education was very nice, but was not sufficient' and that in any case it was too difficult to instil a European spirit into children; above all, he said, the unity of Europe could not be achieved by reason, but only by force. Coppola pointed to the danger represented by Russia, the 'enemy of European civilisation' because of its 'Oriental mystique', and advocated the lesson of Rome. What he meant by this was that Rome would save European civilisation for the fourth time – the Roman Empire, Christianity and the Renaissance being the first three times – by incorporating and reformulating the subversive Oriental mystique, in other words by 'digesting' Socialism into Fascism.[3]

After this intervention, Valéry tried to block the debate, declaring that Coppola's exposé was 'magistral, très élevé et trés étendu', but that it was impossible to discuss it because it was too ample, and he gave the floor to another speaker. Immediately after this, Duhamel intervened on Coppola's speech, asking him what he meant by his reference to the gods still adored by the intellectual community and abandoned by the young.[4] Coppola replied without hesitating: he gave the example of the democratic ideology of equality, and pointed to the contradiction between that old Enlightenment idea and modern European imperialism, and to the vulgarisation of that ideology, i.e. Wilson's principles, now used by Asians against Europe. Again Valéry interrupted the debate, giving the floor to another speaker, but as soon as this was over Julien Benda took up the point made by Duhamel, reminding Coppola that the idea of freedom was not simply one or two centuries old, but that it went back to the Greeks, and was perhaps not yet dead; he then warned against a certain 'famille de penseurs' which had declared the end not only of the idea of freedom but also of the very idea of truth, while 'certain parties in certain countries declare that they want to teach children, in the field of history, the "national truth"'. He was referring to the Action Française and Charles Maurras, greatly admired in certain countries that Coppola knew well, and to the Soviet Union.[5] At this point Coppola launched into a tirade on the fact that a great people recognising a great man as its chief was a great act of freedom. Valéry found a way to conclude the exchange with the pharisaic consideration that nothing expressed the European spirit better than the co-existence of two opposite tendencies, and Coppola commented: 'C'est le caractère dialectique de l'esprit européen', thus giving rhetorical hot air the last word.[6]

There was much in this exchange that related to the points made by Huxley, but he did not intervene. Nor did he comment on the very moving intervention by the novelist Jules Romains, the second time the taboo on politics was broken. Romains was the only voice to clearly describe the predicament in which intellectuals currently found themselves: he abandoned the 'prudence extrême' that Valéry had recommended, and expressed his anguish that their debate risked becoming sterile in not recognising that the European spirit was subordinated to the existence of Europe, and that any thought or action concerning that existence required complete freedom of discussion on its political conditions. What was moving in Romains's earnest declaration was that he accepted that the times required 'prudence extrême', but rejected any spiritual legitimation of the situation through any declaration of the type: 'I have wanted this'. The delegates should, on the contrary, state that they did not accept what was happening, but that at a time when the 'inferior powers of the soul were drawing the peoples of Europe into a vertigo' there was nothing to do but to wait and suffer. Romains clearly saw that the proposals emerging from the conference would be so timid – 'si prudentes, si détournées, si pudiques' – that he despaired they would ever attract the interest of the masses subjected to so many insolent rumours, and asked for another meeting to discuss first of all the political organisation of Europe.[7] Huxley did not react to any of these provocations; his last intervention was instead very diplomatic, rejoicing that everybody had spoken French – a sign that the rationality of the Enlightenment embodied in French had not died out completely – and thanking France for its contributions on behalf of all good Europeans.

The situation at the conference was representative of a wider one for intellectuals and culture in Europe at the time: the aggressive Fascist rhetoric contrasted with vague academic praise of a European universalism, the emptiness of bureaucratic resolutions, silence on the great problems of mass culture, the difficulties, indeed, of mutual understanding even when one language (French) was used. Jules Romains was perfectly right, and perfectly isolated in his recognition. The counterposition which pleased Valéry was not the dialectics boasted of by Coppola, but the polarisation of the forces tearing Europe apart, Fascism, Stalinism, anti-Fascism and anti-Communism. As the years went by, political forces became increasingly penetrating, and at the same time the traditional division between the fields of politics and culture became steadily more blurred. The conference had shown – for those who still doubt it – that there was no neutral international space for the cultural debate. In Britain this illusion perhaps lasted longer, because the intellectual atmosphere was freer from pressures, but the twin processes of political polarisation and of a merger between politics and culture were evident there as well, against the background of a growing interest in the theme of Europe.

The publishing scene in Britain reflected this. A sign can be found in the list of works added to the British Library during the decade. In the period 1931–1935, texts on the history of Europe in the subject index numbered about 150 and those on European politics about 90; in the period 1936–1940 they increased, respectively, to about 190 and 150. As for the quality of the titles, in history there appeared between 1932 and 1938 the great works on Europe by Dawson, Fisher and Croce, and in politics an increasing number of books on the problem of the relationship between dictatorships and democracies as well as on the danger of an impending war. The titles (of books published only in England) reflected a sense of growing anxiety: *End to Illusion: A Study of Post-war Europe* (by L. Schwarzschild, 1934), *Black Hand over Europe* (by H. Pozzi, 1935), *Europe in Crisis* (by R.B. Mowat, 1936), *Europe under the Terror* (by J.L. Spivak, 1936), *Thunder over Europe* (by H. Gigon, 1937), *Fear Came on Europe* (by J. T.

Whitaker, 1937), *Europe into the Abyss* (by S. Forbat, 1938), *The Labyrinth of Europe* (by M. Burn, 1939), *Disgrace Abounding* (by D. Reed, 1939), *Europe's Dance of Death* (by G.T. Garratt, 1940). While the quantity of these books helped make the continent and its problems better known in England, they were repetitive and often full of commonplaces. However, it is possible to discern some important lines of discussion.

The idea of Europe was now torn apart by polarisation, and through that showing its fragility. *The Intelligent Man's Review of Europe To-day* by G.D.H. and Margaret Cole made the point in relation to the geography, history, economy and politics of the continent, starting from the acknowledgment that the advent of Nazism had dealt a heavy blow to European Socialism as a whole.[8] While the Coles envisaged the possibility of 'the advent of a single federation wide enough to embrace the entire European continent', they believed that 'the essential prelude to any collaborative commonwealth of Europe is the establishment of some form of socialism in each European country' – which they hoped would occur without bloodshed – and that 'the hope of making the League of Nations into an effective instrument of internationalism lies in the victory of socialism in enough of the countries which make it up totally to change its character'.[9] The limitation of this concept of united Europe – which subordinated it to the nation and to the victory of socialism – is evident: it had no innate strength that would allow it to oppose the Fascist ideology; conversely, at almost the same time Oswald Mosley started arguing that the only way to achieve a united Europe was through the accession of Fascism to power in the major European countries. Moreover, the Coles declared that for the present the idea of a confederal Europe would have to be conceived in terms which left Britain out; only if a number of British colonies fell or were taken away could Britain be drawn into the circle of the continental system. As for the Soviet Union, there was the eventuality that the smaller states of Eastern Europe would turn Communist, and in that case the USSR would be brought far more into contact with the West. While the Coles did predict some of the future of the world and Europe with far-sightedness and accuracy, the kind of cosmopolitan socialism that they invoked was very vague: they did not say in which countries it would develop, nor how it would challenge the existing Fascist dictatorships.

This genre of work on Europe's state featured forecasts on the near future; many of the books written by political scientists, journalists and historians analysing the political situation in Europe, attempted to assess the chances of war. In the second half of the 1930s this topic became more concrete and down-to-earth than it had been at the beginning of the decade, and the public was eager for information on it. One bestseller in the field was *Inside Europe* by the American correspondent of the *Chicago Daily News*, John Gunther. The book – criticised sharply by the *Fascist Quarterly*[10] – went through 30 impressions between January 1936 and

November 1938, some of them with new material and new prefaces. It was written on the explicit assumption that 'the accidents of personality play a great role in history', and it told the intimate story of the leaders playing decisive roles 'in the stupendous drama of Europe between wars', from France, Spain and Italy to England, Central Europe and the Balkans, through Germany, Poland, Switzerland and the Soviet Union. It was a simple and clever way of proceeding, based on much evidence accumulated through the author's journalistic work, as well as books, pamphlets and newspapers.

Similar, more limited, surveys of European affairs were *Fear Came on Europe* by John T. Whitaker, the American correspondent who had been with the Italian troops in Ethiopia (1936), and Hugh Sellon's *Europe at the Cross Roads* (1937, revised 1938) on political problems concerning France, Italy, Germany, Britain and the League of Nations. Worried about 'the unhappy state of Europe', Sellon – then a lecturer on Foreign Affairs and International Relations at Bonar Law College in Ashridge – sought the hope that, on the basis of the 'essential unity of [its] civilisation', it would be possible to 'build a finer civilisation on mutual respect and toleration', with a particular role assigned to Britain, where 'the European virtues of individual freedom and initiative [were] not as endangered'. Sellon still believed that Britain's insular position gave her protection against military invasion,[11] and that she could act as the decisive element between the ideological extremes of the continent, without having to participate in an armed conflict.

The sense that war was very likely was put forward by the more realistic authors, who warned against a policy of appeasement that would not set precise limits on Fascist expansionism. So did the scholarly work *Britain and the Dictators*, in which the historian R.W. Seton-Watson studied the relationships between Britain and the continental regimes in a vast historical analysis covering Russia, Italy and Germany since 1919. He detected an acute spiritual crisis of public opinion during the years 1936–7, caused by the direct challenge the obscure and nebulous European situation posed to the idea of progress, to liberalism, and to Christianity itself. British foreign policy remained equally obscure and undefined, characterised by an intermittency which exasperated continental Europeans. While Seton-Watson adhered to a policy of non-intervention in Spain – and justified it with his analysis – he believed that it should be made absolutely clear that Britain would never let France and her interests down, and that political realism was not compatible with lack of interest; rather, it involved issuing a clear warning that Britain would be ready to fight rather than to abandon her traditional friends.

These issues even penetrated the travel book genre – real or fictional – which by then included books written by political tourists, now often indicating to readers that the names and occupations of the people met during the journey were disguised. *European Journey* (1934), by Philip Gibbs, was meant to give 'an authentic record of the ideas, hopes and fears moving in the minds of common folk and expressed in wayside conversations' in the villages, cities, inns and market-places of six European countries. In the past the author had had some sympathy for Mussolini, but he now reckoned that Italy was on the verge of a deep economic crisis, and he stigmatised as 'senseless and mean and cruel' the treatment received by Jews in Germany. He returned from his European journey 'with renewed faith in the kindliness, the humour and the shrewdness of ordinary people', who had talked to him about their desire for peace and a decent livelihood. But he also wrote that 'everywhere there is a sense of doom in the minds of men and women', and that the fear of another war 'is haunting and obsessing the mind of Europe to-day', although the standard of living among the working classes had risen during the previous 20 years[12] Going back to England he felt relieved about 'returning to a country free from tyranny, civil strife, and dangerous forces at the flash-point of explosion'.[13] It was of course an illusion that the British could remain aloof from the continent's troubles and conflicts: looking back on his journey, he came to realise that he felt 'unable to see much light ahead with any promise of happiness and peace for the European people'.

In *A Young Man Looks at Europe* (1938), by Robert Young (pseudonym of P.S.R. Payne), the journey began at Verdun, commemorating the 1916 battle where so many Germans and French had died, and then moved to Paris, Munich, Vienna, Budapest, Cracow and Prague. For the author and his two young companions – a French woman and a German man – Europe had become an incomprehensible and mysterious country in which they felt like strangers and aliens. He 'returned to England without any clear idea of the forces working in Central Europe', having found justifications for civil war almost everywhere but noticing that 'everyone was talking about war with a sense of incredulous disbelief',[14] so much so that the whole idea of war had become unreal and few people seemed to take any interest in the current conflict in Spain. Seeing threatening graffiti ('Jude, verrecke!') in blood-red paint on the houses of some Jews in Vienna – 'the blood dripping from the long serif of the J' – they had 'wondered whether this was not the first sign of the final disappearance of European culture'.[15]

Political polarisation was evident even within this genre. Major F. Yeats-Brown, the author of *Bengal Lancer*, who publicly identified with British Fascism, wrote *European Jungle* (1939) where he put to use his having been 'a wanderer through the new and rising nations of Europe' from Russia to Germany and Spain. For him the 'serpent in the European jungle' was Communism, standing for 'the annihilation of Christianity and of our system of civilisation';[16] behind Communism stood the 'children of Israel'. Yeats-Brown disapproved of the German treatment of Jews, but he was staunchly antisemitic, anti-liberal, anti-capitalist, anti-demo-cratic, anti-pacifist and anti-Communist. He declared that he disliked Communism because he disliked any sort of internationalism,[17] and he feared that anti-Fascist propaganda had so anaesthetised the British that they were no longer able to see the incumbent threat to Western civilisation.

The theme of the decay of European civilisation – as already seen from the point of view of the psycho-analytical and psychological debates (see Chapter 2, 'States of Mind') – was to some extent superseded by the discussion on the more immediate problems of war and peace in Europe. However, it was always present to some degree, acquiring, as the years went by, apocalyptic overtones. In 1932 the book by the Spanish philo-sopher Ortega y Gasset, *The Revolt of the Masses*, was published in England and received warmly across the board, from the journal of the New Britain Movement to Eliot's *The Criterion*, which was already in close contact with the *Revista de Occidente* (1923–36), founded by Ortega with the purpose of keeping Spanish readers in touch with the general trend of European thought. Ortega was at that time a Member of Parliament of the Spanish Republic; in the following years he did not take sides in the civil war, with-drawing instead from politics and living abroad from 1936 to 1945. *The Revolt of the Masses* tackled precisely the problem posed by Aldous Huxley at the 1933 Paris conference: the accession of the masses to public life in Europe, i.e. to the political, intellectual, moral, economic and religious aspects of European civilisation, from the highest cultural levels to the daily forms of dress and leisure. By 'Europe' Ortega understood primarily 'the trinity of France, England, and Germany'. In the light of Ortega's vitalistic existentialism, the analysis of the European crisis put together very different phenomena: the rise of the standard of living not only for minorities but for large strata of people; the presence of the 'multitude' in all the places created by civilisation such as theatres, cafés and beaches; the levelling of fortunes, culture and sexes; and, above all, the new psycho-logical condition of the ordinary man, a sort of primitiveness based on self-satisfaction and specialisation, ignoring 'the spontaneous and joyous effort' of training and ascesis. In contrast to all the claims made about the 'Americanisation' of Europe, Ortega stated that the triumph of the masses had come about in Europe for internal reasons, in particular, the wealth and security produced by liberal individualism and scientific research; contrary to the prophets of decadence, he saw in such processes 'a fabu-lous increase of vital possibilities' as well as the risk of Europe returning to barbarism within 30 years. Ortega's solution to all this was Nietzschean: the formation of a European aristocracy ready to overcome nationalism and to build up a united Europe into 'a gigantic continental state'.[18]

*The Revolt of the Masses* brilliantly catalysed themes and motifs which were widespread on the continent as well as in England. It is interesting to compare a British version of some of its points, i.e. a liberal progressive democratic version, such as that proposed in the introduction to *The Intelligent Man's Way to Prevent War*, a collection of essays (including those by Norman Angell, Gilbert Murray, Viscount Cecil and Harold Laski) edited by Leonard Woolf (1934) in the same series as the book by the Coles. The editor summarised the reasons why it could be said that in the years 1923–1933 Europe had taken another step on the road back to barbarism, even bigger than that taken with the First World War: he noted the economic crisis, the political instability, the growing tension between nations, the rise of savage dictatorships and the glorification of Fascist mass-murders, the suppression of liberty, the barbarous persecution of Liberals, Socialists, Pacifists and Jews, and he claimed that all this indicated that the process of breakdown of European civilisation was well under way. Civilisation, said Woolf, was a delicate organisation which was in a continuously precarious state everywhere in the world, since 'we are all of us still half-savages' whose instincts to kill, dominate, persecute and torture could hardly be reconciled with an 'ordered society of humane, educated, intelligent, free, prosperous, and cultured individuals'. The 'intelligent man' – the democratic version of Ortega's aristocracy – was supposed to stand for all this and, through an understanding of what was going on, to react to the 'rebellion of all that is savage in us'.[19] But what was savage in this case was not so much the result of the processes indicated by Ortega, i.e. the development of science and liberalism, as the inner drives, understood in a Freudian sense as the discontents of civilisation.

In the second half of the 1930s the discussion on the crisis of European civilisation could not avoid political polarisation, and this amounted most of the time to a lowering of the level of the debate. One area of resistance was to some extent represented by T.S. Eliot and his *Criterion*. One instance of this was Eliot's reaction to an American book which had met a good deal of critical approval when it was reviewed in London. *Was Europe a Success?* by Joseph Wood Krutch, prefaced by C.E.M. Joad, and endorsed by Albert Einstein and Aldous Huxley on the front flap, posed the question of whether European civilisation was inextricably linked with an inequitable social order, including imperialism, military pride and national spirit. Krutch evidenced the similarities, notwithstanding differences, between those who wanted to save European civilisation as a whole, for instance Eliot and Maurras on the one hand, and Mussolini and Hitler on the other. T.S. Eliot[20] reproached Krutch for his lack of historical sense, his dislike of Christianity, and his static conception of European civilisation. But he especially emphasised that what he found depressing was 'to live in a world in which views which I dislike are opposed by other views which I dislike so much as I dislike Mr. Krutch's'. In the late 1920s *The Criterion* had appealed to a 'Europe of the mind', a republic of letters, 'an appeal to reason rather than an emotional summons to international brotherhood'.[21] In this perspective European consciousness was not a triumphant and positive feeling, but one born of the sense of insecurity and danger which had followed the First World War and the Russian Revolution. It stemmed from the perception, expressed in Valéry's words, that Europe was a small and isolated cape on the Western side of the Asiatic continent. Eliot used the self-consciously European profile of the journal as a weapon to attack various forms of parochialism but also to stigmatise the dominant liberal sentiments in England.[22]

A very similar intention to T.S. Eliot's, but stemming from an opposite political view, was behind the publication of a journal with the title *The European Quarterly: A Review of Modern Literature, Art and Life*, whose editors were Edwin Muir and Janko Lavrin, both from the background to Orage's *New Age* (Muir worked as Orage's assistant). Both of them were also good friends of Mitrinovic, whom Lavrin described as a man with 'a home-made messiah complex' while Willa Muir defined him as 'an entertaining companion because he was such an egregious nonsense-monger'.[23] Edwin Muir (1888–1959) was a self-educated man who, after working as a clerk in various commercial and ship-building offices in Glasgow, became a journalist, translator, and author of fiction, poetry and criticism. He experienced great poverty, and lived in Germany, Czechoslovakia and Austria; he and his wife translated Kafka into English. He took great interest in psycho-analysis and this led him into full analysis and a resulting belief in the possibility of a revolution of human personality. Although he was a life-long socialist, he had nothing in common with the political poets of the 1930s, from whom he was distant both on account of age – he was some 20 years older than the Auden generation – and of his own experience of working-class life.[24] His association with Janko Lavrin (1887–1986) in *The European Quarterly* had more than one meaning: the two shared an interest in psycho-analysis and Janko wrote what he defined as 'psycho-critical studies' of Ibsen, Nietzsche and Tolstoy. Lavrin was also of Slovene origin, educated in Austria, Russia and Scandinavia; he had been a journalist in Russia and a Russian war correspondent in the First World War, and in 1923 became Professor of Slavonic Studies at the University of Nottingham. Therefore he represented that Central and Eastern Europe which was so crucial to the political definition of Europe in a period of Nazi aggression towards that area. Some of his contributions to the journal, such as an article comparing the Russian thinker Vassily Rozanov, 'the Jewish renegade' Otto Weininger and D.H. Lawrence on the question of 'Sex and Eros',[25] were an attempt to combine the comparative analysis of authors from the East and West of Europe with a psycho-literary vision of the motif of erotism.

*The European Quarterly* announced that its purpose was to 'attempt to establish a sympathetic contact between the intellectual life of this country and that of the continent', dealing with the vital problems of the age 'particularly as they are reflected in art and literature'. It promised to publish literary contributions from all the European countries as well as from the United States and to 'try to foster the growth of the European spirit in every sphere of human activity'[26]). It did indeed publish contributions by authors from various countries, from Kafka to Dostoyevsky, and Kierkegaard to Garcia Lorca, as well as articles concerning the current situation in Europe, on topics such as Hitlerism, the Balkans and peace, since its editors believed 'that the realm of literature, art and thought should transcend all national and political boundaries'.[27] The existence of *The European Quarterly* was, however, short-lived: it was published four times between May 1934 and February 1935 and then closed. The editors' belief that a broad cosmopolitanism could be developed in Britain 'which could perhaps counteract and even reconcile the conflicting nationalist passions of Europe' in a 'supra-national European consciousness' leading to 'a free Federation'[28] encountered in the political state of the age conditions most unsuited to its purposes, and efforts had to be abandoned.

The attempt of *The Criterion* itself to express a European consciousness was only partially successful. The journal published texts by writers such as Benda, Cocteau, Croce, Curtius, Hofmannstahl, Malraux, Thomas Mann, Montale, Pirandello, Proust, Max Scheler, Valéry, Wiechert and many other Europeans of varying political and religious views. But by the early 1930s it relied increasingly upon British contributors, and Eliot's hope of forming a 'phalanx' of the best minds of Europe began to collapse together with European civilisation.[29] In January 1939, Eliot wrote, in 'Last Words', the editorial terminating *The Criterion*:

> [in the last eight years] the 'European mind', which one had mistakenly thought might be renewed and fortified, disappeared from view: there were fewer writers in any country who seemed to have anything to say to the intellectual public of another.[30]

It was a 'gradual closing of the mental frontiers of Europe', as he said later, in his radio broadcast to Germany 'The Unity of European Culture' (1946). In this broadcast Eliot also stated, with reference to the intellectual climate of the 1930s, that 'a universal concern with politics does not unite, it divides' and tends to destroy the cultural unity of Europe, and that the confusion between politics and culture is just as much a mistake as that between the material organisation of Europe and Europe as a spiritual organism.[31]

Eliot's apology for Christianity was very different from that of some Fascist intellectuals, for instance in the ideas presented by Douglas Jerrold on the nature of European civilisation as inextricably linked with Christianity; Jerrold advocated as Europe's only hope its return to the Christian order, and to this end found that no harm could come from Fascist Spain and Fascist Italy, while the feared Soviet Russia could well be a source of impending catastrophe.[32] Eliot too believed that European civilisation would disappear with the disappearance of Christianity, but constantly tried to pose the question on the grounds of religious tradition, 'less false' for him than the political one. Eliot, whom Orage had already called 'a good European' in *New Age* in 1921, acknowledged various times that he had been influenced by Christopher Dawson in conceiving of Europe as of a common civilisation, and in recognising the contribution made to European civilisation by the barbaric society that had been the human material on which Christianity grew, a society organised on the principle of kinship and characterised by a spirit of loyalty and devotion to the community.[33] In a radio talk given in February 1937 Eliot spoke of the failure of liberal democracy to sustain the moral and intellectual values which might keep in check the ideologies of Fascism and Communism, and invoked for democratic societies the renunciation of 'wrong ambitions and wrong desires' and the allegiance to God.[34] In March 1939 he gave three lectures in Cambridge, which led to the writing of *The Idea of a Christian Society*, published later in the year, and of *Notes Towards the Definition of Culture* (1948). A passage in *The Idea of a Christian Society* offers a good example of Eliot's attempt to pose questions at a level higher than the political. He says here that his reaction to the acceptance in September 1938 by the European powers of Hitler's occupation of Sudentenland in Czechoslovakia was of distress not due merely to disagreement on political grounds. It was:

> ... a feeling of humiliation, which seemed to demand an act of personal contrition, of humility, repentance and amendment; what had happened was something in which one was deeply implicated and responsible. It was not a criticism of the government, but a doubt of the validity of a civilisation.[35]

In those circumstances it was very difficult to live up to the ideal of unity of culture and variety of loyalties; the 'free play of intellect' which in the past had allowed 'a common concern for the highest standards both of thought and of expression... a common curiosity and openness of mind to new ideas' had been interrupted and 'an international fraternity of men of letters within Europe' no longer existed.[36] Culture was obsessed by politics, for better or worse, and politics was now obliged to deal with aggression and war.

## Mosley and the British Union of Fascists

In his autobiography, published in 1968, Oswald Mosley claimed that the 'motif of Europe' ran through his early speeches,[37] delivered immediately after the First World War:

> They all reiterated the same theme – eschew foreign adventures which are none of Britain's business, look after our own people, conserve our resources, guard our Empire, maintain our strength, develop our vital interests, which are in Europe, and ignore all distractions from these purposes in remote territories.[38]

The 'motif of Europe' as understood by young Mosley does not appear to be very Europeanist from this quotation, although it does correspond rather faithfully to what he was saying at the time, when he advocated an effective League of Nations and isolationism for Britain.[39] Generally, a confusion exists between Mosley's engagement with a united Europe after the Second World War[40] and the presence of a 'Europe theme' in his political action between the wars:

> ... all my life – as my very early speeches show – I felt myself an [sic] European, and as a movement we were greatly interested in keeping peace between Europeans and also in the gradual development of some common aims in European politics.[41]

In the autobiography Mosley also insists on his attempt to become 'fully and completely a European'; the fact that by 1968 he can 'feel equally at home in England, France or Germany' allows him to conclude that 'in a sense all Europe is my home'.[42] Mosley thus projects his alleged Europeanness and Europeanism back onto the interwar years, and exaggerates the relevance and the quality of his European engagement in the 1930s, appropriating the issue of a united Europe.

Oswald Mosley (1896–1980) made his political début as a Conservative immediately after the First World War and tried unsuccessfully to organise a new 'Centre' party under Lloyd George; under the influence of Lord Robert Cecil he also served on the Executive of the League of Nations Union. In November 1920 Mosley 'crossed the floor' and collaborated for some years with the Liberals, although he was elected as an independent. In 1924 Mosley joined the Labour Party, from which he resigned early in 1931, on the basis of ideas which became the Manifesto of the New Party, involving among others John Strachey and Harold Nicolson. The Mosley Manifesto, a mixture of planning and *laissez faire*, proposed a new approach to the economy through a complete reorganisation of industry and agriculture, as well as an institutional change, the creation of a cabinet of five ministers with the power to carry through emergency policies, subject only to the general control of parliament. In his effort to find a third way between capitalism and socialism, Mosley moved rapidly towards Fascism, and a trip to Rome increased his enthusiasm for Mussolini.[43] In October 1932 he launched the British Union of Fascists (BUF), and after Hitler consolidated his power he switched his major allegiance to the Nazis with a shift marked by political antisemitism.[44]

Mosley's idea of Europe during his Fascist period was linked with the question of preserving European peace, for him a major priority, but he took different stands in the course of time. In 1934 he was still in favour of a reconstructed League of Nations, although he also argued that the co-operation between Fascist governments in all great countries would be the surest guarantee of peace, as he wrote in the revised edition of *Greater Britain*, originally published in 1932. But the 'European leadership must rest with the great Powers'[45] and very soon a united Fascist Europe would supersede the League, he believed. In 1936, a crucial year for the development of Mosley's idea of Europe, he declared in one of his speeches:

> the only alternative [to the League] is the union of Europe as opposed to the division of Europe under the old balance of power which now wears the tattered label League of Nations.[46]

In 'The World Alternative', an important statement published in the *Fascist Quarterly* of July 1936, Mosley advocated a return to 'the idea which animated the post-war generation', of 'the union of Europe in a system of public law and order which broadly applied to international affairs the law and sanctions of law commonly employed within each nation'.[47] That idea, Mosley maintained, had been frustrated by the perversion of the League of Nations, so that, 18 years after the end of war, the balance of power which divided Europe into two opposing camps of balancing allies was restored under the auspices of the League.

What this union of Europe amounted to was the establishment of friendly terms between Great Britain and the three other most important nations of Europe; according to such terms, the German colonies would be returned to Germany – which would eliminate the possibility of German expansion in Europe – while the occupation of Abyssinia by Italy would be accepted on the basis that a hostile Italy would be a much greater menace to British trade routes from the base of Sicily than from any base in Abyssinia. With France's accession to Universal Fascism, a four-power *bloc* of Fascist and National-Socialist countries would be created, which would wipe out what Mosley called financial democracy, i.e. the degeneration of democracy whereby the parliamentary system had become totally outdated and dominated by the decisions of international finance on Wall Street and in the City of London. Mosley also insinuated that for European purposes the Caucasus should be in Italian rather than in Bolshevik hands, and that the Ukraine would be better developed by joint action between

Germany and Poland, but he did not go so far as to propose the partition of Soviet Russia, being content to suggest that Russia should 'mind her own business and leave Europe and Western civilisation alone to manage their own affairs'. The persuasive forces behind this suggestion were to be a united Fascist Europe in the West and Japan in the East – a reason for Britain to withdraw its opposition to Japan's entrance into Northern China.[48] Subsequently, Mosley became more explicit in his advocacy of 'the legitimate expansion of Germany in directions the opposite to any threat to French interest'.[49] While in 1932 Mosley's vision had been of a ratio-nalised world economy modelled on a corporate British Empire, by the second half of the decade he was talking of Britain and Germany as the twin pillars of world order.[50]

According to Mosley, the European union he had in mind could extend to embrace and combine with American policy in regions which affected new world interests, towards a comprehensive policy of 'white civilisation' based on the reality of mutual interests and on 'the world creed of the Twentieth Century', which was to have the force of a new reli-gion. This creed included a 'New Europe', which would emerge from the struggle between the old and the new worlds, also defined by Mosley as the 'struggle with the dark enemy of mankind'; he believed that 'deeper than every division of material things is the division of the spirit in the modern Europe'.[51]

This vision was inspired by Mosley's interpretation of Spengler's *Decline of the West*, whereby he believed that the challenge posed by Spengler's diagnosis of European decadence could be taken up 'with the radiant optimism born of man's achievements in the new realm of science' and with the 'undying belief in the invincible spirit of that final product of the ages – modern man'. The capacity of modern man to arrest the decline of Western civilisation would be a blow against the 'materialist doctrines of two Jews', Marx and Freud, which 'have paralysed the intellectual world into the acceptance of surrender to circumstance as an article of faith'.[52] This peculiar interpretation of two doctrines that proposed radical change in their respective fields is an element of Mosley's antisemitic beliefs; the BUF developed antisemitism from 1934 onwards, on the Nazi example,[53] and engaged in a violent campaign against the Jews in East London in 1935–6.

Mosley had first been attracted to Spengler by his 'profound under-standing of Caesarism', which was, however, coupled with Spengler's insufficient appreciation of modern science, while Mosley believed that the union of a Caesarian movement with science was the prime require-ment of the modern age.[54] As the alienation of the BUF from British society increased, especially after the Olympia (a large venue in West London) meeting of 1934 – where the Fascists were responsible for violent attacks on their opponents – 'the apocalyptic critique of European civilisation of

Oswald Spengler was injected to a greater extent into fascist ideology'.[55] Mosley was also influenced by Spengler in his version of an antisemitism not based on race, but on cultural grounds, which allowed for the assimilation of Jews within national cultures, while some of the least viable parts of Spengler's thoughts, such as the belief that there were more similarities between European nations than between groups within a nation, and that cultural contact caused only contamination and decay, provided justifications for Mosley's idea of a united Europe.[56] The example, Mosley repeated over and over, should come from Britain, which should stop all immigration and deport Jews as well as all foreigners 'unless they proved themselves valuable citizens' who put 'Britain first'.[57] This statement, made in 1936, was further developed in 1939: a united Europe should be capable of finding a 'final solution' i.e. a territory where the Jews could create a Jewish National State; but Jews should not ask that such a state be founded at the expense of Arabs.[58] Meanwhile, the British – who had 'created the Empire without race mixture or pollution' – should live up to their racial tradition: 'the unfit will be offered the alternatives of segregation sufficient to prevent the production of unfit children, or voluntary sterilisation'.[59] Indeed, the antisemitism of Mosley and the BUF (more violently emotional antisemitic feelings than Mosley's were expressed within the BUF by William Joyce and A.K. Chesterton) found a context in an existing tradition of social and intellectual antisemitism in Britain, although in the period between the end of the nineteenth century and the Second World War there was no evidence of official government antisemitism.[60]

Mosley's conception of Europe, which excluded Soviet Russia and reduced it to an alliance between four powers, was clearly very narrow. Its reference to spiritual and intellectual terms was vague, and its scope really amounted to legitimating Germany's and Italy's expansionist aims. The argument that Mosley might have been right in believing that Hitler's aims were confined to Central and Eastern Europe and that at almost any time in the 1930s an Anglo-German settlement could have been negotiated on this basis,[61] thus providing 'an alternative history for the nation he loved',[62] ignores the cost of such an alternative – which implied sacrificing the Central and Eastern European regions to the *status quo* of its Western part – for Germany and for Europe. The idea of a New Europe under the banner of Universal Fascism held by Mosley in the second half of the 1930s was exactly the opposite to the ideal of the New Europe presented in the newspaper of that name published in London in the years 1916–1920 on the initiative of the historian R.W. Seton-Watson and other supporters of the small Slav peoples; their aim had been to fight against Pan-Germanism by promoting self-determination and the emancipation of Central and South-eastern Europe from German and Magyar control. In contrast, there were some similarities between Mosley's ideas and Mitrinovic's NEG, in the sense that Mosley had been influenced by some of the thinkers and scientists connected with the NEG, such as Kitson and Hobson, or whose books had been important for Mitrinovic, such as the Social Darwinists, especially Benjamin Kidd and Houston Chamberlain.[63] But the similarities were not based so much on the idea of Europe – centered for the NEG on individual spiritual regeneration – as on the reorganisation of society and the economy; moreover, the NEG always stayed with its ambiguities and never took a Fascist position, with the exception of some individual members, such as Major Fuller, who was an active official in the BUF, a contributor to the *Fascist Quarterly* (his antisemitic articles are quoted in Chapter 3), and the most eminent military adviser to Mosley.

As far as Mosley's relationship with Fascist conceptions of Europe in other countries is concerned, his contacts were more fruitful with the Italians than with the Germans. Let us remember that Mussolini had sponsored the Convegno Volta on Europe in 1932 and met Coudenhove-Kalergi in 1933, while Hitler had mockingly rejected both Pan Europa and Briand's ideas.[64] Some Italian Fascists developed a 'Euro-Fascism' which included Mussolini's proposal for a revision of the Versailles treaties and 'a modicum of political unity', allowing Europe to grasp once again the helm of world civilisation.[65] Contradictory tendencies on the issue of Europe existed among Italian Fascists, while for all of them the fundamental contradiction concerned the question of the equal rights of weaker peoples in a future united Europe. In any case, Mosley contributed to Italian Fascist journals, including *Anti-Europa*, whose editor Asvero Gravelli had been very encouraging to Coudenhove-Kalergi. On the other hand, his dual loyalty to Britain and Germany was criticised by Alfred Rosenberg, the philosopher of the Nazi movement and author of *Krisis und Neubau Europas* (1934), an early propagandist exposition of National Socialist ideology on Europe. In the end, Nazi ideas for Europe, which at a certain point (1943) included the prospect of a federal solution, were nothing more than a disguise for the aggressive aim to create a Germanic Reich.[66]

After the Second World War Mosley developed the idea of a European union and the slogan 'Europe a Nation'. He then admitted 'the true fault of all real National Socialist and Fascist movements', i.e. that 'our political ideology and propaganda were far too Nationalistic even to mould the minds of men in a new sense of European kinship and solidarity'.[67] The New Union of Europe would be able to bring to reality the 'Idea of Kinship', according to which Europe is 'a family of the same stock and kind'; this 'biological approach' was considered by Mosley to be more in accord with fact and nature than any simple ideological conception. Later on Mosley would advocate 'the sanity and balance of the main European tradition' to support his declaration of being as much against licence as against repression: a male tradition, expressed in the principle that for 'men in the classic European tradition... hysteria was excluded, all was ruled by purpose served by character'.[68]

## An impossible task (Margaret Storm Jameson)

In 1933 'an eloquent plea for a united Europe' was written by Margaret Storm Jameson in *Challenge to Death*, a book which, she claims in her autobiography with her usual sarcasm, 'had the effect I expected – none'.[69] This tone is consistent with the literary style of the autobiography – written in the 1960s – in which she portrays her activity in the inter-war period, 'the interregnum', as an enthusiastic militant 'without principles and with the instincts of an anarchist'. The literary identity that Storm Jameson projects in the book is a multiple and complex one; she doubts whether 'there is an I under all the dissimilar "I's"' which through the decades have constituted her personality. One of those "I's", active for some years after 1933, was involved in 'equivocal amity with pacifists and combative supporters of the League of Nations'. But that 'I' immediately splits, as Storm Jameson evidences the contradiction in the policy that she was seeking to pursue at the time in her 'loathing of war': pacifism on the one hand and the armament of the League of Nations on the other. A pacifist could support the idea of an armed League, she writes, only if she assumed that the bombs of the International Air Force would never be dropped.

Storm Jameson's interest in Europe dated from the aftermath of the First World War. An essayist and writer of 45 novels, a lifelong Socialist and Labour supporter, she was active in various left-wing and libertarian causes.[70] She started working with Orage, whom she greatly admired, at *The New Age* in 1913–14, and in 1932 worked with him at *The New English Weekly*. It was in 1919 that she felt for the first time 'the sense, horribly familiar later, of a dark wave of pain, cruelty, fear, gathering force at the other side of Europe and about to rush down'.[71] That sense was induced in her by the realisation, after reading a report in a newspaper, that German and Austrian children were dying of hunger. As was typical of her generosity in supporting causes, she immediately included and went on including in every issue of *New Commonwealth*, the journal she was then sub-editing, 'at least a paragraph about Europe's famished children'. Subsequently, her second marriage, to the historian Guy Chapman in 1925, was one of the factors that turned Storm Jameson outward, towards Europe, although she remained 'Yorkshire to the bone'.[72] In the following years she travelled to France and Germany, and was involved in a number of initiatives taken by writers in defence of peace and against Fascism. With the ascension of Nazism to power, she came to feel 'a genuine loathing for what was being done by barbarians who had taken the Europe of Goethe, Dante, Vico, the very heart of Christian humanism and the classical Renaissance'.[73]

In the autumn of 1933 Philip Noel-Baker, who had been principal assistant to Lord Cecil during the Peace Conference in Paris and British delegate to the Assembly of the League of Nations in 1929–31, asked Storm

Jameson to help him recruit well-known writers in defence of collective security and against war. The writers were invited to a dinner given by Viscount Cecil at the 'imposing and reticent' Wellington Club. Robert Cecil, Viscount Chelwood (1864–1958), was one of the architects of the League of Nations and president of the League of Nations Union between 1923 and 1945; in 1937 he received the Nobel prize for peace. The League of Nations Union (LNU) carried out important work in educating British people on internationalism; however, it 'was so cautious in its advocacy that it remained thoroughly safe and respectable', and in order to keep in touch with those in power, did not follow its analyses through to any unpleasant conclusions.[74] In 1931 the LNU received 406,868 subscriptions, and in the period between November 1934 and June 1935 it conducted the 'Peace Ballot', a campaign in which 38% of the population took part. The ballot indicated that there was considerable public support for collective security, but also that this support was widely assumed to involve little more than economic sanctions backed by naval pressure.[75] This explains why the co-existence of various political positions in an anti-war front was possible for several years.

In her account of the dinner with Cecil and the book that followed, Storm Jameson's literary persona treats herself not only with understatement, but with self-denigration. She says that she accepted Noel-Baker's offer because she was 'incapable of risking his disapproval by refusing'; she was, however, secretly convinced that they 'were throwing sand against the wind', and she made the proposal to edit a symposium on the danger of another war feeling 'cold with the fear of ridicule'.[76] All these touches of uneasiness are very important for underlining an attitude – a mixture of insecurity, desire to please, obliging behaviour, which has often been labelled 'feminine' – on the part both of the subject writing and of the person who was then taking action. This is not only a mechanism of narrative memory, which can be found in a number of memoirs; it is a construction of the public self which takes to an extreme the image of what a woman can be in that historical situation, with all her uncertainties and passions. The definition of such aspects in this construction as traditionally – not essentially – feminine would not have pleased Storm Jameson. She preferred, like other women writers, to skip her first name and use a middle name which could be either male or female,[77] and insisted that she had never thought of herself 'as either male or female. You just go on with what you had to do.'[78] This comment is consistent with the construction of her deprecatory self-image, on which she had started much earlier than when writing her full autobiography, as the connecting pieces in *Civil Journey*, a collection of her essays published in 1939, show. In *Civil Journey* Storm Jameson already exhibited her difficulties with Noel-Baker's proposal, although it is clear that it was she who gave the project its final form: she felt 'nervous' about the dinner, which she found 'rather alarming', she thought 'anxiously' about it and her 'heart sank' when her name was proposed to edit the book which resulted. It is true that Storm Jameson's attitude implies a direct challenge to any traditional definition of the feminine. However, she actually transforms and turns upside down the traditional image of the woman at the service of a political cause – how many women would not recognise in her description the state of mind of female militants before feminism? – as she uses it with a mixture of irony and coquetry.

The book issuing from the dinner 'turned out a frightful labour', involving the handwriting of some 200 letters and negotiating with writers through 'cajoling, explaining, persuading, encouraging', plus putting together the skeleton of the book. The result of all this was *Challenge to Death*, published by Constable in 1934, a collection of essays by a group of very distinguished authors representing different schools of thought – five of whom were Socialists, wrote Storm Jameson[79] – and various fields of activity, such as politics, journalism and culture; a poem was also included: *War Cemetery* by Edmund Blunden. But Storm Jameson's toil was not over. She had first to convince Cecil to write a foreword, sending him the draft of the whole book,[80] and then to convince him to correct what he had written:

> ... it is a great pity that you say at the very beginning of your foreword that you have not read the book... readers will find this discouraging news... Would it be possible for a slight change to be made?[81]

She finally decided to allow Constable to leave out that 'blunt statement', 'since you did not absolutely forbid it'.[82] The published foreword by Lord Cecil begins with the simple statement that 'this book is the outcome of a vivid realisation by its authors of the menace to peace'; it goes on to illustrate the difference between the nationalism which leads to hatred and that which is capable of transcending its duty to one country in order to serve its duty to humanity. Cecil then reminded his readers that the fundamental conception of the League of Nations was to establish an international system of co-operation and to achieve international peace, as inscribed in the preamble of the covenant, which was the League's basis.

Storm Jameson wrote an introductory essay, *The Twilight of Reason*, which 'could have been written either by a devout supporter of the League or an out-and-out pacifist', she acknowledged, and no-one noticed, thanks to her 'fine rhetorics' and fluent writing, the logical gap inherent in an armed league. This essay played on the idea of the universal revolt from reason which was making the intellectual structure of civilisation collapse. The author included in the 'spread of disrespect for reason' throughout Europe the philosophy of Bergson, the novels of D.H. Lawrence, the 'infection' by jazz, this last judgement being a widespread opinion among European intellectuals at the time. The revolt against reason was shared by all countries on the basis of an interdependence which was not merely economic or spiritual: '... in part it is artificial and evil', in other words it was the effect of modernity itself. But the irrational revolt was at its strongest in the Fascist countries (Storm Jameson argued at length with Mussolini's idea of the absolute national state) and lay at the heart of the success of National Socialism, which she considered to be a return to barbarism.

Among the contributors were Vernon Bartlett, the director of the London office of the League for ten years and special foreign correspondent of the BBC; George Catlin (husband of Vera Brittain), pacifist and professor of politics at Cornell University; the scientist Julian Huxley; J.B. Priestley, critic, novelist and dramatist. Four other women contributed essays: Vera Brittain, who wrote on the importance, for the success of the issue of peace, of taking into consideration the 'public mind' (while Noel-Baker wrote on the 'official mind'); Mary Agnes Hamilton, Labour MP and member of the British delegation to the League Assembly in 1929–30, who supported the need for international security, in opposition to 'extreme pacifists'; Winifred Holtby (the very close friend of Vera Brittain), a poet, writer and journalist who supported the cause of disarmament; and Rebecca West, who wrote on 'the necessity and grandeur of the international idea'. Noel-Baker also contributed two essays on the insufficiency of the national air force and the necessity of establishing an international Air Police Force 'ready to take action in any part of Europe'. Storm Jameson was quite right, 30 years later, to point out the deep contrast between such proposals on the one side and the radical pacifist positions of some of the other contributors, such as Brittain, Catlin and Holtby, on the other. Altogether, it was a rather strange book, which illustrated powerfully the differences within the anti-war front.

One further and not minor difference concerned the issue of a united Europe. Cecil and Noel-Baker had been among those who preferred to maintain the frame of the League of Nations than to support fully the novelty of Briand's proposal for a United States of Europe. Storm Jameson, in her final essay, came out in favour of a united Europe, but let its relationship with the League remain vague. In this essay, entitled 'In the End', she pleaded for public opinion 'knowingly to accept the necessity of taking the first steps towards a European union', 'with England its heart'. It was England's duty to assume the responsibility and show 'the bogged and strayed nations of Europe a road to follow'. She argued boldly against the alleged impossibility of such a task: 'the impossibility of any task is no reason for not trying it', because belief and courage do not require the certainty of victory. Some autobiographical touches were crucial to the argument: Storm Jameson spoke as a 'little Englander in love with an England which never was but could be', who had grown up to understand and love Europe while remaining loyal to her roots. From the strength of these roots she drew something which might appeal 'to young men and women' who did not care as much as politicians for victory as a way of securing their places, but who might start action for the sake of the effort itself:

> In my part of England, when anyone says, 'You mustn't do it, it's impossible', we have a way of answering with a kind of shrewd bold conceit, 'Why, it can be *tried*!'
> 'You mustn't dream of it, a united Europe is impossible.'
> 'Why, it can be tried!'

She appealed to 'ordinary men' like herself, who had better heads and less authority 'than the men who misrepresent us at conferences', to rouse themselves from a sleep-walking state. In order to make her appeal stronger, she reminded her readers that 'ordinary men' had on their side 'half a million whose names can be read on memorials in the cities, towns, and small villages of our country'. This was an approach to the idea of a united Europe *quia absurdum* – tried out because impossible – using as levers the desire to live (it was indeed an extreme challenge to death), the sense of local or regional pride, and the local virtues of obstinacy, defiance, and enjoyment of a sense of adventure. The appeal was somehow incomplete – perhaps it would have needed a more literary rather than essay form – and it worked *ex negativo*: it was the last resort to be tried, since nothing else had worked or would work to avoid war. Storm Jameson did not hide the fact that: 'it *may* be too late', but this observation only strengthened the whole argument.

The conception of a united Europe is still unfocused in this piece of 1934, and it becomes clearer only in connection with another essay that Storm Jameson wrote the following year, 1935, 'On Patriotism', where she repeated: 'I am a Little Englander on one side (the left, the side of the heart), and on the other I try to be a good European'. What she proposed, starting from this autobiographical approach and using as examples her own history and observations, was 'an England reformed at home' which would have in this way more authority abroad and provide the basis for a similar reformation in Europe. She was thinking of something that we would call to-day a 'social Europe', restoring some of the obligations of the welfare state to the underprivileged, an ideal which is far from being practised. The autobiographical approach is also used as a rhetorical device, consistently with the ironical mood of her writing, which implies declaring both her passions and her detachment from them. This device allows her to express the possibility of a double identity, which was deeply rooted in Storm Jameson's ambivalence,[83] but here it is no more in the sense of being 'either male or female', rather of establishing a direct link between local and international or multi-national identities.

This approach also allowed Storm Jameson to make an appeal to reason again, a reason which included social and emotional colours. She insisted on the theme of childhood and youth, bringing as examples both her own happy childhood – 'I was born fortunate – that is, in Whitby; and intolerant, that is, a Yorkshireman' – and the case of her son, who was privileged, undergoing a prolonged education at Cambridge, while so many young men had by then been out of work for five or six years. Her argument was that all children should be made able to enjoy the same privileges, and she posed the problem in very simple rational terms and questions: 'if the best milk, clean air, daily baths, warmth, are thought necessary for any child they are necessities for all' or 'which wisdom or justice is there in a society which leaves some boys to rot' while a few get a high level of education? Then her argument developed like a syllogism: first, since 'the English are the subtlest and most nearly civilised of all peoples', they must recognise what a waste it is not to give all children the same training and opportunities; second, since for ill or good England is a part of Europe, she should take 'more part in the business of Europe, interfere more often, and speak in a less lawyer-like and equivocal voice'. England was to start a process aiming to reach a point when all the people of Europe would enjoy the same degree of comfort and security. This project was much more outspoken and complete than the one sketched in 'In the end'; it switched from the political to the social and moral levels, appearing not less impossible than it did before, but explaining much better that the challenge to death could not succeed without challenging also poverty and inequality. Death, Storm Jameson had written in 1934, was also the death of society.

Through these essays Storm Jameson was showing the respect for the public mind that Vera Brittain had asked for when, in her essay included in *Challenge to Death*, she had defended it from the allegations of sentimentality, lack of logic, and attention to irrelevant trifles. Storm Jameson's writing, by giving space to sentiments and to another logic than the official one, a logic where what was 'relevant' and 'irrelevant' changed places, was trying to speak directly to the public mind. At that particular time Margaret Storm Jameson and Vera Brittain shared common beliefs and attitudes as representatives of the war generation (they were born respectively in 1891 and 1893). Their deep intellectual and emotional friendship, begun in the summer of 1927, would last until the early 1940s, when Storm Jameson chose not 'to accept, as genuine pacifists do, anything rather than war' and to abandon pacifism in the booklet *The End of This War* for PEN (she was chair of the English section of PEN between 1938 and 1945). That choice must have been extremely difficult and yet, I believe, inevitable at that point; one can still feel how dramatic the decision on these issues as well as the parting of ways between the two women would have been. Vera Brittain, who described her friend as 'the most honest and uncompromising person I know', had by then seen the gap between the supporters of collective security and the exponents of revolutionary pacifism grow wider and wider from 1938 on with the threat of a second world war.[84]

Among the essays in the collection *Challenge to Death*, Rebecca West also appealed to the public mind, understood in the sense of public opinion, which would be shocked by the proposal to place air power in the hands of an international body. West too included emotions in the concept of the public mind, such as love of country; where the public mind went wrong, she said, was in building on the recognition of the usefulness of nationalism a repudiation of internationalism. Then it should be corrected by the European tradition – of which the English tradition was but one branch – to understand nationalism and internationalism as counterbalances which can keep nations in equilibrium. Now that 'Europe has come to its maturity', a society of nations must be established, wrote West, and an international police force would 'enable all to live in this useful fellowship'.

From her other writings, Storm Jameson appears to have been aware of the contradictions of European civilisation not only where the purposes of Europeanists were concerned. A major contradiction, as evidenced in some of her novels, is the attitude towards the Jews, considered in turn as bringing out both the best and the worst of European civilisation. She criticised European antisemitism and considered 'anti-Semitism in England as symptomatic of cultural values which depend on a mission of superiority and dominance that all nations and all their men and women share to some degree'.[85] Her work showed a constant awareness of the price to be paid by the Jews and democrats of Europe for the failure of Western democracies to contain Hitler.[86] In the 1930s she did everything in her power to help refugees from Germany, although with her typical self-deprecation she expressed her action as having helped 'a few, too few, men and women to escape the hell of German concentration camps, and then to keep them alive', as she wrote later on.[87]

In 1939–40 Storm Jameson took an active interest in federalism, supporting the Federal Union (FU) and its initiatives. When a collection of essays on the aims of FU was edited by Chaning-Pearce, with the contributions of its most important members and sympathisers, he asked Storm Jameson's permission to include an article that she had already published in the *Fortnightly Review* on 'Federalism and a New Europe'. It was a dramatic article, starting with the sentence: 'It is possible that Europe cannot be saved' and the description of a 'future historian, probably Chinese' who assessed the causes of the decay of European civilisation: 'economic nationalism, the shortsightedness or ignorance of some national leaders, the power lust of others'. For Storm Jameson the task of organising Europe was at that point extremely urgent, since 'the choice between anarchy and some measure of federalism cannot wait'. She took a sharp position in the debate of the time on the geographical definition of federation, whether it should include the USA or be a mainly European affair; for her, the latter option was the only viable course of events, while the absolute priority for Europe was 'to cleanse herself of her disease of economic nationalism' before engaging in any co-operation with others. Storm Jameson was ready to accept that European federation should be achieved in stages, but she was convinced that it should at some point include Germany, given 'her energy, her capacity for idealism, her decent virtues'. It should not be forgotten, in order to appreciate her long-sightedness, that Storm Jameson was writing during a war which she rightly defined as 'in effect a civil war' and that she had repeatedly critcised Germany's national culture. As for the form of federation, she proposed a federal European Council with all the main economic, political and military powers, 'the power to control trade and finance, to deal with other states and groups of states, to control and limit armaments, to enforce respect for international law, to control the use of raw materials'. She added to these tasks the emancipation of colonies: 'to govern and educate in colonial territories and to prepare them for self-government', a remarkable aim in a period when European federation was often still understood as simply implying the unification of all the colonial possessions under a united Europe. Finally, Storm Jameson mentioned what she had most at heart: 'to reconstruct and develop certain social services in Europe', giving as examples communications and medicine; these came last only because of the urgencies imposed by war, but there can be no doubt that they were top priorities in Jameson's vision.

Storm Jameson's concept of 'social Europe', as well as her Europeanism *ex negativo* have a particular significance for those who find themselves in a position of exclusion. Women, refugees and the unemployed, for example, would recognise her appeal to redefine Europe, while they would not be very interested in, and indeed might feel hostile to, the construction of a Europe of the privileged. A similar approach was proposed – much later on – by the German Ursula Hirschmann, who had had to escape from Berlin in the 1930s because she was both Jewish and an active anti-Nazi. In 1975 Hirschmann founded in Brussels the association 'Femmes pour l'Europe', with an appeal to a social politics aiming for equality between men and women, for better work conditions, for the active participation of workers in economic and social decisions. She considered herself a 'wandering European' without a language, neither Italian in spite of having Italian children, nor German even if Germany had been her fatherland. In *Noi senza patria* (*We Without a Fatherland*), an unfinished collection of her writings, she wrote, echoing and transforming Marx: '... we are federalists because in a united Europe we have nothing to lose but our chains'.

These messages have a deep resonance today, in spite of the great differences in the international situation. In *Writing in the Margin: 1939*, written soon after the beginning of the Second World War, Storm Jameson designated the duty of the writer in the difficulties of war time: the more difficult it became, 'the more faithfully he must help the movement of ideas in Europe and between Europe and the rest of the world'. He should not think in terms of destroying Hitlerism in one country, but of 'saving the Europe of which England is a part, of imagining for Europe a future' without the poison of nationalism, and of 'pursuing his imagination of Europe to its bounds'.[88] This exhortation did not conceal the grief, despair and pain contained in the writer's situation and task. Storm Jameson's was an enlightening idea of Europe, not strictly political, but valid on the moral, intellectual and emotional planes, connecting Europe with individual lives and with their local and daily dimensions. If this direction of thought were to be developed, it might enable a reply to be given to the questions posed by Virginia Woolf in her *Three Guineas*, written in 1938 as a response to the request that women help prevent the war: the best way to do that, concluded Woolf after a brilliant description of the educated woman's position in British society, was 'by finding new words and creating new methods'. This meant that the principles of justice, equality and liberty should be asserted bearing in mind that 'the public and private worlds are inseparably connected'.[89] It is interesting that women who had such different attitudes to the war and the actions to be taken by women and men in this respect, as Woolf and Storm Jameson both recognised, although from different points of view, the need to connect the private and the public. Storm Jameson's idea of a united Europe was indeed founded on her interpretation of the link between private emotions and daily realities on the one hand, and politics on the other.

## 'In Spain is Europe'

'Europe is absent,' wrote W.H. Auden in the poem *Journey to Iceland*, where he had travelled with Louis MacNeice in the summer of 1936.[90] In that same summer, on 17 July, General Franco rebelled against the Republican Government in Spain and started the civil war. The supra-national significance of this war – a 'dress rehearsal' of the struggle between Fascists and anti-Fascists which was to be the stuff of the European Resistance in the Second World War – was clearly recognised by Carlo Rosselli, the Italian anti-Fascist assassinated by the Mussolini regime in February 1937. While Fascist Italy and Nazi Germany sent arms and troops to support Franco, the democratic governments of France and Britain opted for non-intervention; but many individual citizens of the European countries went to fight on the side of the Republic, constituting the international brigades. Of the 2,000 British citizens who participated in the Spanish Civil War – 500 killed and twelve hundred wounded – about half were Communists, some belonged to the Labour Party or the Independent Labour Party, some to no political party (a few Britons also supported General Franco, as did

Major Fuller, writing afterwards in his support). Eighty percent of the British who joined the international brigades were from the working class, many of them unemployed and from the Distressed Areas.[91] Others were poets, and they expressed in their poetry, published at the time in journals such as *Left Review* and *New Writing*, the sense that the struggle had European dimensions as well as a new meaning for the unity of Europe. At the same time, their poetry also conveys a strong sense of the metamorphosis taking place in the Western conception of love.

'Spain has torn the veil of Europe', wrote Rex Warner (born in 1905) in his poem 'The Tourist Looks at Spain', included in the anthology *Poems for Spain* edited by Stephen Spender and John Lehmann in 1939. The sentence appears the first time as if spoken by the poet, but soon it is echoed by another voice:

> Hear what they say who came from farm and factory,
> the few-weeks soldiers slain
> or kept in the cruel wire, for fear and fury...
> 'In Spain the veil is torn.
> In Spain is Europe. England is also in Spain.'

What is torn is the veil hiding the dark side of civilisation, a side which had been invisible for 'all those of us who loved, who read the classics'. Spain was 'the mirror' showing that 'what we saw dead was all the time alive' and vice versa: behind what was sacred and successful, solemn and venerable, 'the rat-mask waits and odours of what has long gone sour'. Now, 'the people who speak in deeds' announce the possibility of a different civilisation:

> It is we who feel future flowing in our veins
> the past and the pressing present.

In his other poems (published in 1937) Rex Warner envisaged a future which would be very much in contrast with a present where 'our peace is war, our love is hate,/and our beauty is iron' ('Peace'), a present which is 'sad, furious, fatal' ('Future'). This future promised a complete revolution in human relations:

> Women work with men and love is voluntary,
> love is delightful.
> Hate is no more against those who withhold bread;
> those people have gone.
> Love is no more the antidote for terror,
> but is recreation.

And yet, already in the present, the fighters can reverse the past: 'our hate is love' ('The Tourist'). Although the poet's conclusion in 'The Tourist' is that: 'Not for many years now will love be guiltless', he seems to allude to a distant future when love will indeed be guiltless and fulfill the dreams of the present.[92]

A similar awareness, of a precarious privileged moment separating the ages and anticipating a future for a new Europe and a new kind of love, was expressed by the poet John Cornford, killed at Cordova at the age of twenty-one at the end of December, 1936. While at Trinity College, Cambridge, Cornford had organised the University Communist Party which briefly united with the Socialists; he reached the front less than a month after the war began, returned briefly to Britain to organise a group of volunteers, and then went back to Spain.[93] His poem 'Full Moon at Tierz: Before the Storming at Huesca' was written from the Aragon front:

Where, in the fields by Huesca, the full moon
Throws shadows clear as daylight's
The innocence of this quiet plain
Will fade in sweat and blood, in pain...

Now the same night falls over Germany
And the impartial beauty of the stars
Lights from the unfeeling sky
Oranienburg and freedom's crooked scars...

England is silent under the same moon
From Clydeside to the gutted pits of Wales.

This passage, wrote Hynes in *The Auden Generation*, recalls Auden's 1933 poem 'Summer Night', where 'the moon that shines down on lovers in an English garden also climbs the European sky'. It is a Europe soon to be invaded by a second Flood, bursting 'the dykes of our continent', drowning the protected life of the past and opening the way to a new life.[94] We might also recall, among the many references to Europe in Auden's poetry, his poem 'Europe 1936', published in *Time and Tide*, which starts from a moment of recognition and belonging:

Certainly our city: with the byres of poverty down to
The river's edge, the cathedral, the engines, the dogs;
Here is the cosmopolitan cooking,
And the light alloys and the glass.

But the poem ends with a vision of the earth as suspended and lonely, in a gelid universe, precipitating towards a complete change, the direction of which is unpredictable:

... through years of absolute cold
The planets rush towards Lyra in a lion's charge. Can
Hate so securely bind? Are they dead here? Yes.

And the wish to wound has the power. And tomorrow
Comes. It's a world. It's a way.

Cornford begins 'Full Moon' with a vision of time from a very distant age:

The past, a glacier, gripped the mountain wall,
And time was inches, dark was all...

Time moves irresistibly forward breaking down old orders and creating the present:

Time present is a cataract whose force
Breaks down the banks even at its source,

While the future 'has no image in space'. 'We are the future,' says the young poet, coming immediately back to the present: 'the last fight let us face'. In the present, love is linked with trepidation and fear:

The love that tears me by the roots,
The loneliness that claws my guts.

In 'Poem', 'on the last mile to Huesca', he invokes 'the heart of the heartless world', and expresses his fear, begging, in case he were to die: 'don't forget my love'. Here too is the recognition that, while the present allows neither the old forms of love to continue nor new ones to emerge fully, the participation in the struggle gives some foresight into the changes that will take place:

Action intervenes, revealing
New ways of love, new ways of feeling.

The same sense that traditional sentiments are outdated and impotent was expressed by H.B. Mallalieu (born in the USA in 1914 and educated in Britain, where he subsequently worked as a journalist):

Spain, 1938
Pity and love are no more adequate:
They have not saved ten thousand who are dead,
Nor brought relief to peasants who in dread
Gaze at that sky which held their hope of late:
They have not stifled horror or killed hate.
Europe is not impatient of her guilt,
But those on whom her tyranny is built,
By love deserted, have grown desperate.

The passage to Europe is immediate, once more through the mention of the sky, evoking an ancient gesture of people in despair, who look at the sky in search of help or at least consolation. But Europe provides neither; although no longer absent, her presence is passivity and tyranny, inertia and despair. Hers is a threatening presence as announced by the Spanish war: 'the signal was Spain', says Mallalieu in another poem expressing in its very title: 'The future is near us' the sense of an imminent change.[95] Among 'those who caught the signal' were 'those deeply involved with love or with the sun'. In this poem, the change prophesied for the immediate future is an enlargement of the struggle for a European dimension to the most obscure sides of human life. But the prophetic eye of the poet sees further, capturing the dream of a love which outgrows the present:

War is already flagrant in Europe and the black
Night of hatred sets boundaries to delight.
Love is too large in the short day before us,
The islands beyond our reach. Sight is sure.

In Auden's 'Spain', written in April 1937, immediately after his return from the war, to which he had gone in January, the sense of the present is transmitted by the rythmic and obsessive repetition of the words 'But to-day the struggle'. Stanzas cadenced on 'Yesterday all the past' – a yesterday where the whole of civilisation, with its science, economic life, religious feuds and artistic production is concentrated – alternate with the stanzas announcing 'To-morrow, perhaps the future'. In the future – among many other things – lies the possibility of love; the reader does not know how ironical:

To-morrow the enlarging of consciousness by diet and breathing.
To-morrow the rediscovery of romantic love

Just as the present stands between that past and that future, so Spain stands between two continents:

... that arid square, that fragment nipped off from hot
Africa, soldered so crudely to inventive Europe

Beyond the banality of the characterisation of the two continents – although we should remember that Franco had been able to attack the Republic from his base in Africa – Spain is seen to represent the opportunity for change: 'I am your choice, your decision. Yes, I am Spain'. In the end this means that 'on that tableland scored by rivers,/Our thoughts have bodies'.

In many of these poems there is a direct connection between language and experience[96] created by the experience, either actual or mediated by compassion and anger, of the war – a 'literary event' which altered consciousness and engaged the English imagination.[97] The connection between poetry and life made possible by the Spanish Civil War allows for an osmosis between words and deeds, so that deeds take the place of words ('the people who speak in deeds'[98]) and, *vice versa*, words become as significant as deeds. Such are the names of battlefields and places of resistance which have penetrated poetry, for instance in 'Poem of Spring' by Mallalieu:

> Spain rose with menacing thunder of cloud, rumbling over Europe the names of Madrid, of Brunete, of Guadalajara, of Jarama: and from those guns broke the smoke and the shell of to-day.
>
> Austria was down overnight, to our mortuary of names adding Vienna. Prague and Warsaw disappeared in the graveyard of Europe.

In this long poem (published in 1940 in *Letter in Wartime*) Mallalieu looks back at the previous decade – 'ten years ago was a Spring' – from the very beginning of 'these roaring forties'. The acute awareness of time past, present and future, so vivid in so many of these poems, is compressed here in the perception of a decade suspended in a flow of time where the past and the future fuse as if in a dream:

> I remember an earlier summer and the sky blue
> Stretching across peaceful Europe to as blue a sea: or dream of tomorrow's summer
> Vague as unvisited country whose cliffs are edged with sorrow, hearing beyond birds
> Flags of speech proclaiming a new era. Only the present eludes me.

In the present, 'after ten years of the premonition of love and the omens of death', 'love finds no fluent speech to move', with 'the flaming cities and the wounded caterpillars of refugees winding hopelessly across Europe', and Europe is reduced to 'the grave of a continent'.

In another poem included in the same collection, 'To Edward Douse', Mallalieu wrote:

> My hand lies lost in Europe as it writes
> To you who stands as lost:…
> I see the white cities of Europe breaking upon the plain and the rain of shrapnel and splinter

But the Europe of his vision is a Europe animated by its different languages – 'idioms of love' – viewed almost as a living body, stretching in time and space throughout the whole world. This image holds promises for the future, in spite of the terrible present:

1. Europe lies open to the wound of war…
2. … where once we walked in the whale of a continent, soothed by a summer where the smile translated the differing idioms of love:

3. ... where we walked in the sun along the Rhine or climbed towards La Grave: and to-morrow extended as far as the Urals...

5. ... Europe lies back upon its Asian limb and from African skull and the Indian palm the twin Americans grew.

In this poem the European war is perceived by the poet as a civil war, which must be fought as such. Europe has now become the fatherland, the place of belonging. Yet another poem by Mallalieu, which speaks of 'Europe's tomb' and 'love's autumn', still projects the hope of a 'Renewal', when 'you and Europe will return'.

The feeling of internationalism in the Spanish struggle was for many volunteers more or less explicit, as a presupposition and/or a result of their experience of the war. An example is *Homage to Catalonia* by George Orwell, published in 1938, after Orwell had been wounded in the neck and had come back to Britain with his wife. In the book retelling his experience, the word 'Europe' appears for the first time in Chapter 5, which introduces the theme of politics into what has been presented up to that point as a general struggle for freedom. The word is introduced in an appropriate context: 'when the struggle broke out on 18 July it is probable that every anti-Fascist in Europe felt a thrill of hope. For here at last, apparently, was democracy standing up to Fascism'.[99] In the previous 40 pages Orwell has given us a sense of how one could become a European (without ever mentioning this word) in the Spanish war. An example is when in late December 1936 – having just arrived – he briefly meets, in the Lenin Barracks in Barcelona, an Italian militiaman whom he will never see again: neither speaks the other's language, but there is a sudden 'affection' between them, 'as though his spirit and mine had momentarily succeeded in bridging the gulf of language and tradition and meeting in utter intimacy'.[100] Or, when Orwell describes the sense of freedom and the democratic spirit at the front, in spite of terrible hardships, where human solidarity overcame the political divisions among the supporters of the republic, divisions which were so bitter in Barcelona. In his later memories Orwell stretched that human solidarity to include the Fascists, remembering when he refrained from shooting at a man running from a Fascist trench, half dressed and holding up his trousers with both hands as he ran, because 'a man who is holding up his trousers isn't a Fascist, he is visibly a fellow-creature, similar to yourself, and you don't feel like shooting at him'.[101] All through the book, Orwell makes it clear that there was not much space for ideology in the daily reality of the struggle, and that the sense of internationalism was developed implicitly through an accumulation of minor events, such as the ones he described.

While the active dimension of internationality stemming from solidarity is very relevant, and moving, the poems about Spain are at another level. The sense of Europe which they describe is not merely the realisation of the supra-national political dimension of the Spanish Civil War; what emerges in them is the pre-figuration of a different Europe, and a re-founding of European civilisation. It is the feeling that an age is finishing and that something new is necessary, particularly in the fields of inter-subjectivity – of relationships between man and man, and man and woman – and in the way of feeling, that is to say in the field of emotions. Such hope was justified by the changes which took place – even if only for a short period of time – in the Spanish struggle, where the differences of class and gender seemed to be overcome, at least in certain parts of the country.

Love is mentioned many times, both in a general or universal sense and in a specific one, referring to romantic love. In the second sense it appears incongruous in the tragedy of the age and, at the same time, too closely connected with the old world which is collapsing; it needs to be re-discovered, and reinvented, together with human relationships. It is not only war and hatred that destroy love; even before the war – but made visible by it – love was heavily implicated in a civilisation which the poets fought not only to defend, but to change deeply, especially through their poetry. The relationship between European civilisation and love – in the intuitions of the poems – is no longer the exclusive connection between Eurocentrism and a hierarchical love where the subject is on a higher level than the object, but one where Europe is connected fraternally with the whole world and the subjects of love are equal. These intuitions are vague and sometimes rough, but they indicate a sharp change from the core of traditional European civilisation.

To evaluate these intuitions is no simple matter. The achievements of the poems are uneven, both in depth of content and in strength of form; their visions may well be very farsighted, in the same way as utopias are. The Spanish dream collapsed in disaster, not only in the sense that the Republic was defeated, but also because the USSR, which had supplied arms to the Republican Government, destroyed all the solidarity by eli-minating the Anarchists and the Trotskyists, as well as many who were neither. Orwell evoked this tragedy, when he wrote that the Italian he met in the Lenin barracks, who was 'probably a Trotskyist or an Anarchist', had little chance of remaining alive: 'in the peculiar conditions of our time, when people of that sort are not killed by the Gestapo they are usually killed by the GPU'.[102]

If a new feeling of community with ordinary Europeans arose in Britain in the second half of the 1930s as a response to the Fascist menace,[103] we are faced with a paradox. That feeling of community developed exactly when the community was threatened with disappearance: the existence of Europe became real for the British at a moment when the death of Europe was a likely prospect, and indeed it was already under way, if it meant the annihilation of a common space for exchange and understanding. At the same time the very fact that Auden had signalled the absence of Europe indicated that that absence had finally come about. This paradox has not been solved by history, in the sense that it is not clear to what extent European civilisation has survived the experience of Fascism and Nazism, as well as the anti-Fascist retaliations, which sometimes involved atrocity as well. We are still living with the consequences of those events, and the memory of them has not yet been sufficiently elaborated, just as the ideal of regeneration through revolution, from the French to the Russian, has been deeply shaken, and the closer relationship established between democracy and socialism in the European consciousness is still frail and inadequately founded. In this sense the poems about Spain, which express a higher level of imagination about a distant future, give voice to a re-definition of European civilisation, and offer a possible solution of the paradox. The regeneration sought by the poets has not taken place, and a Europe capable of purposefully cherishing feelings of solidarity and the mirage of a different way of loving as integral parts of a new civilisation has not yet emerged. That this mirage appeared to a few, who expressed it in their poetry, is therefore very important for us today; its existence in the imagination is no guarantee of its practical feasibility, but it is a promise in that direction and will turn out to be an illusion only if no further effort is made to create it.

## 'Song of the West' (Margaret Ormiston Curle)

The new closeness to Europe was felt not only on political or politico-cultural grounds, but also in the purely literary field. While the Auden generation fused together the political and the cultural, other writers and poets – of a different generation or gender – expressed a closeness with Europe which was mainly cultural. Margaret Ormiston (the pen-name of Margaret Ormiston Curle) was distant in age and gender from the political poets who wrote about Spain, being a woman born in 1889 and therefore at least the span of a generation older than they. For her, the gender mark is evident in a different way than for political writers such as Vera Brittain and Storm Jameson, principally in the genre in which she expressed herself. She mainly wrote poems and fables for children, of a historical and mythological kind: *Tancred, the Hero, and Other Fairy Tales* (1920), *The Dryad, and other Poems* (1921), *Kerdac, the Wanderer* and *The Golden Fleece* (1924), *Travel Songs and Ballads* (1930). These books were often composed of stories about knights, magic armour, witches, monsters, ogres, dwarfs and dragons narrated in the conventional way usually attributed, in an oleographic way, to grandmothers or aunts narrating to children. Secondly, and despite research efforts, information about her life is very scanty. It is not only women who have vanished from the bio-graphical records – another example in this book is Fedor Vergin – but in

Ormiston Curle's case the disappearance takes on a symbolic meaning because she was a woman. We can allow ourselves to imagine that her life was that of an emancipated woman, since she moved from Scotland to London, apparently lived on her own and did not marry; the lack of information induces a sense of loss and obscurity which is fitting in the light of the new patterns of women's lives from the end of the last century to our own – so often "hidden from history", in the terms used by Sheila Rowbotham. However, her work was not innovative or progressive enough to be included in the collections of inter-war women's poetry, so that there is a complete dearth of critical work on her.

Margaret Curle was born at Harleyburn, Melrose, into a wealthy family with eight servants, the daughter of a man described by the census as a lawyer, banker and solicitor, and of a woman born in India; her grandfather was also a lawyer and her paternal uncle a well-known archaeologist interested in the prehistoric monuments of Scotland. Margaret was educated in Edinburgh, in Dresden and at King's College, London, and lived in London; she is usually indicated as Miss in the biographical records. The dedication of her book of fairy tales, *Tancred*, 'To my nephews and nieces' can probably be taken as a sign of the fact that she had no children. A violinist and a translator of French and German verse, she contributed to many poetry and general magazines and won the Bardic Honour in the Southern Counties, Eisteddfod 1922. The critics praised her sense of melody and the rhythmic lilt of her verse.

Throughout her work – besides dreamy meditations on flowers and harvests – a strong sense of history can be found as well as an interest in legends and myths. The relationship with the past and its contrast with the present appear in various forms in her poems, which take themes such as 'An Aeroplane at Stonehenge' or 'The Old Violin Remembers'. Numerous poems are dedicated to the known and unknown heroes and heroines of the past, with titles like 'Servants of Humanity' and 'Time Dissolving'. The literary achievements of the past are a constantly recurrent theme, for instance in 'To Shakespeare', 'Quixote to Cervantes', and especially 'Walter Scott', this last composed on the centenary of his death (1932). Scott is familiarly called 'Our Brother', but also recognised more formally as:

> The Wizard, our Sir Walter!
> His wand a pen, he wove in magic hues
> The many-coloured pattern of the past;
> Revealer
> Of Scottish type and pith, himself heroic.

All these themes converged into the long poem which Margaret Ormiston published in 1938, 'Europe'. It was composed of 60 iambic pentameter-rhyming quatrains, whose 'onward flowing rhythm suggests well' – in the words of the reviewer in the *Times Literary Supplement* – 'the rapid march of time'.

The first quatrain of the poem introduces the topic of Europe with a sense of belonging, emotional participation and anticipation of the future:

> Our Europe is the theme: from bygone ages,
> Through clan and nation, war, tumultuous surging,
> By evil ways and good, by fools and sages,
> To the young, untested Europe now emerging.

The poet has the sense that something new is appearing in Europe, 'young and untested', and tries to discover its roots by going far back, to the 'island Crete' where 'a people came to knowledge and skill', and from there to Greece, Rome, Syria where the Christian religion originated (does the choice of Syria rather than Palestine indicate a touch of antisemitism?). History unfolds from antiquity to the decline of Rome, when invaders 'lower than the brutes' brought darkness and pillage, and 'the sword of Islam' threatened Europe; among the invaders only the Viking and Teutonic heroes are presented in an admiring way as 'sea-wise, intrepid' (while the Vandals are 'insolent' and the Franks unqualified). In spite of darkness and decline,

> Great dreams were shaping then through pain and toil;
> Men dreamed our Europe one, one State, one church.

Among the men 'whose vision spanned the future', Hildebrand, Charlemagne and Bernard are cited; when chivalry finally appears, it is, predictably within this historical frame, a high point of the story. The voice of the poet, narrating the story of Europe in this long journey through the ages, alternates with other voices, written in italics and characterised by a different metre (fourteeners); these are the choral voices of the peoples she encounters on her journey.

> Now chivalry was rising in the west,
> A scheme of life, a portent, and a power,
> A world in arms, when feudal duty pressed
> On every man, and knighthood came to flower.

> This was the age of building: once again
> The European genius came to bloom,
> But now in dome and cloister, village fane
> And vast cathedral, pinnacle and tomb.

> *'We are hewing, we are carving, we are giving of our best;*
> *We are singing at our labour, we are glorifying the West,...*
> *We are Europe'.*

These last three lines are sung by the obscure people building the cathedrals; they are called in, as the Greeks and Romans were earlier on, as witnesses of history. But they are the first to fully represent the spirit of the continent, who can legitimately not only proclaim, 'We are Europe,' but also declare their self-awareness of collective immortality, since they can 'worship and aspire'.

A list of great men follows, from Saint Francis, Dante and Chaucer to Savonarola, Galileo and Giotto, but 'the humble serf, the tiller of the soil' is not separated from them and can join in their same search. Then 'great nations in the making' are mentioned as well as their colonial achievements, and at this point a parenthesis recognizes that

(For treachery and evil, Europe's name
Was blotted with inexpiable shame!)

But at the same time the 'Western spirit, keen to know, to make' was expressing its creative force and 'swaying Erasmus, Leonardo, Drake'. 'Time hastened' and so does the poem, rushing through the Enlightenment, the French Revolution, Napoleon, and the great composers and artists of the eighteenth and nineteenth centuries. 'And soon the reign of science had begun', the scientists being 'the sons of Europe, her special pride', since science is indeed her specialty: 'Europe was the first to test, to probe' and 'science lured the European mind/To know, to conquer'. 'We are working for the future, for the ages yet unborn,' sing the scientists, promising 'a fairer morn' and giving a spiritualistic interpretation of the developments of nuclear physics:

We have lost the solid atom in the energies that bind;
There is nothing left but thought, and matter merges into Mind!

Again the shortcomings of the course of progress are relegated in parenthesis: 'Europe gained in knowledge (with a dearth,/As yet, of wisdom)', and that part of Europe which does not coincide with 'her offspring, huge and young,/The great Republic of the West' is completely ignored. The whole poem wants to be an epic of Western civilisation, as the title of this subchapter suggests, making a détournement of another poem by Ormiston Curle, 'Song of the West', which was dedicated to the beauties of British Western counties.

Finally the triumphant march is interrupted for the second time (the first interruption was the consequence of the barbaric invasions of the Roman empire), and tragedy emerges in full light with the First World War. It is only at this dramatic point, faced with the extraordinary challenge of the entire European civilisation, that 'sea-engirdled Britain' enters the scene as a nation. British individuals such as Darwin, Turner and Dickens had already appeared; so, significantly, had Simpson, 'finding anodynes for pain'. Sir James Simpson was the first obstetrician to use chloroform for relief in labour pains, against the opposition of obstetricians and the clergy; perhaps his mention in this rather short list of British contributors to European civilisation indicates that the poet had some sense of gender. It is the threat of a fall back into barbarity that moves Britain:

And the beast leapt up, the beast that lurks in man,
And darkness hid the day!

Then Britain rose, defiant, from her sleep
Behind her ships of steel;
While Europe saw the trenches wind and creep,
The old defences reel.

A vast fresco of battle-places and fighting peoples from the whole world, including those from Africa, India and America follows. After all that 'madness and slaughter', the poet contemplates her own time and the landscape she sees is desolate:

The old world passed in flame, but rising from the pyre,
Came gory Russia, drenched in her revolution; Spain,
In anarchy and fear; dictators, aiming higher
Than a sultan or a tsar, impregnable in reign.

The world has lost its way, our Europe lost her soul', concludes the poet, also pointing out the fall of the high hopes raised 'by a solemn pact and League' to end not only the massacre of man by man, but also 'the tortuous ways of old, the falsehood and intrigue' of traditional politics. At this point, the initial vision of a 'young, untested Europe' has given way to a gloomy landscape with threatening prospects, where the positive alternatives appear, after what has been said, less likely to take place than the negative ones:

This Europe sways in fear, while the world, the future wait;
She has torn apart the bands of a creed that once sufficed:
But the deeps remain, the deeps of God. Is it love or hate
That comes, is it war or peace, rule of chaos or Christ?

The set phrases and platitudes do not hide the sense of uncertainty in this last quatrain. Similarly, the stereotyped survey of European civilisation does not conceal a participation in its values, particularly its cultural expressions. The great composers are given a prominent place in the poem's ride through the ages: Bach, Mozart, Beethoven, Schubert and Wagner are mentioned as 'Europe's soul singing'; perhaps Margaret Ormiston, as a violinist, was particularly sensitive to the musicians' contributions to culture and civilisation.

This long poem condenses themes present in her other poems, which pulled together the famous and the obscure, including 'the humble, toiling women, and the mother by the hearth' ('Servants of Humanity'), invoked England to take up her leading role: 'O land, my land, be faithful to thy name,/And guard thine ancient fame!' ('The River Speaks'), and proposed a vision of the history of humanity from the discovery of the wheel to machines cleaving 'through air and ocean' ('Speed'). The expressive form is often trite, but eminently suitable for reading aloud, since it follows the rythm of the spoken word, and has a narrative strength in telling the story. The vision of European civilisation that thus emerges is centred on spiritual and intellectual achievements, from religion and art to science, and is not without moral and political overtones. From her own position, this poet was aware of the processes going on in Europe and of the threats they represented. Her feeling of belonging to this civilisation, and the sense of unity between Britain and Europe, are expressed inequivocably, and the poem could be read as a plea for Britain to take up her responsibilities in the European situation. If this is so, Margaret Ormiston would not have been taking a radical position, but expressing what was becoming a feeling common to a large section of public opinion in Britain, as we have seen.

The fact that she was a relatively successful poet might suggest that at the time it was more difficult for a woman to emerge in a progressive literary environment than in a more traditional one, where women's voices were accepted if they kept to their roles, such as those of well-developed genres. Her poetry is old-fashioned and completely ignores modernism and experimental writing, assuming an unbroken line of poetry from Chaucer to Georgian traditionalism,[104] while it establishes a close correspondence between its boringly regular metres and its high-minded sentiments. In spite of her lack of sophistication and innovation, Margaret Curle put into some of her work an awareness of her epoch and the values of liberalism and patriotism which were corrected by the sense of belonging to a wider culture. Her 'Europe' can perhaps be taken as a sign that even conservative cultured people with no political engagement were experiencing in their own way the new closeness with Europe.

## Destiny of a myth: images of Europa and the bull

The ancient theme of Europa and the Bull, already met with Mottram (see Chapter 1) and Briffault (see Chapter 4), was transformed in the tension between culture and politics of the 1930s. The most striking examples of its political implications for Europe in this period can be found in the works of German painters, such as those by Leo von Koenig in the years 1929–36 and Max Beckmann in 1933[105] (see Figure 3, Chapter 3). Their Europas reflect a sense of violence and horror inspired by the rise of Nazism; no longer portrayed as triumphant women capable of reconciling body and soul, nature and culture, animal and human, they are instead presented as victims of brutal force to which they react in vain. This representation, which is in striking contrast with most artistic production of the previous centuries, can also be found in some of the artists operating in the following years. One of the most explicit is Jacques Lipchitz, a French sculptor of Jewish Lithuanian origin, who created two bronze Europas, one in 1938, a sculpture transmitting a sense of extreme motion and convulsive agitation, and a second one in 1941 – when he fled to the US – where Europa is stabbing the bull. Of this second one, he wrote in his autobiography: 'Europa is fighting against her rapist (Hitler) and trying to kill him'. While the earlier version portrayed many elements of a lyrical interpretation of the myth, in the later one 'Europa has become specifically modern Europe threatened by the powers of evil and fighting for her life against them'. By incorporating all this into his sculptures, Lipchitz was expressing the emotions he felt in relation to the war and the disruption of his own life.[106]

In 1930s Britain we do not find any artistic expressions of the politicisation of Europa and the Bull. Instead there are, on the one hand, examples of a more general connection between the theme and the worry about the decadence of European culture, and on the other the continuation of the tradition using the image of Europa and the Bull decoratively; among instances of the latter, the images connected with the emergence of new media or new forms of mass diffusion of art are particularly relevant.

An example of the former trend is the reappearance of Europa in the work of an Irish poet, Oliver St John Gogarty (1878–1957), who formed part of the Irish literary revival, although he was a satirist of sentimental nationalism. A doctor and literary man, Gogarty was a close friend of W.B. Yeats, who considered him 'one of the great lyric poets of the age', and he was portrayed – much to his irritation – as Buck Mulligan in James Joyce's *Ulysses*. Gogarty served as Senator in the Irish Free State Senate from its foundation in 1922 to its abolition in 1936; kidnapped and threatened with death in 1923 by Republican extremists, he escaped by plunging into the Liffey and swimming away (later he presented a pair of swans to the river in gratitude for having 'saved' him), but shortly afterwards his house was sacked and burned by the IRA. In 1939 he decided to leave Ireland and he remained a resident of New York City until his death.

His poem 'Europa and the Bull' was part of a collection published in New York in 1933 and in Britain in 1938. It is a witty poem, which begins with a squabble between the Phoenician king, father of Europa, and the nurse who should take care of Wide Eyes (a literal translation of one of the recognised etymons for the name 'Europa') since her mother the queen is dead. The king is worried about his daughter being brought up as a boy and expresses it colloquially, portraying Europa as very similar to the girls of the poet's time and their tendency towards emancipation: he blames the

Never-to-be-
Too-much-deprecated
Tendency towards bringing
Only daughters up as boys.

Indeed Europa is presented, while walking and running on the beach with her young companions, as a 'tomboy' or a 'fearless maiden', and at moments similar to the archer goddess Artemis herself. Thus she is completely fearless when

Clear against the bright wall
Of the low horizon
On the bull came, prancing,
Lifting up his knees.
He came on as gaily
As a galley dancing
While its sail is being lowered
And the shouts are from the quays.

Like a man of Yorkshire
Grunting after Christmas,
When the curly foreheads
And the appetites convene.

The two similes reduce the bull's mysteriousness and bring it close to us, particularly the second, which lowers the tone with familiar terms such as 'Yorkshire' and 'Christmas' and 'low' terms such as 'grunting', which equates human and animal appetites. The light and mocking tone applied to classical subjects is typical of Gogarty, who had a solid classical foundation and excelled in the use of epigrams, aphorisms and the mock-heroic genre. His comic ploy was to treat the myth in terms of certain conventions of a modern provincial society.[107] The metres (dactyls and iambi) convey with their rapid rythm a sense of movement and amusement:

But she held on lightly
To the garlands on the gilded
Horn, more blunt, but stronger
Than the horns of buffalo.

The mention of garlands and gilded horns reminds us of the tradition of representations of Europa, including that of Veronese, although this joking tone soon gives way to serious invective.

The poet intervenes directly and compares the mythical past with his own age: he prefers 'the days in which/Such miracles were common' to his own, and he takes as typical of his time the teacher 'Who maintains the World was made/According to the word/Of men who separate Mankind/

From Universal Nature'. At this point the serious tone suddenly reverts
again to a mocking one, referring not to the ancient but to the present myths:

> For what eloping god to-day
> Would turn into a Ford?

This tone alternates with the strong invective, which starts again, revealing
the object of the poet's attack. The Age of Faith of the past was much
happier than the present one:

> When, if there's faith about,
> 'Tis not in gods by girls transformed,
> But Jewish mathematic.

'Jewish mathematic' may be understood as a reference to Einstein's
physics – with a touch of antisemitism? – while the men who separate
mankind from nature are the scientists. Gogarty shared with his friend
Yeats (who received the Nobel prize for literature in 1923, and who, from
1922 to 1928, also sat in the Senate of the Irish Free State) the polemics
against science, and believed that the crisis of Western values was connected with it. This serious intermezzo is soon closed by the final stanza,
where a more decided resumption of the mocking tone brings Europa
close to our time once more:

> What about her father?
> Formal proclamation
> That is was her nurse's
> Fault was no excuse
> In the eyes of 'County',
> Nor a consolation;
> But glory when the Church declared
> His son-in-law was Zeus!

What brings Europa nearer to the present is the petty bourgeois version of
the drama – gossip, quarrels, excuses – but what remains far away is the
beauty of the white bull 'With the purple-vested/Girl upon his
back,/Laughing when he dipt down,/Laughing when he bellowed'. The
retrieval of the mythical past takes place in a climate of conservatism,
where the joking tone reinforces, by contrasting with it, the vehemency of
the invective; the alternation of the two tones reflects Gogarty's desire to
write poetry that 'might provide a means of escape from petty concerns
and transient enthusiasms', as he wrote to a friend in the 1930s, and his
participation in current events and the destiny of Western culture. This
attitude is consistent with his feeling that the violence unleashed on the
century permitted no return to the past except in the imagination.

Gogarty and Yeats shared the theme of Europa as well as another similar one, that of Leda and the Swan, although Yeats had given a different image of Europa in a sequence composed in 1929 (and originally published in 1932 as *Words for Music Perhaps*), where she was introduced by 'Crazy Jane', a character based on an old woman – a 'local satirist' 'with an amazing power of audacious speech' – who lived close to the poet's castle at Gort. In one of the ballads dedicated to Crazy Jane, this hint was made at the end of one stanza:

> Great Europa played the fool
> That changed a lover for a bull.
> *Fol de rol, fol de rol.*

The last line is a refrain composed of meaningless words as in old ballads, with the purpose of making the poem brighter and more clearly like a song. In another poem, Crazy Jane, reproved by the Bishop for her irreverence, maintains that woman is better served by a human lover than by a divine one like the Bishop's loud, overbearing God. This mention of Europa touches one of Yeats's recurrent themes, the escape through irreverence, from the hegemony of orthodox christianity; in this light Europa appears foolish in her preference for a god to a man, in contrast with Gogarty's Wide Eyes, who reconciles 'mankind with universal nature'.

As the decade went by, the image of Europa was appropriated by the new media. Photography was in the process of being transformed by colour, and one of the pioneers of experiments with it in the early 1930s was Yevonde Cumbers (1893–1975), known professionally as Madame Yevonde; technical research was very important in her work, and she worked closely with the inventor of the VIVEX process, Dr D.A. Spencer, to develop the full potential of colour photography. Inspired by the 'Olympian party', a charity ball held in March 1935 at Claridge's, she had the idea of photographing society ladies dressed up as figures from classical mythology. In July 1935 she held an exhibition at her studio in Berkeley Square on 'Goddesses and Others'. The vividly-coloured prints bore images of Lady Mosley (Diana Mitford) as Venus, Mrs Anthony Eden as the Muse of History, the Duchess of Wellington as Hecate, and so on. 'Europa' (365 x 252mm) was represented by a Mrs Donald Ross, whose beautiful torso embraced a stuffed bull. Even if the influence of Surrealists on Yevonde was to be fully activated only one year later, with the opening of the International Surrealist Exhibition by André Breton, she was quite ready for it: the bunch of fake flowers on the bull's head, the empty look of the woman, the artificiality and stillness of the composition resemble a commercial use of surrealist montages. The air of publicity does not conceal a sense of estrangement somehow strengthened by touches of caducity - like the haircut or the mannered gestures typical of the age. It may well be that nineteenth-century painting inspired Yevonde in her quest to represent mythological themes,[108] but the difference induced by the new medium is striking. The construction of the image by traditional mythological painting idealised it, polishing it and giving it a less transient tone. This type of photography maintains the ephemeral signs of the age and of the individual, although redeemed to a certain extent by the humourous treatment of the fleeting beauty of the flesh, but the divine has definitely gone from this sort of representation.

There could be no better illustration of the destiny of the image of Europa in late-1930s Britain: the mythical creature is incarnated in an obscure upper-middle-class English woman whose regular features express her contented possession of the bull. This one has the resigned and stiff look of a stuffed animal, slightly embarrassed and out of place in this situation, without any hint that at some point he might be Zeus. We know from Madame Yevonde that it was very difficult to find the bull: the directors of the Natural History Museum were scandalised by the idea of one of their animals being used in a photographer's studio, while colonial and travel bureaux and shops offered rhinos or elephants, elks, moose and antelopes, but no bulls: the bull was very rarely stuffed in England. Finally, Yevonde's prop woman found an emporium of stuffed animals used for films in Camden Town, where she hired the bull for ten shillings and sixpence, and she brought 'him back in a taxi with as much triumph as ever He felt when he galloped away with Europa'.[109]

While the images of 'Goddesses and Others' were completely secularised, they gave space to women's dreams of dressing up and transvesting themselves as fantastic creatures; this type of photography – for which only wealthy or famous people posed – came close, however, to mass culture inasmuch as Yevonde's sitters became somehow similar to characters of comic-strips. Yevonde liked to free her own and her sitters' imaginations in experimenting with their own images; the 'incongruity of the ingredients'[110] used in these portraits as well as in her 'still-life fantasies' confirmed the fantastic nature of her 'realistic' style. As she wrote in her memoir, she was 'a photographer who happens to be a woman' and she had taken up photography with the definite purpose of making herself independent. Born into a prosperous middle-class family (her father was the director of a firm manufacturing printing inks), Yevonde had studied in Belgium and Paris. A good friend of Rebecca West, in the decade berteen 1910 and 1920 she had formed part of the suffragist movement, sold *The Suffragette* on street-corners and marched in processions; in 1921 she was the first woman to address the Congress of the Professional Photographers' Association with a speech on 'Photographic Portraiture from a Woman's Point of View'. She had decided not to marry, but in fact did so when she met the author and journalist Edgar Middleton; however, she later wrote: 'if I had to choose between marriage and a career I would choose a career, but I would never give up being a woman'.[111] Her life reflects the contradictions of a working woman: she had no children, and said that she regretted only the loss of the 'physical experience and mystery' but that spiritually it did not worry her at all.[112] Her work certainly displays many influences, among them that of Man Ray, but also had its own distinct style, both in her portraits for society ladies and celebrities, and in commercial advertising, which included magazine assignments with *Sketch and Tatler* and *Fortune*.

Europa appears once again in another example of the mixture between new forms of mass culture and artistic production for the wealthy. Frank Dobson (1886–1963), considered during the 1920s and 1930s one of the Britain's finest modern sculptors, was also a designer of fabrics, which were produced either by Allan Walton Textiles (during the 1930s a number of textile manufacturers invited artists to design fabrics in an attempt to raise the standards of textile design) or were printed by his wife Mary. The second range of textiles were produced from lino block carved by Dobson – an appropriate technique for a sculptor – and printed on fairly coarse natural linen with printer's ink, using one or two blocks and the same number of colours; some were purchased by the Victoria and Albert Museum. Among these was the textile 'Europa and the Bull', produced in 1938, possibly designed to be seen not hanging as a curtain but flat as a bedspread or as upholstery. The image is printed in a light but intense blue for Europa and a deep tobacco brown for the bull. The design (30 x 30cm) has a dynamic effect, the bull in full flight and Europa leaning over it, the scene 'dramatically encapsulated within a jagged circle'.[113] This textile predates a terracotta on the same subject produced by Dobson in 1946, very different, with the bull leaning massively over the woman, a figure of great power, contrasting strongly with the stylised elegance of the textile (Plate 4). This is due to the medium and the repetition of the motif: the critics had pointed out since the beginnings of Dobson's career that the forms he created were conditioned from their very conception by the substance in which they were expressed.[114]

Dobson began to show his work at the Friday Club, the exhibiting society founded by Vanessa Bell, and it was the critics Roger Fry and Clive Bell who were largely responsible for the success of his early career. Bell praised Dobson's simplicity, 'which sublimates away all unessential details', and considered him an aesthetician almost exclusively preoccupied with pure form. During the 1930s Dobson joined the fight against Fascism as a member of the Artists' International Association which supported democracy in Spain; in 1939 he took part in an exhibition called 'Art for the People' with Henry Moore, Duncan Grant, Vanessa Bell and Ben Nicholson among others,[115] and in 1942 he accepted an Associateship of the Royal Academy.

The use of a dramatic image for interior decoration was not a novelty in itself, since Europa and the Bull had been a frequent subject of the minor arts from the Renaissance onwards: it had been treated in all sorts of materials and used as a decoration on tapestries, chests, cups and vases, plates, clocks, cameos, embroidered covers, jewelry containers and all types of boxes, medals and playing cards (*Die Verfuehrung*). The novelty was in the commercialisation of the image for a potentially vast middle-class public, since Dobson's textiles were sold at Fortnum & Mason's contemporary decoration department and at Heals textile shop. One would be tempted to suppose that as the years went by the unconscious connection between Europa and Europe would become more evident and that therefore a purely decorative use of the motif reflected an escape from this connection – but the temptation must be resisted, as the case of Dobson contradicts this easy hypothesis. This artist was anti-Fascist, but did not see in the image of Europa and the bull any overt reference to the European situation. However, it is true that his charging and steaming bull is a fierce image and his Europa a 'femme chancelante' (to use the title of one of Max Ernst's paintings whose staggering woman with open arms is similar to Dobson's Europa), while his later statuette is a dramatic representation of the scene with the woman in a subordinated position. But the use of an ancient and dramatic image infinitely repeated on upholstery shadows the sense of tragedy and induces a sort of indifference, perhaps a sign of the times and of the destiny of the work of art in the age of mechanical reproduction, when resulting products can be sold on a large scale. This idea of art for popular consumption was more potential than real in the case of Dobson's textile, but this implicitly showed the ambivalence of the new forms of culture and art in transforming an ancient image.

## Active solidarity (Friends of Europe and Federal Union)

In the mid-1930s the slogan of a 'united Europe' took on a new meaning linked to the Nazi rise to power, although the concept it represented was often rather vague and its aims not very well defined. In British progressive circles a 'united Europe' came above all to mean solidarity against Nazism and Fascism, and the issue of Europe was increasingly identified with that of Germany. This was the case of the Friends of Europe, an association which in 1933 started publishing a series of pamphlets, with the purposes of counteracting Nazi propaganda, opposing the domination of Europe by any one power and working for a union of Europe based on respect for law and for the rights of small nations. The secretary of this association was the socialist Rennie Smith, who had previously been a staff member of the International Federation of Trade Unions, General Secretary of the National Peace Council, and a Labour Member of Parliament. Smith's political itinerary ranged from pacifist positions, supporting the League of Nations and the initiative in favour of 'General

Disarmament NOW' in 1927[116] to the conviction that 'only success in arms can avert' Nazi domination[117] in 1939.

The first 'Friends of Europe' pamphlets included Wickham Steed's *The Future in Europe* (October 1933), in which he analysed the danger posed by German militarism and proposed that Britain contribute to the establishment of an international commonwealth based upon the League of Nations covenant and a common law punishing nations for offences against peace; at that point, he wrote, 'Europe, having 'found herself', would again become the centre and hearth of the world's civilisation'. Another pamphlet, also dating to October 1933, presented Albert Einstein's talk *'Europe's Danger; Europe's Hope'* delivered to some 10,000 people at a meeting organised at the Royal Albert Hall by the Refugee Assistance Fund. Einstein, who had decided not to go back to Germany after the Nazi accession to power, counterposed the submissiveness and servility instilled into youth by the current German Government to the 'consciousness of personal responsibility of the true European man', and proposed a future 'when Europe is politically and economically united'. In a later pamphlet (*Germany, Great Britain and the League of Nations*, June, 1935), Anthony Eden confirmed that the only possible collective peace system was the League of Nations, but that a new commitment should be made in order to make it effective.

Between 1933 and 1939 more than 70 'Friends of Europe' pamphlets were published, most of which dealt with aspects of Nazi propaganda, and which translated into English excerpts from the works of the racial doctrines of Alfred Rosenberg (1936–37) and documents illustrating the struggle of the German church against Nazism (1939). The booklet *History on a Racial Basis* by the Nazi Johann von Leers (1936) was prefaced by the scientist Julian Huxley, elder brother of Aldous, who had written, together with the anthropologist A.C. Haddon and the biologist and sociologist A.M. Carr-Saunders, a refutation of Nazi racial doctrines: *We Europeans. A Survey of 'Racial' Problems* (1935). By harshly criticising the ideas of 'race' and 'blood', the three authors stressed the contrast between the family, an ancient biological factor, and the nation-state, a modern conception and product - in contrast to the Fascist pseudo-science which insisted on a connection between the two (we have seen Mosley using 'the idea of kinship' to define the bond among Europeans). According to Huxley and his collaborators, 'race' proved to be a misleading term, and the question of 'race-mixture' turned out to be primarily a matter of nationality, class or social status.[118] The 'Europeans' were in reality an incredible mixture of tribes and cultures, particularly in those areas where a high degree of civilisation had been reached – good examples of this were to be found in Provence and the British Isles. The Jews were no more a distinct 'race' than the Germans or the English; biologically it was as misguided to speak of a 'Jewish race' as of an 'Aryan race'.[119] The Nazi ideal of the superior

Teutonic race was ironised in this book in the proposition of 'a composite picture of a typical Teuton from the most prominent of the exponents of this view. Let him be as blond as Hitler, as dolicocephalic as Rosenberg, as tall as Goebbels, as slender as Goering, and as manly as Streicher.'[120] The book made an appeal to tolerance, diversity and multiculturalism, and expressed the hope that 'crosses between groups or classes of markedly different ethnic groups within the same country' would in the future blur social barriers.

Huxley, prefacing von Leers, reminded his readers that such 'pseudo-scientific rubbish' was designed especially for use in German schools. The education of young people was a constant worry of Friends of Europe, who also published a history handbook for German teachers explaining how to focus European history on the idea of race (1937) and a handbook for the training work of the Hitler Youth (1940). The state of German universities was mentioned as a motive for serious concern in the pamphlet containing the exchange of letters between Thomas Mann and the Dean of the Philosophical Faculty of the University of Bonn, which was prefaced by J.B. Priestley (1937). Mann, in exile and deprived of German citizenship, had been informed by the Dean that his name had been struck off the roll of honorary doctors. He replied with a letter in an elevated tone, in which he spoke in a moving way of what it meant to a writer to be exiled from his people and his language; Mann challenged the effrontery of the current German leaders in confusing themselves with Germany, and wished for 'Germany's voluntary return to the European system, her reconciliation with Europe'.

Friends of Europe also published a monthly newsletter, with a good coverage of books on Europe, Germany and Fascism. In October 1939, the association founded the monthly *Europe Tomorrow*, intending to work 'for a United Europe, based on respect for law and for the rights of small nations'. In 1939 they published in their 'War Series' pamphlets *A Free Czechoslovakia and a Free Germany in a Free Europe* by Eduard Benes and Jan Masaryk. At the same time the fortnightly *Free Europe: Central and Eastern European Affairs* started to appear (until 1945–46); this published contributions by Labour politicians such as C.R. Attlee, Archibald Sinclair, J.H. Harley, and Arthur Greenwood, as well as by some Liberals such as Wickham Steed. Within the British Labour movement there were individuals, such as G.D.H. Cole, and groups, such as the Independent Labour Party, which supported the idea of European unity.[121]

In the course of the 1930s Britain gave its active solidarity to many 'good Europeans' who took refuge there, either to escape Nazi persecution, such as the Austrian writer Stefan Zweig, or to pursue Europeanist activities, such as Coudenhove-Kalergi. Zweig moved to England in 1934, and in 1940 became naturalised before leaving for America. In his autobiography he acknowledged that Britain had allowed him to maintain his physical and spiritual freedom, but he also added that he found witnessing the credulity of British people towards Hitler very distressing. He pointed out that he had lived in Britain for many years knowing very few British people; while they were very generous to refugees, he felt an insurmountable separation between those like himself who had already experienced the impact of Nazism and those who still maintained the illusion that it would expand exclusively towards Russia.[122]

Coudenhove-Kalergi, who had changed his mind in the late 1930s, after the Nazi foundation of Greater Germany, and included Britain in his revised project for Pan Europa, paid numerous visits to Britain in 1938 and 1939. In June 1938 he was invited to give a speech at the British Institute of International Affairs (Chatham House), which had been founded by the former Liberal minister Lord Lothian and Lionel Curtis, who had been active in the *Round Table* (see Chapter 2) and who abandoned imperial for international federalism in 1938. During the inter-war years, the principal area of interest for Chatham House – which had taken over the legacies of groups such as Round Table and the first New Europe[123] – had been that of Anglo-American relations; the Institute laid the cultural and material basis on which would develop an Anglo-American Atlantic policy and in the spring of 1939 Lord Lothian was appointed ambassador to the US.[124] The invitation to Coudenhove-Kalergi was therefore an important sign of a new direction of interest. In his speech at Chatham House, Coudenhove-Kalergi, introduced by Rennie Smith, no longer advocated a purely continental European federation based on a French/German axis, but instead a direct British participation in Pan Europa and Britain's leadership of the continent. A year later, in June 1939, he again gave a speech at Chatham House and expressed his disagreement with any attempt to involve the USA in a European federation, as it was proposed by Clarence K. Streit in his book *Union Now*.[125] Coudenhove-Kalergi met Winston Churchill, Alfred Duff Cooper and Anthony Eden, and participated in founding a British Pan-European Committee which included L. Amery, Edward Grigg, Arthur Salter, Harold Nicolson, Gilbert Murray, and Walter Layton.[126] In October 1939 he gave written form to his new ideas in an English publication, *Europe Must Unite*.

The idea of federation was widely discussed in Britain in the year leading up to, and the early part of, the Second World War, with various positions conflicting in the public arena. The initiative which was most important in defining Europe was the foundation, between September and December 1938, of the Federal Union (FU) by some young pacifists and federalists from Oxford and Cambridge – Derek Rawnsley, Charles Kimber and Patrick Ransome – soon to be joined by older political men such as Lionel Curtis, Lord Lothian and Wickham Steed; a committee of advisers was formed of Curtis, Steed and the Socialist Barbara Wootton. FU 'Statement of Aims' advanced the proposal that national sovereignty be overcome and replaced with a federation dealing with 'such common affairs as defence and order, currency, trade, communications and migration' and endowed with the power of taxation and borrowing. No definition of the geographical limits of such a federation was made, and in fact disagreement existed within the FU over whether the union should extend to the world or Europe or promote an Atlantic union with the USA. In any case, the FU grew rapidly and gained a high level of popular support, with supporters from many walks of life: novelists, musicians and academics; among the professional politicians involved were Clement Attlee, Harold Wilson and Ernest Bevin (General Secretary of the Transport and General Workers' Union; in 1927 the TUC had passed a resolution moved by him calling for the creation of a United States of Europe). Among sympathisers with the FU's idea of federation were Julian Huxley, Arnold Toynbee, Storm Jameson, J.B. Priestley, Leonard Woolf, C.E.M. Joad, E.M.W. Tillyard and George Catlin; here there reappear the names of people who had been active during the decade in various forms of Europeanism. One of the Vice-Presidents of Federal Union, the politician Niall MacDermot, was a member of Mitrinovic's NEG.[127] On the other hand, the FU did not attract the sympathy of the League of Nations Union, which however avoided antagonizing it.[128]

There were also strong criticisms of the FU: John Strachey attacked it, maintaining that only socialism could save the world from war, and H.G. Wells – whose writings had convinced so many that national sovereignty was the fundamental cause of war – defined its effort as puerile and as offering 'the cheapest dope', while the writer John Middleton Murrey considered the FU utopian and yet 'the most promising means of focusing public attention on the necessity for a true international community'. On the question of the relationship between socialism and federalism raised by John Strachey in *Federalism and Socialism*, 1940 – in which he considered the two completely distinct and mutually exclusive – Barbara Wootton replied, in *Socialism and Federation*, that what he proposed was 'an unnatural and unnecessary choice'.[129] Wootton, who was initially Research Officer for the Labour Party and the Trades Union Congress, and then Director of Studies for Tutorial Classes at the University of London, argued for a European, or at least Western European federation to be formed at the end of the war.[130] She put forward a programme with three essential points: first came civil and political freedom, next social and economic needs, third the creation of a supra-national authority. After being the Chairman of the FU provisional Executive Committe, Barbara Wootton became Chairman of its National Council until 1943. She wrote in her autobiography about this period: 'to all of us in Federal Union, federation was a step towards world government... but to the hard-headed practical men we were all alike; a hopeless lot of woolly idealists... Practical men in positions of power can always demonstrate the impracticability of idealistic proposals by the simple device of making sure they are never tried'.[131]

By the summer of 1939 FU membership was at more than 2,000, with local branches organising meetings and debates; a weekly *Federal Union News* was published in 3,000 copies because of restrictions on paper, although it reached a wider readership; an FU bookshop and two clubs were also created. By the beginning of February 1940 there were 204 branches and more than 8,000 members; the FU was to reach a membership of 12,000, with 300 branches and bridgeheads in Paris and Geneva. A Federal Union Research Institute was also created, directed by William Henry Beveridge, rector of Oxford University, which organised conferences gathering well-known scholars such as the economist F.A. von Hayek and the anthropologist Lucy Mair. The FU acted as a catalyst for ideas which had already been relatively widespread in Britain for some decades,[132] but the wide scope of its policy hosted disagreement which led to division after the war on the issue of Europe or world federation,[133] reflecting dissent in large sections of public opinion. Part of the importance of the FU lay precisely in its providing a forum for debate and disagreement about the scope of federation.

The discussion on these themes was very lively in Britain at this time and a large literature was produced by representatives both of liberal and socialist thought. The debate brought together themes and people who had advocated some form of federalism for years and young people on the public scene for the first time. In 1939, Clarence B. Streit, Geneva correspondent of the *New York Times*, published *Union Now*, which called for a democratic federal union of nations along the Atlantic sea-board as the first step towards a world government. Lionel Curtis and Lord Lothian were very receptive to these ideas, while others in the FU preferred a European-oriented federation. William Burnley Curry, a young recruit to the FU and headmaster of the progressive co-educational Dartington Hall School in Devon, published *The Case for Federal Union* (1939) which reached a very large audience: 100,000 copies in six months (in spite of Harold Nicolson dismissing Curry's book as 'thoughtless'). Curry was influenced by Streit in advocating a federation of democracies, but included Germany in his scheme in order to 'detach the German people from Hitler', thus moving towards the advocacy of a European federation.[134] Curry's book appealed forcefully to emotions as well as to rationality; it started with quotations from Rainer Maria Rilke ('A War-Time Letter') and Bertrand Russell, and included as a Foreword 'An Open Letter to John Citizen' which challenged everyone between twenty-five and forty years of age

> [not] to prefer the claptrap of nationalism, your separatisms, your petty jealousies and your patriotic vanities, to that creative life of peace and happiness and plenty that is there, within our grasp, if only we would unite with our fellow-men throughout the world.

Lord Davies, who had founded the New Commonwealth Society with the aim of creating an international police force and court, published *A Federated Europe* in 1940: 'Europe,' he wrote, 'is a community of people possessing a historical background and the nucleus of a common civilisation', but also a geographical expression inhabited by very diverse peoples, living in a perpetual state of anarchy and currently divided into two camps, totalitarian and democratic. Davies considered the USA and the British Dominions to be the two major examples of federalism; as a start he proposed an Anglo-French constitution either federate or confederate, the former involving the direct representation of the people and the latter the direct representation of their governments. While he found it difficult to include either the Fascist totalitarian states or the Soviet Union in his plan for a federated Europe, he did consider Turkey 'part of Europe'.

The Australian lawyer and FU activist Ronald Gordon Mackay, in *Federal Europe* (1940) criticised the Briand Memorandum of 1930 because it had maintained the absolute sovereignty of the member states, and instead proposed 'a common government for Great Britain, France and Germany as it was before the annexation of Austria' as a nucleus around which a larger organisation might grow, including Austria, Czechoslovakia, Northern Ireland, Poland, but also the dominions, Australia, Canada, New Zealand, and South Africa (white population only). Subsequently, the other European states with their colonies would be invited to accede to the federation, although not the Soviet Union. The constitutional lawyer and reader in English Law at LSE, W. Ivor Jennings, also an FU member, in *A Federation for Western Europe* (1940) took a different view. Western Europe should regard itself as a nucleus for expansion and not an end in itself, but a time could be foreseen when the admission of the USA would be a good way of redressing the balance after the possible inclusion of the enormous population of Soviet Russia. On the question of totalitarian states, Jennings admitted that 'one would make many compromises in order to bring in Italy, Spain and Portugal'.

While the political relevance of the FU has been studied,[135] its reverberations on cultural grounds have attracted less attention, although they are equally important and interesting. Some indications of this can be found in the volume edited by Chaning-Pearce and which appeared in January 1940, where an essay by Storm Jameson was republished. *Federal Union: A Symposium* presented writings by well-known members and supporters such as Jennings, Robbins, Curry, Mackay and Wickham Steed on the past and future of federalism, its practice and theory. In this last section, some contributions focussed on the cultural aspects of federalism. Reviving the debate on the psychological problem at the heart of the prevention of war, William Brown, reader in Mental Philosophy at Oxford, explained the necessity of controlling the unconscious mind and its 'innate conservative tendencies', hoping that the establishment of a Federal Union would make the sublimation of aggressive tendencies easier; with the new feeling of security granted by an international government, he believed, aggressiveness would be channelled along the paths of scientific research, social reform and the combating of disease. Sir John Boyd Orr, director of the Rowett Research Institute, Aberdeen, was convinced that if a federation of democratic nations with a common fighting force were created, science would help to strengthen its position, raising the standards of living, lengthening the average lifespan of life by at least another 20 years, and generally making utopia possible in many fields. Writing on federalism and education, Grace E. Hadow, Principal of the Society of Oxford Home Students – who died before the publication of the book and to whose memory it was dedicated – expressed the hope of 'beginning a new movement quietly and humbly' and her strong belief that 'Federal Union bases its faith in the first place on the individual', individuals being considered in their relations not only to their family or nation, but to the world. Hadow boldly proposed that teachers should present to children – who were 'practical creatures' – the conception of an active citizenship of the world, helping them, at a time when exchanges with other countries were still difficult, to realise that children in other countries were not potential enemies but fellow-citizens. If 'in totalitarian countries mere babes are made into miniature soldiers,' she wrote, why was it not possible to teach children in democratic countries to see their individuality as a voluntary contribution to the common stock, not confined to their own country?

However, the most interesting analysis in the collection on cultural grounds was that by J.B. Priestley on 'Federalism and Culture'. Priestley, a novelist, playwright and essayist, who had also worked as a junior clerk in a wool firm, and participated in the First World War, being wounded twice, took a direct and dramatic approach to the question. There was a time, he wrote, when nationalism was a great cultural force, capable of inspiring poets, musicians, painters; but now the arts were internationalised: 'no man produces a book, a play, a symphony, a show of pictures, a film, withour owing something to every corner of Europe. It is impossible to enter the world of arts without strolling across half a dozen frontiers.' While the arts had become international, this did not necessarily mean 'cosmopolitan', i.e. not belonging to any particular region or without any local attachments (cosmopolitanism in this sense was attributed by Priestley to the Jews). Were it not for this touch of antisemitism, his ideas could have been acceptable:

> ... once we are free of the age-long dog-fight of the nations [...] we can attend to what is in all truth our own bit of the world, our own hills and dales and woodlands, our own wind and rain, our own folk whom we know by name, the near magical world in which we spent our childhood, and out of our interest, attachment and love can come flowering all the arts... I want to stick like

glue to Yorkshire pudding, cheese with apple tart, and the broad vowel sounds of my own North-country speech, but I want to do it in a wide federation of peoples, all equally attached to some charming nonsense of their own, but all loyal to the federal idea.[136]

In the collection, the only two essays to make explicit reference to Europe are those by Brown and Priestley; the issue of federalism inflamed sentiments and minds also perhaps because it was rather vague and expressed humanistic aspirations of a general kind.

It is no surprise that the idea of a European federation enjoyed a brief period of success in Britain, but, after producing a literature which influenced British political thinking at the time, has been more or less forgotten. In spite of the dislike for federalism in Britain, there was a federalist trend in British political culture at that time, from the Round Table to the FU; while most of the federalist groups were limited to intellectual circles and had a relatively short life, becoming educational organisations as a result of their political failure, the FU was an exception in that it gained popular support. The Foreign Office paid serious attention to the idea of federalism for the first time in the history of the empire, not only as a result of Chatham House but also because of the popular support for the FU. This was essentially a movement of young men, and it expressed the revolt of the younger generation against the policy which had brought about the war. It focussed on mobilising public consent for the federalist project, while leaving the federalists of the older generation to overcome the resistance of diplomacy and politicians, but this ideological gap between the two generations weakened the FU.[137]

The international reverberations of the movement of ideas around a federal Europe in Britain in the years 1939–40 were important. The British debate offered an advanced basis on which the positions of great federalists such as Altiero Spinelli and Jean Monnet would develop in the aftermath of the Second World War. During the war, the intellectual and friendly anti-Fascist networks provided the channels through which these ideas could travel. For instance, Luigi Einaudi, the liberal economist and first president of the post-war Italian republic, sent two or three books on English federalist literature to Ernesto Rossi, then confined on the island of Ventotene for his opposition to Fascism. Among the books there was Lionel Robbins's *The Economic Causes of War* (1939) which called for European federation if European civilisation was not to perish, without concealing that this was no easy task: 'we have a common culture. But we have no common language. We have a common history. But it is riven by fratricidal quarrels'. Rossi and his fellow prisoner Altiero Spinelli found those books inspiring for their *Manifesto di Ventotene* of 1941, which advocated European federation; it was also the basis for another manifesto drafted in Geneva in 1944, when leaders of resistance circuits from eight occupied countries (and two members of the German underground movement) met secretly and called for a federal union of European peoples.[138] Even today in Italy, British contributions to federalist thought are referred to as the 'Anglo-Saxon Federalist School' and considered most illuminating in the evolution of European federalist thought.[139]

Another instance of the widespread influence of federalist ideas is a New Europe Circle which existed in the international community in London between 1940 and 1942 as an informal organisation; it set up study groups on peace and on economic and financial problems, with the aim of achieving the highest standard of living compatible with the current technical means of production. Civil servants of the governments of several of the allied nations such as Belgium, Czechoslovakia, the Netherlands, Norway, Poland, Greece and France, in exile because of German occupation of their countries, participated in these meetings, and planned control on investment, migration, agriculture and trade.[140] It is remarkable that they chose, in those emergency circumstances, a name which promised a future not only for their countries, but for a higher form of community.

### Notes on Chapter 6

1   *L'Avenir*, p 134
2   *Ibidem*, p 143
3   *Ibidem*, p 175ff
4   *Ibidem*, p 188ff
5   *Ibidem*, p 198ff
6   *Ibidem*, p 210
7   *Ibidem*, p 298ff
8   Cole 1933, Preface, p 8
9   *Ibidem*, pp 780–3
10  *Fascist Quarterly*, II, 1936
11  Sellon, p 285
12  Gibbs, p 440
13  *Ibidem*, p 449
14  Young, p 311
15  *Ibidem*, p 334
16  Yeats–Brown, p 336
17  *Ibidem*, p 28
18  Ortega y Gasset, pp 9–11; 49; 40; 136
19  Woolf L., p 8ff
20  *Criterion*, XV, LX, 1936
21  *Criterion*, VI, August 1927

22   Collini
23   Rigby, p 61
24   Gardner
25   *European Quarterly*, I, 2, 1934
26   *European Quarterly*, I, 1, 1934
27   *Ibidem*
28   "Great Britain and Europe", by A Continental, *European Quarterly*, I, 3, November 1934
29   Ackroyd, pp 248; 221
30   *Criterion*, XVIII, LXXI, pp 271–2
31   Eliot, *Notes towards the Definition of Culture*
32   Jerrold, *The Necessity of Freedom*
33   Smith, pp 22; 82–3
34   Ackroyd, p 242
35   Eliot, *Christianity and Culture*, pp 50–51
36   Eliot, *Notes*, p 121
37   Mosley, *My Life*, pp 108, 383
38   *Ibidem*, p 108
39   Skidelsky, p 123
40   Mosley Nicholas 1983, p 300
41   *My Life*, p 349
42   *Ibidem*, p 431
43   Cross, p 56
44   Benewick, pp 161–2
45   Chesterton, p 161
46   *My Life*, p 382
47   Mosley, "The World Alternative", p 377
48   *Ibidem*, p 392
49   Mosley, *Tomorrow We Live*, p 66
50   Webber, p 122
51   *Tomorrow We Live*
52   *Ibidem*, p 71
53   Mandle, p 23
54   *My Life*, p 323
55   Thurlow, p 108
56   *Ibidem*, p 110
57   Mosley, *Fascism: 100 Questions*, Points 94 and 95
58   *Tomorrow We Live*, p 60
59   Mosley, *Fascism: 100 Questions*, Points 93 and 76
60   Holmes, pp 179; 189–190; 227
61   Skidelsky, p 427
62   Lewis, p 200
63   Hayes, pp 177–9
64   Salewsky, p 37

65   Cofrancesco, p 180
66   Kluke quoted by Salewski, p 37
67   Mosley, *Union of Europe*
68   *My Life*, pp 240; 245
69   Storm Jameson, *Journey*, p 328
70   Montefiore
71   *Journey*, p 156
72   Feinstein
73   *Journey*, p 295
74   Birn, p 2
75   Ceadel 1993, pp 171–2
76   *Journey*, Chapter 7
77   Showalter, p 59
78   Labon, p 42
79   Add. Mss. 51193 (1), Letter of 6 September 1934
80   *Ibidem*, Letter of 3 May 1934
81   *Ibidem*, Letter of 16 August 1934
82   *Ibidem*, Letter of 6 September 1934
83   Lassner 1998, p 68
84   Brittain, *Testament of Experience*, p 168; Berry and Bostridge
85   Lassner 1992, p 188
86   Montefiore, p 40
87   Storm Jameson, *Journey*, p 344
88   Storm Jameson, *The Writer's Situation*, pp 199–200
89   Woolf V., pp 162–4
90   Auden, *Letters from Iceland*, p 26
91   Branson and Heinemann, p 342
92   McLeod
93   *Left Review*, 3, 1, February 1937
94   Hynes, pp 133–4
95   *Poets of Tomorrow*
96   Spender and Lehmann, p 11
97   Hynes, p 242
98   Warner
99   Orwell, p 48
100  *Ibidem*, p 7
101  *Ibidem*, p 231
102  *Ibidem*, p 243
103  Hynes, pp 176; 312–4
104  Montefiore
105  Kampmeyer-Kaeding; Salzmann
106  Lipchitz, p 151
107  Carens
108  Salway, p 43

109 Yevonde, p 237
110 Gibson
111 Yevonde, p 284
112 *Ibidem*, p 283
113 Batho
114 McLagan quoted by Jason, p 39
115 Jason
116 Smith R., *General Disarmament or War?*
117 'Declaration of Intents', *Europe Tomorrow*, 1, 1939
118 Huxley and Haddon, p 282
119 *Ibidem*, p 274
120 *Ibidem*, pp 25–26
121 Newman
122 Zweig, *The World of Yesterday*, Chapter XVI
123 Martel
124 Bosco 1994, Introduction
125 *Ibidem*, pp 321–5
126 Coudenhove–Kalergi, *J'ai choisi*, Chapter XXII
127 Mayne & Pinder
128 Birn, p 206
129 Wootton 1943, p 284
130 Wilford
131 Wotton 1967, p 98
132 Bosco 1992
133 Kimber
134 Lipgens 1986, p 75
135 Mayne & Pinder; Bosco; Lipgens 1986
136 Priestley, p 99
137 Bosco 1992, pp 202–4
138 Mayne & Pinder, pp 84–5
139 Bosco 1992
140 Evans

# CHAPTER 7

# 'I LOVE YOU MORE THAN MY NATIONALITY'

At the end of 1936, an event took place in Britain which can be usefully adopted to introduce the last chapter of this book. On 10 December 1936, Edward VIII, king since January of the same year, abdicated, and in a farewell speech to the nation declared that he could not be happy without the woman he loved. This woman, Wallis Simpson, with whom he had fallen in love in the early 1930s and whom he married in June 1937, was an American twice divorced and therefore not considered a suitable Royal consort. The abdication was the conclusion of an intricate story which is not yet completely clear, and in which allegiances were complex. While most ordinary people were for the king, most important people were against him;[1] among his supporters was Sir Oswald Mosley, among his opposers the Archbishop of Canterbury and the Prime Minister.[2] Public opinion, not only in Britain but worldwide, was ready to accept the romantic version of the story: the sacrifice of a kingdom for love, and the media did much to support this view. Some politicians, however, had different worries: not only did some Socialists see in Edward VIII an incipient Fascist leader, but it was also generally apparent that he differed from his government's position on the crucial question of a possible war with Germany, since both the King and Mrs Simpson were known to have very good relationships with the Nazis, from the German ambassador in London, von Ribbentrop, to Hitler himself.

The whole story is significant, from our point of view, for various reasons: insofar as it concerned public opinion, it showed the mythological resonance of romantic love, since vast masses in the world accepted such news as plausible; but it also showed the intertwining of love and politics, in various and not always explicit ways. This mixture was still evident in a 1996 BBC documentary which considered Edward VIII 'one of the great romantics' and at the same time used as its title 'The Traitor King'. Last but not least the king represented a love for Germany which was not new in his family: his mother was a German princess, and he was a descendant of the royal houses Hanover and Saxe-Coburg. The name he bore for the rest of his life, Duke of Windsor, had been chosen by George V for the British royal house to replace Saxe-Coburg-Gotha during the First World War in response to wartime anti-German feelings.

A mixture of private and public, love and politics, British and German can be found at a more day-to-day level in the story which follows. In Catherine and Konrad's vicissitudes, I believe, there is a European specificity, although marked by the particular meeting of two European nationalities; their encounter happened to be across the European divide of the time, and their love story bears more than one sign of the European tradition and of its crisis.

In the early spring of 1938 a British woman and a German man started writing to each other, having met in Zuers, a resort in the Austrian Alps. They differed widely in age and relatively in social status, since Catherine, born in 1910, was the daughter of a lieutenant colonel and belonged to a landowning family in England with Irish blood, while Konrad, born in 1896, was a count descended from a famous and prestigious German household. His family, known since the thirteenth century, had its roots and estates in Northern Germany, and in the course of the centuries many of its members had occupied important positions as public functionaries, especially as diplomats. With the death of his father, Konrad – who had an older brother and four sisters – had inherited 2,800 hectares of land.

The correspondence between Catherine and Konrad soon became one of love which lasted for many years; it illustrates with great vividness what it meant to live through a love relationship with a European dimension. Significant as it is on these grounds, the relationship between the two is exceptional. Only because of their social status – and at the same time because of their individual peculiarities – was the relationship possible in the form it took. Thanks to its exceptional character, the correspondence throws light on some of the issues that we have found in novels and essays of the period, and shows the deep links between the literary imagination and the imaginary present in daily life.

In the first few months, letters from Catherine (the first is dated 25 March 1938, when she took the initiative to start the correspondence) were more numerous than those from Konrad, and were written from various tourist and health resorts, as she moved from the Hotel Bellevue, Kleine Scheidegy, to the Hotel du Lac in Interlaken, and then to London, Paris, Steeg, Bath and Venice. Catherine writes light-hearted letters about her life of parties and leisure, and treats the relationship with Konrad as an adventure, signing herself as 'Deine Erste Englische Frau', an epithet half affectionately, half jokingly repeated by him: 'my first english "maidly"'.[3] From other hints to be found here and there in the letters, it appears that the two correspondents had been enjoying a reciprocal frankness and complicity, confiding to each other the number and nationalities of previous lovers. Catherine did not mind writing that she got 'plastered' at parties, and introduced an almost naive touch of seduction, as when she sent Konrad a photograph of herself on a glacier in shorts and sleeveless top (April 12, 1938). Fewer letters came from Konrad, who seemed to prefer to send cards, both from Munich and from his own estate in Northern Germany.

After Catherine's visit to the estate, which lasted a few 'lovely weeks', according to Konrad, from May 27 to some time in June, Catherine's tone changed from the light description of daily leisurely life to that of the love letter, although not a stereotypical one. On July 23, she wrote from Wickham Market, Suffolk:

> My darling – 'Pig,' I said, when I went down to the hall at dawn this morning and there was no letter from you! Early this morning I had the most horrible dream all about you. Do you know when dreams shatter you so much that you wake up in a sweat! I dreamt that when I arrived on August 2nd you were perfectly horrible to me – and I said 'Well, why ask me to come and see you?' and you answered that you were like that and there was no accounting for your moods! Then some woman had kind tone – and then I woke up.

Catherine's fears as expressed in her dream at least partially referred to her plan to go to Brioni for a summer holiday, and on her way there to stop in Hamburg for two days and meet Konrad. Evidently she felt she was exposing herself too much. The degree of intimacy that the two had reached, expressed in a sort of code usual in lovers' letters ('Love from that Verdammt No 61'), and which was consistent with the type of emancipation Catherine was openly embodying ('I promised you would be my 25th and last – I mean it' [30 July, 1938]), still left some doubts as to whether it would lead where she really wanted: 'I pray and pray to God that you will perhaps think you could marry me in the end,' she wrote in the same letter. After the two days together, Konrad asked for 'time to find out if it would work,' adding that Catherine did 'not realise at all how difficult the question is'; however, the only difficulty he openly mentioned was the problem of how it would be for her to live in his family house not only for the few lovely weeks in the summer, but throughout the lonely and harsh winters (8 August, 1938).

Konrad worried about the possibility of Catherine adjusting her lifestyle to the German winter and society. She was a very independent young woman, her independence having been made economically possible by the inheritance that her father had left her at his death when she was eighteen; emotionally, she did not seem to have very strong links with either her mother or her two sisters. Catherine had first attended a school in Suffolk, where dance and drawing were taught, and then the Slade School of Fine Arts – part of University College, London – where she enjoyed painting particularly. She had also gone for two terms to a finishing school in Paris where she met another young woman, Grace, with whom she was to remain good friends for the rest of her life. Grace, who shared with Catherine a background of English country life, had wider cultural interests than Catherine, in literature, history and art, and she went to Oxford University, where she obtained a degree. The two young women could not have been more different, but they liked each other and shared the mixture of emancipation and convention (reminiscent of the protagonist of Mottram's *Europe's Beast*) that characterised the women of their social rank at that time: for instance they drove cars, but did not wear trousers. For sports such as skiing (Catherine was a brilliant skier) and hunting (which they frequently did) they wore various types of breeches. The two women travelled widely together, developing – in Grace's memory – a good exchange: 'I used to teach her history of art. She liked learning and had a very good visual memory. We never bored each other.' In 1935, the two of them flew to Johannesburg, landing in the desert, for the wedding of a mutual friend.

We can measure the distance between the lives of women of different social classes, if we remember that less privileged women in the interwar period found themselves obliged to work hard and undergo deprivation and loss; if there was some similarity between women of the middle and lower classes in the new possibilities of leisure for the young and in the more widespread attention to smartness and efficiency in their domestic and personal appearance,[4] for women of the upper classes the change was not so great, except that 'everybody could now have a larger variety of clothes' (Grace). Like 20 percent of her contemporaries, Catherine had been wearing lipstick on her pleasant if not really beautiful face before going to Germany; when she found out that Hitler was against it, 'she came back and never wore it again'. Catherine dressed her wonderful figure in hand-made tweed skirts and hand-made shoes, so that her appearance conveyed the idea that she was a free woman, although neither frivolous nor light. Free she certainly was to lead an international lifestyle, travelling to resorts and friends' houses all over Europe. She extended such freedom to her attitude to sex, by not needing to call it 'love'. Finally, as her friend Grace remembered, 'she had an iron-head and could drink everybody under the table'.

In a letter written on 15 August 1938, Catherine insisted on the idea of changing her lifestyle; as a sign of this intention she germanised her name, and signed herself as 'the ex vamp Katharina' (a name that she subsequently used often in her correspondence with Konrad). By that time she declared she was spending 'the whole day rushing to ask if there are any letters,' but perhaps not the nights, since the same letter of 19 August, from Brioni, mentioned 'so many parties and excitements' and described

> ... the most terrific party given by the Duke of Spolleto [sic] – only about 20 people were asked. I say it was just like an 18th century orgie! We had it all in a private home – delicious food and lots of drink – and then everyone did a dance or sang something – and I did my rumba on the piano – and it was just like saying 'Now which woman do you want'.

Whether this tone was meant to stir some jealousy in Konrad or whether it was simply due to Catherine's naturally outspoken manner, is impossible to say. Hints of eroticism and coquetry are scattered in the letters, with remarks like 'I am entirely brown all over. I want you to see it before it faids [sic]'. Konrad seemed to enjoy her letters, which he read 'several times'(18 August). Catherine's life of amusement was suddenly interrupted by an appendix operation at the end of August (Konrad learned this from a telegram sent to him by Contessa Cavalli, one of Catherine's friends in Brioni), after which she convalesced in Italy. At the Grand Hotel in Venice, Catherine had an altercation with some Italians, as she reported in one of her letters to Konrad:

> How your allies the Italians dislike the Germans my darling – they can't see them! I get awfully pompous when people run down the Germans because I always take it as a personal insult because of you my dear! (3 September).

This remark gave Konrad an occasion to disclose a certain sense of European identity, as we would say today:

> What the Italians think of us I know. To me it always seems funny that well educated people can dislike any other European nation entirely. I think one finds lots of nice people in every country and lots of horrid ones. You are a darling to defend us. (9 September).

From Venice, Catherine moved to Villa Motta at Travedona, in the lake region, where she was startled, when listening to the English news on the radio, at the 'filthy war hysteria in London', which contrasted with the relaxed Italian atmosphere, at least to her eyes ('in this country they don't bother at all'). However, she had made her choice, and her first loyalty was now not to Britain: 'if there's a war I'm coming straight to you' (20 September). Since the summer, she had been saying that all she needed of England were her bank account and her dentist (6 July).

By early November, however, Catherine was back in London, where Konrad came to visit her: 'Mummy thought you were charming and I so adored having you in England' (8 November). The relationship was finally going in the direction Catherine wanted most: marriage. She was dreaming of 'lovely children and a lovely home', and yearning for a process of identification with her beloved that would change her into a new and better woman: 'you are good and sweet and kind and you would make me good and sweet and kind' (19 November). However, before the intention to marry could become in any way official, she was asked by Konrad to ascertain her family roots. No matter how much in love Konrad was – and he certainly was – and how much he regretted the tendency of the international situation away from peace (on 21 November he wrote: 'what a pity the political atmosphere has changed so much since Muenchen', referring to the agreement on Czechoslovakia reached between Britain, France, Germany and Italy in September) he placed a racial condition on their marriage:

> My darling if you should have the slightest suspicion that there was any non arian blood in your family please do tell me. The worst thing that could happen would be to find out after we have been married, because then we would have to be divorced. So clear everything as much as possible before: you must not say it is too expensive, nothing is to [sic] expensive to find out these things. Lots of kisses I am longing to see you (23 November 1938).

Catherine at first reacted rather lightheartedly ('on Mummy's side I have a little Medici blood' [9 November]) and then did her best, in spite of the difficulties, to find all the certificates that Konrad wanted. She sent her parents' birth certificates, but she still had to get the christening and marriage certificates both of her parents and her grandparents. She managed to go back to her great-grandfather, but obtaining the documents was not easy. It was a problem not only of cost – £50 up to that point – but of bureaucratic complications and a lack of co-operation by British professionals, sometimes dictated by anti-racialist feelings:

> ... the solicitor who is collecting the birth certificate was quite sniffy when I asked about the Jew. He said: 'Most of us are very glad if we have a little Jewish blood in our veins – it makes us better business men'! Anyway there isn't any Jew in them.

Konrad replied that it had always been a custom of his family 'to know quite a lot about the ancestors'. That he did not seem to see the difference between trying to exclude racial factors and trying to ascertain aristocratic ancestry is an indication of how even non-Nazis could accept the ideology of aryanism in Germany in the 1930s.

On 24 November Catherine sent her mother's marriage certificate, insisting that the engagement be announced, and Konrad finally lessened his demands:

> I hope you understood that we could announce the engagement the moment I had all the certificates of your parents and grand-parents and that we could try to find out more about the elder generation later (28 November).

But the tension between the two had reached a high point and produced a major crisis in the relationship, although this was on a different subject. Konrad had written a letter expressing some fears about Catherine's reputation, suggesting that it was now necessary for her to distance herself from 'all sorts of customs and things one liked', to be 'double careful' and to remember how easily her reputation could be spoiled by certain people who knew Konrad's best friends (23 November). He had perhaps been subjected to some malevolent gossip, and, feeling 'frightened', asked Catherine for reassurance that she would be 'clever and nice if I tell you you cant do something you want to do'. They also had a telephone conversation, during which it is likely that her motives for marrying him were discussed, since immediately afterwards Catherine wrote to Konrad that she could not 'be treated like that' – without trust – but she would condescend, if he 'hated' her being in London, to move to Suffolk. However, her protest was vibrant:

> I love you more than anything else in the world – more than my independence – more than my nationality – and yet you still think that I am gold digging and title digging (27 November).

Konrad apologised, on the grounds that he had been very depressed and wanted to share that depression with her too, an attitude that would later come to be Catherine's own. The accusation that she was gold- and title-digging was probably wrong, since Catherine was very proud both of her cosmopolitan experience and of her English gentry heritage ('just as good as German aristocracy', in Grace's words) and did not feel she was 'marrying up'. Even so, a marriage with a German count with the kind of wealth and fame that Konrad's family had was quite prestigious at the time. This observation is not meant to suggest that Catherine was not in love, but her letters of this period suggest that her love was exalted by the aura around German aristocracy. However, it should also be remembered that after the First World War there were strong anti-German feelings in Britain, and Catherine was showing her usual attitude of independence by not taking any notice of those feelings. She could count on the fact that the British royal family had been Anglo-German for a long time, and the tradition reflecting this was present in literature in memoirs, autobiographies, and novels.

Among the most famous examples of this tradition was Elizabeth von Arnim's humorous account – published anonymously in 1898 – of her married life in Pomerania, where she had defied both the climate and social conventions by dedicating all her time to cultivating a garden. She had been born in Australia, brought up in England, and had married

Count von Arnim-Schlagentin. Her witty story of life with the count, whom she nicknamed the Man of Wrath, illustrated many aspects of daily life and Weltanschauung in which the Germans and the English were at odds, although reconcilable and even deeply compatible on many grounds. A more recent example of Anglo-Germanity was described by Robert Graves in his well-known *Good-Bye to All That*, which included a report on his experience of the First World War, which he fought on the Somme. Graves introduced himself insisting on his German inheritance, from Saxon country pastors to the historian Leopold von Ranke, the great-uncle to whom he claimed he owed his historical method. Leopold's brother, Heinrich – Graves' grandfather – married a Lutheran Schleswig-Dane, while one of their children – Graves's mother – married an Irishman and moved to England. Graves thought he derived 'the pride to be in the service of humanity' from the von Rankes, and a tradition of individualism from his Irish-Scottish blood. He was no exception to the stereotype representing Germany as discipline and continuity, and England as freedom and progress. However, he did not refer to the two countries as wholes; he reported that, when he had been fighting against the Germans (and it is noticeable that he does not show any sign of hatred towards the enemy), he and his fellows-in-arms had drawn up a list of 'the cleanest troops in trenches, taken in nationalities'. Actually, the criteria included both religion and region, with the descending order as follows: English and German Protestants; Northern Irish, Welsh and Canadians; Irish and German Catholics; Scottish; Mohammedan Indians; Algerians; Portuguese; Belgians; French. As for atrocities, 'the troops that had the worst reputation for acts of violence against prisoners were the Canadians (and later the Australians)'.[5] We will not comment on these self-explanatory hierarchies, but just notice the type of solidarity they confirm along lines of North and South, Protestant and Catholic, elements that corrected the insistence on nationality. It should be recalled at this point that both Konrad and Catherine belonged to the first category, English and German Protestant, even if their letters rarely mention their religious beliefs.

A third example in our short digression on Anglo-German marriages is the story of Madeleine Kent, who in 1938 published a book that was reprinted three times in quick succession, with the significant title *I married a German*, in which she related her experience of living in Dresden in the years 1931–36. Even Madeleine, whose husband was a confirmed Social-Democrat and a pacifist later obliged to flee from Germany on account of Nazi persecution, still felt the fascination of his 'once noble family' that had owned vast estates in Saxony (his great-uncle had been the Kaiser's aide-de-camp, his grandfather and father cavalry officers, and he himself was born in a *Schloss*). A common theme with the representations that we have already encountered emerges from her description of the 'Saxons', i.e. the more accentuated subordination of women to their husbands in

Germany than in England. However, Madeleine Kent's perspective in marrying a German was much more idealistic than Catherine's; she too had wished at times that she was not British, but in the sense of wanting to be a citizen of the world, and she believed that there was 'something enlarging about having a claim to two nationalities'.[6] This dream collapsed, and later Madeleine regretted having given up her nationality in order to marry Hans; her book ends with the couple escaping from Nazi Germany to free England, where 'a gentle Immigration Officer' remarks: 'And you, madam, were British?' 'Yes, I'm British...' is the spontaneous reply, claiming back her nationality.

Catherine did not mind signing away her British nationality – according to her friend Grace because she 'was too practical' – nor did she seem to care about the repressive system in Germany, which was by then recognised internationally. Inasfar as we can understand Catherine's motivations, her love had a genuine core, and so had Konrad's, whatever influence the context of the contemporary imaginary played on them and their relationship. The image of the German count for her, and that of the independent and outspoken young British woman for him, certainly played a part in their falling in love, although they were not the only reasons for their mutual interest. In the end the crisis between them was resolved and the engagement announced (6 December). This marked a turning-point in the correspondence, which took on a more intimate tone, with affectionate sexual allusions. Konrad:

> ... the tiny thing is getting frightfully impatient and telling me he is not so tiny at all every day. He asks me every day, where you are and sends viele Gruesse [many greetings] (8 December).

> Catherine:
> I hope we'll be quite ideal swine – and have lots of ideal children... with hundreds of kisses – and an extra special kiss for the Baby (2 January).

This type of language is frequently used in love letters, to make sexual and sensual allusions, including childish words, secret expressions and dialect.[7] In lovers' letters, terms from private jargon, diminutives and pet names are alternated with childish expressions, either words pronounced as a child would pronounce them or words that are traditionally used only with children and by children. The phenomenon could be interpreted as one of the variants of 'regression' to childhood, which is an essential component of falling in love and a way of establishing a passionate bond. In the linguistic expression of the love letters between Catherine and Konrad, it is not the lovers themselves who are changed into babies, but parts of their bodies which are tranformed into little humans or animals ('the Baby, the Mouse'). Jumping to this degree of intimacy apparently created some fears in Konrad. After making an allusion of a similar kind, he added:

I can write this because I think they don't open letters in this country. I always am afraid they open them.

There was nothing at all in their letters that might have disgraced him with the German authorities. However, Konrad's fear is an indication of the widespread terror which encompassed everyday (and every night) life in Nazi Germany at the time. It is worth mentioning that two members of his family, belonging to a different lineage – both high-level diplomats – had resigned their posts in 1933 in opposition to Nazism; one went into voluntary exile and died in Switzerland in 1939, the other was repeatedly arrested by the Gestapo and was assassinated in 1945. Konrad was not that kind of man. He was disenchanted, after having served as an SA ('Sturmabteilung', the early Nazi militia), and at the time he met Catherine he was neither strongly pro- nor anti-Nazi, while he was very worried about the Russian regime and its possible expansion. Therefore Konrad accepted what was happening in Germany with a sort of passivity, never showing any sign of rebellion or even dissension. However, at that time he was like everybody else under the Nazi pressure on public opinion – perhaps he felt even more exposed because of his social position – and this pressure, coupled with his worries about his possible marriage, resulted in confusion between the public and the private that fostered fear.

At the end of 1938 and the beginning of 1939 Konrad was still afraid that marriage between him and Catherine would not work out, and he again became very depressed by this thought, despite the fact that Catherine was sure that the marriage would solve all their conflicts, and that it would bring her a sense of peace: 'I promise that I won't ever let my devil come out again'. This promise was made on 2 January 1939; a few days later, on 10 January, they married in England and Catherine moved to Konrad's family estate in northern Germany (the Bismarcks lived next door, 'but they were so awful that they could not be considered very good society' [Grace]). The correspondence was then interrupted and taken up again only at the end of that year; by then Konrad was involved in the war, which had started in September 1939, and it was now Catherine's turn to feel very depressed at her husband's absence. Konrad was an Obersturmbannfuehrer in the SA and a lieutenant in the reserve of a cavalry regiment, two positions that were not very high up, given the importance of his family; this could be interpreted as another indication that he did not support the Nazi regime with great conviction, and that he accepted it in a rather resigned or opportunistic way.

By the beginning of 1940, Catherine's handwriting on the headed paper of the family house shows a remarkable change, becoming more homogeneous and tidy. She was pregnant and took a trip to Munich, where she began to feel much better. Konrad remarked that it was 'a great pity' that his wife disliked the family house so much, and thought it was mainly due to difficulties with servants. It was, however, more than that. By May 1940 Catherine was having dreams that reflected an inner conflict, showing that in the end national blood is not water:

> ... last night I dreamt that the Germans marched into Holland and that Queen Wilhelmina, looking perfectly frightful, stood on the HauptBanhof in Amsterdam with a gun in her hand saying that if the Germans were coming she was going to fight them personally! (May 1).

This dream, as she wrote it to Konrad, is another striking indication of the way that public preoccupations can intrude upon the inner life of the individual. In it, the national and private are mixed in a vivid way: a royal woman, armed, defends the Central Station (a point of departure towards England?) against the Germans (Konrad among them?); it is easy to suggest Catherine's identification with that 'frightful' and courageous lady. According to an interpretation of dreams collected by Charlotte Beradt in Nazi Germany during the period 1933–39, the foreigners who appeared in those dreams were ideal and independent contrasting figures, thus representing the ideal ego of an internal and external migration.[8] All in all the dreams showed the penetration of propaganda and terror into the niches of daily life, only apparently private, an extraordinary testimony of the degree of totalitarianism.

The private conflict going on within Catherine at the time was that, while she felt in some ways as unhappy as the dream showed, she was by now becoming very fond of the family house. She was investing a great deal of energy in restoring it, a job which she was good at, since she had both good taste and experience in the field of interior decoration (she had developed this by working in London at Peter Jones store for John Fowler, a well-known interior decorator who had done many large houses and her own flat). With Konrad away she felt insecure, despite her pregnancy; whether this would turn out to be her best investment depended entirely on the sex of the infant:

> Of course if 'little Konrad's a girl I'll die of disappointment... if anything happened to you and I had a girl I wouldn't have any right to the home any more.

It turned out to be a boy, born shortly after the sudden death of Konrad's mother on 4 June 1940; her grandson Alexander was born in the Luebeck hospital between the second half of July and early August.

Catherine breast-fed Alex for only four months, defying the doctor's advice and widespread practice of the time, another sign of her independent temperament. From the beginning Alex had a nurse, whose political attitudes gave the couple a chance to express their own. In her letter of 23rd August to Konrad, Catherine mixed politics and nursery:

... today the old man in Mecklenburg promised the war would be over with England – and it isn't!...

Darling Axel Poo gets sweeter every day. He really is a poppet. The nurse has now got a photograph of Uncle Percy up in the nursery – not hung on the wall – quite a small one on the table! The weather my darling is suicidal.

Konrad replied on 1 September:

How good that you like the nurse. I only fear that if she is such a hot N... she wont look at the bible and wont teach Zweg to say his prayers, but one neednt worry about that yet.

Among the various family nicknames, such as 'Zweg' or Alex for Alexander, 'Uncle Percy' was the name that the two used to designate Hitler. The tones used here indicate that at that point they were not particularly pro-Nazi, whatever they might have felt in the past. Catherine, who had always been rather unpolitical, had been through a period of admiration for the Nazis when they had come to power. Now, however, religion was more important for her and Konrad: she not only went to church, but also ran a Church Society. Maybe other factors were also at work in reducing her admiration for Hitler. When, after the war, her friend Grace asked her whether she had known of the persecutions, camps, and executions, she replied that she had seen people at the station with striped jackets, adding that she did not know about the camps, but had understood that something was going on. Certainly she had feared the consequences of the Nazi war for herself and her family.

Catherine's sense of nationality was not totally dead even at the conscious level, since she wrote:

You know I can't help thinking that they are not finding the conquest of England so easy after all – it seems (3 September, 1940).

But she was worried that Konrad might be sent to fight England; in that case, she would prefer to 'know the worst' as early as possible.[31] However, Konrad remained posted in Norway, a relatively secure place, for a long time, and Catherine's loyalties were not put to that test. At this point, she and her husband had been married for 19 months, but of these they had been together only 11 months. Their letters were frequent and affectionate, with the usual allusions to the mouse, and dreams of a 'lovely holiday, just enjoying life' (Konrad, 4 September, 1940). However there was some tension between the two: Catherine wanted to order some jewels that Konrad thought too expensive and complained about not having seen, while he was buying a platinum fox brooch for her birthday; they discussed the matter in their letters – not an easy task – and finally she gave up, reminding him that she had been 'madly economical – never spend a penny' (10 July 1941).

He called her 'my dear bad tempered girl', and when she received the platinum fox, she wrote that she hardly deserved such presents.

In 1941 Catherine expressed the fear that Konrad might be sent to Finland, and felt relieved that he was still in Norway, a comparatively less dangerous place (1 July). His letters described going hunting for elks, and spending some afternoons on the beach; he was able to send chocolate as well as sardines and stockings. Konrad was wondering 'how long this russian [sic] affair will last', while Catherine believed it 'will soon be over', but he was sure that 'Amerika will come in soon' (10 July, 1941). By the second half of July 1941 Catherine's letters started mentioning hardships at home more often: the peasants, she said, were depressed as they felt sure that as soon as the corn was cut the English would start bombing. She was buying everything she could – paper, matches, pullovers – in order to be ready for the worst. But at the end of August Catherine was still decorating the house, and having quite substantial restorations made, such as lowering the ceiling in the *Saal*, putting a tiled floor and a big frigidaire in the kitchen, and redoing the servants quarters putting in a bathroom. This was a field in which she felt sure of herself ('I know I have good taste about houses'), and she was also feeling optimistic about her relationship with her husband, whom she 'was missing very much':

I feel I have fewer complexes about you and 'bed' now (31 August).

It is interesting to note *en passant* that a psycho-analytical term like 'complex' had worked its way into the daily speech of the times. The use of the term, which originated with Neisser (*Individualitaet und Psychose*) in 1906, had been established by Jung in 1907 (*Ueber die Psychologie der Dementia Praecox*), and was used by 1928 in a publication like *Punch*, in the context: 'a fond aunt with a commiseration complex' (8 February). Catherine and Konrad used it frequently, both in the English and German form.

Konrad went home for leaves, which were not always peaceful, although once in a while they were good and happy times for both. However, the couple's hope of having a second child was frustrated. After each leave Konrad received letters from Catherine stating that she was in bed 'with the Curse' and their 'efforts to produce a Snooks no 2 *had* ended in nothing'. As a consequence, she felt it was all 'very sad and disappointing'. By the autumn of 1941 Catherine was living through a period of acute nostalgia for England, and she became more aware of differences of national attitude, her regret including a feeling for her Irish descent. She expressed it all with her usual frankness and sometimes tough language:

Darling I am so homesick. I long for home, and cosy teas, and Janet, and cinemas, and no rows and arrangements – and all my friends how I long for it all (19 October).

[I] rather long for the casual line, and hot live, atmosphere of the Irish [by contrast with a 'well organised and clean country'] ... I long for the sea and rolling green hills and mists, and beautiful casualness (22 October).

It is noticeable how an English woman of a totally different intellectual and cultural capacity had a few years earlier expressed a similar contrast. Alix Strachey, spending a year in Berlin being psycho-analysed by Karl Abraham, had written to her husband James in 1925:

I do think the English splendid in their madness... & nobody outside has any Ahnung [inkling] of it. I miss it terribly. The Germans are very, very simpleminded.[9]

Saving music & intellect – which may be everything – they [the Germans] are hopeless. They've simply not the remotest idea of how to conduct their lives. It makes me weep to see their attempts.[10]

Catherine rediscovered her traditions in unforeseen ways, such as when she identified with an English woman who scandalised the high society by not appearing to mourn her husband properly:

... it is really her English way – because English people are always brought up not to show their feelings – and so we don't take mourning very seriously. Darling I do so long for normal people again – not these Germans. I long for men who make compliments – and women that don't look like cows. I like my life really, and the simple people – but oh these bloody awful *Adel* [aristocrats] with all their pretensions and conventions (2 December).

Thus she ended up scorning that very aristocratic German society which she had so longed to enter.

During the autumn of 1941 the hardships of the war were felt: 'there was nothing to buy for Christmas' (26 October), news kept coming about friends who had died or disappeared, rows were breaking out between neighbours. Konrad commented: 'I have the impression that slowly but surely all the people at home get mad' (27 October). Still, the big family house had many reserves; in November they killed some of their geese and ducks to make preserves. Under the pressure Catherine was discovering new skills and finding herself up to her models:

I am really quite clever at getting things I sometimes think! I am reading 'Gone with the wind' again. There is a great similarity between myself and Scarlet O'Hara – only I have more conscience than she had – but we have the same toughness and determination. I think it must be our Irish blood! (25 November).

It is possible that many women found the image of the unscrupulous, vigorous and beautiful Scarlet helpful, in the struggle to procure food for their families under the growing hardships. Margaret Mitchell's book had come out in 1936, and it became the biggest bestseller published up to that time, selling a million copies in the first six months; a film was made of it in 1939. Catherine's reasons for identifying with Scarlet can be easily guessed: Scarlet represented not only women's determination to survive with their dear ones, but also that 'unsatisfied desire'[11] that Catherine knew only too well.

America was creeping into European daily life and culture. Alex, now almost one-and-a-half years old, sang with the radio and shook 'his head in syncopated rythm, like an American chorus girl' (Catherine, 10 December, 1941). But the United States were drawn into the war, after Japan's sudden attack on Pearl Harbour, on 7 December 1941. Konrad felt

> rather furious with the americans. They are such a boasting lot and always believe they won the last war. So it will be a good lesson for them if they get to know a bitt [sic] more of war trouble (16 December, 1941).

Konrad did not go home for Christmas that year, but he had a short leave immediately after. Letters were now taking 'an awfull [sic] time', and life under war conditions was getting worse and worse. In March and April 1942 there were air-raids on Luebeck, the German town close to the family estate. Catherine was appalled by the consequences and afraid that they might stir ill-feeling against somebody like her, who belonged to the country that had bombed the town:

> [everyone is] upset because of this GHASTLY thing in Lübeck. I may not write about it – but it's the worst thing that has happened. Hitler and Goering have both been in Luebeck. Of the seven church spires, one is left standing. They are dust [all shops burnt out]
> … wish you were here in case people are nasty to me (3 April 1942).

Konrad replied that she needn't be afraid, but advised her to 'be a little careful with speaking english in trains and at places where people are who dont know you' (12 April). And in fact, all in all, Catherine was not given trouble over her being English in daily life. Two months before this, Catherine had told Konrad a story about a friend of hers living in Germany – presumably married to a German – who had been called 'Englische Schwein' by some Hitlerjugend in Lueneburg. The story went that Hitler had come to hear of this, was absolutely furious, and had insisted on knowing the names of the boys, so that they could be punished (25 January). There was also a remarkable legend that friendship between Germany and Britain was 'one of the Führer's dearest wishes' and that Hitler 'again and again held out the olive branch to [the British], and again and again he met with nothing but rebuff'. The legend is used ironically by Christabel Bielenberg, another Anglo-Irishwoman who had in 1932 married a German lawyer, later associated with resistance circles, and had lived with him and their three sons in Germany; the above quotations are some of the expressions she used when interrogated by the Gestapo in January 1945.[12]

The strain on the issue of nationality became more pronounced with the bombing by the British. Catherine experienced moments of fear and horror for the 'terrible bangs and shooting' alternating with a sense of relief for 'how lucky we are' in comparison with 'how much misery there is in the world' (9 and 11 April). She had developed an interpretation of the epoch in which she was living, after some discussion with a friend who had put forward the theory of the end, in February 1942, of the 2,000-year-long Wassermann period. Catherine derived the following set of ideas from him as well as from her own reasoning:

> I believe it will be the end of Patriarchy which came with Christ, who was of course the founder of Patriarchy. What could be more Patriarchal than the Christian laws of marriage and morality? I expect there will be again a matri-archal age – and something quite quite new in the way of religion etc. All this is my own idea – and I believe it is rather true (6 April).

Incoherent as this vision was, and although no further mention is made of these questions in the letters, the above passage is an indication of Catherine's belief in some sort of vindication of women, and a justification of her own sense of independence. She was coming to believe that she could really be 'in ruhe [peace] alone – quite alone or with my own country women – or with you quite alone. Other Germans depress me utterly – ausser [except] tante Trude' (17 April). These sentiments developed into a complicated, and to Konrad rather threatening, form of self-reflection.

Since October 1941, Catherine had been re-reading their entire correspondence, which was somehow the history of their relationship. She found that her own letters had gone from being 'witzig' [witty] and gay to being 'a bore'. Her forays into the recent past brought to the surface memories of a more distant period, and Catherine had a vivid dream about her former lover Roger and his wife, who in the dream had come to Germany. She took the dream as a bad omen, as if something might have happened to Roger, and spent many evenings reading over all the love letters she had received from him. Those evenings opened up a world very different from her daily life, which 'consists of tiny sorgens [worries] that surround one and everyone else' (it is to be noticed how often at this point German words appear in Catherine's letters, sometimes like here with no capital initial and with an anglicised form of the plural). Although it may strike us as peculiar, it became quite natural that Catherine would include those evenings in her letters to her husband, not only because she probably had no-one else to talk to, but also, and perhaps more importantly, because the evenings belonged to the world of correspondence to which Konrad also belonged, a world different from actual life. Writing letters opened up communication with Scarlet O'Hara as well as with Catherine's past and her present dreams. A sign of this was that when she was so depressed she could not write. But it might have been quite upsetting for Konrad to get letters which included passages like this concerning Roger:

> He wrote splendid letters that man. Reading his letters makes me wonder why we didn't go on – ours was such a tremendous love – it wasn't sensual – it was complete love mental and physical – and we were so constructive to one another trotz [even though] that I was <u>so</u> young. It is nice to know that one has at one time in one's life been so much loved. He wrote so often… it was 1930, 31, 32
> …he really broke my heart for ever – and yet I think it would have been dreadful if I had married him then…
> He was my big love… Roger created me – really (17 April).

The letter continued comparing at length her feelings for Roger and for Konrad, the latter being 'utterly' respected and admired by her, not enough of a compliment for a loving husband. In another letter, written a few days later, on 22 April, she could say that she loved him, but had 'great sehnsucht [nostalgia] for the past at the moment', because everything was changing so fast and the future was so uncertain. Reconsidering her whole life with a sharp sense of self-understanding Catherine felt that it had gone full circle:

> I am very grateful to you and the war for bringing back the real me – the one that used to be in embryo long ago when Roger knew me – and which died when he grew out of loving me – and I grew into a sophisticated gay girl – now I am back at the beginning again.

Now we are getting to the heart of this correspondence, where important events take place, events of the heart and the psyche, and strong emotions are expressed. The difficulty of exchanging letters increased: not only did it take much longer, but there was little paper to write on, and Konrad frequently ran out of pens and had to use a pencil or to stop writing because the candles were finished. However, the exchange went on with depth and sincerity, as the two correspondents tried to understand themselves and each other better. To the three letters of 17, 21 and 22 April, which Konrad received together, he replied earnestly, appreciating 'such nice long and interesting letters'. Then he too went through a reconstruction of the history of their relationship. Konrad remembered that the first year had been 'awfull', and thought that the separation had allowed them to find their 'personalities back again'. He was sadly aware of the fact that it was difficult 'if a girl has really been in love with a man to be married to another man', and the difficulty was worse 'if he comes from quite different surroundings, from a different country and people and if he is as old as I am'. It was so much easier, Konrad wrote, to have an affair and to pick up only the nice moments of life. What is striking in Konrad's letter is the mixture of resignation and despair in relation to love and marriage; here, the role of distance and separation is crucial. Only by living far away, he wrote:

> I could begin to love you again at short moments, when I had the feeling that perhaps you loved me a little, for instance the moment you met me when I came on leave. But darling you have <u>never</u> looked at me with loving eyes like other women do if they are in love. Mostly you dont look at me at all and if you do your eyes seem to be dead and your soul isnt in them and I cant get hold of you or get near you.

This tone of deep regret for not feeling loved pervaded the whole letter, but with no recrimination. Konrad declared that in spite of all this he was glad that Catherine was his wife and appreciated the changes she had undergone in the last two years, showing qualities that she had wanted to hide before, when she had chosen to appear as a lighthearted girl who only wanted amusement. In spite of these reassuring observations, Konrad showed his dismay about his own image as projected by his wife, and wondered whether it was she who did 'not quite understand me or am I such an empty person? Perhaps you are right, I dont know'. This letter was written on 27 April 1942; on the following day Konrad added some lines, saying that he hoped he had not offended Catherine and mentioning that he had lots to do and some difficulties with odd colonels. His sense of identity was evidently shaken, as a short comment showed: '[I] sometimes think I am good looking'. He had asked for leave, but was not given it because of his duties ('you have got such an important husband!') (10 May); he regretted having written that 'very silly letter' and was afraid it had spoiled the relationship:

> I wonder if you will like me still, when I come. It is curious that I easily feel old and a complete Trottel [idiot] when I am with you and I dont at all with other people (3 May).

Finally, Konrad got his leave and stayed at home for a month, during which they 'got on so well together'. Immediately afterwards, however, Catherine complained: '... we have failed again – today I got the 'Curse'... I am so disappointed that we can't reproduce ourselves again. It is such a waste of time – and so sad for Alex.' Konrad replied that it was 'very triste!', but it was the type of *Pech* (misfortune) that happened often with human beings and highly-bred animals. Meanwhile the war was intensifying, and Catherine understood from Hitler's speeches that there was no hope of it ending that year 1942. Rostock was in ashes, she wrote, Cologne had been bombed very badly; it was expected that very soon they would get only 200 grams of meat and much less bread (30 April). Germany was, however, having 'great successes in Africa', which Catherine found 'exciting' (22 June and 3 July). But by mid-July there were no potatoes, very few vegetables, and no fruit (19 July).

Catherine had been thinking that from England's point of view the war would have probably finished 'without Churchill'. Yet, in spite of distancing herself from Britain, she still considered it a form of 'utter tactlessness' that a visitor from the Nachrichten Truppe [signal troops] 'started holding forth about the fantasticness of Germany – the new Europe – poor England etc' (25 June). It might have been interesting to hear what he had to say about the 'new Europe' and whether he was echoing Goebbels's ideas about 'the Europe of the future'. In 1940 Goebbels had expressed the view that 'at the moment when British power is collapsing' Germany had the opportunity, together with Italy, to reorganise Europe under their leadership, so that in 50 years people would no longer think in terms of countries but of continents 'and European minds will be filled and swayed by quite different, perhaps much greater problems'.[13] In any case Catherine felt offended – she who referred to Germans as 'us' – and both she and her friend Paula expressed their reaction with such giggles that Paula had to leave the room.

The correspondence between Konrad and Catherine went on for a while with routine news, but by October a new crisis was looming. Catherine began it by reporting the opinion of her friend Janet, who had been to visit her, that she was much nicer and much less nervous than when Konrad was at home. In her letter, Catherine suggested that she was now so used to being alone a lot that she really needed it, and began a dream-like digression – perhaps written in the evening again – that led her to compare her marriage with her ideal image of it, faithful to the romantic stereotype:

> I must say I do think marriage in these days is death and romance.

She mixed the possibility of rejuvenating her relationship with Konrad –

> I think we shall have to go away somewhere when the war is over and try and recapture romance... we do need to recapture Romance

– with her desire for new scenery and a new relationship:

> Affairs always take place in hotels, and so one has no household cares... I should love a tremendous flirt at the moment – it would do me a lot of good.

By then her comparison between the Germans and the English was ambivalent, defining the former as sentimental but with no imagination, the latter *vice versa*. However, she concluded the letter with an appeal that she and Konrad 'must be a perfectly harmonious pair – for the children – or rather I must pull myself together – I wish I could – Darling, please make me madly in love with you' (12 October).

This type of appeal, implying a need that is unsatisfied, is doomed to failure, because it triggers a spiral of fear, guilt and recrimination. Konrad was no exception. He declared he would 'try to answer' and showed his embarassment by hinting that 'one never knows who reads these letters'. He also mentioned that Catherine loved to boss and wanted to manage his life for him, but he also felt guilty because during his last leave, after an illness, his 'sexiness wasnt as strong as it used to be'. Konrad recognised they should 'try to recapture Romance' and proposed a trip to the Woerther See after the war. He was troubled that she felt unhappy and feared that if she had a flirt, she would also have an affair and never really go back to him (25 October). In reply, Catherine recapitulated her attitude to love and friendship in a strikingly articulate way, and she was very lucid about her narcissism as the basis of her relationships with men:

> You see darling I am a person who has always – and _always_ will, find antici-
> pation better than realisation – and I am a person who is really happier with
> women than with men. Men have only one use for me – and women I always
> find delightful companions and amusing to talk to – men bore me utterly as
> people. I know that they interest me if they talk about 'me' and flatter 'me' –
> because I am an egocentric, and flourish only in an atmosphere of admiration.

Catherine acknowledged that she had been in love only 'about twice' in her life, and that she had 'been disillusioned too often'. She felt she was happier in the family house with Alex than she had ever been, but sometimes she longed for her 'gypsy life'. Her need for romance was translated into national difference: she was longing 'for England – and the romanticness of the English countryside', while Germany had '<u>no</u> romance for her'. She believed it was her husband's fault, 'who had never made it romantic for her'. Catherine also brought up the old story of Konrad's fear that she would behave badly and accused him of having made her ashamed her past 'affairs and past sexiness'. Her resentment surfaced after four years, and took the form of a reproach to Konrad that he had made her somehow 'unnatural', and terrified of sex: 'you gave me a complex – and I don't suppose I shall ever get over it'. The family house had been just hard work. 'All that is death to romance,' Catherine said, while she needed romance to be alive:

> I long for a great great love to tear at my soul and make me miserable – and to
> make me so blissfully happy that I really feel alive again. I want someone to
> vitalise me. You, my darling, devitalise me. I don't know why... with you I so
> often feel, with a terrible sadness, that I am missing something. I am so utterly
> not 'in love' with you - though I love you - and need you – and would be mis-
> erable not to have you.

These declarations – which could appear like requests, as Konrad himself had thought, to have one's way clear to a flirtation – might have never come up in daily life, but letter-writing, by offering an opportunity for psychic self-analysis, gave them a chance, a sort of legitimation. They were mixed up with petty observations on daily things, like Konrad's lack of punctuality, untidiness, habit of eating too much 'and piling up your plate with potatoes and mashing them up – talking and drinking with your mouth ful [sic]', all amounting to 'a complete lack of self-discipline' (4 November). A few days later Catherine felt worried that perhaps she 'shouldn't have written so much in *her* last letter' (8 November) or even 'shouldn't have written that letter' at all (12 November).

Through this letter and the other ones in the same tone, Catherine was placing herself, at least partially, in a tradition of stereotypes about the relationships between the Germans and the English. One major example of this tradition is Elizabeth von Arnim, already been mentioned in relation to her book on being married to a German aristocrat, and her attempt to grow a garden in Pomerania. Attitudes to gardening were, in the literary conventions that Elizabeth shared, important marks of differences between nationalities, and were presented with an irony that did not hide the symbolic value of, for instance, 'arranging the poor plants like soldiers in a review'[14] or the subtle implications of attitudes to roses, which Germans would imprison in hot-houses, while a shrewd Englishwoman would dare to make them face the winter under fir branches and leaves, which they all survived, 'looking as happy and as determined to enjoy themselves as any roses, I am sure, in Europe'.[15] The teasing way in which Elizabeth wrote of German life – terribly boring Sundays, horrid meals followed by heavenly music, stern ladies who disapproved of her garden – and of her husband, the Man of Wrath, throws a sympathetic light upon the differences between Germans and English, implying that after all they really can get along very well together, if the English use their sense of humour. She remarked that her husband shared the idea that 'every German woman has learned to cook',[16] while she seemed to be 'the only one who was naughty and wouldn't'; Catherine too did not know how to cook, although she had developed into a perfect hostess in running the home and was a 'tremendous boss' to the servants according to her friend Grace. The literary version of Count von Arnim showed some similarities with Konrad, as the Count 'persisted in holding his glass in his left hand at meals, because if he did not his relations might say that marriage has improved him, and thus drive the iron into his soul'.[17] Catherine and Konrad were less ironic, but they would have understood the predicament perfectly.

Konrad was wise enough not to try answering the 'long letter of November 4' because he was 'not in the mood and, sad to say, it seems rather hopeless'. But he still said he loved her 'for being so honest' (15 November). The old feeling of complicity between them, and his appreciation of her frankness never totally disappeared. Perhaps, if he had been attracted by the independent young woman who liked 'playing with fire', as she described herself, he still found some attraction, not without pain, in her desire to revive those years. At this point she took a trip to Berlin, did some shopping and went to parties, but she returned home having 'seen how beastly people are' and appreciating Konrad all the more (20 and 23 November, 3 December). Konrad, on the contrary, felt 'so fed up with everything', because the eldest officer after him had left (24 November), and one 'so very seldom met decent people' – talking of the last three years – 'one nearly never meets anybody of ones own Gesellschaft' (7 December). He asked Catherine to send him playing cards. She was now longing to comfort him and pleaded guilty once more: 'I really feel such a beast dearest that I wrote you that letter'; as for the cards, 'one can't get such a thing here anymore – for love or money' (6 December). But she sent him parcels of 'nice things to eat and to smoke', while he reciprocated with a Norwegian wool jacket which had been exchanged for one of her earrings. Thus the relationship continued, with its ups and downs, tenderness and tension. Some of Konrad's leaves went very well, like the one in March and April 1943, after which Catherine wrote: 'we have got over our Complexen' (14 April) and Konrad: 'I had the feeling that you loved me just as much as I love you' (16 April).

That the letters between her and Konrad were constituting a world with its own coherence and dynamics was very clear to Catherine. At the beginning of 1943 she arranged them all 'in the right order' and justified her effort with the legitimation of much autobiographical writing:

> If there is no fire, or revolution, to destroy them it ought to be very interesting for the Zukunft [future]. As no one can deny that we live in stirring times (12 January).

Around them 'the war really was beginning'. In the 'hellish Stalingrad affair' many friends and people from Konrad's regiment were killed, and 'the whole situation was rather alarming'. The only problem, Konrad thought, was to stop the Bolsheviks 'koste es was es wolle' [let it cost what it may], and he was glad that his 'strong government' reacted immediately in the only right way, one of the few times he ever expressed such feelings (7 and 21 February).

The need to save letters at such a time went slightly further than the reasons given by Princess Marie Bonaparte, in an article written just before the beginning of the war, about the tendency of some of her acquaintances to save their correspondences. The 'genuinely positive element which makes a person keep papers' was, for her, unquestionably a matter of narcissism projecting itself beyond life, in the individual's hope 'to go on living in some form or other and in spite of everything': 'time appears to be conquered, for one's voice, fixed on paper, has by this means survived'.[18]

According to Bonaparte, the 'hoarder of papers' was usually a good correspondent, with a certain degree of exhibitionism as well as a general inclination towards the preservation of possessions. This description fits well with what we know about Catherine. The very fact that she kept all their letters in perfect order tells us something of her attitude; this was confirmed by her friend Grace, who remembered her as very tidy, and as polishing her suitcase every night during their trips. Her care in letter-writing and keeping letters was not, however, linked with a literary inclination. She read the novels that were popular at the time, *Gone with the Wind* as we have seen, as well as a more popular type of literature about waitresses who married aristocrats. But she did have a cult for the writings that she and her correspondents produced, thanks to which she transmitted them to us, thus creating, as Marie Bonaparte writes, a sense of communion in 'the battle against oblivion'. This task often seems to be left to women. Other correspondences indicate a gender division of labour whereby both men and women save letters but it is the latter that reorganises, orders and binds them together.[19]

One of the main strains in the relationship between Catherine and Konrad was the frustration of their hope to have more children. Catherine felt jealous of women who did, and finally decided to go to a Frauenartzt [gynaecologist] in Hamburg, who discovered that it was almost a physical impossibility for her to have a child, because her 'womb was tipped too far back' (9 June). He advised an operation, which she decided to have done in mid-July in a private clinic in Goettingen, as she considered it too dangerous to go to a hospital in Hamburg on account of the bombing. Although the operation cost 1500RM, she was proved to have taken the right decision in avoiding Hamburg. Once back at home, she was shocked by the effects of the bombs, and felt 'it must be the end of the world':

> Oh my darling you don't know, and you can't ever imagine what it is like here... Hamburg is <u>nothing</u>, literally nothing left – und es herrscht dort ein Elend der nicht zu beschreiben ist [desolation and misery rule there, which are indescribable] (28 July).

The sudden switch to German is indicative of her participation in the tragedy of German towns bombed by the British and Americans. Konrad also wrote in German sometimes, but Catherine used only a few German words here and there. She reported that Alex too was terrified, and that he trembled and cried, repeating: 'Flieger wachen oder kaput' [pilots stay awake or kaput]. Communication was becoming increasingly difficult. Both Catherine and Konrad complained that they did not receive news about each other, but they kept writing and sending letters all the same, not knowing whether they would arrive or not. Konrad sent Catherine lists of letters that he had mailed to her: 'am 13, 19, 29 Juli und am 8 u 12

August' (18 August); the lists indicate the great importance attached to each letter, the symbolic value it had as an object connecting two beings even if it repeated the content of other letters. The relationship of the letters with time was also of extreme importance: it was essential for both correspondents to write and to receive letters every few days, or at least to know that they had been written.

The habit of making lists is part of the etiquette of long and frequent correspondences, as both published and unpublished sets of letters testify. In our case, the list indicated that Konrad shared in his own way Catherine's care for keeping a full record of their correspondence and relationship. Konrad feared that some of his last letters had been destroyed in the Hamburg bombing, but actually it was the letter of the 19 July that went missing – or at least that is not present in the existing collection – the one that contained birthday wishes for Catherine and for Alex. Sometimes letters arrived, but in the wrong order: Konrad received Catherine's letter of the 19th on the 28th August, and on the 29th her letter of the 28 July; this required a readjustment of the internal scansion between the rhythms of life and those of letter-writing. It was just one of the reasons why Catherine felt 'it is so difficult to write letters these days', the other reason being that 'so much has happened that one doesn't know where one is' (5 August). There was 'so much to be talked about' and at the same time 'in such a hopeless world – everyone says that they simply cant write letters' (23 August and 3 September). More than once during September 1943 Catherine scribbled some words on a checkered piece of paper to send to Konrad, and the words included something like: 'Darling, I am so dreary I can't write' (7, 8 and 10 September). The same tones can be found in letters written by British women from their country to their husbands and lovers during World War II: 'Oh darling Ive such a lot to tell you, but I just feel too sick at heart to start', wrote bus conductress Hetty Spear from Bristol some time between 1940 and 1944.[20] But there is often more tenderness in these less literate letters than in Catherine's; she never wrote, like Hetty did: 'without your own man you feel sort of lost, I dont mind dying but I do want to be with you, it wouldn't matter much would it if we were together'. Catherine's forms of expression as well her own feelings towards Konrad were more contradictory, as the next episode shows.

By 23 October 1943, Konrad was in a small Albanian 'Gott-verlassen Gebirgsdorf' [God-forsaken mountain village], plunged in the middle of partisan war, in a world where 'at every moment a partisan shoots at one'. There he had the occasion to confirm his ideas about educated Europeans: the Italian officers with whom he had to do were in the majority 'ganz nette Leuten' [quite nice people], particularly their commander in chief, Captain R., 'a lovely typical italian [sic] tenor', and they all spent a rather fine Christmas together. At first Catherine could not get used to the idea that from the 'comparative sicherheit [safety] in Norway' Konrad now was in continuous danger (31 October 1943). Then she went to the opposite extreme: 'I am probably a widow by now – and I am trying to get used to the idea – because I am sure it will happen sooner or later... please come back home just once more' (3 December). Konrad took her awkwardness in good humour; on the 29th he wrote:

> the last letters from you are dated dec. 3 and 8 [the latter is not in the dossier]. In the first you see me killed and in the second you got plastered. I must say no behaviour for a widdow!! [sic]'

On 10 January 1944, Catherine calculated that, although it was their fifth wedding anniversary, they had had about one and a half years of married life together. She was at the moment without servants and had two children to look after, Alex and Franz, possibly the child of a friend, since later the same year in June Catherine was again complaining about the 'failure' of their encounter in May; she had 'the Curse', and asked Konrad, who by then was in Bromberg, to 'please go to a doctor'. Catherine felt 'very nervous': she had been re-reading all Roger's letters once more, feared that she had been 'beastly' to Konrad 'ueber Pfingsten' [over Whitsun], but was praying him to '<u>please</u> not have affairs with other women, because I should hate it' (31 May and 8 June).

That summer they had some good times together. Konrad was at home for Catherine's birthday at the end of July, when they had 'the nicest party we have ever given' (5 August). Alex was by then four years old, and his father asked for a snapshot of him. Being in Bromberg allowed Konrad to make quick visits home, as well as telephone calls that did not, however, always work, since the connection was often bad. Things seemed to be better between them, but he felt he wanted more warmth from her, 'a look, a glance, a gesture'. She thought that things were made complicated by his being 'so sensitive'; his oversensitivity provoked her 'to be beastly' (2 November), quite a possible dialectic in relationships:

> You say I never talk seriously to you, but darling I feel we understand each other so well that it's somehow not necessary. I very rarely talk seriously to anyone – either I don't talk at all or I talk nonsense. So please believe that I love you.

By the beginning of 1945 Catherine had to face one more major problem. She had been assigned 25 'Fluechtlinge' [refugees] to put up, but on 13 February she had '28 people upstairs!'. They were 'very nice', she wrote, but she did not know what they were to eat. Among them there were two secretaries, who typed some of Catherine's letters. After March 1945, the correspondence was interrupted, because Konrad was wounded in April near Frankfurt am Oder; his next letter is dated 2 July 1945, while there are no more letters from Catherine in the file until October 1947. The letters that follow are much more erratic and less numerous than the previous ones, and cover the period up to 1966; this time it is Catherine who is away from home. She is travelling to London, Suffolk and Paris, from where she describes films, plays and exhibitions, while Konrad replies from home.

These last letters provide us with an epilogue to the story. Catherine addressed them to 'Konrad and all'. We deduce from the letters that Catherine finally had a second child, but she still tried to have more; in May 1950, she went to see 'a little Viennese Jew who was the biggest authority on fertility in England' and who wanted a sample of Konrad's 'sperm by aeroplane'. An exchange between Konrad and Catherine that took place in May 1952 serves as an adequate conclusion to their story. Catherine was in England, and reacted to some remark by her husband with a summary of their marriage, while reiterating an ancient theme:

> You always behave and talk as though our marriage was the biggest failure in History – and actually though it has had terribly dark and beastly moments I think it hasnt been all that bad – not any more beastly than practically every-one's marriage has been if they were honest enough to admit it. It is of course a grievous pity that 'bed' is such a flop with us – but apart from that (I admit a major tragedy) – maddening though we can both be to each other – I wouldn't want to be married to anyone else…
>
> I am envious of all those baby producers. I really am. Do you think there is the faintest hope of our producing again if we really made an effort?…
>
> I do think of you with the greatest affection and love – you extraordinary old Bear (6 May).

Konrad, for his part, summarised his own attitude in such a way as to confirm that their relationship was still very much alive, in spite of all the disappointments and disillusionment:

> Bei allem Trennenden habe ich doch noch immer eine Stelle fuer Dich in meinem Herzen. Einen seelischen Kontakt zwischen uns herzustellen, dazu gehoert sehr viel Kraft u. Liebe. Und er ist nun mal Vorbedingung fuer alles andere, auch alles Koerperliche. Dann wuerden wir vielleicht sogar nochmal ein Kind produzieren, vielleicht! Wollen wir hoffen, dass wir nochmal zu einer Einheit werden (22 May).[21]

A comparison of the outcome of Konrad's and Catherine's love with that of others confirms that to establish and maintain a relationship between partners of different nationalities was extremely difficult for people in different social conditions. The story of John Dossett-Davies and Ellen Monnich, whose letters were partially published, is an example of this. John had met Ellen in Goettingen where he went after being demobilised, fell in love with her and believed that their love was important in the effort needed to avoid the repetition of the devastation of Europe.[22] But he had not anticipated the strength of anti-German feelings in England, and at the time felt it impossible to know how quickly these would subside. So he wrote a letter to Ellen ending the relationship without giving her the true reason: 'half of me says I was acting responsibly, half that it was cowardly',[23] and they never met again. Their story reminds us that, even if many international marriages and relationships were happy, the Second World War had shown a European dimension of love to be a dream of the past or of the future, and not a reality for most people at the time.

## Notes on Chapter 7

1   Graves and Hodge
2   Muggeridge
3   Respectively April 2, the fourth letter from Catherine, and April 9, the first letter from Konrad. Quotations from the letters follow the spelling of the original faithfully, including some minor errors by the correspondents in using each other's language.   The word 'maidly', which means 'resembling a maid', is obsolete in English; it is more likely that Konrad anglicised a German expression such as Maedchen or Maedel.
4   Alexander, pp231ff and 205
5   Graves 1929, pp 233–6
6   Kent, p 15
7   Dondeynaz
8   Koselleck, p xxiv
9   Strachey, J. and A. (see Sources, Ch. 7), pp 211–2
10   *Ibidem*, p 98
11   Belsey, pp 39–41
12   Bielenberg, pp 234–5
13   Lipgens 1985, pp 73–5
14   Arnim, p 24
15   *Ibidem*, p 21
16   *Ibidem*, p 152
17   *Ibidem*, pp 170–1
18   Bonaparte, p 237
19   Dondeynaz, p 29
20   Figes, p 268
21   Translation: Despite all that is separating us I am keeping a place for you in my heart. A lot of energy and strength is needed for our souls to meet. And this is after all the precondition for everything else, including everything physical. Then we might even produce a child, maybe! Let us hope that we will once again become one.
22   Day-Lewis, p 214
23   *Ibidem*, p 219

# Epilogue

## Europe as Fatherland

A strong feeling of belonging to Europe had developed in a minority of British people between the end of the 1930s and the beginning of the 1940s, one strong enough to push them to fight the Second World War with the intention of saving Europe from Fascism. Among them was the handful of British volunteers who worked with the Special Operations Executive (SOE), a secret military service set up by Winston Churchill in 1940 with a high degree of autonomy and the objective of 'setting Europe ablaze', i.e. to carry out clandestine operations and co-ordinate with resistance movements. Basil Davidson, who was one of those recruits, wrote of those who volunteered to work in SOE that 'not fighting for the all-European cause so much despised by current chauvinism would have seemed disgraceful to them'.[1] He deems it 'quite strange' that historiography has paid so little attention to this phenomenon; one reason for this might have been the Cold War and its paralysing effects on political thought, while another factor, both cause and result, was the fact that the new European consciousness usually existed in an implicit way and was only made explicit much later on.

Davidson, born in 1914, left school at 16, did various jobs, became a socialist and started a writing career at the *Economist* in 1938.[2] In December 1939 he was recruited by what later became the SOE and was sent first to Hungary, then parachuted into Yugoslavia, where he fought beside the partisans during 1943 and 1944. From January 1945 to the end of the war in May, he fought with the Italian resistance in Liguria.[3] In the 1950s he wrote on Africa and supported the liberation movements of the then Portuguese colonies, producing important books and text-books on the history of Africa.

According to Davidson,

> ... the European idea derived, insofar as it took shape in those years, from rejection and hatred of what the Nazi-Fascists were doing or trying to do. And this

307

is why the politics of 'communism' and/or anti-communism had, really, very little to do with all that time.[4]

The Nazis had created a kind of united Europe under their rule which 'was called *Festung Europa*, Fortress Europe'. This made the British realise how close Britain was to Europe, indeed a part of it, and was the incentive for them to imagine a different Europe and to fight for it. For this reason Davidson changed the meaning of the initials SOE to 'Special Operations Europe', which became the title of an autobiographical memoir on his experience of the resistance in Italy. In this book he expressed the view that the resistance movements in Europe 'had every essential in common' and 'depended on the voluntary participation of very large numbers of people who were "non-political" in any party sense. They fought in 'the belief that freedom, the rule of law, is a supreme good in itself' and were engaged in a democratising process, at the same time clearing 'a space for civic decency and even progress' and extracting 'hope and human value from the misery of the war'.[5]

Another man fought in the SOE with similar feelings: Frank Thompson. He was born in 1920, the son of two missionaries who had worked in India and had returned to England in the 1920s, when Edward John Thompson took a part-time job at Oxford teaching Bengali and Indian history. Frank's younger brother, Edward P., has written that theirs was 'a home which was supportive, liberal, anti-imperialist, quick with ideas and poetry and international visitors'.[6] Frank attended an élite preparatory school in Oxford, won a scholarship to Winchester and entered Oxford University, again on a scholarship, in 1938. There he was, with Iris Murdoch and Michael R.D. Foot,

> ... part of a small, intensely self-conscious, intensely intellectual group of friends, each of whom in series appeared to be in a state of unrequited, desperate and voluble passion for each other. Every one seemed to have been in love with the wrong person.[7]

Frank was then 'pining green with Iris, who was gently sympathetic but not at all helpful'; this was the foundation for a close friendship, which gave rise to a correspondence during the war; in the autumn of 1943 he wrote to Iris expressing his envy for her and Michael 'doing important things like falling in and out of love – things which broaden and deepen the character more surely than anything else' and adding: 'I can honestly say I've never been in love'.[8] In fact he lamented in his letters, especially to Iris, the monotonous masculinity of military culture.[9]

In 1939, at the age of 19, Frank Thompson volunteered for the Royal Artillery. Earlier that year he had been 'converted' by Iris Murdoch and had joined the Communist Party. However, he never was an orthodox Communist, and he does not seem to have had any contact with the

Communist Party of Great Britain after March 1941, when he left England for the Middle East as a lieutenant in a small communications and intelligence unit known as the GHQ Liaison Regiment (or Phantom). He served in the Western Desert, Egypt, Iran, Iraq, Jordan, Syria, the Lebanon, Palestine and Sicily. In the second half of 1943 he succeeded in transferring from GHQ liaison to the work of the SOE and in late January 1944 he was parachuted into South Serbia; he then entered Bulgaria and fought with the Bulgarian partisans. He was captured with a group of them on 31 May and, after a show trial at Litakovo, executed, in uniform, by the pro-Axis government on 5 June;[10] in the trial which condemned him to death he declared himself a Communist.

Frank Thompson too had developed the feelings of a Europeanist in response to Nazism. Foot, a close friend and school-mate at Winchester, remembers that some of their teachers there had a strong influence on Frank and himself in this respect: particularly Oakeshott, Leeson the headmaster, and Donald McLachlan 'helped to make Frank an anti-Nazi, and to give him some early glimmerings of the resistance struggle'; all of them 'in their three quite different ways talked and thought as Europeans'.[11] Frank's memories of Winchester were still very vivid during the war and he often evoked the Wykehamist tradition as having given him 'a strong intolerance of all folly, especially of folly which involved cruelty' and a sense of history and of proportion 'reminding one at every turn of one's own unimportance'. At one point, when he was lying in a field in Sicily under threat of bombing, he reflected that some of the Winchester dons, 'if they heard that I was lying in a Sicilian meadow by full moonlight, would be crazy with jealousy'.[12] Although he recognised that 'the culture one imbibed at Winchester was too nostalgic',[13] he believed that 'the classics, as taught at Winchester, certainly gave one a sense of belonging to an area that had been ruled by Rome, and had retained some degree of cultural coherence ever since'. Thus, this European consciousness was grounded in the classics more than in the Middle Ages, although Frank had read Dawson's *The Making of Europe*, as Foot remembers (he himself started to read this book, but found it antipathetic to his own Protestant and anti-Fascist beliefs and so did not finish it).

Other influences on Frank Thompson were those of Gilbert Murray and T.E. Lawrence, both neighbours and friends of his family, the former transmitting a sense of classicism, the latter personifying resistance. A most powerful influence, which probably helped to develop a European consciousness, was that of the Spanish Civil War, in which a friend of Frank and his family, Antony Carritt, to whom he dedicated a poem, died. In 1943, while in Malta, he remembered 'those men who, in the sierras and on the banks of the Ebro, bore the heat of the day alone' and declared his conviction that 'those of us who came after were merely adopting an idea that *they* proved – that freedom and Fascism can't live in the same world, and that the free man, once he realises this, will always win'.[14]

These themes can be found in his writings, edited by his mother and brother. Frank Thompson was a European in many ways, in the sense of the 'good European' of the past, but also of the new European of the future. He had a strong sense of history and of the continuity of European civilisation, from the time when 'the Greeks fought at Scamander and Marathon' to his own. Sicily – where he landed in July 1943 – reminded him of Pindar's eulogies, Aeschylus's grave, Frederick and Mathew Arnold. When, on approaching the island, he exclaimed: 'By Jove it was good to be back in dear old Europe!',[15] the mention of the Greek god was no empty rhetorical device; he was imagining Vulcan and Persephone and Ares as direct interlocutors, and he read their action in the Sicilian landscape. It was an animated nature which surrounded him as he lay all night on the ground while air-raids took place on the nearby port: 'I trusted Faunus to protect me. Nor was my confidence misplaced'.[16] This perception of the past was the foundation of a sense of belonging which brought together those who came from the same heritage: 'the more I see people, the more I love and value Europeans'. This remark is immediately followed by very positive remarks about Americans and New Zealanders, but Frank Thompson felt increasingly that he had 'a whole world of sympathies and sentiments in common with the folk of Europe and Asia – but precious little with the newer continents', because he deeply valued the sharing of a common past.

His Europe was, however, not only the Europe of the Mediterranean, inherited from the ancient classics; it was also very much Central and Eastern Europe, including Russia, and that is one reason why his concerns are so close to those of Europeans now willing to integrate the Eastern and Western parts of Europe. When Frank cried: 'how much I miss Europe,' he added that he was thinking of 'the real Europe, lying on an axis from York to Yaroslav – the Europe of bears and fir forests, of beefy, rosy-cheeked people, who eat heavily and drink good heavy drink'.[17] Thompson admired the courage of the peoples of Eastern Europe – 'Aren't the Slavs a splendid lot?' – and especially praised the Poles, but also the Czechs and the Serbs, while recalling that it was not 'the first time that the Slavs have thrown their bodies between Europe and destruction'.[18] He often reflected on how much these peoples, but also the Norwegians, Greeks, Dutch, French, Belgians and people of occupied Russia, were suffering at the time.[19] He was continuously comparing his lot with that of 'most Europeans' and finding that he had 'an extremely easy war'; when he felt this way, it was often of the people of Eastern Europe that he was thinking, imagining what the cold must have been like in Russia. Frank expressed a particular fondness for the 'Russkies', whose bravery in the war he greatly admired and he spent time trying to envisage ways of increasing the solidarity between Britain and Russia. His notion of Europe was not narrowly geographical: when in Tel Aviv, he expressed this by claiming: 'I like the Jewish atmosphere. The Jews are a lively, intelligent and European people' (but he hated Zionism and could not be reconciled with Islam).

He had indeed very much in mind the future of Europe. Between June and October 1943 he already had the sense that 'a chemical change was taking place in Europe' which made it impossible to go back to the old ways, an epochal change comparable to 'the end of the last Ice Age, when the glaciers receded and restored to Europe her freedom'.[20] This change could only be brought to a good end, he believed, by the popular leftist movements: 'Europe's health can be restored only by the working-class movement',[21] and the 'Western virtues' of 'concern for human life, dignity and liberty' – which he believed had almost disappeared from European civilisation since it had tolerated mass unemployment and Fascism – could only be revived on a radical socialist foundation. Thompson admired Soviet Russia, but his constant capacity to distinguish between ideologies and peoples led him to criticise Russian socialism for having lacked humanity and kindliness in its treatment of the Polish landowners transferred to labour camps in the Urals after the German occupation.[22] He felt very strongly that 'a Socialist should confine his hatred to systems, and judge every individual on his own merits'. His communism was combined with a deep sense of democracy and he had inherited from his family the best of the liberal tradition. According to Foot, who was never a Communist, if Frank had known of the gulag, he would not have hesitated to denounce it.[23]

Frank Thompson's love for Europe and his concern for its future found expression through his excellent proficiency in languages: he knew Latin and ancient and modern Greek (composing fluent Greek and Latin verse at the age of ten or eleven), Italian, French, German, Russian, Bulgarian, Polish and Serbo-Croat, as well as having a smattering of Arabic. During the war he seized all possible chances to better his knowledge: 'most of my spare time I spend fooling about with languages',[24] finding all sorts of people to teach him, and continuing to teach himself by listening to various languages and accents on the radio. Communication was a priority in his planning for the future, and he thought about having 'the news read in accents ranging from Priestley's as the most patrician', including some 'broad Yorkshire accents'.[25] He also wanted to propose that the BBC broadcast, as often as twice a day, a programme of old English songs and madrigals, in order to help the British people to become more aware of their national tradition and be proud of it.

In addition, he connected two major concerns, communication and education, in 'an idea for promoting the solidarity of Europe'.[26] According to his plan, after the war all schoolchildren should be given a thorough grounding in one language from each of the three main language groups in Europe. English and German children should be taught French and Russian; Russian, Bulgarian and Serbian children should learn French and German; French, Italian, Spanish and Rumanian children should be taught German and Russian (Italian, he thought, would have been a more satisfactory key to the romance languages, but French was such a universal language that one had to teach it). Afterwards, they should be able to reach a workmanlike standard in any other language in those groups after two months' hard full-time study. Special regulations should be made for the countries and languages not falling into the three groups. A law would oblige everybody wishing to stay more than three months in a European country to pass a language test at the end of the first three months. Thompson attributed so much importance to languages because his concern was to find ways to overcome misunderstanding and ignorance of one another between Europeans, who often did not even understand the need they had of each other. This was particularly true, he thought, for 'the English, whom Europe understands so little and yet needs so much (I need hardly say that this state of affairs is reciprocal)'.[27]

Frank Thompson's Europe was not only a Europe of the mind but very much a Europe of the heart, of which he spoke with real passion: 'Europe is the one subject of which I never tire, about which I could read or write, listen or speak almost *ad infinitum*', he wrote in January 1943, when he was giving lectures to his squadron about occupied Europe and the underground struggle.[28] When considering the attraction of going to China and studying its culture, he realised that he was 'too heavily involved in Europe already', and would not want to waste his ability to read so many European languages; 'besides, I'm too fond of Europe,' he added, imagining himself after the war spending two years at Oxford or London, then going to Beograd or Sofia, and then perhaps ending up in a Hungarian gaol – irony intervenes to check his daydreaming. In February 1943 he read the proposal of a United States of Europe in one of G.D.H. Cole's books, probably *Europe, Russia and the Future* (1941), in which Cole argued that a Europe made up of independent national socialist republics would be unable to make any effective provision for the development of Europe's economic resources and envisaged a Western European union, not necessarily covered by a single unified economic plan although possibly built upon Socialist foundations. Cole's book, written shortly after the Nazi attack on Russia and addressed to fellow socialists,[29] and its appeal to 'think supra-nationally, democratically, and realistically' found a ready listener in Frank. He was enthused by 'the pleasant prospect' that a supra-national union of Western Europe raised:

> How wonderful it would be to call Europe one's fatherland, and think of Krakow, Munich, Rome, Arles, Madrid as one's own cities! I am not yet educated to a broader nationalism, but for a United States of Europe I could feel a patriotism far transcending my love for England. Differences between

European peoples, though great, are not fundamental. What differences there are serve only to make the peoples mutually attractive. Not only is this Union the only alternative to disaster. It is immeasurably more agreeable than any way of life we have known to date.

These words signal a deep change of perspective from the pre-war writings on a united Europe, which had insisted on it as the only way to avoid disaster. Now, in the middle of disaster, a young man was talking about emotions and pleasure – the pleasure which could be drawn from the multiplicity of Europe, of its peoples, languages and cities, and from the mutual attraction between its cultures and peoples. Frank was already experiencing that new kind of patriotism for which he felt 'not yet educated' in his daily life. When in July 1943 he was sent to Sicily, after two years of absence from Europe, he talked with one of his companions about 'why we were so glad to be going back to Europe', and of the physical joy of this return:

> ... when we were still about 50 yards away the overpowering, aromatic scent of the Mediterranean littoral – in this case citrus and wild mint – came out to us and lapped around us. Europe's greetings to her returning sons.

The sense of being at home persisted, in spite of going through a battle and seeing comrades wounded and killed. He dreamt of coming back to Sicily for his honeymoon, when he would 'take my wondering young bride down to Avola and show her the beach where I landed'. Irony immediately comes in again to correct the dream and he figures that this future wife might be a Chinese girl with seven years of war against his 'paltry four' or a 'hard-bitten young ambulance-girl who drove all through the London blitz'.[30] Whether this imaginary young bride could coincide with Iris Murdoch, who some decades later would remember their liaison as 'We weren't engaged, but we hoped to get married',[31] is perhaps not so important. What matters is that Thompson seemed to be developing a view of love which went beyond longing and desire based on distance, towards a fully reciprocated relationship.

Where his enthusiasm for Europe was concerned, Thompson was not blind to conflicts between Europeans, and foresaw 'an embittered and factious post-war Europe', but he nourished a general optimism towards the future, convinced as he was that men who want to be free win in the long run: 'the future *does* look very fine. It's a grand world we'll be a-building, and the business of building will be far more interesting and exciting than any of the so-called 'adventures' that war brings.'[32] The anticipation of this distant future allowed him to express his sense of European identity eloquently: 'My eyes fill very quickly with tears when I think what a splendid Europe we shall build (I say Europe because that's the only continent I really know quite well) when all the vitality and talent of its indomitable people can be set free for co-operation and creation' (January 1944).[33] The observation in parenthesis, in spite of its apparent banality, is very important: it reminds us that every sense of belonging or identity finds its roots in an initial limitation which is not only due to choice, or 'elective affinity'. It is 'given', either biologically or culturally, and must be accepted as such; the awareness of such acceptance of roots and boundaries is crucial in order to avoid believing that one's sense of belonging is based on position of superiority in a hierarchy.

This point is also what allows the passage from Europe to the world and *vice versa*. Thompson's passion for Europe and Europeans was firmly grounded in a double feeling towards all fellow beings; on the one hand he really enjoyed them: 'I never fail to be amazed at how nice people are',[34] and their variety, which he shared. Writing to Iris Murdoch on 1 December 1943, after having observed that 'one lives really far too little', he said that for him the moments of real life were when he met a friend or when 'for a flickering moment, I realise that I am a man in a townful of varied men, and that this on the whole is a rather good thing'.[35] On the other hand he felt compassion for the others: compassion for the homesickness of the soldiers, whose letters he had to censor as an officer, compassion for his comrades ('my major has been captured, poor old boy'[36]), for the prisoners and for those he met during the war: when the Sicilians who have just shot at the British suddenly ask for mercy, he feels 'pity for these Sicilians, so utterly has Mussolini ruined their lives and their self-respect'. But he also had a general compassion for humankind, for how much men had suffered 'for millennia', growing up and dying 'in filth and flies and stench'.[37]

At the same time, his Europeanness opens up a strong sense of 'the Unity of Man' as a whole, a unity demonstrated by the war: 'my chief intellectual interests are in the earth and the people on it'.[38] This was coupled with care and attention for the single individual: 'how helpless and how lonely the individual human being is';[39] however, he was rather suspicious of psycho-analysis and preferred individuality 'not messed about by continued psychological kit-inspections',[40] saying of himself: 'I'm very little of an introvert', an assertion which sounds like a defence of his own idealism. However, this aversion for introspection did not reduce in the least his interest in and solidarity with human beings. An example of his attitude to even the smallest person can be found in an episode which took place during the invasion of Sicily, when an eight-year-old girl became indignant because the soldiers had borrowed her jug for wine and protested loudly to them. Thompson wondered whether something similar might have happened when the Germans took Smolensk, or the Japanese Peiping or the Italians Addis Ababa, and commented: 'Perhaps so. Girls of eight are indomitable the world over. We hastened to give her back her jug...'[41]

In spite of his excellence and his extreme drive for perfection – dictated by very high idealism and by his family education – Frank

Thompson was also very human, with a capacity to stir deep sympathy. Some of his most moving notes are the ones indicating weaknesses or daily habits, such as his nightmares, when being trained for parachuting: 'during the night I must have done at least twenty descents',[42] or his sensitivity to animals and flowers. In his war diary he wrote of 'dwarf toad-flax, purple stock, small marigolds, red and yellow ranunculus, and even small blue irises' as well as of his memories of blackthorn – a symbol of English spring for him; just before leaving Cairo for Serbia in January 1944, he rejoiced that on a short walk through the vineyards he had found 'nineteen different species of wild flower in bloom', some flamboyant, although he was more interested in certain humbler flowers that he had not seen for three years, such as 'groundsel, shepherd's purse, red fumitory and lesser celandine'.[43] It was his thirst for knowledge and learning that was exercised through this interest for life, and which nourished his desire to 'build a new communal ethics' extending to the whole environment, since his priorities were '1) people... 2) animals and flowers'.[44]

His brother Edward, who was three-and-a-half years younger, was serving in Italy at the time when Frank died. Much later he used his historical expertise in trying to clarify the circumstances of his death and the variations in his brother's fame in Bulgaria: ranging from exalted national hero to silence, depending on the policy of the regime in power. Edward Thompson has reconstructed as far as possible the last weeks of Frank's life with the Bulgarian partisans, when he went into Bulgaria from South Serbia, having not received any instructions from SOE headquarters in Cairo. At that time Bulgaria was patrolled by its Fascist army and gendarmerie, working under the control of Gestapo agents, and the situation of the Bulgarian partisans was desperate; and in the case of the group which Frank had joined connections had been cut, a part of their forces swept away, and they were betrayed. According to E.P. Thompson, the decision to execute Frank was not taken by a local captain but by a higher authority: 'at that point in the war it seems inconceivable that the authorities would have ordered the execution of a British officer in uniform if some gesture or signal had not passed which offered them some licence'.[45] This hypothesis makes Frank's death even more cruel. The hope on which he had based his action in Bulgaria, of a general armed uprising, proved unfounded, as General Tempo, Supreme Commander of the National Liberation Party of Macedonia, had foreseen in trying to warn Frank that setting off for the interior of Bulgaria was foolhardy.[46]

The hope or illusion that pushed Frank Thompson to ignore this warning included a vision of Europe reaching its autonomy through the integration of its Eastern and Western parts, a task to which, had he lived, he would have certainly devoted all his energies. In Thompson's notion of Europe, two elements were essential, solidarity and the confidence in a new Europe. The sense of solidarity is well expressed in a poem that he composed in Malta in July 1943, picking up a phrase from one of his mother's letters: 'the strong joy of your returning'. He anticipates a return where he and his family will 'climb the hill together, the four of us', but the dominant, although almost unspoken, feeling in the poem is that his destiny is linked with that of millions of Europeans and that he can envisage his return only in a liberated Europe. Only then could he dream of a return to 'peace, not trying to be a soldier' and of going back to the lovely countryside of England:

> In that cool heaven of my yearning
> To rest with eyes half-closed and savour,
> Along with millions Europe over,
> The still strong joy of our returning![47]

The confidence in a new Europe is expressed in his Christmas message to his family in 1943, which has been quoted many times and gives the title to the memoir edited by his mother and brother:

> There is a spirit abroad in Europe which is finer and braver than anything that tired continent has known for centuries, and which cannot be withstood… It is the confident will of whole peoples, who have known the utmost humiliation and suffering and have triumphed over it, to build their own life once and for all.

The following day he wrote to Iris Murdoch some very simple words, which summarised the feelings of many Europeans at the time: 'we must crush the Nazi and build our own life anew'.[48] What is most striking in this confidence is the notion that the hope to take one's life into one's own hands is not based on any triumphalistic ideology, but on the struggle against humiliation and suffering. Everybody would be able to have access to building a Europe of this kind, and it would be a Europe open to people from the whole world.

In our course of research, Basil Davidson and Frank Thompson represent the importance of the resistance to Nazi-Fascism which helped to 're-create a sense of European feeling and interest'; even if its military impact in battlefield terms was 'puny', the Resistance had great strength in moral and political terms.[49] Frank Thompson is very close to have become a mythical figure, both in the memory of those who were young with him and remember his exuberance and intelligence and in the reconstruction of biographers.[50] He symbolises a period when the hope for the unity and regeneration of Europe was not yet broken by disillusionment about Russian Communism. Frank Thompson's story also allows us a final consideration on the connection between love and Europe that we have been searching out. He had known the type of love which was for so long considered the utmost of European civilisation, unrequited ecstatic longing, but he had come to consider it not as 'love'; he was preparing for something else. That other love, as well as the other Europe he had in mind, has remained part of the future.

## Notes on Epilogue

1   Davidson 1996
2   Bygrave
3   Davidson 1946 and 1980
4   Basil Davidson, Letter of 25 February 1997
5   Davidson 1980, pp 228–9; 278
6   Thompson E., p 47
7   *Ibidem*, p 55
8   *Ibidem*, p 77
9   *Ibidem*, p 74
10  Foot 1990, pp 205–6
11  M. D. Foot, Letter of 15 June 1997
12  *There is a Spirit in Europe* (see Sources, 329) pp 111; 133
13  *Ibidem*, p 12
14  *Ibidem*, p 134
15  *Ibidem*, p 121
16  *Ibidem*, p 133
17  *Ibidem*, p 75
18  *Ibidem*, p 38
19  *Ibidem*, p 46
20  *Ibidem*, p 16
21  *Ibidem*, p 85
22  *Ibidem*, p 88
23  M. D. Foot, Letter of 15 June 1997
24  *There is a Spirit in Europe*, p 171
25  *Ibidem*, p 68
26  *Ibidem*, p 83
27  *Ibidem*, p 122
28  *Ibidem*, p 79
29  Newman M.
30  *There is a Spirit in Europe*, p 118
31  Inglis, p 10
32  *There is a Spirit in Europe*, p 141
33  *Ibidem*, p 20
34  *Ibidem*, p 102
35  *Ibidem*, p 164

36  *Ibidem*, p 47
37  *Ibidem*, p 62
38  *Ibidem*, p 47
39  *Ibidem*, p 88
40  *Ibidem*, p 48
41  *Ibidem*, p 130
42  *Ibidem*, p 150
43  *Ibidem*, p 172
44  *Ibidem*, p 19
45  Thompson E., p 97
46  Vukmanovic, p 315
47  *There is a Spirit in Europe*, p 135
48  *Ibidem*, p 169
49  Foot 1976, p 319
50  Inglis

# Sources and References

The traditional historiographical distinction between sources – understood as primary – and references – understood as secondary – is no longer clearcut as it was in the past. The boundaries between the two change according to the object and the method of historical study. The distinction I make here is between a category of 'sources' referring to coeval materials used as support of the interpretive thesis, such as texts by an author and reviews of these texts, and one of 'references' including all material, both coeval and subsequent, useful for establishing the context. This general separation has been sometimes modified by pragmatic considerations on what was more convenient in terms of quotations and for readers; for instance, texts used in more than one chapter go into References.

## Sources

Chapter 1

Among Mottram's books, I have used:
The *Spanish Farm* Trilogy (*The Spanish Farm*, 1924, *Sixty-four Ninety-four*, 1925, *The Crime at Vanderlyndens*, 1926), Chatto & Windus, London 1927; quoted respectively in the Penguin edition of 1938 for the first volume and in the original edition for the second and third ones;
*The English Miss*, Chatto & Windus, London 1928;
*Europa's Beast*, Chatto & Windus, London 1930;
*Autobiography with a Difference*, Hale, London 1938;
*Vanities and Verities*, 3 vols, Hutchinson, London 1958.

Book reviews of *Europa's Beast* – as collected in the Chatto & Windus archive, now at the Library of the University of Reading – are the following, in the order of their appearance:

*Harpers's Bazaar*, April 1930;
*Birmingham Gazette*, 24 April 1930;
*Evening Standard*, 24 April 1930;
*Daily Express*, 25 April 1930 (by Harold Nicolson);
*Daily Sketch*, 25 April 1930;
*Dundee Evening Telegraph*, 25 April 1930;
*Referee*, 27 April 1930;

*Yorkshire Post*, 30 April 1930;
*Daily Herald*, 1 May 1930 (by G.G.);
*Everyman*, 1 May 1930;
*Times Literary Supplement*, 1 May 1930;
*Liverpool Post*, 2 May 1930;
*Norwich Mercury*, 2 May 1930;
*The Times*, 2 May 1930;
*Lowestoft Journal*, 3 May 1995;
*The Observer*, 4 May 1930 (by Gerald Gould);
*Sunday Times*, 4 May 1930 (by Ralph Straus);
*East Anglian Daily Times*, 5 May 1930;
*Birmingham Post*, 6 May 1930;
*Inverness Courier*, 6 May 1930;
*Punch*, 7 May 1930;
*Manchester Guardian*, 9 May 1930 (by C.M.);
*Time and Tide*, 9 May 1930;
*Country Life*, 10 May 1930 (by V.H.F.);
*John O' London's Weekly*, 14 May 1930 (by Lydia Languish);
*The Northern Echo*, 14 May 1930;
*Glasgow Herald*, 15 May 1930;
*The Manchester Guardian Weekly*, 16 May 1930;
*Oxford Mail*, 16 May 1930;
*Week-End Review*, 17 May 1930;
*Evening Express*, 20 May 1930;
*Gownsman*, 24 May 1930;
*The Nation and The Atheneum*, 24 May 1930;
*The New Statesman*, 24 May 1930;
*Sphere*, 24 May 1930;
*Sketch*, 28 May 1930;
*The Daily Mail*, 30 May 1930;
*Daily News*, 31 May 1930;
*Bookman*, June 1930;
*The Scottish Banker*, June 1930;
*Vogue*, 11 June 1930;
*The Spectator*, 21 June 1930;
*Scots Observer*, 26 June 1930 (by G.M.L.).

The film *Roses of Picardy* (1927) based on *The Spanish Farm* is missing, but stills can be viewed in the collection of the British Film Institute. The film received the following reviews:
*Bioscope*, v. 71, no. 1073, May 5, 1927;
*Kinematograph Weekly*, no. 1046, May 5, 1927;
*Picturegoer*, v. 13, no. 78, June 1927;
*The Sketch*, 18 May 1927 (by Michael Orme).

Chapter 2, 2

By Christopher Dawson I have used the following texts:
*Christianity and Sex*, Faber & Faber, London 1930 (a later and shorter version of this booklet, with the title *The Patriarchal Family in History*, is included in *The Dynamics of World History*);
*The Making of Europe: An Introduction to the History of European Unity*, Sheed & Ward, London 1932;
*The Modern Dilemma: The Problem of European Unity*, Sheed & Ward, London 1932;
*The Spirit of the Oxford Movement*, Sheed & Ward, London 1933;
'Interracial cooperation as a factor in European culture', in Reale Accademia d'Italia, Fondazione Alessandro Volta, Convegno di Scienze Morali e Storiche, 14–20 novembre 1932, Tema: *l'Europa*, vol. I: *Atti preliminari*, vol. II: *Allegati*, Roma 1933;
*Medieval Religion (The Forwood Lectures 1934) and Other Essays*, Sheed & Ward, London 1934;
'The Church and the Dictators', four articles in *Catholic Times*, April 27, May 4, 11, 18, 1934;
*Religion and the Modern State*, Sheed & Ward, London 1935;
'Spain and Europe', *Catholic Times*, 12 March, 1937;
*Beyond Politics*, Sheed & Ward, London 1939;
*The Judgement of the Nations*, Sheed & Ward, London 1942;
*The Dynamics of World History*, Sheed & Ward, London 1957.

I have considered the following book reviews of *The Making of Europe*, in order of appearance:
*Times Literary Supplement*, 23 June, 1932
*English Review*, LV, July–December 1932 (by H.A.L. Fisher);
*Spectator*, 20 August, 1932 (by Aldous Huxley);
*Cambridge Review*, LIV, 1315, 14 October 1932 (by G.G. Coulton);
*Criterion*, XII, XLVII, January 1933 (by F. McEachran);
as well as Vera Brittain's review in *Time and Tide* ('Modern Europe Adrift', May 17, 1929) of another book by Dawson, *Progress and Religion*;
*Revue critique d'histoire et de littérature*, 1934, pp 169–170 (by E. Gilson).

Chapter 2, 3

The Libraries of the Institute of Psycho-analysis and of the Analytical Psychology Club were essential for providing not only books and periodicals, but also subject indexes and guides to the relevant literature.

Chapter 3

The Archives of the New Atlantis Foundation in Ditchling, Sussex, are an invaluable resource for research on Mitrinovic, the Adler Society and New Europe. The list of the lectures given at the Adler Society and at the New Europe group as well as the typewritten copies of many of them and handwritten notes taken after them

can be found there. The Foundation keeps the list of sources as classified by Mitrinovic, the pamphlets and leaflets, and much correspondence. A series of pamphlets based on the annual Foundation lectures and the periodical publication *New Atlantis Bulletin* are produced by the Foundation; among the pamphlets I found particularly useful Farrington Benjamin, *The New Atlantis of Francis Bacon*, 1964; Violet MacDermot, *The Social Vision of Alfred Adler*, 1980; Ellen Mayne, *The Christian Philosophy of Vladimir Solovyov*, 1957; David Shillan, *The Order of Mankind as Seen by Auguste Comte*, 1963. Most of Mitrinovic's writings have been republished in Mitrinovic Dimitrije, *Certainly, Future. Selected Writings*, East European Monographs, Boulder, New York 1987;
*Idem, Lectures 1926–1950*, New Atlantis Foundation in association with J.B. Priestley Library, University of Bradford, 1995.

Books donated from his library are held by the J.B. Priestley Library, University of Bradford, West Yorkshire.

The British Library in London has a copy of the pamphlet *Integration of Europe*; enclosed in it is a letter by Reginald Wrugh to the Head of Acquisitions, dated 1988, where he evokes some of the activities of the NEG and a speech given by Annie Besant on 'The United States of Europe', but he dates it 1923 or 1924.

Obituaries of Geddes, Kitson and Soddy were published in *The Times*, respectively on 18 April 1932, 4 October 1937 and 24 September 1956.

Chapter 4

Briffault's papers were donated to the British Library by his daughter Joan Briffault Hackelberg on 18 February 1975 and are kept in the Department of Manuscripts under the heading Add. 58440-58441-58442-58443. They include letters to and by Briffault, as well as various documents concerning him and his family.

Herma Briffault's papers are kept at the New York Public Library, Department of Manuscripts, 135F6, Files 1–8. They include a resumé of all the books she ghosted and edited, as well as of her translations of books by authors such as Marguerite Duras, Colette, and Sartre, very often redoing bad translations by other people, so that she was rarely given a recognition. The manuscript of her research (done in 1947–50, when she collaborated as a research analyst in the Pentagon project *The Encyclopaedia Arctica*) on the Russian-American Telegraph Arctic Expedition in 1864–67 was never published.

The archives of the publishing house Hale, that printed *Europa* and *Europa in Limbo* in Britain, were destroyed by fire and war as well as lost in moves. Therefore no data are available on the circulation of those books in the U.K., except those contained in the B.L. archive.

I have used the following books by Robert Briffault:
*The Making of Humanity*, Allen & Unwin, London 1919;

*Psyche's Lamp: A Revaluation of Psychological Principles as Foundation of All Thought*,
Allen & Unwin, London 1921;
*The Mothers: A Study of the Origins of Sentiments and Institutions*, Allen & Unwin,
London 1927, 3 vols;
*Sin and Sex*, with an introduction by Bertrand Russell, Allen & Unwin, London
1931;
*Europa. A Novel of the Days of Ignorance*, both editions: Scribners, New York 1935,
and Hale, London 1936;
*Europa in Limbo*, both editions: Scribners, New York 1937, and Hale, London 1937;
*Reasons for Anger. Selected Essays*, Hale, London 1937;
*Les Troubadours et le sentiment romanesque*, Editions du Chêne, Paris 1945.

Book reviews (in chronological order of appearance):
*Times Literary Supplement*, 14 July 1927 (on *The Mothers*)
*Times Literary Supplement*, 26 March 1931 (on *Sin and Sex*)
*Time*, 9 September 1935 (on the American edition of *Europa*)
*Times Literary Supplement*, 18 January 1936 (on *The Collapse of Traditional Civilisation*)
*New Statesman*, 19 September 1936 (Peter Quennell on *Europa*)
*Spectator*, 2 October 1936 (Peter Burra on *Europa*)
*Time and Tide*, 3 October 1936 (Edith Shackleton on *Europa*)
*Times Literary Supplement*, 17 October 1936 (on *Europa*)
*New Statesman and Nation*, 16 October 1937 (Cyril Connolly on *Europa in Limbo*)
*Times Literary Supplement*, 16 October 1937 (on *Europa in Limbo*)
*Time*, 27 September 1937 (on the American edition of *Europa in Limbo*)


Chapter 5

I have consulted the documents concerning C.S. Lewis at the archive of Oxford
University Press, File 811562, and Lewis's letter to Denis de Rougemont in the
Neuchâtel archive of the de Rougemont Papers.

The following texts by C.S. Lewis have been used:
*The Allegory of Love: A Study in Medieval Tradition*, Oxford University Press 1958 (1st
edition 1936);
'Christianity and Culture', *Theology*, XL, March 1940, pp 166–79;
'A Letter', *ibidem*, June 1940, pp 475–77;
'Peace Proposals for Brother Every and Mr. Bethell', *ibidem*, XLI, December 1940,
pp 339–48;
book review of *Passion and Society* by Denis de Rougemont, *ibidem*, June 1940, pp
459–61;
*The Four Loves*, Fount, London 1977 (1st edition 1960): this book is based on ten
radio talks about love, which were given by Lewis at the request of the Episcopal
Radio-TV Foundation in 1959, Atlanta, Georgia;
*Surprised by Joy: The shape of my early life*, Bles, London 1955;
*Letters*, edited and with a Memoir by Warren H. Lewis, revised and enlarged
edition ed. Walter Hooper, Collins, London 1988;
the opinion on the Common Market was published by *Encounter*, XIX, 6, December
1962, p 57.

For the reception of *The Allegory of Love*, the following reviews have been consulted (in chronological order of appearance):
*John O'London's Weekly*, 18 April 1936;
*Daily Telegraph*, 5 June 1936 (Harold Nicolson);
*Times Literary Supplement*, 6 June 1936;
*The Sunday Times*, 28 June 1936 (G.M. Young);
*London Mercury*, 34, July 1936, pp 270–1 (E.H.W. Meyerstein);
*Observer*, 23 August 1936 (B. Ifor Evans);
*Nottingham Journal*, 28 August 1936 (R.M. Hewitt);
*Spectator*, 4 September 1936 (William Empson);
*Notes and Queries*, 3 October 1936, pp 250–1;
*Review of English Studies*, 13, October 1937, pp 477–9 (Kathleen Tillotson);
*New York Herald Tribune*, 18 October 1936 (Albert Guerard);
*Criterion*, 16, January 1937, pp 383–8 (Vera S.M. Fraser);
*Journal of English and Germanic Philology*, January 1937 (Edgar C. Knowlton);
*Medium Aevum*, VI, 1, February 1937, pp 34–9 (O.Elton), pp 34–40;
*Speculum*, April 1937;
*American Historical Review*, 43, October 1937 (Gray C. Boyce), pp 103–4;
*Modern Language Notes*, November 1937 (Thomas A. Kirby).

Some of these reviews have been reprinted in:
Watson George (ed.), *Critical Essays on C.S. Lewis*, Critical Thought Series no 1, Scolar Press, Aldershot 1992, with the addition of:
*English* I, 1936, The English Association, Mona Wilson, pp 344–5;
*Modern Language Review*, 32, 1936 (G.L. Brook), pp 287–8.

On Lewis I have consulted the following bibliographies:
*C.S. Lewis, An Annotated Checklist of Writings about him and his Works*, compiled by Joe R. Christopher and Joan K. Ostling, Kent State University Press, 1972;
*C.S. Lewis, A Bibliography*, brought up to date by Walter Hooper, Aidan Mackey, Bedford 1991;
*C.S. Lewis, A Reference Guide*, by Susan Lowenberg, Halland Maxwell Macmillan, New York-Toronto 1993.

Besides Cantor, Veldman and Wilson (see References), I used the following:
Christopher Joe R., *C.S. Lewis*, Twayne, Boston 1987;
Cobb Lawrence W., 'Courtly Love in *The Allegory*', *Mythlore*, 14, Autumn 1987, pp 43–54, 55;
Gilbert Douglas and Kilby Clyde S., *C.S. Lewis: Images of His World*, Eerdmans, Grand Rapids, Mich. 1973;
Green Roger Lancelyn and Hooper Walter, *C.S. Lewis: A Biography*, 1974;
Hannay Margaret Patterson, *C.S. Lewis*, Ungar, New York 1981;
Rossi Lee D., *The Politics of Fantasy. C.S. Lewis and J.R.R. Tolkien*, UMI Research Press, Ann Arbor, Mich. 1984;
Sayer George, Jack, *C.S. Lewis and His Times*, Macmillan, London 1988.

The poem 'Estat ai en greu cossirier' is quoted in Provençal from *Trobairitz* by Angelica Rieger, and in English from *The Women Troubadors* by Meg Bogin,

Paddington Press, London, 1976. The other two Provençal poems are quoted from *La poesia dell'antica Provenza. Testi e storia dei trovatori*, ed. Giuseppe E. Sansone, vol. I, Guanda, Milan 1984; the English versions are from Pound's translations in *Proença*.

Chapter 6, 1

The data on the books concerning Europe are based on:
Subject Index of the Modern Works added to the Library of the British Museum in the Years 1931–35, and
Subject Index of the Modern Works added to the Library of the British Museum in the Years 1936–1940, Pordes, London 1965

The review of Ortega y Gasset's *The Revolt of the Masses*, in *New Britain*, I, 3, 24/5/1933, was written by Frank Watson, and that in the *Criterion*, XII, XLVI, 1933, pp 144–6, by Frank MacEachran

Chapter 6, 2

I have used the following writings by Oswald Mosley:
*Fascism: 100 Questions Asked and Answered*, B.U.F Publications, London, March 1936;
'The World Alternative. European Synthesis within the Universalism of Fascism and National Socialism', *Fascist Quarterly*, II, 31, July 1936, pp 377–95;
*Tomorrow We Live*, Greater Britain Publications, June 1938;
*Union of Europe: Extension of Patriotism Idea of Kinship*, reprinted from *Mosley Newsletter*, Mosley Publications, Ramsbury 1947;
*My Life*, Nelson, London 1968.

Mosley's article 'Modern Dictatorship and British History' was published in *Antieuropa*, September 1933-XI (V, 5–9, pp 271–4).

Chapter 6, 3

Margaret Storm Jameson's letters to Lord Cecil are kept at the British Library Department of Manuscripts, under the heading Add. Mss. 51193 (1).

Of her writings I have used the following:
Jameson Margaret Storm (ed.), *Challenge to Death*, Constable, London 1934 (her writings in *Challenge to Death* were republished in *Civil Journey* where they are connected by autobiographical notes);
Ead., *Civil Journey*, Cassell, London 1939;
Ead., 'Federalism and a New Europe', in Melville Chaning-Pearce (ed.), *Federal Union: A Symposium*, Lothian Foundation Press, London 1991 (reprint of 1940 edition), pp 249–262, originally in *Fortnightly Review*, 147, January 1940;
Ead., *The Writer's Situation and Other Essays*, Macmillan, London 1950;
Ead., *Journey from the North*, vol. I, Virago, London 1984 (1969)

Chapter 6, 5

I have not been able to find the date of Margaret Ormiston Curle's death, but I would like to thank the institutions which replied kindly to my queries:
Blackwell Publishers, Oxford
Devon County Central Library, Exeter
Devonshire Association for the Advancement of Science, Literature and the Arts, Exeter
Devonshire Press, Torquay
Edinburgh University Library
General Register Office for Scotland, Edinburgh
Glasgow University Library
National Library of Scotland, Edinburgh
National Library of Wales, Aberystwyth
Scottish Borders Council, Melrose
Scottish Genealogy Society, Edinburgh
Scottish Record Office, Edinburgh
Society of Authors, London

The information on her was found in:
*Who's Who in Literature*, 1934;
*Who Was Who Among English and European Authors 1931–1949*, 1978.

A biographical note on her uncle Alexander Ormiston Curle can be found in *Scottish Biographies*, 1938.

Margaret Ormiston Curle published the following books:
*Travel Songs*, Devonshire Press, Torquay n.d.;
*The Dryad and Other Poems*, Erskine MacDonald, London 1921;
*The Golden Fleece: A Poem*, Merton Press, Abbey House, Westminster SW1 1924;
*Kerdac, the Wanderer*, A.H. Stockwell, London 1924;
*Tancred, the Hero, and Other Fairy Tales*, A.H. Stockwell, London 1920;
*Europe*, Shakespeare Head Press, Oxford 1938.

Chapter 6, 6

The poem 'Europa and the Bull' by Oliver St John Gogarty was originally published in his *Selected Poems*, MacMillan, New York 1933; a revised and enlarged edition of the collection was published with the title *Others to Adorn*, Rich & Cowan, London 1938. For biographical information on Gogarty I used the books by J.B. Lyons, *Oliver St John Gogarty*, Bucknell University Press, Lewisburg 1976, and *Oliver St John Gogarty: A Biography*, Blackwater, Dublin 1980.

Frank Dobson's textile is kept at the Victoria and Albert Museum. The photograph *Europa and the Bull* by Yevonde is at the National Portrait Gallery.

Chapter 6, 7

The association 'Friends of Europe', which had its offices in London at 122 St Stephen's House, Westminster, published more than seventy pamphlets between 1933 and 1939. They can be consulted in the library of the London School of Economics, which also has copies of the newsletter of the association and of the monthly *Europe To-Morrow*.

## Chapter 7

The letters between Catherine and Konrad are kept in the Department of Manuscripts at the British Library, although part of them will be accessible only in 2014. The names used in this chapter are pseudonyms.

Other contemporary love letters are quoted from the following collections:
Day-Lewis Tamasin (ed.), *Last Letters Home*, Macmillan, London 1995
Figes Eva (ed.), *Women's Letters in Wartime 1450–1945*, HarperCollins, London 1993
Strachey James and Alix, *Bloomsbury/Freud: Letters 1924–25*, ed. Perry Meisel and Walter Kendrick, Basic Books, New York 1985

Correspondances have been studied very little for what concerns the twentieth century. One of the rare examples is Section III of Bossis Mireille (ed.), *La lettre à la croisée de l'individu et du social*, Kimé, Paris, 1994

## Epilogue

I am most thankful to Basil Davidson for his letters, particularly that of 25 February 1997 concerning SOE's European inspiration. Frank Thompson's papers are in the Bodleian, but not yet classified; when they are usable, some of the hypotheses made in this Epilogue on his Europeanist thought might be confirmed and enlarged. For the moment this chapter is based on published material, particularly his own writings included in the book edited by his mother and brother:
Thompson Theodosia J. and Thompson Edward P., *There is a Spirit in Europe... A Memoir of Frank Thompson*, Gollancz, London 1947, besides conversations with and letters from Professor Michael R.D Foot (particularly his letter of 15 June 1997), Dorothy Thompson and Simon Kusseff.

# References

Ackroyd Peter, *T.S. Eliot*, Penguin 1984

Adkins Francis James, *Europe's New Map*, Noel Douglas, London 1925

Agnelli Arduino, 'Da Coudenhove-Kalergi al piano Briand', in Sergio Pistone (ed.), *L'idea dell'unificazione europea dalla prima alla seconda guerra mondiale*, Fondazione Luigi Einaudi, Torino 1975, pp 39–57

Alexander Sally, *Becoming a Woman*, Virago, London 1994

Amery Leo S., 'The British Empire and the Pan-European Idea', *Journal of the Royal Institute of International Affairs*, 1, IX, January 1930

Angell Norman, *The International Anarchy* and *Educational and Psychological Factors*, in Woolf Leonard, respectively pp 19–66 and 456–98

Annan Noel, *Our Age: The Generation That Made Post-War Britain*, HarperCollins, London 1995 (1990)

(von) Arnim Elizabeth, *Elizabeth and her German Garden*, Virago, London 1994, (1898)

Auden Wystan Hugh, *Selected Poems*, Faber & Faber, London 1979;

*Idem*, and MacNeice Louis, *Letters from Iceland*, Faber & Faber, London 1937

[L']*Avenir de l'esprit européen*, Société des Nations, Institut International de Coopération Intellectuelle, Paris 1934

Balzaretti Ross, 'The Creation of Europe', *History Workshop*, 33, Spring 1992, pp 181–196

Barraclough Geoffrey, *European Unity in Thought and Action*, Blackwell, Oxford 1963

Bataille Georges, *Le Collège de Sociologie*, Mardi 4 juillet 1939, in Denis Hollier (ed.), *Le Collège de Sociologie 1937–1939*, Gallimard, Paris 1995

Batho Howard, 'Textiles by Frank Dobson', *Journal of the Decorative Arts Society*, 17, 1993, pp 34–41

Bauer Victor M., *Europe: A Living Organism*, New Europe, London 1933

Baynes Helton Godwin, *Analytical Psychology and the English Mind*, essay in *Idem*, *Analytical Psychology and the English Mind and Other Papers*, Methuen, London 1950, pp 34–60 (originally published in the Festschrift *Die Kulturelle Bedeutung der komplexen Psychologie*, Springer, Berlin 1935);

*Idem*, *Germany Possessed*, Jonathan Cape, London 1941

Beck William S., *Organismo*, in *Enciclopedia Einaudi*, vol. X, Einaudi, Torino 1980, pp 135–177

Beddoe, Deirdre, *Back to Home and Duty: Women between the Wars 1918–1939*, HarperCollins, London 1989

Behr Shulamith, 'Wassily Kandinsky and Dimitrije Mitrinovic: Pan-Christian Universalism and the Yearbook *Towards the Mankind of the Future through Aryan Europe*', *Oxford Art Journal*, 15, 1, 1992, pp 81–88

Belloc Hilaire, *Europe and the Faith*, Burns & Oates, London 1962 (the Prologue, *The Catholic conscience of history*, first appeared in 1920 as a series of lectures to a Catholic historical society in London);

*Idem*, *The Crisis of Our Civilization*, Cassell, London 1937

Belsey Catherine, *Desire. Love Stories in Western Culture*, Blackwell, Oxford 1994

Benewick Robert, *Political Violence and Public Order: A Study of British Fascism*, Allen Lane, London 1969

Bennett Henry Stanley, *George Gordon Coulton 1858–1947*. Proceedings of the British Academy, London 1947

Beradt Charlotte, *Das Dritte Reich des Traums*, Suhrkamp, Frankfurt am Main 1966

Berdyaev Nicolaj, *The End of Our Time*, Sheed & Ward, London 1933

Bergonzi, Bernard, *Reading the Thirties. Texts and Contexts*, MacMillan, London 1978

Berki R.N., *Marxism and European Unity*, in Stirk 1989, pp 41–64

Berry Paul and Bostridge Mark, *Vera Brittain: A Life*, Chatto & Windus, London 1995

Besant Annie, *The United States of Europe*, Theosophical Publishing House, Adyar, Madras 1928

Bhagavan-Dasa, *The Science of the Emotions*, 3rd edition, Theosophical Publishing House, Adyar, 1924

Bielenberg Christabel, *The Past is Myself*, Corgi, London 1994

Birn Donald S., *The League of Nations Union 1918–1945*, Clarendon Press, Oxford 1981

Bloch R. Howard, *Medieval Misogyny and the Invention of Romantic Love*, University of Chicago Press, Chicago 1991

Boardman Philip, *Patrick Geddes Maker of the Future*, Introduction by Lewis Mumford, University of North Carolina Press, Chapel Hill 1944

Boase Roger, *The Origin and Meaning of Courtly Love. A Critical Study of European Scholarship*, Manchester University Press, Manchester 1977

Bonaparte Marie, 'A Defence of Biography', *International Journal of Psycho-Analysis*, July–October 1939, Vol. XX, Part 3 and 4, pp 231–240

Bosco Andrea, *Lord Lothian. Un pioniere del federalismo 1882–1940*, Jaca, Milano 1989;

Idem, *The Federal Idea: The History of Federalism from Enlightenment to 1945*, vol. I, Lothian Foundation Press, London-New York 1991;

Idem, (ed.), *Federal Union and the Origins of the 'Churchill Proposal': The Federalist Debate in the United Kingdom from Munich to the Fall of France 1938–1940*, Lothian Foundation Press, London 1992;

Idem, *Chatham House and Federalism*, in Andrea Bosco and Cornelia Navari (eds), *Chatham House and British Foreign Policy 1919–1945*, Lothian Foundation Press, London 1994, pp 319–34

Bottome, Phyllis, *Alfred Adler Apostle of Freedom*, Faber & Faber, London 1939

Bowen Stella, *Drawn from Life. Reminiscences*, Collins, London 1941

Boyce Robert, 'Britain's First "No" to Europe: Britain and the Briand Plan, 1929–30', *European Studies Review*, 1, 10, Jan. 1980, pp 17–45;

Idem, *British Capitalism and the Idea of European Unity Between the Wars*, in Stirk 1989, pp 65–83;

Idem, *Was there a 'British' alternative to the Briand Plan?*, in Peter Catterall with C.J. Morris (eds), *Britain and the Threat to Stability in Europe, 1918–45*, Leicester University Press, London-New York 1993

Braidotti Rosi, *Commento alla relazione di Adriana Cavarero*, in Maria Cristina Marcuzzo e Anna Rossi-Doria (eds), *La ricerca delle donne. Studi femministi in Italia*, Rosenberg & Sellier, Torino 1987, pp 188–202;

Ead., *Nomadic Subjects*, Columbia University Press, New York 1994

Brands Marten Cornelius, *Europe halved and united: from a split object to a restored cultural identity?*, in A. Rijksbaron, W.H. Roobol, M. Weisglas (eds), *Europe from a Cultural Perspective: Historiography and Perceptions*, Nijgh & Van Ditmar, Amsterdam 1987, pp 73–83

Branson Noreen and Heinemann Margot, *Britain in the Nineteen Thirties*, Weidenfeld & Nicolson, London 1971

Breton André, *L'amour fou*, Gallimard, Paris 1937

Brittain Vera, *Halcyon or the Future of Monogamy*, Kegan Paul, New York 1929; Ead., *Testament of Experience. An Autobiographical Story of the Years 1925–1950*, Virago, London 1993 (1957)

Brown William, *Federalism and Psychology*, in Chaning-Pearce, pp 83–91

Brugmans Henri, *L'idée européenne 1920–1970*, De Tempel, Bruges 1970

Bugge Peter, *Europe 1914–1945: the nation supreme*, in Kevin Wilson and Jan van der Dussen (eds), *The History of the Idea of Europe*, Routledge, London and New York 1993, pp 83–149

Burke Edmund, *Writings and Speeches*, vol. IX, Clarendon Press, Oxford 1991

Buxton Charles Roden, *Inter-continental Peace*, in Woolf Leonard, pp 199–255

Bygrave Mike, 'A Lion for Africa', *Guardian Weekend*, 15 February 1997

*Cahiers jungiens de psychanalyse*, 82, 1995: 'Jung et l'histoire, les années 30'

Cairns Huntington, *Robert Briffault and the Rehabilitation of the Matriarchal Theory*, in Harry Elmer Barnes (ed.), *An Introduction to the History of Sociology*, University of Chicago Press 1948, pp 668–676

Calverton Victor Francis, *The Bankruptcy of Marriage*, Macaulay, New York 1928

Cantor Norman F., *Inventing the Middle Ages: The lives, works, and ideas of the great medievalists of the twentieth century*, William Morrow, New York 1991

Carens, James F., *Surpassing Wit: Oliver St. John Gogarty, his Poetry and his Prose*, Gill and Macmillan, Dublin 1979

Carlton David, *MacDonald versus Henderson: the foreign policy of the second labour government*, MacMillan, London 1970

Ceadel Martin, *Supranationalism in the British peace movement during the early twentieth century*, in Bosco 1991, pp 169–192;

Idem, *A Pro-War Peace Movement? The British Movement for collective Security (1936–1939)*, in Maurice Vaisse, *Le pacifisme en Europe des années 1920 aux années 1950*, Bruylant, Bruxelles 1993, pp 167–192

Chabot Jean-Luc, *L'idée d'Europe unie de 1919 à 1939*, Thèse pour le doctorat d'état en science politique, Université de Grenoble, 1978

Chaning-Pearce Melville (ed.), *Federal Union: A Symposium*, Lothian Foundation Press, London 1991 (reprint of 1940 edition)

Cheikh-Moussa Abdallah, 'Le masque d'amour', *Intersignes*, 6–7, printemps 1993: *L'amour et l'Orient*

Idem.., 'La négation d'Eros', *Studia islamica*, LXXII, Maisonneuve et Larose, Paris 1990

Chesterton Arthur K., *Oswald Mosley: Portrait of a Leader*, Action Press, London 1937

Churchill Winston, 'The United States of Europe', *Saturday Evening Post*, 15 February 1930 (also in Ducci Roberto, Olivi Bino (eds), *L'Europa incompiuta*, Cedam, Padova 1970, pp 28–39)

Cioran Emile Michel, *La tentation d'exister*, Gallimard, Paris, 1956

Cocks Geoffrey, '<<Sur un reve de plats jetés par la fenêtre>>: de la psychanalyse dans la société et la vie politique en Europe, 1900–1939', *Revue Internationale d'Histoire de la Psychanalyse* 5, 1992

Cofrancesco Dino, *Ideas of the Fascist Government and Party on Europe*, in Walter Lipgens (ed.), *Documents on the History of European Integration*, vol. I, de Gruyter, Berlin-New York 1985, pp 179–199

Cole George Douglas Howe, *Europe, Russia, and the Future*, Gollancz, London 1941

*Idem*. and Margaret, *The Intelligent Man's Review of Europe To-day*, Gollancz, London 1933

Collini Stefan, *The Dream of a European Literary Review: T.S. Eliot and 'The Criterion'*, in Bock Hans Manfred, Racine Nicole, Michel Trebitsch (eds), *Les revues européennes de l'entre-deux-guerres*, Maison des Science de l'Homme/IMEC, Paris 1998

Coudenhove-Kalergi Richard N., *Pan-Europe*, PUF, Paris 1988 (1923)

*Idem*, *Held oder Heiliger*, Pan-Europa Verlag, Wien-Paris-Leipzig 1927;

*Idem*, *Europe must Unite*, Mayflower Press, Plymouth 1939;

*Idem*, *J'ai choisi l'Europe*, Plon, Paris 1952

Cross Colin, *The Fascists in Britain*, Barrie and Rockliff, London 1961

Crozier Andrew, *Britain, Germany and the dishing of the Brian Plan*, in Preston King and Andrea Bosco (eds.), *A Constitution for Europe: A Comparative Study of Federal Constitutions and Plans for the United States of Europe*, Lothian Foundation Press, London 1991, pp 213–230

(La) Curne de Sainte Palaye Jean Baptiste, *Histoire littéraire des troubadours*, Slatkine Reprints, Genève 1967 (1774)

Curry William Burnlee, *The Case for Federal Union*, Penguin 1939

Davidson Basil, *Partisan Picture*, Bedford Books, Bedford 1946

*Idem*, *Special Operations Europe: Scenes from the Anti-Nazi War*, Gollancz, London 1980

*Idem*, 'Goodbye to Some of That', *London Review of Books*, 22 August 1996

Davies David (Lord), *A Federated Europe*, Gollancz, London 1940

Dawson William Harbutt, 'The Disunited States of Europe', *Contemporary Review*, 138, July 1930, pp 14–21

Day Susanne R., *Where the Mistral Blows: Impressions of Provence*, Methuen, London 1933

De Martino Ernesto, *La fine del mondo. Contributo all'analisi delle apocalissi culturali*, Einaudi, Torino 1977

Defries Amelia, *The Interpreter Geddes. The Man and His Gospel*, Routledge, London 1927

Delanty Gerard, *Inventing Europe. Idea, Identity, Reality*, Macmillan, London 1995

Denomy Alexander J., 'Fin'Amors: the Pure Love of the Troubadours, Its Amorality, and Possibile Source', *Mediaeval Studies*, VII, 1945;

*Idem*, *The Heresy of Courtly Love*, Peter Smith, Gloucester, Mass. 1965

Deschamps Etienne, *Quelle Afrique pour une Europe unie?*, in Michel Dumoulin (ed.), *Penser l'Europe à l'aube des années Trente*, Nauwelaerts, Bruxelles 1995, pp 95–150

Donaldson Ethelbert Talbot, 'The Myth of Courtly Love', from *Speaking of Chaucer*, Athlone Press, 1970, pp 154–163

Dondeynaz Rosalba, *Selma e Guerrino. Un epistolario amoroso (1914–1920)*, Marietti, Genova 1992

Dowson Jane (ed.), *Women's Poetry of the 1930s. A Critical Anthology*, Routledge, London 1996

Dronke Peter, *Medieval Latin and the Rise of European Love-Lyric*, 2 vols, Clarendon Press, Oxford 1965 and 1966;

*Idem*, *The Medieval Lyric*, Hutchinson University Library, London 1968

Duranton Henri, *L'interprétation du mythe troubadour par le Groupe de Coppet*, in Le Groupe de Coppet 1977, pp 349–373

Dyson Freeman, *Disturbing the Universe*, Harper & Row, New York 1979

Eddy Sherwood, *The Challenge of Europe*, Allen & Unwin, London 1933

Eder Montagu David, *Psychoanalysis in relation to politics*, in Jones 1924, pp 128–68

Elias Norbert, *Die höfische Gesellschaft*, Suhrkamp, Frankfort a/M 1983;

*Idem, Über den Prozess der Zivilisation, ibidem*, 1982

Eliot Thomas Stearns, *Christianity and Culture*, Harcourt, Brace & Co, New York 1940

*Idem, Notes towards the Definition of Culture*, Harcourt, Brace & Co, New York 1949

Ellenberger Henri F., *The Discovery of the Unconscious*, Fontana, London 1994 (1970)

Ellis Havelock, *Views and Reviews: A Selection of Uncollected Articles 1884–1932*, vol. II, Second Series: 1920–1932, Desmond Harmsworth, London 1932, Ch. 20 (originally published in the New York *Birth Control Review*, September 1928)

Engels Frederic, *The Origins of the Family, Private Property and the State*, Lawrence and Wishart, London 1940

Evans Archibald A., *The 'New Europe' Circle in London*, in Bosco 1992, pp 71–77

Farrington Benjamin, *The New Atlantis of Francis Bacon*, Tenth Foundation Lecture, New Atlantis Foundation, Richmond Hill, Surrey, 1964

Fauriel Claude, *Histoire de la poésie provençale*, 3 vols, Labitte, Paris 1846

Feinstein Elaine, Preface to Margaret Storm Jameson, *Love in Winter* (1935), Virago, London 1984

Felman Shoshana, *On Reading Poetry: Reflections on the Limits and Possibilities of Psychoanalytical Approaches*, in Joseph H. Smith (ed.), *The Literary Freud: Mechanisms of Defense and the Poetic Will*, Yale University Press, New Haven-London 1980, pp 119–148;

*Ead., To Open the Question*, pp 5–10, and *Turning the Screw of Interpretation*, pp 94–207, in Felman (ed.), *Literature and Psychoanalysis: The Question of Reading: Otherwise*, Johns Hopkins University Press, Baltimore-London 1982

Firestone Shulamith, *The Dialectics of Sex: The Case for Feminist Revolution*, Morrow, New York 1970

Fisher Herbert A.L., *A History of Europe*, Eyre and Spottiswoode, London, 1936

Fletcher J. Gould, *Europe's Two Frontiers*, Eyre & Spottiswoode, London 1930

Foerster Rolf Hellmut, *Europa: Gechichte einer politischen Idee*, Nymphenburger, München 1967

Foot Michael R.D., *Resistance. An analysis of European Resistance to Nazism 1940–1945*, Eyre Methuen, London 1976;

*Idem, Special Operations Executive 1940–1946*, Mandarin 1990

Ford Ford Madox, *Provence from Minstrels to the Machine*, Lippincott, London 1935

Fornari Franco, *The Psychoanalysis of War*, Indiana University Press, Bloomington and London 1975 (1966)

Fortescue Lady, *Perfume from Provence*, Blackwood, Edinburgh and London 1935

Fowler Bridget, *The Alienated Reader: Women and Romantic Literature in the Twentieth Century*, Harvester Wheatsheaf, New York-London 1991

Freud Sigmund, *Das Unbehagen in der Kultur und andere Kulturtheoretische Schriften*, Fischer, Frankfurt/am Main 1994, *Einleitung* by Alfred Lorenzer and Bernard Goerlich, pp 7–28 (for the English translation I refer to *Civilization and Its Discontents*, SE, Norton, London 1989)

Fuller John Frederick Charles, *Atlantis, America and the Future*, Kegan Paul, Trench, Trubner & Co, London 1926;

*Idem, 'The Cancer of Europe', Fascist Quarterly*, I, 1, January 1935;

*Idem, Memoirs of an Unconventional Soldier*, Ivor Nicholson & Watson, London 1936;

*Idem, The Conquest of Red Spain*, Burns Oates & Washburne, London 1937;

*Idem, Das Problem Europa. Ein englischer Soldat über den Sinn des Krieges*, Nibelungen Verlag, Berlin-Leipzig 1944

Fussell Paul, *Abroad: British Literary Traveling Between the Wars*, Oxford University Press, 1980

Gaitskell Hugh, *Four Monetary Heretics – Douglas Soddy Gesell Eisler*, Christie, Christchurch, New Zealand 1969

Gardner Helen, *Edwin Muir. The W.D. Thomas Memorial Lecture Delivered at the University College of Swansea on Dec. 8, 1960*, University of Wales Press, Cardiff 1961

Geddes Patrick and Thompson John Arthur, *The Evolution of Sex*, Humboldt, New York 1890 (1889)

Gibbs Philip, *European Journey: Being the narrative of a journey in France, Switzerland, Italy, Austria, Hungary, Germany and the Saar in the spring and summer of 1934*, Heinemann and Gollancz, London 1934

Gibson Robin and Roberts Pam, *Madame Yevonde*, National Portrait Gallery, London 1990

Gimbutas Marija, *The Civilization of the Goddess*, Harper, San Francisco 1991

Glass Stanley Thomas, *The Responsible Society: The Ideas of the English Guild Socialist*, Longmans, London 1966

Glover Edward, *War, Sadism and Pacifism: Further Essays on Group Psychology and War*, George Allen and Unwin, London 1933;

*Idem*, 'War and Pacifism: Some Individual (Unconscious) Factors', *Character and Personality*, 1936, IV, pp 305–318;

*Idem, Psychoanalysis in England*, in Franz Alexander, Samuel Eisenstein, Martin Grotjahn (eds), *Psychoanalytic Pioneers*, Basic Books, New York-London 1966;

*Idem*, 'Bibliography', *Psycho-analytic Quarterly*, 38, 1969, pp 521–548;

*Idem*, and Ginsberg Morris, *A Symposium on the Psychology of Peace and War*, A reprint from the *British Journal of Medical Psychology*, XIV, III, 1934

Goldenberg Naomi R., 'A Feminist Critique of Jung', *Signs*, 2, 2, 1976 (see as well the comment on her article by Barbara E.Chesser and Goldenberg's reply in *Signs*, Spring 1978)

Goldstein Erik, *The Round Table and the New Europe*, paper presented at the Tenth Lothian Conference on 'The Round Table Movement, the Empire/ Commonwealth and British Foreign Policy', 22–23 March 1996, London

Goldstein Leonard, 'The Revolution through English Eyes', *Wissenschaftliche Zeitschrift der Paedogogischen Hochschule Potsdam*, 11, 3, März 1967, pp 197–202

Gossman Lionel, *Medievalism and the Ideologies of the Enlightenment. The World and Work of La Curne de Sainte-Palaye*, Johns Hopkins, Baltimore 1968

Graves Robert, *Good-Bye to All That. An Autobiography*, Jonathan Cape, London 1929;

*Idem, The White Goddess. A historical grammar of poetic myth*, Farrar, Straus & Giroux, New York 1995 (1948)

*Idem*, and Hodge Alan, *The Long Week-End: A Social History of Great Britain 1918–1939*, Faber & Faber, London 1941

Green Martin, *Children of the Sun: A Narrative of Decadence in England after 1918*, Pimlico, London 1977

Greer Germaine, *The Female Eunuch*, McGibbon & Kee, London 1970

*(Le) Groupe de Coppet*, Actes et documents du deuxième Colloque de Coppet, 10–13 juillet 1974, Slatkine, Genève, and Champion, Paris 1977;

*(Le) Groupe de Coppet et l'Europe 1789–1830*, Actes du V Colloque de Coppet, Tübingen, 8–10 juillet 1993, Touzot, Paris 1994

Gunn Peter, *Vernon Lee Violet Paget 1856–1935*, Oxford University Press 1964

Gunther John, *Inside Europe*, Hamish Hamilton, London 1936

Hacking Ian, *Rewriting the Soul: Multiple personality and the sciences of memory*, Princeton University Press, Princeton 1995

Hadow Grace E., *Federalism and Education*, in Chaning-Pearce, pp 107–113

Hamilton Alastair, *The Appeal of Fascism. A Study of Intellectuals and Fascism*, Blond, London 1971

Hampden Jackson J., *Europe since the War. A Sketch of Political Development 1918–1939*, Gollancz, London 1933

Harding Mary Esther, *The Way of All Women. A Psychological Interpretation*, Longmans, Green & Co., London 1933

Hastings Beatrice, *The Old 'New Age': Orage I – and Others*, Blue Moon Booklet no 16, London 1936

Hayes Paul, *The Contribution of British Intellectuals to Fascism*, in Lunn and Thurlow

Heater Derek, *The Idea of European Unity*, Leicester University Press, Leicester and London 1992

Heerfordt Christian Frederik, *A New Europe*, George Allen & Unwin, London 1925; new edition *A New Europe II*, with *A Sketch of the Constitution of such a Federation*, Robert Holden, London 1926

Herodotus, *Histories*, with an English translation by A.D. Godley, Heinemann, London 1975

Hillman James, *Saggio su Pan*, Adelphi, Milano 1977 (the Italian edition has a preface which does not appear in the original edition *An Essay on Pan*, 1972)

Hinshelwood Robert D., 'Psychoanalysis in Britain: Points of cultural access, 1893–1918', *International Journal of Psycho-Analysis*, 76, 1, Feb. 1995

Hirschmann Ursula, *Noi senzapatria*, Il Mulino, Bologna 1993

Hitchcock James, *To Tear Down and to Build Up: Christianity and the Subversive Forces in Western Civilization*, in *Christopher Dawson's Insight: Can a Culture Survive the Loss of its Religious Roots?*, The Proceedings of the Wethersfield Institute, vol. 7, Ignatius Press, San Francisco 1995

Hittinger Russell, *Christopher Dawson on Technology and the Demise of Liberalism*, in *Christopher Dawson's Insight: Can a Culture Survive the Loss of its Religious Roots?*, The Proceedings of the Wethersfield Institute, vol. 7, Ignatius Press, San Francisco 1995

Hobman Joseph B. (ed.), *David Eder. Memoirs of a Modern Pioneer*, Foreword by S. Freud, Gollancz, London 1945

Hobson Samuel George, National Guilds and the State, Bell, London 1920;

*Idem, The House of Industry. A New Estate of the Realm*, King, London 1931;

*Idem, ABC of Modern Socialism*, House of Industry League at the National Trade Union Club, London 1937;

*Idem, Pilgrim to the Left. Memoirs of a Modern Revolutionist*, Edward Arnold, London 1938

Holder Alan, *Three Voyagers in Search of Europe. A Study of Henry James, Ezra Pound, and T.S. Eliot*, University of Pennsylvania Press, Philadelphia 1966

Holloway David (ed.), *The Thirties. A Chronicle of the Decade*, Simon & Schuster, London 1993

Holmes Colin, *Anti-Semitism in British Society 1876–1939*, Arnold, London 1979

Howorth Muriel, *Pioneer Research on the Atom. Rutherford and Soddy in a glorious chapter of science: The life story of Frederick Soddy*, New World Publications, London 1958

Huddleston Sisley, *Europe in Zigzags. Social, Artistic, Literary and Political Affairs on the Continent*, Lippincott, Philadelphia & London 1929

Hueffer Francis, *The Troubadours. A History of Provençal Life and Literature in the Middle Ages*, Chatto & Windus, London 1878

Hutchinson Paul, *The United States of Europe*, Willett, Clark & Colby, Chicago 1929

Huxley Julian S. and Haddon A.C., *We Europeans: A Survey of 'Racial' Problems*, with a Chapter on 'Europe Overseas' by A.M. Carr-Saunders, Kraus Reprint, New York 1970 (Jonathan Cape, London 1935)

Hynes Samuel, *The Auden Generation. Literature and Politics in England in the 1930s*, Bodley Head, London 1976

Illouz Eva, *Consuming the Romantic Utopia: Love and the cultural contradictions of capitalism*, University of California Press, Berkeley 1997

*In commemoration of Professor Frederick Soddy*, no date, no place, British Library pamphlet P204930

Inglis Fred, *Biography I: The Short Happy Life of Frank Thompson*, in Idem, *The Cruel Peace. Everyday Life in the Cold War*, Aurum Press, London 1992

*Is the Catholic Church Antisocial? A Debate between G.G. Coulton and Arnold Lunn*, Burns Oates and Washburne, London 1946

Jacoubet Henri, *Le genre troubadour et les origines françaises du romantisme*, Société d'Edition 'Les Belles Lettres', Paris 1929

James Edwin O., *The Cult of the Mother-Goddess*, Thames and Hudson, London 1959

Jameson Margaret Storm, *Journey from the North*, vol. I, Virago, London 1984 (1969)

Jankowiak William (ed.), *Romantic Passion: A Universal Experience?*, Columbia University Press, New York 1995

Jason Neville, *The Sculpture of Frank Dobson*, The Henry Moore Foundation in association with Lund Humphries, London 1994

Jeanroy Alfred, *La poésie lyrique des troubadours*, 2 vols, Privat, Toulouse, and Didier, Paris 1934

Jennings W. Ivor, *A Federation for Western Europe*, Cambridge University Press, 1940

Jerrold Douglas, *The Necessity of Freedom. Notes on Christianity and Politics*, Sheed & Ward, London 1938

Johnstone, Richard, *The Will to Believe. Novelists of the Nineteen Thirties*, Oxford University Press, Oxford-New York 1984

Jones Ernest (ed.), *The War Neuroses*, International Psychoanalitical Press, London-Vienna 1919

Idem, (ed.), *Social Aspects of Psychoanalysis*, Williams & Norgate, London 1924;

Idem, book reviews of Freud/Einstein letters and of Glover's *War, Sadism and Pacificism*, in the *International Journal of Psycho-analysis*, no 14, 1933, pp 418–421;

Idem, 'How can civilisation be saved', IJP, 24, 1943

Julliard Jacques, 'Sur un fascisme imaginaire, à propos d'un livre de Zeev Sternhell', *Annales E.S.C.*, 39, 4, juillet–aout 1984

Jung Carl Gustav, *Civilization in Transition*, Bollingen Series, Princeton University Press (the numbers indicate the paragraph, not the page),
vol. 10, 1964:
*Woman in Europe*, 1927,
*The Swiss Line in the European Spectrum*, 1928;
*Archaic Man*, 1931,
*The Spiritual Problem of Modern Man*, 1931,
*Wotan*, 1936;
vol. 11:
*Psychology and Religion: East and West*, 1958:
*Psychotherapists or the Clergy*, 1932;
vol. 13:
*Alchemical Studies*, 1968:
*Commentary on the Secret of the Golden Flower*, 1931,
*Richard Wilhelm: In Memoriam*, 1931;
vol. 18:
*The Symbolic Life*, 1954:
*The Tavistock Lecture II (Discussion)*, 1935
*Idem*, and Kerényi Karoly, *Einführung in das Wesen der Mythologie*, Routledge and Kegan Paul, London, 1951 (1940–41)
Kakar Sudhir and Ross John M., *Tales of Love, Sex and Danger*, Oxford University Press, 1992 (1986)
Kampmeyer-Käding Margret, *Europa, das verführende Weib: Malerei und Graphik um 1900*, in *Die Verführung der Europa*, Staatliche Museen Preussischer Kulturbesitz Kunstgewerbemuseum-Propylaeen Verlag, Berlin 1988, pp 187–199
Keating John, *The British Experience: Christian Democrats without a party*, in David Hanley (ed.), *Christian Democracy in Europe: A Comparative Perspective*, Pinter, London-New York 1994
Kent Madeleine, *I Married a German*, Allen & Unwin, London 1938
Kerényi, Karoly, *Die Mythologie der Griechen. Die Goetter – und Menschheitsgeschichten*, Rhein Verlag, Zurich 1951
Kestner Joseph A., *Mythology and Misogyny*, University of Wisconsin Press, Madison 1989
Kimber Charles, *Federal Union*, in Peter Catterall with C.J. Morris (eds), *Britain and the Threat to Stability in Europe, 1918–45*, Leicester University Press, London and New York 1993, pp 105–111
King Norman, *Le Moyen Age à Coppet*, in *Le Groupe de Coppet* 1977, pp 375–399
Kitson Arthur, *A Letter to H.R.H. the Prince of Wales on the World Crisis – Its Cause, and Remedy*, July 4th, 1931, Alden Press, Oxford
Klein Melanie, *The Psycho-Analysis of Children*, Virago Press, London 1989 (1932); *Ead.*, *The Selected Melanie Klein*, Penguin 1991
Koehler Erich, *Sociologia della fin'amor. Saggi trobadorici*, Liviana, Padova 1976
Koselleck Reinhart, Preface, in Beradt
Krutch Joseph Wood, *Was Europe a Success?*, Methuen, London 1935
Kubie Lawrence S., 'Edward Glover: A Biographical Sketch', *The International Journal of Psycho-Analysis*, 54, 1973, pp 85–94
Kushner Tony, *The Persistence of Prejudice. Antisemitism in British society during the Second World War*, Manchester University Press, Manchester 1989

Labon Joanna, 'Tracing Storm Jameson', *Women: a cultural review*, 8, 1, 1997, pp 33–47

Lassner Phyllis, *A Cry for Life: Storm Jameson, Stevie Smith, and the Fate of Europe's Jews*, in M. Paul Holsinger and Mary Ann Schofield (eds), *Visions of War. World War II in Popular Literature and Culture*, Bowling Green State University Popular Press, Bowling Green, Ohio, 1992, pp 181–190;

Ead., *British Women Writers of World War II: Battlegrounds of their Own*, MacMillan, London 1998

Lasswell Harold D., *Psychopathology and Politics*, The University of Chicago Press, Chicago 1977 (1930)

Lauter Estella and Schreier Rupprecht Carol (eds), *Feminist Archetypal Theory. Interdisciplinary Re-Visions of Jungian Thought*, University of Tennessee Press, Knoxville 1985

Lee Vernon (Violet Paget), *Euphorion: being Studies of the Antique and the Mediaeval in the Renaissance*, 2 vols, T.Fisher Unwin, London 1884

*Left Review*, vol 3, no. 1, February 1937: 'John Cornford 1913–1937', pp 67–68

Lehmann Andrew G., 'Reflections on *Europa*', in Peter M.R. Stirk (ed.), *European Unity in Context: The Interwar Period*, Pinter, London-New York 1989, pp 99–109

Lehmann John (ed.), *New Writing in Europe*, Pelican 1940

Lewis David S., *Illusions of Grandeur. Mosley, Fascism and British Society, 1931–81*, Manchester University Press, Manchester 1987

Light, Alison, *Forever England. Femininity, Literature and Conservatism Between the Wars*, Routledge, London and New York 1991

Lipchitz Jacques with H.H. Arnason, *My Life in Sculpture*, Thames and Hudson, London 1972

Lipgens Walter, *A History of European Integration*, vol. I: *1945–1947 The formation of the European Unity Movement*, Clarendon Press, Oxford 1982;

*Idem*, (ed.), *Documents on the History of European Integration*, vol. I, Walter de Gruyter, Berlin-New York 1985

*Idem*, (ed.), *Documents on the History of European Integration*, vol. 2: *Plans for European Union in Great Britain and in Exile 1939–1945*, de Gruyter, Berlin-New York 1986 (pp 23–204 are dedicated to Federal Union and federalism in 1939–45 Britain)

Lombard Alfred, *Un mythe dans la poésie et dans l'art. L'enlèvement d'Europe*, La Baconnière, Neuchâtel 1946

Loubet del Bayle Jean-Louis, *Les non-conformistes des années 30*, Seuil, Paris 1969

Lunn Kenneth and Thurlow Richard C. (eds), *British Fascism: Essays on the Radical Right in Inter-War Britain*, Croom Helm, London 1980

MacEachran Frank, *The Destiny of Europe*, Faber & Faber, London 1932;

*Idem*, *The Unity of Europe*, Search (for NEG), London 1933

MacKay Ronald W.G., *Federal Europe: Being the case for European Federation together with a draft constitution of a United States of Europe*, Michael Joseph, London 1940

Maidenbaum Aryeh and Martin Stephen A. (eds), *Lingering Shadows. Jungians, Freudians, and Anti-Semitism*, Shambala, Boston-London 1991

Mairet Philip, *Pioneer of Sociology. The Life and Letters of Patrick Geddes*, Lund Humphries, London 1957

*Idem*, *Autobiographical and Other Papers*, Carcanet, Manchester 1981

Makin Peter, *Provence and Pound*, University of California Press, Berkeley 1978

Malinowski, Bronislaw, *Sex and Repression in Savage Society*, Kegan Paul, London 1927

Mallalieu Herbert B., *Letter in Wartime and Other Poems*, The Fortune Press, London 1940
Mancini Mario, *Il punto su: I trovatori*, Laterza, Roma-Bari 1991
Mandle W.F., *Anti-Semitism and the British Union of Fascists*, Longmans, London 1968
Marcelli Umberto, *Il Gruppo di Coppet e il concetto di nazionalità*, in *Le Groupe de Coppet* 1977, pp 401–415
Martel Gordon, *From Round Table to New Europe: Some Intellectual Origins of the Institute of International Affairs*, in Bosco & Navari 1994, pp 13–39
Martin Wallace, *The New Age under Orage: Chapters in English Cultural History*, Manchester University Press, Manchester 1967
Mayne Richard and Pinder John, *Federal Union: The Pioneers: A History of Federal Union*, MacMillan, London 1990
McDougal Stuart Y., *Ezra Pound and the Troubadour Tradition*, Princeton University Press, 1972
McLeod Alan L., *Rex Warner as Poet*, in McLeod (ed.), *The Achievement of Rex Warner*, Wentworth Press, Sydney 1965, pp 74–82
Menolocal Maria Rosa, *The Arabic Role in Medieval Literary History: A forgotten Heritage*, University of Pennsylvania Press, Philadelphia 1987
Merejkowski Dmitri, *The Secret of the West*, Jonathan Cape, London 1933
Merricks Linda, *The World Made New: Frederick Soddy, Science, Politics, and Environment*, Oxford University Press 1996
Mirkine-Guetzevitch Boris and Scelle Georges, *L'Union Européenne*, Librairie Delagrave, Paris 1931
Mitchell Juliet, *Women: the Longest Revolution. Essays on Feminism, Literature and Psychoanalysis*, Virago, London 1984;
*Ead.*, Introduction to *The Selected Melanie Klein*, Penguin 1991
Money-Kyrle Roger, *Aspasia. The future of amorality*, Kegan Paul, London 1932
*Idem*, review of *A Symposium on the Psychology of Peace and War* (see Glover and Ginsberg), *International Journal of Psycho-analysis*, 16, 1935, pp 491–2
Montagu M.F. Ashley, *Marriage, Past and Present*, Sargent, Boston 1956
Montefiore Janet, *Men and Women Writers of the 1930s: The dangerous flood of history*, Routledge, London 1996
Mosley Nicholas, *Beyond the Pale: Sir Oswald Mosley and family 1933–1980*, Secker & Warburg, London 1983;
*Idem.*, *Hopeful Monsters*, Mandarin 1991
Muggeridge Malcolm, *The Thirties: 1930–1940 in Great Britain*, Collins, London 1967 (1940)
Mulloy John J., *Continuity and Development in Christopher Dawson's Thought*, in *Christopher Dawson, The Dynamics of World History*, Sheed & Ward, London 1957, pp 413–468
Mumford Lewis, *Patrick Geddes, Victor Branford, and Applied Sociology in England: the social survey, regionalism, and urban planning*, in Barnes Harry Elmer (ed.), *An Introduction to the History of Sociology*, University of Chicago Press 1948, pp 677–695
Navari Cornelia, *The origins of the Briand plan*, in Bosco 1991, pp 211–237
Nelli René, *L'érotique des troubadours*, Toulouse, Privat 1963
Neumann Erich, *The Great Mother: An Analysis of the Archetype* (trans. by R. Mannheim), Routledge & Kegan Paul, London 1955

Newman Francis X. (ed.), *The Meaning of Courtly Love. Papers of the first annual conference of the Center for Medieval and Early Renaissance Studies. State University of New York at Binghamton*, March 17–18, 1967, State University of New York Press, Albany 1968

Newman Michael, 'British Socialists and the Question of European Unity, 1939–45', *European Studies Review*, 10, 1980, pp 75–100

Nietzsche Friedrich, *Jenseits von Gute und Böse*, de Gruyter, Muenchen 1993; *Beyond Good and Evil*, translated by R.J. Hollingdale, Penguin 1990 (the first number in parenthesis refers to the paragraph in the German edition and the second to the page of the English edition)

Nott C.S., *Further Teachings of Gurdjieff: Journey through this world*, Weiser, New York 1969

*Idem, Biographical Note*, in A.R. Orage, *On Love*, Janus Press, London 1970

Novalis, *Christianity, or Europe*, translated from the German by the Rev. John Dalton, The Catholic Series, John Chapman, London 1844

Oakley Amy, *The Heart of Provence*, D. Appleton–Century, New York-London 1936

Oliver James, *Christopher Dawson: The Historian of Ideas*, in Scott, pp 211–215

Orage Alfred R., *Friedrich Nietzsche: The Dionysian spirit of the Age*, Foulis, Edinburgh 1906;

*Idem, On Love, with some aphorisms and other essays*, Samuel Weiser, New York 1970 (1932);

*Idem, Selected Essays and Critical Writings*, ed. by Herbert Read and Denis Saurat, Books for Libraries, Freeport, N.Y., 1967 (1935)

*Idem, Political and Economic Writings*, Stanley Nott, London 1936

Orr John Boyd, *Federalism and Science*, in Chaning-Pearce, pp 101–6

Ortega y Gasset José, *The Revolt of the Masses*, Allen & Unwin, London 1932

Orwell George, *Homage to Catalonia*, and *Looking back on the Spanish Civil War*, Penguin 1964 (original edition Martin Secker & Warburg 1938)

Palme Dutt R., 'Notes of the month', *Labour Monthly*, vol. 13, no. 3, March 1931

Paris Gaston, 'Lancelot du Lac. II. *Le Conte de la Charrette*', *Romania*, XII, 48, octobre 1883

Paz Octavio, *La llama doble. Amor y erotismo*, Cìrculo de Lectores, Barcelona 1993

Peattie Louise Redfield and Peattie Donald Culross, *The Happy Kingdom: A Riviera Memoir*, Blackie, London-Glasgow 1935

Pegg Carl H., *Evolution of the European Idea, 1914–1932*, University of North Carolina Press, Chapel Hill and London 1983

Pellegrini Carlo, *Madame de Staël e il gruppo di Coppet*, Patron, Bologna 1974

Pick Daniel, '<<Pourquoi la guerre?>>: Freud-Einstein et le XIXe siècle', *Revue Internationale d'Histoire de la Psychanalyse*, 5, 1992

Pinder John, *Federalism in Britain and Italy: Radicals and the English Liberal Tradition*, in Stirk 1989, pp 201–223;

*Idem, The federal Idea and the British liberal tradition*, in Bosco 1991, pp 99–118

*Poets of Tomorrow*, Hogarth Press, London 1939

Pogson Beryl, *Maurice Nicoll: A Portrait*, Vincent Stuart, London 1961

Poliakov Léon, *Histoire de l'antisémitisme*, tome IV: *L'Europe suicidaire 1870–1933*, Calman-Lévy, Paris 1977

Pound Ezra, *Proença*, in *The Spirit of Romance*, Peter Owen, London 1960 (1910), pp 39–63

*Idem, Psychology and Troubadours, ibidem*, pp 87–100;

*Idem, Personae*, New Directions, New York 1971 (1926, 1935);

*Idem, Ford Madox Hueffer and the Prose Tradition in Verse*, in *Pavannes and Divisions*, Knopf, New York 1918, pp 129–37;

*Idem, Troubadours: Their Sorts and Conditions, ibidem*, pp 166–85;

*Idem, The Cantos*, New Directions, New York 1975

Priestley John B., *Federalism and Culture*, in Chaning-Pearce, pp 93–99

Prince G. Stewart, 'Jung's Psychology in Britain', in Michael Fordham (ed.), *Contact with Jung. Essays on the Influence of His work and Personality*, Tavistock, London 1963

Rapp Dean, 'The Early Discovery of Freud by the British General Educated Public, 1912–1919', *Social History of Medicine*, 3, 2, August 1990, pp 217–243

Rappard William, *Uniting Europe: The Trend of International Cooperation since the War*, Oxford University Press, Oxford 1930

Raynouard François, *Choix des poésies originales des troubadours*, réimpression de l'édition 1816–1821, Biblio-Verlag, Osnabrück 1966, 6 tomes

Reuter Timothy, 'Medieval Ideas of Europe and their Modern Historians', *History Workshop*, 33, Spring 1992, pp 176–180

*Revue internationale d'histoire de la psychanalyse*, 5, 1992: special issue on *L'engagement sociopolitique des psychanalystes*

Rieger Angelica, *Trobairitz: Der Beitrag der Frau in der altokzitanischen höfischen Lyrik. Edition des Gesamtkorpus*, Niemeyer, Tübingen 1991

Rigby Andrew, *Initiation and Initiative: An Exploration of the Life and Ideas of Dimitrije Mitrinovic*, East European Monographs, Boulder, New York 1984

Roobol W.H., *Europe in the historiography between the World Wars*, in Rijksbaron et al., pp 52–61

Rose Jacqueline, *States of Fantasy*, Clarendon Press, Oxford 1996

Rowbotham Sheila, *Hidden from History*, Pluto Press, London 1973

Rubin Miri, 'The Culture of Europe in the Later Middle Ages', *History Workshop*, 33, Spring 1992, pp 162–175

Russell Bertrand, *Marriage and Morals*, George Allen & Unwin, London 1929

*Idem, Autobiography*, Unwin, London 1978 (1967–69)

Rutherford Harry C., *The Religion of Logos and Sophia: From the Writings of Dimitrije Mitrinovic on Christianity*, New Atlantis Foundation, Norfolk Lodge, Richmond Hill, 1966

*Idem, General Introduction*, to D. Mitrinovic, *Certainly, Future*, 1987 (see Sources, 3);

*Idem, The Ideas of Dimitrije Mitrinovic. Writings by Harry Rutherford 1973–1991*, New Atlantis Foundation in association with J.B. Priestley Library, University of Bradford, 1997

Salewski Michael, Introduction and *Ideas of the National Socialist Government and Party*, in Lipgens 1985, pp 37–178

Salter Arthur, *The United States of Europe and Other Papers*, George Allen & Unwin, London 1933

Salway Kate, *Goddesses & Others: Yevonde: A Portrait*, Balcony Books, London 1990

Salzmann Siegfried, *Europa und der Stier im Zeitalter der industriellen Zivilisation*, in S. Salzmann (ed.), *Mythos Europa. Europa und der Stier im Zeitalter der industriellen Zivilisation*, Catalogue of the Exhibition held at Kunsthalle Bremen August 1988, pp 84–94

Samuels Andrew, *The Political Psyche*, Routledge, London 1993;

*Idem*, 'The Professionalization of Carl G. Jung's Analytical Psychology Clubs', *Journal of the History of the Behavioral Sciences*, 30, 1994

Schapiro Barbara Ann, *Literature and the Relational Self*, New York University Press, New York 1994

(de) Schlegel August Wilhelm, *Observations sur la langue et la littérature provençales*, Librairie Grecque-Latine-Allemande, Paris 1818

Schlesinger Bruno, *Christopher Dawson and the Modern Political Crisis*, Dissertation submitted to the Graduate School of the University of Notre Dame, Indiana, 1949

Scott Christina, *A Historian and His World: A Life of Christopher Dawson 1889–1970*, Sheed & Ward, London 1984

Searle Arthur, 'Letters of Robert Briffault', *The British Library Journal*, 1977, 3, pp 169–176

Seeley John R., 'United States of Europe', *Macmillan's Magazine*, March 1871, pp 436–448

Segal Julia, *Melanie Klein*, Sage, London 1992

Sellon Hugh, *Europe at the Cross-Roads*, Hutchinson, London 1938

Selver Paul, *Orage and the New Age Circle: Reminiscences and Reflections*, Allen & Unwin, London 1959

Seton-Watson Robert W., *Britain and the Dictators: A Survey of Post-War British Policy*, Cambridge University Press, Cambridge 1938

Shand Alexander Faulkner, *The Foundations of Character: Being a Study of the Emotions and Sentiments*, MacMillan, London 1914 (revised edition 1920)

Showalter Elaine, *A Literature of Their Own: From Charlotte Brontë to Doris Lessing*, Virago, London 1978

Sieburth Richard (ed.), *A Walking Tour in Southern France: Ezra Pound among the Troubadours*, New Directions, New York 1992

Singer Irving, *The Nature of Love*, vol. 2: *Courtly and Romantic*, University of Chicago Press, Chicago 1984

*Idem*, vol. 3: *The Modern World*, 1987

(de) Sismondi Jean Charles Simonde, *De la littérature du midi de l'Europe*, Treuttel et Würtz, Paris-Strasbourg 1813

Skidelsky Robert, *Oswald Mosley*, Papermac, London 1981

Sloan Pat, 'An "Unknown Soldier" in the Battle of Ideas', *Marxism Today*, VI, May 1962, pp 154–159

Smith Carol H., *T.S. Eliot's Dramatic Theory and Practice*, Princeton University Press, Princeton 1963

Smith Rennie, *General Disarmament or War?*, Allen & Unwin, London 1927;

*Idem*, *Peace Verboten*, 'Fight for Freedom' Publications, Hutchinson, London 1943

Soddy Frederick, *The Impact of Science upon an Old Civilisation*, Hendersons, London 1928

*Idem*, *Money versus Man. A Statement of the World Problem from the Standpoint of the New Economics*, Elkin Mathews & Marrot, London 1931

*Idem*, *Poverty Old and New*, published for the New Europe group by Search, London 1932

Spender Stephen and Lehmann John (eds), *Poems for Spain*, Hogarth Press, London 1939

Spengler Oswald, *The Decline of the West* (transl. by Charles Francis Atkinson), 2 vols, Allen & Unwin, London 1926–29

Spivak Gayatri Chakravorty, *Can the Subaltern Speak?*, in Nelson Cary and Larry Crossberg (eds), *Marxism and the Interpretation of Culture*, University of Illinois Press, Urbana 1988, pp 271–313

(de) Staël Madame, *De l'Allemagne et des moeurs des Allemands*, in *Oeuvres complètes*, vol. X and XI, Treuttel et Würtz, Paris 1820

Stalley Marshall, *Patrick Geddes: Spokesman for Man and the Environment*, Rutgers University Press, New Brunswick, N.J.1972

Steele Tom, *Alfred Orage and the Leeds Arts Club 1893–1923*, Scolar Press, Aldershot, Hants 1990

Steiner Riccardo, 'Quelques observations sur l'engagement sociopolitique des psychanalystes britanniques après la seconde guerre mondiale', *Revue Internationale d'Histoire de la Psychanalyse*, 5, 1992

Stendhal (Henry Beyle), *De l'amour*, Kraus Reprint 1968 (Paris 1822, 1834, 1842)

Sternhell Zeev, *Ni droite ni gauche: L'idéologie fasciste en France*, Seuil, Paris 1983

Stirk Peter M.R., 'Introduction: Crisis and Continuity in Interwar Europe', in Stirk 1989, pp 1–22;

*Idem*, (ed.), *European Unity in Context: The Interwar Period*, Pinter, London and New York 1989

Stopes Marie Carmichael, *Married Love: A New Contribution to the Solution of Sex Difficulties*, Putnam, London 1927/18th edition and 1940/24th edition (original edition 1918)

Story William Wetmore, *Poems*, Houghton, Mifflin & Co., Boston-New York 1896, vol. II: *Monologues and Lyrics*

Stout George Frederick, *Alexander Faulkner Shand*, in *Proceedings of the British Academy*, vol. XXII, Milford, London, Oxford University Press 1937

Strachey John, *Federalism or Socialism*, Gollancz, London 1940

Streit Clarence K., *Union Now: A Proposal for a Federal Union of the Democracies of the North Atlantic*, Jonathan Cape and Harper, London and New York 1939

Suttie Ian D., *The Origins of Love and Hate*, Free Association Books, London 1988 (1935)

Symons Julian, *The Thirties: A Dream Revolved*, Faber & Faber, London 1975 (1960)

Taylor Gordon Rattray, *Biographical Note*, in the abridged edition that he edited of *The Mothers*, Allen & Unwin, London 1952, pp 21–25; 'Introduction', *ibidem*, pp 9–20

Taylor Richard and Melchior Claus (eds), *Ezra Pound and Europe*, Rodopi B.V., Amsterdam-Atlanta 1993, particularly the following essays:
Nadel Ira B., *'Nothing but a nomad': Ezra Pound in Europe (1898–1911)*, pp 19–330;
Dennis Helen M., *Is Wyatt to Petrarch as Ezra Pound to Arnault Daniel?*, pp 33–50;
Emmitt Helen V., *'Make-strong old dreams': Ezra Pound and European Aestheticism*, pp 191–205

Thompson Edward P., *Beyond the Frontier. The politics of a failed mission: Bulgaria 1944*, Merlin Press, Stanford University Press 1997

Thurlow Richard C., *The Return of Jeremiah: the Rejected Knowledge of Sir Oswald Mosley in the 1930s*, in Lunn and Thurlow

Toynbee Arnold J., *Survey of International Affairs 1931*, Royal Institute for International Affairs, Oxford 1932

Trotsky Leon, *Europe et Amérique*, Librairie de l'Humanité, Paris 1926; English edition: *Europe and America*, Pathfinder Press, New York 1971

Tyldesley Mike, 'The House of Industry League: Guild socialism in the 1930s and 1940s', *Labour History Review*, 61, 3, Winter 1996, pp 309–321

Vegetti Finzi Silvia, *Storia della psicoanalisi*, Mondadori, Milano 1986

Veldman Meredith, *Fantasy, the Bomb, and the Greening of Britain*, Cambridge University Press, Cambridge 1994

Vergin Fedor, *Subconscious Europe*, Jonathan Cape, London-Toronto 1932 (translation by Raglan Somerset of *Das Unbewusste Europa. Psychoanalyse der Europäischen Politik*, Hess, Wien-Leipzig 1931)

Vukmanovic Svetozar, *Struggle for the Balkans*, Merlin Press, London 1990

Walsh Maurice N., 'The Scientific Works of Edward Glover', The *International Journal of Psycho-Analysis*, 54, 1973, pp 95–102

Warner Rex, *Poems*, Boriswood, London 1937

Warton Thomas, *The History of English Poetry from the close of the 11th to the commencement of the 18th century*, London 1774–81

Webber G.C., *The Ideology of the British Right 1918–1939*, Croom Helm, London 1986

Webster Charles K., *The League of Nations in Theory and Practice*, George Allen and Unwin, London 1933

Wehr Demaris S., *Jung & Feminism: Liberating Archetypes*, Routledge, London 1988

Weil Simone, *En quoi consiste l'inspiration occitanienne?* and *L'agonie d'une civilisation à travers un poème épique*, in *Ecrits historiques et politiques*, Gallimard, Paris 1960

Westermarck Edward, *Three Essays on Sex and Marriage*, MacMillan, London 1934, pp 163–335

White Cynthia L., *Women's Magazines 1693–1968*, Michael Joseph, London 1970

White Ralph, *The British response to the Briand plan*, in Bosco 1991, pp 237–262

Whitmont Edward C., *Return of the Goddess*, Routledge, London 1983

Wilford R.A., 'The Federal Union Campaign', *European Studies Review*, 10, 1980, pp 101–114

Wilhelm James J., 'Pound and the Troubadours. A Review', *Paideuma*, 2, 1, Spring 1973, pp 133–7

Williams Linda Ruth, *Critical Desire: Psychoanalysis and the Literary Subject*, Arnold, London 1995

Wilson Andrew N., *C.S. Lewis: A biography*, Flamingo, London 1991

Wise Leonard, *Arthur Kitson, Great Monetary Reformers no. 2*, Holborn, London 1946;

*Idem., Frederick Soddy, Great Monetary Reformers no. 3*, Holborn, London 1946

Wood Linda, *British Films 1927–1939*, British Film Institute, London 1986;

*Ead.* (ed.), *The Commercial Imperative in the British Film Industry: Maurice Elvey, a case study*, BFI, London 1987

Woodruff Douglas, Introduction to Belloc, *Europe and the Faith*

Woolf Leonard (ed.), *The Intelligent Man's Way to Prevent War* (Essays by N. Angell, G. Murray, C.M. Lloyd, C.R. Buxton, Viscount Cecil, W. Arnold-Forster, H.J. Laski), Gollancz, London 1934

Woolf Stuart, 'The Construction of a European World-View in the Revolutionary-Napoleonic Years', *Past and Present*, 1992, 137, pp 72–101

Woolf Virginia, *Three Guineas*, Penguin 1978 (1938)

Wootton Barbara, *Socialism and Federation*, in Patrick Ransome (ed.), *Studies in Federal Planning*, MacMillan, London 1943, pp 269–98 (first published in 1941 by MacMillan as Federal Tract No. 6);

*Ead., In a World I Never Made: Autobiographical reflections,* Allen & Unwin, London 1967

Yeats William Butler, *The Poems,* edited by Daniel Albright, J.M. Dent, London 1990

Yeats-Brown Francis C., *European Jungle,* Eyre & Spottiswoode, London 1939

Yevonde, *In Camera,* John Gifford, London 1940

Young Robert, *A Young Man Looks at Europe,* Heinemann, London 1938

Ziffren Abbie, *Biography of Patrick Geddes,* in Stalley 1972

Zweig Stefan, *The World of Yesterday. An Autobiography,* University of Nebraska Press, Lincoln and London 1943

# Index

Refugees Assistance Fund
  meeting 268
Renaissance 224
  classical 239
  Club 145
Rennell of Rodd, Lord 71
Rennert, Hugo 213
Republican United States of
  Europe 57
*Review of Reviews* 52–3, 56, 58–60
*La Revista de Occidente* (1923–36)
  65, 229
*Revue critique d'histoire et de lit-
  térature* 68
Ribbentrop, Joachim von 280
Rickman, John 87–8
Rieder (publishers) 68
Rieger, Angelica, trobairitz's
  corpus 21, 213
Rilke, Rainer Maria 272
Riou, Gaston, *Europe ma patrie*
  138
Ritz, César, biography (1936) 178
Rivière, Joan 83
Robbins, Lionel
  *Federal Union: A Symposium*
    273
  *The Economic Causes of War*
    (1939) 275
Romains, Jules 224–5
  *Men of Good Will* 172
Roman Empire 223, 258
Romanticism 200
Rome
  Convegno Volta (1932) 71–3,
    238
  Excelsior Hotel 72
  Palazzo Farnese 72
  writers 202
Rosenberg, Alfred 71, 269
  *Krisis und Neubau Europas*
    (1934) 238
  racial doctrines (1936–37) 268
*Roses of Picardy* (1927) 32, 35
Rosicrucianism 110
Ross, Mrs Donald 264
Rosselli, Carlo 247
Rossetti, Dante Gabriel 207
Rossi, Ernesto 275
  and Altiero Spinelli, *Manifesto
    di Ventotene* (1941) 275
Rostock 297
The Round Table group 81, 275
*Round Table* journal 54, 270
Rowbotham, Sheila 256
Rowett Research Institute 274

Royal
  Academy 266
  Albert Hall, Refugees
    Assistance Fund meeting
    268
  Institute of International
    Affairs (Chatham House)
    54, 81
Rozanov, Vassily 231
Rudel, Jaufre 194, 207, 214
Rumel, Walter Morse 215
Ruskin, John 108–9, 135, 166,
  200
Russell, Bertrand 75, 77–8, 131,
  272
  Guild socialism 109
  introduction to *Sin and Sex* 183
  *Marriage and Morals* (1929) 48,
    76
Rutherford, Ernest 134
Rutherford, Harry 123–5

Sabines 5
Saint Francis 258
St Michael's Abbey 190–1
Sainte-Palaye, Jean Baptiste La
  Curne de (1697–1781) 2,
    204–5
  *Histoire littéraire des trouba-
    dours* (1774) 201
  *Mémoires sur l'ancienne cheva-
    lerie* (1753) 201
Millot, abbé 201–2
Salisbury, Lord 163
Salter, Sir Arthur 61, 140, 270
Sappho 193, 203
*Saturday Evening Post* 61
Savonarola 258
Saxe-Coburg-Gotha 281
Scandinavian
  bards 202
  Initiative, United States of the
    European Nations 56–7
Scheler, Max 232
Schirach, Baldur von 210
Schlegel, August Wilhelm 205,
  209
  *Leben und Werke der
    Troubadours* (1829) 207
  *Observations sur la langue et la
    littérature provençales*
    (1818) 205
Schlegel, Friedrich 205
Schlesinger, Bruno 73
Schopenhauer, Arthur 117
Schubert, Franz 259
Schuman, Robert 65
Schwarzschild, L., *End to
  Illusion: A Study of post-war
  Europe* 225

*Scots Observer* 30
Scribner, Charles 176–7, 180
Second World War 8, 20, 92,
  271, 303, 306–7
Seeley, John 52
Seignobos, Charles 53
Sellon, Hugh, *Europe at the Cross
  Roads* (1937 revised 1938)
  227
Selver, Paul 112
Serbia 53
  London Legation 112–13
  queen 170
Seton-Watson, R.W.
  *Britain and the Dictators* 227
  New Europe 237
  *New Europe Journal* 53–4
Shackleton, Edith, *Time and Tide*
  172
Shakespeare Company 113
Shand, Alexander Faulkner
  (1858–1936) 151–2, 158
  *The Foundations of Character…*
    (1914) 151
Shaw, George Bernard 55
  *The New Age* 109
Sheed & Ward (publishers) 66–7
Shelley, Percy Bysshe 77
Shepard, Dr William Pierce 213
Sicily, invasion of 314
Simpson, Sir James 258–9
Simpson, Wallis 280
Sinclair, Archibald, *Free Europe:
  Central and Eastern
  European Affairs* 269
Singer, Irving 8–9
Sisam, Kenneth 190
Skene, Geoffrey 28–30, 32–5, 36,
  37–42, 44–6, 48
*Sketch* 266
Slade, Frank 120
Slade, Lilian 23, 120, 136–7
  lectures on
    'Dialectics of Emotions'
      121–2
    'Woman and Society' 121
Slade School of Fine Arts 283
Slavonic
  culture 106
  and East European Studies,
    School of 54
  peoples 53, 237
Smith, Justin, *Troubadours at
  Home* (1898) 214
Smith, Rennie 267, 270
  *Painless Motherhood* 143
Smuts, Jan Christian 122
Social Darwinists 238
socialism 89, 109, 226, 271